THE WORKING WRITER

with College Writer's Reference

TAKEN FROM

The Working Writer
Third Edition

Toby Fulwiler

The College Writer's Reference
Third Edition

Toby Fulwiler
Alan R. Hayakawa

SPECIAL EDITION PUBLISHED FOR LANSING COMMUNITY COLLEGE

Cover Art: "Providence" by George Delany

Taken from:

The Working Writer, Third Edition
by Toby Fulwiler
Copyright © 2002, 1999, 1995 by Pearson Education, Inc.
Published by Prentice-Hall
Upper Saddle River, New Jersey 07458

The College Writer's Reference, Third Edition
By Toby Fulwiler and Alan R. Hayakawa
Copyright © 2002, 1999, 1996 by Pearson Education, Inc.
Published by Prentice-Hall
Upper Saddle River, New Jersey 07458

This special edition published in cooperation with Pearson Custom Publishing.

Printed in the United States of America

10 9 8 7 6 5 4 3 2 1

Please visit our web site at www.pearsoncustom.com

ISBN 0-536-70200-4

BA 995647

 PEARSON CUSTOM PUBLISHING
75 Arlington Street, Suite 300, Boston, MA 02116
A Pearson Education Company

CONTENTS

PART ONE

☙ ☙ ☙

THE ELEMENTS OF COMPOSITION

Source: *The Working Writer,* Third Edition by Toby Fulwiler, published by Prentice-Hall.

❧ 1 ❧
College Writing

I am the absolute worst writer. I will never forget when I had to write my college essay. I thought it was good and then I brought it downstairs to have my parents read it and they tore it apart. By the time they were finished with it, I had to rewrite it five times. I was so mad, but the weird part was, the final copy was exactly what I wanted to say. They had to tear it out of me.

JESSICA

I like to write. Writers are nothing more than observant, perceptive, descriptive people.

PAT

You can count on one thing, attending college means writing papers—personal and critical essays in English, book reviews and reports in history, research reports in psychology and sociology, position papers in political science, lab reports in biology, and so on. Some of these assignments will be similar to those you've done in high school, some will be new, and all will be demanding.

When I asked a recent class of first-year college students to talk about themselves as writers, several began by describing their habits and attitudes: John, for example, said he wrote best "under pressure," while Kevin wanted to write at his own pace, on his own time, and "hated deadlines." Becky preferred writing when she "felt strongly or was angry about something," Doug when the assignment "asked for something personal," but Lisa enjoyed writing any paper so long as the "assignment was clear and fair."

Other students talked about where and when they wrote. Amy, for example, said she did most of her writing "listening to classical music and, if it is a nice day, under trees." Jennifer felt "most comfortable writing on her bed and being alone." Dan said he could write anywhere, so long as he had "a good computer," and José, "as long as it was after midnight." In fact, there proved to be as many different perspectives on being a writer as there were students in the class.

✂ WHY IS WRITING HARD?

Even professional authors admit that writing is not easy. In writing this book, I en-countered numerous problems, from organizing material to writing clearly to finding time and meeting publication deadlines. What, I wondered, did first-year college writers find difficult about writing? Were their problems similar to or different from mine? Here is what they told me:

Jennifer: "I don't like being told what to write about."

Amy: "I never could fulfill the page requirements. My essays were always several pages shorter than they were supposed to be."

Jill: "I always have trouble starting off a paper . . . and I hate it when I think I've written a great paper and I get a bad grade. It's so discouraging and I don't under-stand what I wrote wrong."

Omar: "Teachers are always nitpicking about little things, but I think writing is for communication, not nitpicking. I mean, if you can read it and it makes sense, what else do you want?"

Cara: "I hate revising. I had this teacher in high school who insisted we rewrite every paper over and over again, and that got really boring. Once I've said what I have to say, I don't have anything else to say."

Mike: "If I'm in a bad mood or don't have the right beginning, I find myself stum-bling and not giving a hoot about whether it's right or not."

Kennon: "Putting thoughts down on paper as they are in your mind is the hardest thing to do. It is like in music—to make the guitar make the sound you imagine in your head, to make the words on the page paint the picture in your head."

I wasn't surprised by these answers, since I, too, remember wondering: What did teachers want? How long was enough? How do you get thoughts into words? Why all the nitpicking?

✂ WRITING 1

What do you find difficult about writing? Do you have a problem finding subjects to write about? Or do you have trouble getting motivated? Or does something about the act of writing itself cause problems for you? Explain in your own words by writ-ing quickly for five minutes without stopping.

✂ WHAT DO YOU LIKE ABOUT WRITING?

Though any writer will tell you writing isn't easy, most writers will also describe it as interesting and exciting. So I asked our first-year students what it was about writing that gave them pleasure.

Jolene: "If I have a strong opinion on a topic, it makes it so much easier to write a paper."

Rebecca: "On occasion I'm inspired by a wonderful idea. Once I get going, I actually enjoy writing a lot."

Casey: "I enjoy most to write about my experiences, both good and bad. I like to write about things when I'm upset—it makes me feel better."

Darren: "I guess my favorite kind of writing is letters. I get to be myself and just talk in them."

Like my students, I prefer to write about topics that inspire or interest me, and I find personal writing such as letters especially easy, interesting, and enjoyable.

✑ WRITING 2: EXPLORATION

What kind of writing do you most enjoy doing? What do you like about it: Communicating? Exploring a subject? Playing with words? Something else?

✑ WHAT SURPRISES ARE IN STORE?

At the same time I was teaching these first-year students, I was also teaching an advanced writing seminar to seniors. Curious about their attitudes toward writing, I asked them: "What has surprised you the most about writing in college?"

Scott: "Papers aren't as hellish as I was told they'd be. In fact, I've actually enjoyed writing a lot of them—especially after they were done."

Aaron: "My style has changed a lot. Rather than becoming more complex, it's become simpler."

Kerry: "The most surprising and frustrating thing has been the different reactions I've received from different professors."

Rob: "I'm always being told that my writing is superficial. That I come up with good ideas but don't develop them."

John: "The tutor at our writing lab took out a pair of scissors and said I would have to work on organization. Then she cut up my paper and taped it back together a different way. This really made a difference, and I've been using this method ever since."

Chrissie: "Sharing papers with other students is very awkward for me. But it's extremely beneficial when I trust and like my group, when we all relax enough to talk honestly about one another's papers."

As you can see, most advanced students found ways to cope with and enjoy college writing. Several reported satisfying experiences sharing writing with each other. I'm sorry that some students, even in their last year, could not figure out what their instructors wanted—there *are* ways to do that.

✺ WHY IS WRITING SO IMPORTANT?

I also asked these advanced students why, in their last year, they had enrolled in an elective writing class: "What made the subject so important to you?"

Kim: "I have an easier time expressing myself through writing. When I'm speaking, my words get jumbled—writing gives me more time, and my voice doesn't quiver and I don't blush."

Rick: "Writing allows me to hold up a mirror to my life and see what clear or distorted images stare back at me."

Glenn: "The more I write, the better I become. In terms of finding a job after I graduate, strong writing skills will give me an edge over those who are just mediocre writers."

Amy: "I'm still searching for meaning. When I write I feel I can do anything, go anywhere, search and explore."

Angel: "I feel I have something to say."

Carmen: "It's simple, I love words."

I agree, easily, with virtually all of these reasons. At times writing is therapeutic, at other times it helps us clarify our ideas, and at still other times it helps us get and keep jobs.

✺ WHAT THE SENIORS ADVISE

Since my advanced students had a lot to say about writing, I asked them to be consultants: "What is your advice to first-year college writers?" Here are their suggestions:

Aaron: "Get something down! The hardest part of writing is starting. Forget the introduction, skip the outline, don't worry about a thesis—just blast your ideas down, see what you've got, then go back and work on them."

Christa: "Plan ahead. It sounds dry, but planning makes writing easier than doing laundry."

Victor: "Follow the requirements of the assignment to the T. Hand in a draft for the professor to mark up, then rewrite it."

Allyson: "Don't think every piece you write has to be a masterpiece. And sometimes the worst assignment turns into the best writing. Don't worry about what the professor wants—write what you believe."

Carmen: "Imagine and create, never be content with just retelling a story."

Rick: "When someone trashes your writing, thank them and listen to their criticism. It stings, but it helps you become a better writer."

Jason: "Say what you are going to say as clearly and as straightforwardly as possible. Don't try to pad it with big words and fancy phrasing."

Angel: "Read for pleasure from time to time. The more you read, the better you write—it just happens."

Kim: "When choosing topics, choose something that has a place in your heart."

These are good suggestions to any writers: Start fast, think ahead, plan to revise and edit, listen to critical advice, consider your audience, be clear, read a lot. I hope, however, that instructors respond to your writing in critically helpful ways and don't "trash" it or put it down. Whether or not you take some of the advice will depend on what you want from your writing: good grades? self-knowledge? personal satisfaction? clear communication? a response by your audience? When I shared these suggestions with first-year students, they nodded their heads, took some notes, and laughed—often with relief.

೨ WRITING 5: EXPLORATION

What else would you like to ask advanced college students about writing? Find a student and ask; report back.

೨ WHAT ELSE DO YOU WANT TO KNOW?

I knew that my first-year students had already received twelve years' worth of "good advice" about learning to write, so I asked them one more question: "What do you want to learn about writing that you don't already know?"

Emma: "Should I write to please the professor or to please myself?"

José: "I'm always being told to state my thesis clearly. What exactly is a thesis and why is it so important?"

Jolene: "How do I develop a faster way of writing?"

Amy: "Is there a trick to making a paper longer without adding useless information?"

Sam: "How do I learn to express my ideas so they make sense to common intelligent readers and not just to myself?"

Scott: "How can I make my writing flow better and make smooth transitions from one idea to the next?"

Terry: "I want to learn to like to write. Then I won't put off assignments until the last minute."

Jennifer: "I have problems making sentences sound good. How can I learn to do that?"

John P.: "I would like to develop some sort of personal style so when I write people know it's me."

Jeff: "I want to become more confident about writing research papers. I don't want to have to worry about whether my documentation is correct or if I've plagiarized or not."

Woody: "Now that I'm in college, I would like to be challenged when I read and write, to think, and ask good questions, and find good answers."

Pat: "I don't want to learn nose-to-the-grindstone, straight-from-the-textbook rules. I want to learn to get my mind into motion and pencil in gear."

Heidi: "I would love to increase my vocabulary. If I had a wider range of vocabulary, I would be able to express my thoughts more clearly." *(I'm not sure this book addresses that directly, but the more reading and writing you do, the more words you'll learn!)*

Jess: "I'm always afraid that people will laugh at my writing. Can I ever learn to get over that and get more confident about my writing?"

I can't, of course, guarantee that if you read *The Working Writer* your writing will get easier, faster, longer, clearer, or more correct. Or, for that matter, that your style will become more personal and varied, or that you will become a more confident and comfortable writer—no handbook can do that for you. Becoming a better writer depends on your own interest and hard work. It will also depend on your college experience, the classes you take, and the teachers with whom you study. However, whether in class or on your own, if you read this text carefully and practice its suggestions, you should find possible answers to all these questions and many more.

I admit that there was at least one student's concern for which I really had no good response. Jessica wrote, "My biggest fear is that I'll end up one semester with four or five courses that all involve writing and I'll die." Or maybe I do have a response: If you become comfortable and competent as a writer, you'll be able to handle all the writing assignments thrown your way. Even if you can't, Jessica, you won't die. It's just college.

∂ SUGGESTIONS FOR WRITING AND RESEARCH

Individual

1. Interview a classmate about his or her writing experiences, habits, beliefs, and practices. Include questions such as those asked in this chapter as well as others you think may be important. Write a brief essay profiling your classmate as a writer. Share your profile with a classmate.

2. Over a two-week period, keep a record of every use you make of written language. Record your entries daily in a journal or class notebook. At the end of two weeks, enumerate all the specific uses as well as how often you did each. What activities dominate your list? Write an essay based on this personal research in which you argue for or against the centrality of writing in everyday life.

Collaborative

As a class or in small groups, design a questionnaire to elicit information about people's writing habits and attitudes. Distribute the questionnaire to both students and instructors in introductory and advanced writing classes. Compile the results. Compare and contrast the ideas of students at different levels and disciplines and write a report to share with the class. Consider writing a feature article for your student newspaper or faculty newsletter reporting what you found.

Chapter

✌ 2 ✌

College Reading

Now that I'm in college, I would like to be challenged when I read and write,
to think, and ask good questions, and find good answers.

WOODY

To read and write well in college means to read and write critically. In fact, a major goal of most college curricula is to train students to be critical readers, writers, and thinkers so they can carry those habits of mind into the larger culture beyond college. What, you may ask, does it mean to be critical? How does being a critical reader, writer, and thinker differ from being a plain, ordinary, everyday reader, writer, and thinker?

Being critical in writing means making distinctions, developing interpretations, and drawing conclusions that stand up to thoughtful scrutiny by others. Being critical in reading means knowing how to analyze these distinctions, interpretations, and conclusions. Becoming a critical thinker, then, means learning to exercise reason and judgment whenever you encounter the language of others or generate language yourself.

Most of *The Working Writer* explores strategies for helping you become an accomplished critical writer. This chapter, however, explores strategies for helping you become a more accomplished critical reader and emphasizes as well the close relationship between critical reading and critical writing.

✌ WRITING 1

Describe yourself as a reader, answering some of these questions along the way: How often do you read on your own? What kinds of reading do you do when the choice of reading material is up to you? Where and when do you most commonly do your reading? What is the last book you read on your own? Who is your favorite author? Why?

∾ UNDERSTANDING WRITTEN TEXTS

To understand a text, you need some context for the new ideas you encounter, some knowledge of the text's terms and ideas, and knowledge of the rules that govern the kind of writing you're reading. It would be difficult to read Mark Twain's novel *The Adventures of Huckleberry Finn* with no knowledge of American geography, the Mississippi River, or the institution of slavery. It would also be difficult to read a biology textbook chapter about photosynthesis but know nothing of plants, cell structure, or chemical reactions. The more you know, the more you learn; the more you learn, the more careful and critical your reading, writing, and thinking will be.

Many college instructors will ask you to read about subjects that are new to you; you won't be able to spend much time reading about what you already know. To graduate, you've got to keep studying new subjects that require, first, that you understand what you read and, second, that you can critically assess and write about this new understanding. As you move through the college curriculum, you will find yourself an expert reader in some disciplines, a novice reader in others, and somewhere in between in the rest—often during the same semester.

If getting a college degree requires that you read one unfamiliar text after another, how can you ever learn to read successfully? How do you create a context, learn a background, and find the rules to help you read unfamiliar texts in unfamiliar subject areas? What strategies or shortcuts can speed up the learning process? Let's consider some strategies for doing this.

As an experiment, read the following short opening paragraph from an eight-paragraph *New York Times* story titled "Nagasaki, August 9, 1945." When you have finished, pause for a few moments, and think about (1) what you learned from it, (2) how you learned what you learned, and (3) what the rest of the story will be about.

> **In August 1945, I was a freshman at Nagasaki Medical College. The ninth of August was a clear, hot, beautiful summer day. I left my lodging house, which was one-and-one-half miles from the hypocenter, at eight in the morning, as usual, to catch a tram car. When I got to the tram stop, I found that it had been derailed in an accident. I decided to return home. I was lucky. I never made it to school that day.**
>
> MICHAITO ICHIMARU

How did you do? It is possible that your reasoning went something like mine, which I reconstruct here. Note, however, that although the following sequence presents ideas one after the other, that's not how it seemed to happen when I read the passage for the first time. Instead, meaning seemed to occur in flashes, simultaneously and unmeasurably. Even as I read a sentence for the first time, I found myself reading backward as much as forward to check my understanding. Here are the experiences that seemed to be happening.

1. I read the first sentence carefully, noticing the year 1945 and the name of the medical college, "Nagasaki." My prior historical knowledge kicked in as I *identified* Nagasaki, Japan, as one of the cities on which the United States dropped an atomic bomb at the end of World War II—though I did not remember the precise date.

2.   I noticed the city and the date, August 9, and wondered if that was when the bomb was dropped. I *asked* (silently), "Is this a story about the bomb?"

3.   Still looking at the first sentence, a reference to the writer's younger self ("I was a freshman"), I guessed that the author was present at the dropping of this bomb. I *predicted* that this would be a survivor's account of the bombing of Nagasaki.

4.   The word *hypocenter* in the third sentence made me pause again; the language seemed oddly out of place next to the "beautiful summer day" described in the second sentence. I *questioned* what the word meant. Though I didn't know exactly, it sounded like a technical term for the place where the bomb went off. Evidence was mounting that the narrator may have lived a mile and a half from the exact place where the atomic bomb detonated.

5.   In the next-to-last sentence of the paragraph, the author says that he was "lucky" to miss the tram. Why, unless something unfortunate happened to the tram, would he consider missing it "lucky"? I *predicted* that had the author gone to school "as usual" he would have been closer to the hypocenter, which I now surmise was at Nagasaki Medical College.

6.   I then *tested* my several predictions by reading the rest of the story, which you, of course, could not do. My predictions proved correct: Michaito Ichimaru's story is a firsthand account of witnessing and surviving the dropping of the bomb, which in fact killed all who attended the medical college, a quarter of a mile from the hypocenter.

7.   Finally, out of curiosity, I looked up Nagasaki in the *Columbia Desk Encyclopedia* and *confirmed* that 75,000 people were killed by this second dropping of an atomic bomb, on August 9, 1945; the first bomb had been exploded just three days earlier, on August 6, at Hiroshima.

You'll notice that in my seven-step example some parts of the pattern of identifying/questioning/predicting/testing/confirming occur more than once, perhaps simultaneously, and not in a predictable order. This is a slow-motion description—not a prescription or formula—of the activities that occur in split seconds in the minds of active, curious readers. No two readers would—or could—read this passage in exactly the same way, because no two readers are ever situated identically in time and space, with identical training, knowledge, and experience to enable them to do so. However, my reading process may be similar enough to yours that the comparison will hold up: reading is a messy, trial-and-error process that depends as much on prior knowledge as on new information to lead to understanding.

Whether you read new stories or watch unfamiliar events, you commonly make meaning by following a procedure something like mine, trying to identify what you see, question what you don't understand, make and test predictions about meaning, and consult authorities for confirmation or information. Once you know how to read successfully for basic comprehension, you are ready to read critically. Learn the following reading strategies to improve your reading comprehension:

1.   *Identify.* Read first for what you recognize, know, and understand. Identify what you are reading about. Read carefully—slowly at first—and let meaning take hold where it can.

2. *Question.* Pause, and look hard at words and phrases you don't know or understand. See if they make sense when you reread them, compare them to what you do know, or place them in a context you understand.

3. *Predict.* Make predictions about what you will learn next: How will the essay, story, or report advance? What will happen? What theme or thesis will emerge? What might be the point of it all?

4. *Test.* Follow up on your predictions by reading further to see if they are correct or nearly correct. If they are, read on with more confidence; if they are not, read further, make more predictions, and test them. Trial and error are good teachers.

5. *Confirm.* Check your reading of the text with others who have also read it and see if your interpretations are similar or different. If you have questions, ask them. Share answers.

ᴠᴠ WRITING 2

Select a book you have been assigned to read for one of your courses and find a chapter that has not yet been covered in class. Read the first page of the chapter and then stop. Write out any predictions you have about where the rest of the chapter is going. (Ask yourself, for example, "What is its main theme or argument? How will it conclude?") Finish reading the chapter and check its conclusion against your predictions. If your predictions were close, you are reading for understanding.

ᴠᴠ READING CRITICALLY

How people read depends on what they're reading; people read different materials in different ways. When they read popular stories and magazine articles for pleasure, they usually read not to be critical but to understand and enjoy. In fact, while pleasure readers commonly go through a process similar to the one described in the last section—identifying, questioning, predicting, and testing—they usually do so rapidly and unconsciously. Since such reading is seldom assigned in college courses, whether they go further to confirm and expand their knowledge depends solely on their time, energy, and interest.

When people read college textbooks, professional articles, technical reports, and serious literature, they read more slowly and carefully to assess the worth or validity of an author's ideas, information, argument, or evidence. The rest of this chapter describes the strategies that lead readers from *understanding* texts to *interpreting* and *evaluating* them *critically,* paying special attention to the strategies of *previewing, responding,* and *reviewing.*

Although critical reading is described here as a three-stage process, it should be clear that these activities seldom happen in a simple one-two-three order. For example, one of the best ways to preview a text is to respond to it briefly as you read it the first time; as you respond, you may find yourself previewing and reviewing, and so on. But if you're not engaging in all three activities at some time, you're not getting as much from your reading as you could.

Previewing Texts

To be a critical reader, you need to be more than a good predictor. In addition to following the thread of an argument, you need to evaluate its logic, weigh its evidence, and accept or reject its conclusion. You read actively, searching for information and ideas that you both understand and can make use of—to further your own thinking, speaking, or writing. To move from understanding to critical awareness, you plan to read a text more than once and more than one way, which is why critical readers *preview* texts before reading them from start to finish.

To understand a text critically, plan to preview before you read, and make previewing the first of several steps needed to appraise the value of the text fully.

First Questions

Ask questions of a text (a book, an article, a Web page) from the moment you look at it. Ask first questions to find general, quickly gleaned information, such as that provided by skimming the title, subtitle, subheads, table of contents, or preface.

- What does the title suggest?
- What is the subject?
- What does the table of contents promise?
- What is emphasized in chapter titles or subheads?
- Who is the author? (Have I heard of him or her?)
- What makes the author an expert or authority?
- How current is the information in this text?
- How might this information help me?

You may not ask these first questions methodically, in this order, or write down all your answers, but if you're a critical reader you'll ask these types of questions before you commit too much time to reading the whole text. If your answers to these first questions suggest that the text is worth further study, you can continue with the preview process.

Second Questions

Once you've determined that a book or article warrants further critical attention, it's very helpful to skim selected parts of it to see what they promise. Skim reading leads to still more questions, the answers to which you will want to capture on note cards or in a journal.

- Read the prefatory material: What can I learn from the book jacket, foreword, or preface?
- Read the introduction, abstract, or first page: What theme or thesis is promised?
- Read a sample chapter or subsection: Is the material about what I expect?
- Scan the index or chapter notes: What sources have informed this text? What names do I recognize?
- Note unfamiliar words or ideas: Do I have the background to understand this text?
- Consider: Will I have to consult other sources to obtain a critical understanding of this one?

Previewing *Iron John*

One of my students gave me a book called *Iron John*. To find out more about the book, I previewed it by asking first questions and second questions, the answers to which I've reproduced here for illustration.

ANSWERS TO FIRST QUESTIONS

- The title *Iron John* is intriguing and suggests something strong and unbreakable.
- I already know and admire the author, Robert Bly, for his insightful poetry, but I've never read his prose.
- The table of contents raises interesting questions but doesn't tell me much about where the book is going:
  1. The Pillow and the Key
  2. When One Hair Turns Gold
  3. The Road of Ashes, Descent, and Grief
  4. The Hunger for the King in Time with No Father
  5. The Meeting with the God-Woman in the Garden

ANSWERS TO SECOND QUESTIONS

- The jacket says, "*Iron John* is Robert Bly's long-awaited book on male initiation and the role of the mentor, the result of ten years' work with men to discover truths about masculinity that get beyond the stereotypes of our popular culture."
- There is no introduction or index, but the chapter notes in the back of the book (260–267) contain the names of people Bly used as sources in writing the book. I recognize novelist D. H. Lawrence, anthropologist Mircea Eliade, poet William Blake, historian/critic Joseph Campbell, and a whole bunch of psychologists, but many others I've never heard of. An intriguing mix.

This preview, which took maybe ten minutes, confirmed that *Iron John* is a book about men and male myths in modern American culture by a well-known poet writing a serious prose book in friendly style. Apparently, Bly not only will examine current male mythology but will make some recommendations about which myths are destructive and which are constructive.

Previewing is only a first step in a process that now slows down and becomes more time-consuming and critical. As readers begin to preview a text seriously, they often make notes in the text's margin or in a journal or notebook to mark places for later review. In other words, before the preview stage of critical reading has ended, the *responding* stage has probably begun.

৬৬ **WRITING 3**

Select any unfamiliar book about which you are curious and preview it, using the strategy of first and second questions discussed in this section. Stop after ten minutes, and write what you know about the text.

Responding to Texts

Once you understand, through a quick critical preview, what a text promises, you need to examine it more slowly, evaluating its assumptions, arguments, evidence, logic, and conclusion. The best way to do this is to *respond,* or "talk back," to the text in writing.

Talking back can take many forms, from making margin notes to composing extensive notebook entries. Respond to passages that cause you to pause for a moment to reflect, to question, and to read again, or to say "Ah!" or "Aha!" At points of high interest, take notes.

If the text is informational, try to capture the statements that pull together or summarize ideas or are repeated. If the text is argumentative (and many of the texts you'll be reading in college will be), examine the claims the text makes about the topic and each piece of supporting evidence. If the text is literary (a novel, play, or poem), pay extra attention to language features such as images, metaphors, and crisp dialogue. In any text, notice words the author puts in **boldface** or *italic* type: They have been marked for special attention.

Note what's happening to you as you read. Ask about the effect of the text on you: How am I reacting? What am I thinking and feeling? What do I like? What do I distrust? Do I know why yet? But don't worry too much now about answering all your questions. (That's where reviewing comes in.)

The more you write about something, the more you will understand it. Using a reading journal is a good way to keep your responses together in one place that you can return to when writing an essay or research paper. Write each response on a fresh page and include the day's date, the title, and author. Write any and all reactions you have to the text, including summaries, notes on key passages, speculations, questions, answers, ideas for further research, and connections to other books or events in your life. Note especially ideas with which you agree or disagree. Explore ideas that are personally appealing. Record memorable quotations (with page numbers) as well as the reasons they strike you as memorable.

The following brief passage from Bly's *Iron John* is an example of a text to respond to.

> **The dark side of men is clear. Their mad exploitation of earth resources, devaluation and humiliation of women, and obsession with tribal warfare are undeniable. Genetic inheritance contributes to their obsessions, but also culture and environment. We have defective mythologies that ignore masculine depth of feeling, assign men a place in the sky instead of earth, teach obedience to the wrong powers, work to keep men boys, and entangle both men and women in systems of industrial domination that exclude both matriarchy and patriarchy. . . .**
>
> **I speak of the Wild Man in this book, and the distinction between the savage man and the Wild Man is crucial throughout. The savage soul does great damage to soul, earth, and humankind; we can say that though the savage man is wounded he prefers not to examine it. The Wild Man, who has examined his wound, resembles a Zen priest, a shaman, or a woodsman more than a savage.**

When you want to read a text such as this critically, do so with pen or pencil in hand. Mark places to examine further, but be aware that mere marking (underlining, checking, highlighting) does not yet engage you in a conversation with the text. To converse with the text, you need to engage in one or more of the following activities actively: probing, annotating, cross-referencing, and outlining. The following sections illustrate full responses for each activity; in reality, however, a reader would use no more than one or two of these techniques to examine a single text critically.

Probing

You probe a text when you raise critical questions about the text and see if you can answer them. *Probing* is, in essence, asking deeper questions than those asked in previewing. What you ask will depend, of course, on your reason for reading in the first place. Here, for example, are the questions I raised about the *Iron John* passage:

- Bly refers to the dark side of men; does he ever talk about the dark side of women? How would women's darkness differ from men's? What evidence for either does he provide?
- Bly suggests that part of men's dark behavior is genetic, part cultural; where does he get this information? Does he think it's a 50/50 split?
- What "defective mythologies" is Bly talking about? Does he mean things like religion and politics, or is he referring to nursery rhymes and folktales?
- Bly generalizes in his opening sentence, "The dark side of men is clear"—in most sentences actually. Will subsequent chapters support these statements or are we asked to accept them on faith?
- I like the dimension Bly makes between "Wild" and "savage" men. Did he coin the terms or are they used pervasively in mythology in the same way? I wonder how sharp the line really is between the two.

Those are five good questions to ask about the passage; however, any other reader could easily think of five or more. These questions are "critical" in the sense that they not only request further information from the book—which all readers need to request—but also challenge the text's terms, statements, and sources to see if they will stand up under sharp scrutiny.

The questions are written in my own language. Using your own words helps in at least three ways: it forces you to articulate precisely; it makes the question *your* question; and it helps you remember the question for future use.

Annotating and Cross-Referencing

Annotating, or talking back to the author in the margins of the text, is an excellent way to make that text your own, a necessary step in understanding it fully. Annotating is easier if you have your own copy of the text; otherwise you can make your annotations on Post-it Notes or in a notebook with page numbers marked. As a critical reader, you can annotate the following:

- Points of agreement and disagreement
- Exceptions and counterexamples
- Extensions and further possibilities
- Implications and consequences
- Personal associations and memories
- Connections to other texts, ideas, and courses
- Recurring images and symbols

To move beyond annotating (commenting on single passages) to *cross-referencing* (finding relationships among your annotations), devise a coding system to note when one annotation is related to another and thus identify and locate different patterns in the text. Some students write comments in different-colored ink—red for questions, green for nature images, blue for speculations, and so on. Other students use numbers—1 for questions, 2 for images, and so on.

In *Iron John,* for example, the term *Wild Man* occurs on pages 6, 8–12, 14, and 26–27, in other chapters, and in the title of the book's epilogue. A critical reader would mark all of these. In addition, the related term *Hairy Man* occurs on pages 5, 6, and 11, and so on. In cross-referencing, I noted in the margins when the two terms occurred together.

Outlining

Another way of talking back to a text is *outlining.* This involves simply writing out a condensed version of the opening sentence or topic sentence of each paragraph, capturing its essence, as I did for the two paragraphs from *Iron John:*

1. The dark side of men
2. The savage man versus the Wild Man

Of course, two paragraphs are simply a start; outlining ten or more paragraphs provides a real clue to the author's organizational pattern. Once you have outlined an article or chapter, you will remember that text better, be able to find key passages more quickly, and see larger patterns more easily.

✍ WRITING 4

Keep a reading journal for one article, chapter, or book that you are assigned to read this semester. Be sure to write something in the journal after every reading session. In addition, annotate and cross-reference the text as you go along to see what patterns you can discover. Finally, make a paragraph outline of the text. Write about the result of these response methods in your journal. Did they help? Which ones worked best?

Reviewing Texts

To *review* you need both to reread and to "re-see" a text, reconsidering its meaning and the ideas you have about it. You need to be sure that you grasp the important points within the text, but you also need to move beyond that to a critical understanding of the text as a whole. In responding, you started a conversation with the text so you could put yourself into its framework and context; in reviewing, you should consider how the book can fit into your own framework and context. Review any text you have previewed and responded to as well as anything you've written in response: journal entries, freewriting, annotations, outlines. Keep responding, talking back to the text even as you review, writing new journal entries to capture your latest insights.

Reviewing can take different forms depending on how you intend to use the text—whether or not you are using it to write a paper, for example. In general, when reviewing a text you have to understand what it means, to interpret its meaning, to evaluate its soundness or significance, and to determine how to use it in your own writing.

Reviewing to Understand

Reviewing to understand means identifying and explaining in your own words the text's main ideas. This task can be simplified if you have outlined the text while responding or have cross-referenced your annotations to highlight relationships among ideas. In reviewing to understand, you can reread portions of articles that you previewed, considering especially abstracts, if there are any; first and last paragraphs; and sections titled "Summary," "Observations," or "Conclusions." In a book, you can reconsider the table of contents, the introductory and concluding chapters, and central chapters that you recognize as important to the author's argument or theme.

Reviewing to Interpret

Reviewing to interpret means moving beyond an appreciation of what the text *says* and building your own theory of what the text *means*. An interpretation is an assertion of what you as a reader think the text is about.

In reviewing to interpret, look over any of your journal entries that articulate overall reactions to the text's main ideas. What did you see in the text? Do you still have the same interpretation? Also reread key passages in the text, making sure that your interpretation is reasonable and is based on the text and is not a product of your imagination.

If you plan to write a critical paper about a text, it's a good idea to confirm your interpretation by consulting what others have said about that text. The interpretations of other critics will help put your own view in perspective as well as raise questions that may not have occurred to you. Try to read more than one perspective on a text. It is better to consult such sources in this reviewing stage after you have established some views of your own, so that you do not simply adopt the view of the first expert you read.

Reviewing to Evaluate

Reviewing to evaluate means deciding whether you think the text accomplishes its own goals. In other words, is the text any good? Different types of texts should be judged on different grounds.

ARGUMENTS.   Many texts you read in college make arguments about ideas, advancing certain *claims* and supporting those claims with *evidence*. A claim is a statement that something is true or should be done. Every claim in an argument should be supported by reliable and sufficient evidence.

At the responding stage, you probably started to identify and comment on the text's claims and evidence. In reviewing, you can ask the following questions to examine and evaluate each part of the argument to see whether it is sound:

* Is the claim based on facts? A *fact* is something that can be verified and that most readers will accept without question. (Fact: The title of the book is *Iron*

John; the author is Robert Bly; it was published in 1990; the myth of Iron John is found in several ancient folktales that have been written down and can be found in libraries; and so on.)

- Is the claim based on a credible inference? An *inference* is a conclusion drawn from an accumulation of facts. (Bly's inferences in *Iron John* about the warrior in modern man are based on his extensive study of ancient mythology. His inferences have a basis in the facts, but other readers might draw other inferences.)
- Is the claim based on opinion? An *opinion* reflects an author's personal beliefs and may be based on faith, emotion, or myth. Claims based on opinion are considered weak in academic writing. (Bly's "dark side of men" is metaphorical and not factual. Some readers would consider it a fair inference based on the savage history of humankind; others would dismiss it as Bly's opinion, based on emotion rather than on facts and careful reasoning.)

All three types of evidence—facts, inference, and opinions—have their place in argumentative writing, but the strongest arguments are those that are based on accurate facts and reasonably drawn inferences. Look out for opinions that are masquerading as facts and for inferences that are based on insufficient facts.

INFORMATIONAL TEXTS.   In reviewing informational texts, like reviewing argumentative texts, you need to make sure that the facts are true, that inferences rely on facts, and that opinions presented as evidence are based on expertise, not emotion. Informational texts don't make arguments, but they do draw conclusions from the facts they present. You must decide whether there are enough reliable facts to justify these conclusions. Consider also whether you think the author is reliable and reasonable: Is the tone objective? Has all the relevant information been presented? Is this person an expert?

LITERARY TEXTS.   Short stories, poems, and plays don't generally make arguments, but they do strive to be believable, to be enjoyable, and to be effective in conveying their themes. One way to evaluate literature is to reread journal entries in which you responded to the author's images, themes, or overall approach. Then look through the text again, guided by any annotations you've made, and ask whether you think the author's choices were good ones. Look in particular for repeated terms, ideas, or images that will help you see the pattern of the text as a whole. Evaluating literature is often very personal, relying on individual associations and responses, but the strongest critical evaluations are based on textual evidence.

Reviewing to Write

Reviewing a text to use in writing your own paper means locating specific passages to quote, paraphrase, or summarize in support of your own assertions about the text. When you quote, you use the exact language of the text; when you paraphrase, you restate the text in your own words; when you summarize, you reduce the text to a brief statement in your own words. When you identify a note card that contains a passage to quote, paraphrase, or summarize, make sure that you have recorded the page on which the passage occurs in the text so you can find it again and so you can prepare correct documentation.

☞ READING AND WRITING

Reading and writing, like producing and consuming, are two sides of the same coin. When you study one, you inevitably learn more about the other at the same time. The more you attend to the language of published writers, the more you will learn about your own language. The more you attend to your own written language, the more you will learn about the texts you read.

In fact, many of the reading strategies you use to understand and evaluate published texts work equally well when reading your own writing. You can preview, respond to, and review your own or your classmates' writing to gain a critical understanding of your writing and to discover strategies for effective revision.

☞ SUGGESTIONS FOR WRITING AND RESEARCH

Individual

Select a short text. First, read it quickly for understanding. Second, read it critically as described in this chapter. Finally, write a short (two-page) critical review of the text, recommending or not recommending it to other readers.

Collaborative

As a class or in small groups, agree on a short text to read and write about according to the preceding directions. Share your reviews in small groups, paying particular attention to the claims and evidence each writer uses in his or her review. Rewrite the reviews based on the responses in the groups.

College Journals

*Journal writing forces me to think about the problems I'm having
with a paper. It's almost a relief, like talking to a friend. I have a
conversation with myself and end up answering my own questions.*

PETER

Journals allow people to talk to themselves without feeling silly. Writing in a journal helps college students think about what is happening in their personal and academic lives—an especially important activity for first-year students coping with a new, often bewildering and exciting environment. Sometimes students focus their journal writing narrowly, on the subject matter of a single discipline; at other times they speculate broadly, on the whole range of academic experience; at still other times they write personally, exploring their private thoughts and feelings.

College instructors often require or recommend that students keep journals to monitor what and how they are learning. Just as often, however, students require journals of themselves, realizing that journals are useful and easy to keep whether they're handed in or not.

❧ CHARACTERISTICS OF JOURNALS

In simplest terms, journals are daily records of people's lives (*jour* is French for "day"). Journals are sometimes called *diaries, daybooks, logs, learning logs,* or *commonplace books.* No matter what you call them, the entries written in them are likely to include whatever thoughts, feelings, activities, or plans are on your mind when you sit down to write. In this sense, a journal can be whatever you want it to be, recording whatever snippets of life you find interesting and potentially useful. Certain characteristics, however, remain true for most journals.

Sequence

You use a journal to capture your thoughts sequentially, from one day to the next, though you may not write in it every day. Over time the entries form a cumulative record of what's on your mind. Dating each entry allows you to compare ideas to later and earlier ones and provides an ongoing record of your constancy, change, or growth. You thus end up documenting your learning over the course of a semester or a project.

Audience

Journals are written to help writers rather than readers. A journal is a place for you to explore what's important to you, not to communicate information or ideas to someone else. While you may choose to share entries with readers whom you trust, that is not the reason you keep a journal. A journal assigned by an instructor who intends to read it may initiate an informal conversation between you and the instructor. As such, it has much in common with notes, letters, and other informal means of communication. Some instructors ask to see sample entries rather than read the whole journal. In most cases, required journals receive credit but not a specific grade.

Language

Journal writing is whatever writers want it to be. There usually are no rules; you choose your own language and your own subjects. (The exception may be an assigned journal.) Your focus should be on *ideas* rather than on style, spelling, or punctuation. In journal writing, simply concentrate on what you want to say and use the word, spelling, or punctuation that comes most readily to mind.

Freedom

Students usually are free to practice, discover, rehearse, and even get things wrong in journals without being penalized. Used in this way, journals are practice and discovery books: You can put new concepts into your own language, try out new lines of reasoning or logic, and not worry about completing every thought. If something doesn't work the first time, you can try it again in subsequent entries—or abandon it entirely. In a journal, you always have the freedom to try again.

◌ WRITING 1

Describe your experiences or associations with journals. Have you ever kept one for school before? In which class? With what result? Have you ever kept one on your own? With what result? Do you still keep one? What is it like?

ᔛ USING JOURNALS IN COLLEGE

Academic journals differ from diaries, daybooks, and private journals in important ways. Whereas diaries and the like may record any and all events of the writer's day, academic journals focus more consistently on ideas under study in college.

Academic journals also differ in important ways from class notebooks, which record the instructor's words rather than the writer's. Academic journals might be called "learning logs" because they record the writer's own perceptions about the business of learning, including reactions to readings, impressions of class, and ideas for writing papers.

Academic journals might be described as a cross between private diaries and class notebooks. Like diaries, journals are written in the first person about ideas important to the writer; like class notebooks, they focus on a subject under study in a college course. I might diagram academic journals like this:

Diary → Academic journal ← Class notebook

Academic journals are most often associated with writing classes, but they can be worthwhile in other classes, too, because they help students become better thinkers and writers.

Journals in the Writing Class

Journals are often assigned in writing classes both to help students discover, explore, advance, and critique their specific writing projects and to help instructors monitor and informally assess students' development as writers.

You can use your journal to find topics to write about, to try out introductions and arguments to use in a paper, to record relevant research and observations, to assess how a paper is turning out, and to make plans for what to do next. In the following journal entry, John tells himself what to do in the next draft of a paper describing his coaching of an eighth-grade girls' soccer team:

> 9/16 I'm going to try to use more dialogue in my paper. That is what I really think I was missing. The second draft is very dull. As I read it, it has no life. I should have used more detail.
>
> I'll try more dialogue, lots more, in draft #3. I'll have it take place at one of my practices, giving a vivid description of what kids were like.
>
> I have SO MUCH MATERIAL. But I have a hard time deciding what seems more interesting.

John's entry is an excellent example of a writer critically evaluating himself and, on the basis of that evaluation, making plans to change something.

Use your journal to record regularly what you are learning in class as you read the textbook, participate in class discussion, read other student papers and models of good professional writing, and review your own writing. Near the end of John's writing course, he reflected in his journal about what he'd learned so far.

> 11/29 I've learned to be very critical of my own work, to look at it again and again, looking for big and little problems. I've also learned from my

writing group that other people's comments can be extremely helpful—so now I make sure I show my early drafts to Kelly or Karen before I write the final draft. I guess I've always known this, but now I actually do it.

↷ WRITING 2

Keep a journal for the duration of a writing project, recording in it all of your starts, stops, insights, and ideas related to the project. At the end, consider whether the journal presents a fair portrait of your own writing process.

Journals Across the Curriculum

Journals are good tools for learning any subject better. They are especially useful in helping you clarify the purposes of a course, pose and solve problems, keep track of readings, raise questions to ask in class, practice for exams, and find topics for paper assignments.

In science or mathematics, when you switch from numbers to words, you often see the problem differently. In addition, putting someone else's problem into your own words makes it your problem and so leads you one step further toward a solution. Ross made the following entry in a journal for a first-year biology course. He was trying to connect what he was learning in the class to what he knew from fishing.

> 10/7 I noticed that saltwater barracudas resemble freshwater pike, pickerel, and muskies. As a matter of curiosity, are these different species analogous—that is, equally successful forms but of different evolution, which converged toward similitude? Or are they of common heritage, homologous?

One of the best uses of a journal is to make connections between college knowledge and personal knowledge—each reinforces the others, and the connections often lead to greater total understanding. Once Ross finds the answer to his questions, he will be more likely to remember this information than information about which he cannot make personal connections.

When you record personal reflections in a literature or history journal, you may begin to identify with and perhaps make sense of the otherwise distant and confusing past. When you write out trial hypotheses in a social science journal, you may discover good ideas for research topics, designs, or experiments. Whether or not an instructor assigns a

↷ WRITING 3

Think of a course you are taking that does not require a journal. Could you find a use for a journal in that class? What topics would you explore? Write about something in the course that you have not fully figured out. Or keep a journal for a week or two and see if it helps your understanding of the course. After doing so, consider how it worked. Did you find out something interesting? Explain.

journal, keeping one will help you raise, reflect on, and answer your own questions in almost any course.

Double-entry Journals

A double-entry journal can help you separate initial observations from later, more reflective observations. To make such a journal, divide each page in a notebook with a vertical line down the middle. On the left side of the page, record initial impressions or data observations; on the right side, return as often as necessary to reflect on the meaning of what you first recorded.

While the idea of a double-entry journal originated in the sciences as a way for lab scientists to collect data at one time and to speculate about them later, these notebooks also serve well in other courses. In a literature class, for example, you can make initial observations about the plot of a story on the left, while raising questions and noting personal reflections on the right.

The example on page 28 is a sample journal entry by Susan, a first-year college student, who read Alice Walker's novel *The Color Purple* for the first time. In the left column, she recorded the plot; in the right column, she noted her personal reaction to what she was reading.

The reason Susan took such careful notes in a double-entry journal is that she intended to write an interpretive paper about the novel. You can see the value of a reader monitoring his or her reactions with such care, even noting which pages raise which questions. When Susan began to write her paper, these journal entries helped her to find a thesis and to locate particular passages in the novel to support her thesis.

ᴥ **WRITING 4**

Keep a double-entry journal for two weeks. On one side of the page, include notes from books you are reading or lectures you are attending. On the other side, write your own thoughts or reactions to those notes. At the end of two weeks, assess the value of this technique for your own understanding of the course material.

Personal Journals

Personal journal writing also has many powerful benefits for students and other writers. In personal journals writers can explore their feelings about any aspect of their lives—being in college, prospective majors, getting along with a roommate, the frustration of receiving a low grade on a paper, the weekend party, or a new date. Anne, a student in a first-year writing class, put it this way:

> Writing is a release, a way of expressing myself, and a way for me to be
> introspective. It helps me find meaning in my thoughts and gets me
> through hard times.

28

Summary	What I think
pp. 3–12. Celie's mother is dying so her father starts having sex with her. She got pregnant by him twice, and he sold both of her babies.	Why did Celie's father sell her kids?
Celie's mother died and he got married again to a very young girl.	How could Mr. take Celie if he wanted Nettie so much?
Mr. is a man whose wife died and he has a lot of children. He wants to marry Celie's sister Nettie. Their father won't let him.	I think Celie's father is lowdown and selfish. A very cruel man.
He says Nettie has too much going for her so he lets him have Celie.	
pp. 13–23. Celie got married to Mr., and his kids don't like her. While Celie was in town she met the lady who has her kids. She was a preacher's wife. Nettie ran away and came to stay with Celie. Mr. still likes her and puts her out because she shows no interest in him. Celie tells her to go to the preacher's wife's house and stay with them because she was the only woman she saw with money.	I think it's wrong to marry someone to take care of your children and to keep your home clean.
	I think Celie was at least glad to know one of her children was in good hands.
	I am glad Nettie was able to get away from her Dad and Mr., hopefully the preacher & wife will take her in.
pp. 24–32. Shug Avery, Mr.'s old friend and also an entertainer, came to town. Mr. got all dressed up so he could go see her, he stayed gone all weekend. Celie was very excited about her.	How could he go and stay out with another woman all weekend? Why didn't he marry Shug?
	Why was Celie so fascinated with Shug?

When you keep a journal in a writing class, it's a good idea to mark off a section for personal entries. Whether you share these with your instructor should be your choice. In the following example, Amy was writing more about herself than her writing class; however, she chose to share the entry with her instructor anyway.

> 11/12 I think I should quit complaining about being misunderstood . . . since I don't try very hard to be understandable, it's no wonder people don't. I just get ticked because more people don't even seem to try to understand others. So many people talk instead of listening. (I think I'm scared of the ones who listen.)

✌ WRITING 5

Keep a personal journal for two weeks, writing faithfully for at least ten minutes each day. Write about your friends, family, future, work, money, frustrations, successes, failures, plans, dates, movies—whatever is on your mind. After two weeks, reread all of your entries and assess the value of such a journal to you.

✌ EXPERIMENTING WITH JOURNALS

If you are keeping a journal for the first time, write often and regularly on a wide variety of topics, and take risks with form, style, and voice. Notice how writing in the early morning differs from writing late at night. Notice the results of writing at the same time every day, regardless of inclination or mood. Try to develop the habit of using your journal even when you are not in an academic environment. Good ideas, questions, and answers don't always wait for convenient times. Above all, write in your journal in your most comfortable voice, freely, and don't worry about someone evaluating you. The following selection of journal entries illustrates some of the ways journals can be especially helpful.

Inventing

Journals can help you plan and start any project by providing a place to talk it over with yourself. Whether it's a research paper, a personal essay, or a take-home exam, you can make journal notes about how to approach a project, where to start, or whom to consult before beginning a draft. Here are two entries from Peter's journal in which he tried to discover a research paper topic for his first-year writing class:

> 10/8 The first draft of this research paper is really difficult: how can you write about something you aren't even interested in? It was not a good idea to pick "legalization of marijuana" just because the issue came up in class discussion. I'm afraid my paper will be all opinion and no facts, because I really don't feel like digging for these facts—if there are any.

> 10/12 Well, I switched my research topic to something I'm actually interested in, a handicapped children's rehabilitation program right here on campus. My younger brother was born deaf and our whole family has pitched in to help him—but I've never really studied what a college program could do to help. The basis of my research will be interviews with people who run the program—I have my first appointment tomorrow with Professor Stanford.

Sometimes planning means venting frustration about what's going wrong; at other times it means trying a new direction or topic. Peter does both. Journal writing is ultimately unpredictable: your writing doesn't come out neat and orderly, and sometimes it doesn't solve your problem, but your journal provides a place where you can keep trying.

Learning to Write

Part of the content of a writing course is the business of learning to write. In other courses, part of the content is learning to write papers about specific topics. You can use a journal to document how your writing is going and what you need to do to improve it. In the following example, Bruce reflects on his experience of writing a report:

> 10/3 I'm making this report a lot harder than it should be. I think my problem is I try to edit as I write. I think what I need to do is just write whatever I want. After I'm through, then edit and organize. It's hard for me though.

Bruce chastises himself for making his writing harder than need be but at the same time reminds himself about the process he learned in class that would help his report writing. Journals are good places to monitor your own writing process and document what helps you the most.

Writing to Learn

Journal writing can help you discover what you think. The act of regular writing certifies thoughts and even causes new ones to develop. In that sense, journal writing is strategy for starting in new directions (see Chapter 9). In the following example, Julie, who kept a journal about all the authors she studied in her American literature course, noticed a disturbing pattern and wrote in her journal to make some sense of it:

> 5/4 So far, the first two authors we have to read have led tragic, unhappy lives. I wonder if this is just a coincidence or if it has something to do with the personality of successful writers. Actually, of all people, writers need a lot of time alone, by themselves, thinking and writing, away from other people, including, probably, close family members. The more I think about it, writers would be very difficult people to live with, that's it—writers spend so much time alone and become hard to live with. . . .

Julie used the act of regular journal writing to discover and develop ideas, make interpretations, and test hypotheses. Writing to learn requires you to trust that as you write, ideas will come—some right, some wrong; some good, some bad.

Questioning and Answering

A journal is a place to raise questions about ideas or issues that don't make sense. Raising questions is a fundamental part of all learning: the more you ask, the more you learn as you seek answers. In the following example, Jim wrote in his journal to figure out a quotation written on the blackboard in his technical writing class:

> 9/23 "All Writing Is Persuasive"—It's hard to write on my understanding of this quotation because I don't think that all writing is persuasive. What about assemblies for models and cookbook recipes? I realize that for stories, newspaper articles, novels, and so forth that they are persuasive. But is all writing persuasive? I imagine that for assemblies and so forth that they are persuading a person to do something a particular way. But is this really persuasive writing?

While Jim began by writing "I don't think that all writing is persuasive," he concluded that even assembly instructions "are persuading a person to do something a particular way." The writing sharpened the focus of Jim's questioning and made him critically examine his own ideas, leading him to reconsider his first response to the quotation.

Catching Insights

College is a good place to develop a wider awareness of the world, and a journal can help you examine the social and political climate you grew up in and perhaps took for granted. Jennifer used her journal to reflect on sexist language, recording both her awareness of sexist language in society as well as her own difficulty in avoiding it:

> 3/8 Sexist language is everywhere. So much so that people don't even realize what they are saying is sexist. My teacher last year told all the "mothers-to-be" to be sure to read to their children. What about the fathers? Sexist language is dangerous because it so easily undermines women's morale and self-image. I try my hardest not to use sexist language, but even I find myself falling into old stereotypes.

Evaluating Classes

Journals can be used to capture and record feelings about how a class is going, about what you are learning and not learning. In the following entry, Brian seemed surprised that writing can be fun:

> 9/28 English now is more fun. When I write, the words come out more easily and it's not like homework. All my drafts help me put together my thoughts and retrieve memories that were hidden somewhere in the dungeons of my mind. Usually I wouldn't like English, like in high school, but I pretty much enjoy it here. I like how you get to hear people's reactions to your papers and discuss them with each other.

Entries like this can help you monitor your own learning process. Instructors also learn from candid and freely given comments about the effects of their teaching. Your journal is one place where you can let your instructor know what is happening in class from your point of view.

Clarifying Values

Your journal can be a record of evolving insight as well as the tool to gain that insight. You might ask yourself questions that force you to examine life closely: "If my house were on fire and I could save only one object, what would it be?" or "If I had only two more days to live, how would I spend them?" I used my journal to wrestle with the next direction my life would take:

> 3/12 Do I really want to switch jobs and move to North Carolina? The climate is warmer—a lot longer motorcycle season—and maybe this time we'd look for a farm. But Laura would have to start all over with her job, finding new contacts in the public school system, and we'd both have to find new friends, new doctors, dentists, auto mechanics, get new driver's licenses.
> In truth, we really like Vermont, the size, the scale, the beauty, our house, and Annie is just starting college. Money and sunshine aren't everything. . . .

What you read here is only one entry from nearly a month's worth of writing as I tried to figure out what to do with an attractive job offer. In the end, and with the clarifying help of my journal, I stayed put.

Letting Off Steam

Journals are good places to vent frustration over personal or academic difficulties. College instructors don't assign journals to improve students' mental health, but they know that journals can help. Kenyon wrote about the value of the journal experience:

> 10/14 This journal has saved my sanity. It got me started at writing. . . . I can't keep all my problems locked up inside me, but I hate telling others, burdening them with my problems—like what I'm going to do with my major or with the rest of my life.

In many ways, writing in a journal is like talking to a sympathetic audience; the difference, as Kenyon noted, is that the journal is always there, no matter what's on your mind, and it never gives you grief.

Finding Patterns

The very nature of the journal—sequential, chronological, personal—lends it to synthesizing activities, such as finding patterns or larger structures in your learning over time. Rereading journal entries after a few weeks or months can provide specific material from which you can make generalizations and hypotheses. Each individual act of summary becomes a potential thread for weaving new patterns of meaning. Near the end of an American literature course, Maureen summarized the journal's cumulative power this way:

> 5/2 I feel that through the use of this journal over the weeks I have been able to understand certain aspects of each story by actually writing down what I like, and what I don't. . . . Many times I didn't even realize that something bothered me about a story until I put down my feelings in words. I wasn't even sure how I even felt about *The Sun Also Rises* until I kicked a few ideas around on paper. Now I plan to write my take-home exam about it. In short, this journal has really helped me understand this class.

Recording Change

Sometimes it's hard to see how a journal functions overall until you reread it at the end of a term and notice where you began and where you ended. All along your writing may have been casual and fast, your thoughts tentative, your assessments or conclusions uncertain. But the journal gives you a record of who you were, what you thought, and how you changed. Rereading a term's entries may be a pleasant surprise, as Jeff found out:

> 11/21 The journal to me has been like a one-man debate, where I could write thoughts down and then later read them. This seemed to help clarify many of my ideas. To be honest there is probably fifty percent of the journal that is nothing but B.S. and ramblings to fulfill assignments, but that still leaves fifty percent that I think is of importance. The journal is also a time capsule. I want to put it away and not look at it for ten or twenty years and let it recall for me this period of my life.

ℐ LETTERS FROM JOURNALS

Sometimes, instead of turning in your journal for an instructor to check, you will be asked to write a class letter to your instructor, addressing him or her personally, about issues related to the course—perhaps issues captured in your journal. What I like about this use of journals is that all your thoughts and insights remain private unless you choose to share them with a specific and known audience. An audience is the only real difference between a class letter and a journal entry—the former written to someone else, the latter to yourself.

As an instructor, I appreciate getting letters that are informal, personal, honest, and that contain some references to and insights about course materials: readings, class discussion, subject matter. In other words, I enjoy hearing from my own students about all the ideas for journal writing already explored in this chapter, the only difference being that these are intentionally shared with me. If you are asked to share letters with an instructor, consider the following:

1. Address your instructor personally, including references to common experience or shared ideas, single-space, and sign your name.
2. Focus on course ideas rather than your private life, but include incidents from your private life when they are relevant to course material.

3. Avoid being overly general: Include references to specific passages in the readings or specific incidents in the class.
4. Ask real questions or pose real problems that you hope to have answered.
5. Write informally, in your natural voice, but revise and edit enough so that your language is clear and coherent.

When I receive letters, I either write back a single letter to the whole class, quoting passages from different students so the whole class can be brought into the conversation, or I write brief responses on each letter and return every letter to the sender. I count the letters as I do journals, quantitatively: Students get credit for simply doing them, not grades on specific content.

Increasingly, my students and I share e-mail messages, which is a wonderfully quick and efficient way of conversing about specific ideas, questions, or problems related to the course. E-mail writing may resemble journal writing in that it is usually informal and unrevised; however, like talking on the telephone and writing letters, the addition of a specific audience means that even this most informal language needs to be clear, correct, and respectful. A loose version of the guidelines above would cover e-mail writing as well.

ᛒ SUGGESTIONS FOR WRITING AND RESEARCH

Individual

1. Select a writer in your intended major who is known for having written a journal (for example, Mary Shelley, Ralph Waldo Emerson, Virginia Woolf, or Anaïs Nin in literature; Leonardo da Vinci, Georgia O'Keeffe, or Edward Weston in the arts; B. F. Skinner or Margaret Mead in the social sciences; Charles Darwin or Marie Curie in the sciences). Study the writer's journals to identify the features that characterize them and the purpose they served. Write a report on what you find and share it with your class.
2. At the end of the semester, review your journal and do the following: (a) put in page numbers, (b) write a title for each entry, (c) make a table of contents, and (d) write an introduction to the journal explaining how it might be read by a stranger (or your instructor).
3. Review your journal entries for the past five weeks, select one entry that seems especially interesting, and write a reflective essay of several pages on it. How are they different? Which is better? Is that a fair question?

Collaborative

Have each student agree to bring a typed copy of one journal entry written during the term. Exchange entries in writing groups or in the whole class and discuss interesting features of the entries.

Chapter

❧ **4** ❧

The Elements of Composition

I find it very confusing moving from one professor to another.
They all expect different things. I still haven't learned yet what
makes a "good" paper as opposed to a "bad" paper.
JENNIFER

Why do teachers always make you write about what they want you
to and never what you want to? What is the writing for anyway?
ERIC

I would like to develop some sort of personal style so
when I write people know it's me.
JOHN

The focus, structure, and style of every paper you write are determined by your situation—why you are writing (purpose) and to whom (audience). Taken together, purpose and audience largely determine the voice in which you write. While this chapter asks you to consider each of these fundamental elements of composition in isolation, in truth, experienced writers usually think about them subconsciously and simultaneously. In any case, I believe the following discussion may be useful when you are assigned to write an academic paper.

❧ **WRITING FOR A PURPOSE**

People write to discover what's on their minds, figure things out, vent frustrations, keep records, remember things, communicate information, shape ideas, express feelings, recount experiences, raise questions, imagine the future, create new forms—and simply for pleasure. They also write when they're required to in school, to demonstrate knowledge and solve problems. But no matter what the task, writers write better when they do so purposefully—when they know what they want to accomplish. This section examines three broad and overlapping stages of writing: discovering, communicating, and creating. It discusses strategies to accomplish each one effectively.

Writing to Discover

Writing helps people discover ideas, relationships, connections, and patterns in their lives and in the world. In college, students write to discover paper topics, develop those topics, expand and explain ideas, and connect seemingly unrelated material in coherent patterns. In this sense, writing is one of the most powerful learning tools available.

Writing is especially powerful because it makes language and therefore thoughts stand still, allowing thoughts to be examined slowly and deliberately, allowing ideas to be elaborated, critiqued, rearranged, and corrected. Playwright Christopher Fry once said, "My trouble is that I'm the sort of writer who only finds out what he is getting at by the time he's got to the end of it." In other words, his purpose and plan become clear only after he has written a whole draft; he knows that the act of writing will help him find his way. But rather than considering this inventive power of writing "troublesome," to use Fry's words, you can consider it a solution to many other problems. Once you know that writing can generate ideas, advance concepts, and forge connections, then you can use it deliberately and strategically to help you write college papers.

Discovery can happen in all writing. Any time you write, you may find new or lost ideas, implications, and directions. However, sometimes it pays to write with the specific intention of discovering. Discovery writing is often used before actual drafting to explore the subject and purpose of a paper or to solve writing problems once drafting and revising have begun.

↩ WRITING 1

Describe a time when you used writing for discovery purposes. Did you set out to use writing this way, or did it happen accidentally? Have you used it deliberately since then? With what results?

Writing to Communicate

The most common reason for writing in college is to transmit ideas or information to an audience. College students write essays, exams, and reports to instructors, as well as letters, applications, and résumés to potential employers. The general guidelines for such writing are well known: Communicative writing needs to be obviously purposeful so both writer and reader know where it's going. It needs to be clear in order to be understood. It needs to include assertions supported by evidence in order to be believable. And it needs to be conventionally correct in terms of spelling, mechanics, and grammar in order to be taken seriously. While there are interesting exceptions to these guidelines (see Chapter 24), they are the rule in most academic writing situations.

Thesis-Based Writing

Many academic assignments ask you to write *thesis-based* papers, that is, papers that assert, explain, support, or defend a position or idea. Your assertion about the idea or position is called the paper's *thesis*. Since most academic papers are assigned so that instructors can witness and assess student knowledge, stating a thesis makes clear what, exactly, the paper's claim or position is. The thesis, broadly speaking, is the place to summarize the main idea to make it explicit to readers. For example, the thesis of this chapter is stated in the first paragraph: that *the focus, structure, and style of papers are determined by purpose and audience.* This claim is then supported throughout the rest of the chapter.

Some thesis-based papers present the thesis first, usually in the opening paragraph to tell readers what's coming. Such *thesis-first* papers are common in academic as well as technical and scientific writing because they emphasize the transmission of an idea or information clearly, directly, and economically, thus helping readers get rapidly to the point. In contrast, *delayed-thesis* papers do not state conclusions up front but examine a variety of conditions or circumstances to be considered before a decision is made. Such papers emphasize the process by which the writer discovered knowledge as much as the knowledge itself. Whether first or delayed, a thesis-driven paper explicitly answers the critical reader's question "So what?" Why does this paper exist? What's it about? Common thesis-based assignments in college include the following, which are examined in more detail in subsequent chapters:

- *Explaining ideas.* The purpose of explaining something is to make it clear to somebody who knows less about the subject than you do. You explain best by following a logical order, using simple language, and providing illustration and examples of what you mean.
- *Arguing positions.* The purpose of arguing is to persuade readers to agree with your position. College assignments frequently ask you to explore opposing sides of an issue or several different interpretations of a text and then to take a stand advocating one point of view.
- *Interpreting texts.* The purpose of interpreting a text is to explain to others what the text means, to tell why you believe it means this, and to support your reading with reasons based on evidence from the text.

Question-Based Writing

Still other papers assigned in college may have, as their larger purpose, more personal or reflective dimensions, and never directly state a thesis at all. Such exploratory papers might pose questions to which specific answers are illusive or examine dimensions of the writer's self in relation to the larger world. These *question-based* papers might be said to emphasize the play of the writer's mind more than the direct transmission of knowledge. However, these papers, too, answer—though less directly—the critical reader's questions "So what? Why does this paper exist? What's it about?" Common question-based assignments include the following, which are examined in more detail in subsequent chapters:

- *Recounting experience.* People narrate personal stories to share common experiences with others and to learn, in the telling, the meaning of those experiences for themselves.

- *Exploring identity.* People examine their own lives to find out important things about who they are, how they got that way, or where they're going next.
- *Profiling people.* Writers profile other people to find out how other lives are lived, valued, and expressed, and, in the process, to learn about our shared culture.
- *Reflecting on the world.* Writers speculate, muse, and ponder about an infinite number of ideas and issues in our world, and share them with others, to find out what these ideas mean and what, along the way, the world means.

ᕗ WRITING 2

When is the last time you wrote to communicate something? Describe your purpose and audience. How successful were these acts of communication? How do you know?

Writing to Create

When you write to imagine or create, you often pay special attention to the way your language looks and sounds, its form, shape, rhythm, images, and texture. Though the term *creative writing* is most often associated with poetry, fiction, and drama, it's important to see any act of writing, from personal narratives to research essays, as creative.

When you write to create, you pay less immediate attention to your audience and subject and more to the act of expression itself. Your goal is not so much to change the world or to transmit information about it as to transform an experience or idea into something that will make your readers pause, see the world from a different angle and perhaps reflect upon what it means. You want your writing itself, not just the information it contains, to affect your readers emotionally or esthetically as well as intellectually.

In most college papers, your primary purpose will be to communicate, not to create. However, nearly every writing assignment has room for a creative dimension. When writing for emotional or esthetic effect in an otherwise communicative paper, be especially careful that your creativity serves a purpose and that the communicative part is strong on its own. You want your creative use of language to enhance, not camouflage, your ideas.

INTENSIFYING EXPERIENCE. When Amanda recounted her experience picking potatoes on board a mechanical potato harvester on her father's farm, she made her readers feel the experience as she did by crafting her language to duplicate the sense of hard, monotonous work:

> Potatoes, mud, potatoes, mud, potatoes, that was all I saw in front of me. They moved from my right side to my left, at hip level. A conveyor belt never stopping. On and on and on. The potatoes passed fast, a constant stream. My hands worked deftly, pulling out clods of dirt, rotten potatoes, old shaws, and anything else I found that wasn't a potato. It was October, the ground was nearly frozen, the mud

was hard and solid. Cold. Dirt had gotten into my yellow and yet brown rubber gloves, had wedged under my nails, increasing my discomfort.

This is a creative approach to essay writing because the writer uses a graphic, descriptive style to put readers at the scene of her experience rather than summarizing it or explaining explicitly what it meant to her.

EXPERIMENTING WITH FORM.   Keith created a special language effect in an otherwise traditional and straightforward academic assignment by writing a poetic prologue for a research essay about homeless people in New York City. The full essay contains factual information derived from social workers, agency documents, and library research.

> The cold cement
> no pillow
> The steel grate
> no mattress
> But the hot air
> of the midnight subway
> Lets me sleep.

Using the poetic form creates a brief emotional involvement with the research subject, allowing readers to fill in missing information with their imaginations. Note, however, that the details of the poem (*cold cement, steel grate, subway*) spring not from the writer's imagination but from his research notes and observations.

ᴽ WRITING 3

Describe a time when your primary purpose in writing was to create rather than to discover or communicate. Were you pleased with the result? Why or why not?

ᴽ ADDRESSING AUDIENCES

The better you know your audience, the better you're likely to write. Whether your writing is judged "good" or not depends largely on how well it's received by the readers for whom it's intended. Just as you change the way you speak depending on the audience you're addressing—your boss, mother, instructor, friend, younger brother—so you change the way you write depending on the audience to whom you're writing. You don't want to overexplain and perhaps bore the audience or underexplain and leave it wanting.

Speakers have an advantage over writers in that they see the effect of their words on their listeners and can adjust accordingly. A puzzled look tells the speaker to slow down, a smile and nod says keep going full speed ahead, and so on. However, writers can only imagine the reactions of the people to whom they're trying to communicate.

I believe all college papers need to be written to at least two audiences, maybe more: first, to yourself, so you understand it; second, to your instructor who has asked you to write it in the first place. In addition, you may also be writing to other students or for publication to more public audiences. This chapter examines how expectations differ from one audience to the next.

Understanding College Audiences

It might help to think of the different audiences you will address in college as existing along a continuum, with those closest and best known to you (yourself, friends) at one end and those farthest from and least known to you (the general public) at the other end:

Self—Family—Friends—Instructor—Public

While the items on your continuum will always differ in particulars from somebody else's, the principle that you know some audiences better than others will always be the same and will influence how you write. The audience of most concern to most college students is the instructor who will evaluate their learning on the basis of their writing.

> ✍ **WRITING 4**
>
> Think back over the past several weeks and list all the different audiences to whom you have written. To whom did you write most often? Which audiences were easy for you to address? Which were difficult? Why?

Shaping Writing for Different Audiences

To shape your writing for a particular audience, you first need to understand the qualities of your writing that can change according to audience. The context you need to provide; the structure, tone, and style you use; and your purpose for writing can all be affected by your audience. (Structure, tone, and style are important elements of voice.)

CONTEXT.   Different audiences need different contexts—different amounts or kinds of background information—in order to understand your ideas. Find out whether your readers already know about the topic or whether it's completely new to them. Consider whether any terms or ideas need explaining. For example, other students in your writing group might know exactly whom you mean if you refer to a favorite singer, but your instructor might not. Also consider what sort of explanation would work best with your audience.

STRUCTURE.   Every piece of writing is put together in a certain way: some ideas are discussed early, others late; transitions between ideas are marked in a certain way; similar ideas are either grouped together or treated separately. How you structure a paper depends in large part on what you think will work best with your particular audience. For example, if you were writing an argument for someone who disagrees with your position, you might begin with the evidence with which you both agree and then later introduce more controversial evidence.

TONE.   The tone of a piece of writing conveys the writer's attitude toward the subject matter and audience. How do you want to sound to your readers? You may, of course, have a different attitude toward each audience you address. In addition, you may want different audiences to hear in different ways. For example, when writing to yourself, you won't mind sounding confused. When writing to instructors, though, you will want to sound confident and authoritative.

STYLE.   Style is largely determined by the formality and complexity of your language. You need to determine what style your readers expect and what style will be most effective in a given paper. Fellow students might be offended if you write in anything other than a friendly style, but some instructors might interpret the same style as disrespectful.

PURPOSE.   The explicit purpose of your writing depends more on you and your assignment than on your audience. However, certain purposes are more likely to apply to particular audiences than others. Also, there are unstated purposes embedded in any piece of writing, and these will vary depending on whom you're addressing. For example, is it important that your readers like you? Or that they respect you? Or that they give you good grades? Always ask yourself what you want a piece of writing to do for or to your audience and what you want your audience to do in response to your writing.

Let's follow the way writing generally needs to change as you move along the scale away from the audience you know best, yourself.

WRITING TO YOURSELF.   Every paper you write is addressed in part to yourself, and some writing, such as journals, is addressed primarily to yourself. However, most reports, essays, papers, and exams are also addressed to other people: instructors, peers, parents, or employers. Journal writing is your opportunity to write to yourself and yourself alone. When you write to yourself alone, you don't need to worry about context, structure, tone, or style; only purpose matters if you are the sole reader. However, if you make a journal entry that you might want to refer to later, it's a good idea to provide sufficient background and explanation to help you remember the event or the idea described if you do return to it. When you are the reader of your own writing, choose words, sentences, rhythms, images, and punctuation that come easiest and most naturally to you.

WRITING TO PEERS.   Your peers are your equals, your friends and classmates, people of similar age, background, or situation. Some of your assignments will ask you to consider the other students in the class to be your audience, for example, when you read papers to each other in writing groups or exchange papers to edit each other's work.

The primary difference between writing to yourself and writing to peers is the amount of context and structure you need to provide to make sure your readers understand you. If your paper is about a personal experience, you need to provide the explanations and details that will allow readers who did not have your experience to fully understand the events and ideas you describe.

If your paper is about a subject that requires research, be sure to provide background information to make the topic comprehensible and interesting in a structure (for example, chronological order, logical order, cause-effect sequence) that makes sense. Be direct, honest, and friendly; peers will see right through any pretentious or stuffy language.

You usually write to peers to share a response to their writing, to recount an experience, to explain an idea, or to argue a position. In a writing class, the most important implicit purpose is probably to establish a good working rapport with your classmates by being honest, straightforward, and supportive.

WRITING TO INSTRUCTORS.   Instructors are among the most difficult audiences for whom to write. First, they usually make the assignments, so they know what they want, and it's your job to figure out what that is. Second, they often know more about your subject than you do. Third, different instructors may have quite different criteria for what constitutes good writing. And fourth, each instructor may simultaneously play several different roles: a helpful resource, a critic, an editor, a coach, and, finally, a judge.

It is often difficult to know how much context to provide in a paper written for an instructor unless the assignment specifically tells you. For example, in writing about a Shakespearean play to an English professor, should you provide a summary of the play when you know that he or she already knows it? Or should you skip the summary information and write only about ideas original with you? The safest approach is to provide full background, explain all ideas, support all assertions, and cite authorities in the field. Write as if your instructor needed all this information and it were your job to educate him or her.

When writing papers to instructors, be sure to use a structure that suits the type of paper you are writing. For example, personal experience papers are often chronological, reports may be more thematic, and so on. (The chapters in Part Two describe conventional structures for each type of paper discussed there.)

One of your instructor's roles is to help you learn to write effective papers. But another role is to evaluate whether you have done so and, from a broader perspective, whether you are becoming a literate member of the college community. Therefore, your implicit purpose when you write to instructors is to demonstrate your understanding of conventions, knowledge, reasoning ability, and originality.

WRITING TO PUBLIC AUDIENCES.   Writing to a public audience is difficult for all writers because the audience is usually both diverse and unknown. The public audience can include both people who know more and those who know less than you; it can contain experts who will correct the slightest mistake and novices who need even simple terms explained; it can contain opponents looking for reasons to argue and supporters looking for reasons to continue support. And you are unlikely to know many of these people personally.

You usually have some idea of who these anonymous readers are or you wouldn't be writing to them in the first place. Still, it is important to learn as much as you can about any of their beliefs and characteristics that may be relevant to the point you intend to make. What is their educational level? What are their political, philosophical, or religious beliefs? What are their interests?

When you don't know who your audience is, provide context for everything you say. If you are referring to even well-known groups such as the NCAA or ACLU, write out the full names the first time you refer to them (National Collegiate Athletic Association or

American Civil Liberties Union). If you refer to an idea as postmodern, define or illustrate what the term means. (Good luck!) Your writing should be able to stand by itself and make complete sense to people you do not know.

Your purpose and structure should be as clear as possible, with your opening paragraph letting this audience know what's to come. Your tone will depend on your purpose, but generally it should be fair and reasonable. Your style will depend on the publication for which you are writing.

> ### ᔕ WRITING 5
>
> How accurate do you find the preceding discussion about different college audiences? Describe circumstances that confirm or contradict the description here. If instructors are not your most difficult audience, explain who is.

ᔕ FINDING A VOICE

Each individual speaks with distinctive voice. Some people speak loudly, some softly, others with quiet authority. Some sound assertive or aggressive while others sound cautious, tentative, or insecure. Some voices are clear and easy to follow while others are garbled, convoluted, and meandering. Some create belief and inspire trust while others do not.

An individual's voice can also be recognized in the writing he or she produces. A writer's voice, like a person's personality, is determined by factors such as ethnic identity, social class, family, or religion. In addition, some elements of voice evolve as a writer matures, such as how one thinks (logically or intuitively) and what one thinks (a political or philosophical stance). Writers also can exert a great deal of control over their language. They create the style (simple or complex), the tone (serious or sarcastic), and many other elements. Writers try to be in control of as many elements of their writing voice as they can.

Defining Voice

The word *voice* means at least two distinctly different things. First, it is the audible sound of a person speaking (*He has a high-pitched voice*). Speaking voices distinguish themselves by auditory qualities such as pitch (high, low, nasal), pace (fast, slow), tone (angry, assertive, tentative), rhythm (regular, smooth, erratic), volume (soft, loud), and accent (Southern, British, Boston). Applied to writing, this meaning cannot be taken literally; unless writers read their work aloud, readers don't actually hear writers' voices. However, the language on the page can re-create the sound of the writer talking. Careful writers control, as much as they can, the sound of their words in their readers' heads.

Second, *voice,* especially when applied to writing, suggests who a person is and what he or she stands for. Written voices convey something of the writers behind the words, including their personal, political, philosophical, and social beliefs. In addition, writers' beliefs and values may be revealed in the way they reason about things, whether they do so in an orderly, scientific manner or more intuitively and emotionally.

⨪ **WRITING 6**

In your own words, describe the concept of voice. Do you think writers have one voice or many? Explain what you mean.

⨪ **ANALYZING VOICE**

Readers experience a writer's voice as a whole expression, not a set of component parts. However, to help you understand and gain control of your own voice, let's examine the individual elements that combine to make the whole.

TONE. Tone is your attitude toward the subject and audience: angry, anxious, joyous, sarcastic, puzzled, contemptuous, respectful, friendly, and so on. Writers control their tone, just as speakers do, by adopting a particular perspective or point of view, selecting words carefully, emphasizing some words and ideas over others, choosing certain patterns of inflection, and controlling the pace with pauses and other punctuation. For example, note how your tone might change as you speak or write the following sentences:

- The English Department was unable to offer enough writing courses to satisfy the demand this semester.
- Why doesn't English offer more writing courses?
- It's outrageous that so many students were closed out of first-year writing courses!

To gain control of the tone of your writing, read drafts of your paper aloud and listen carefully to the attitudes you express. Try to hear your own words as if you were the audience: decide whether the overall tone is the one you intended, and reread carefully to make sure every sentence contributes to this tone.

STYLE. Style is the way writers express themselves according to whom they are addressing and why. Style is found in the formality or informality, simplicity or complexity, clarity or muddiness of a writer's language. For example, in writing to a friend, you may adopt an informal, conversational style, characterized by contractions and simple, colloquial language:

John. Can't make it tonight. Spent the day cutting wood and am totally bushed.

In writing to instructors, however, you may be more formal, careful, and precise:

Dear Professor James,

I am sorry, but my critical essay will be late. Over the weekend, I overextended myself cutting, splitting, and stacking two cords of wood for my father and ended up with a sprained back. Would you be willing to extend the paper deadline for one more day?

In other words, the style you adopt depends on your audience, purpose, and situation. To gain control of your style, think about how you wish to present yourself, and shape your words, sentences, and paragraphs to suit the occasion.

STRUCTURE.   The structure of a text is how it's put together: where it starts, where it goes next, where the thesis occurs, what evidence fits where, how it concludes. Structure is the pattern or logic that holds together thoughtful writing, revealing something of the thought process that created it. For example, a linear, logical structure may characterize the writer as a linear, logical thinker, while a circular, digressive structure may suggest more intuitive, less orderly habits of mind. Skillful writers, of course, can present themselves one way or the other depending on whom they're addressing and why.

The easiest way to gain control of an essay's structure is to make an outline that reveals visually and briefly the organization and direction you intend. Some writers outline before they start writing and stick to the outline all the way through the writing. Others outline only after writing a draft or two to help control their final draft. And still others start with a rough outline they continue to modify as the writing modifies thought and direction.

VALUES AND BELIEFS.   Your values include your political, social, religious, and philosophical beliefs. Your background, opinions, and beliefs will be part of everything you write, but you must learn when to express them directly and when not to. For example, including your values would enhance a personal essay or other autobiographical writing, but it may detract attention from the subject of a research essay.

To gain control of the values in your writing, consider whether the purpose of the assignment calls for an implicit or explicit statement of your values. Examine your drafts for words that reveal your personal biases, beliefs, and values; keep them or take them out as appropriate for the assignment.

AUTHORITY.   Your authority comes from confidence in your knowledge and is projected through the way you handle the material about which you are writing. An authoritative voice is often clear, direct, factual, and specific, leaving the impression that the writer is confident about what he or she is saying. You can exert and project real authority only over material you know well, whether it's the facts of your personal life or carefully researched information. The more you know about your subject, the more clearly you will explain it, and the more confident you will sound.

To gain control over the authority in your writing, do your homework, conduct thorough research, and read your sources of information carefully and critically.

↭ **WRITING 7**

Describe your own writing voice in terms of each of the elements outlined in this section (tone, style, structure, values, authority). Then compare your description with a recent paper you have written. In what ways does the paper substantiate your description? In what ways does it differ from your description? How do you account for any differences?

ॐ SUGGESTIONS FOR WRITING AND RESEARCH

Individual

1. Select a topic that interests you and write about it in each of the three modes described in this chapter. First, begin with discovery writing to yourself, perhaps in a journal. Second, write a letter to communicate with somebody about this interest. Third, write creatively about it in a short poem, story, or play. Finally, describe your experience writing in these different modes.

2. Select a paper you have written recently for an instructor audience and rewrite it for a publication, choosing either a student newspaper or a local magazine. Before you start, make notes about what elements need to be changed: context, structure, tone, style, or purpose. When you finish recasting the paper to this larger, more public audience, complete collaborative assignment 3. Make final revisions, taking into account your partner's observations, and send your paper to the publication.

3. Collect and examine as many samples of your past writing as you have saved. Also look closely at the writing you have done during this term. Write a paper in which you describe and explain this history and evolution of your voice and the features that most characterize your current writing voice.

Collaborative

1. Select a topic that your whole writing group is interested in writing about. Divide your labors so that some of you do discovery writing, some do communicative writing, and some write creatively. With scissors and tape, combine your efforts into a single coherent, creative piece of college writing, making sure that some of every member's writing is included in the finished product. Perform a reading of this collage for the other groups; listen to theirs in return.

2. In a group of five students, select a topic of common interest. Write about the topic (either as homework or for fifteen minutes in class) to one of the following audiences: yourself, a friend who is not attending your school, your instructor, an appropriate magazine or newspaper. Share your writing with one another, and together list the choices you needed to make for each audience.

3. Exchange recently written papers with a partner. Examine your partner's paper for the elements of voice. In a letter, each of you describe what you find. How does your partner's perception of your voice match or differ from your own? Now do individual assignment 2, including your partner's assessment as part of your analysis.

Chapter

ᖷ 5 ᖷ

The Working Writer

Is writing a matter of learning and practice, or are good writers born?

Ross

While there is no one best way to write, some ways do seem to work for more people in more situations than do others. Learning what these ways are may save you some time, grief, or energy—perhaps all three. This chapter describes the sometimes exciting, sometimes tedious, and always messy process of working writers, taking a close look at the various phases most writers go through, from planning and drafting through researching, revising, and editing. If you're interested in improving your writing, examine closely your own writing process: Describe how you do it, identify what works and what doesn't, then study the ideas and strategies that work for others—some of these are bound to help you.

What are your writing habits? What do you do, for example, when you are assigned to write a paper due in one week? Do you sit down that day and start writing the introduction? Or do you sit down but do something else instead? If you don't work on the assignment right away, do you begin two days before deadline, or is your favorite time the night before the paper is due? Do you write a few pages a day, every day, and let your paper emerge gradually? Or do you prefer to draft it one day, revise the next, and proofread it just before handing it in?

What writing conditions do you seek? Do you prefer your own room? Do you like to listen to certain kinds of music? Do you deliberately go somewhere quiet, such as the library? Or do you prefer a coffee shop, a cafe, or a booth at McDonald's?

With what do you write? Your own computer or the school's? Your old Smith Corona portable typewriter or a pencil on tablets of lined paper? Or do you first write with a favorite pen and then copy the result onto a computer?

Which of the habits or methods described here is the right one? Which technique yields the best results? These are trick questions, since different ones work best for different individuals. There is no single best way to write. People manage to write well under wildly different conditions.

The rest of this chapter identifies five discrete but overlapping and often nonsequential phases of the way writers work—planning, drafting, researching, revising, and editing—and explains how computers have become critical tools in this process.

ॐ OWN THE ASSIGNMENT

To understand and take seriously assignments given by other people, you need to do more than merely react to them. You need to make them your own. One way of owning an assignment is to figure out how doing the assignment benefits you in some way—answers a nagging question, is fun or challenging, helps somebody you care about. Another way of owning an assignment is to break it down to a manageable size so you can handle it with the information and time available. In addition, you may also find a way of doing the assignment that's original and creative—an approach more likely than not to spark interest in your reader.

A good way to own any assignment is to write about it, using your own words to help find an angle or approach that is comfortable, sensible, or interesting. You can do this in a journal, log, or notebook, keeping a methodical record of thoughts about the assignment. Can you restate the assignment in your own words? Can you break it into component parts? Can you limit the scope or size?

In Assignment 1, find an experience that you want to explore and learn from. Then ask whether it might be of interest to others either because it's common and they could identify with it or because it's unusual and they could learn from it. You've got to want to learn from the experience yourself and at the same time make others want the same thing. For example, in writing about a sport, the time you sat on the bench may have taught you lessons as important as those you learned scoring the winning field goal. Your experience of a typical day on the job may provide insights just as interesting as those gained from the day the store caught fire. You can own your topic by writing about your insider knowledge, including unfamiliar details that make the experience come alive for your readers.

Taken from: *The Working Writer,* Second Edition by Toby Fulwiler.

༭ **WRITING 1**

Answer the questions posed on the opening pages of this chapter and describe your own work as a writer: Where, when, and how do you usually write? What are the usual results? With what do you need some extra help?

༭ **PLANNING**

Planning consists of creating, discovering, locating, developing, organizing, and trying out ideas. Writers are doing deliberate planning when they make notes, turn casual lists into organized outlines, write journal entries, compose rough drafts, and consult with others. They also are doing less deliberate planning while they walk, jog, eat, read, browse in libraries, converse with friends, or wake up in the middle of the night thinking. Planning involves both expanding and limiting options, locating the best strategy for the occasion at hand, and focusing energy productively.

Planning comes first. It also comes second and third. No matter how careful your first plans, the act of writing usually necessitates that you keep planning all the way through the writing process, that you continue to think about why you are writing, what you are writing, and for whom. When writers are not sure how their ideas will be received by someone else, they often write to themselves first, testing their ideas on a friendly audience, and find good voices for communicating with others in later drafts.

During the planning process for the first edition of *The Working Writer,* for instance, I was trying out ideas and exploring broadly and also narrowing my thinking to focus both on my purpose as a writer and the purposes that handbooks serve. I had to consider the audience: Who uses textbooks? I had to find my voice not only as a classroom teacher but as a writer: Would I be friendly and casual or authoritative and serious? I spent some time inventing and discovering ideas, figuring out what kind of information readers require, how much of this information I already knew, and where to find what I didn't know.

Strategies for Planning

1. Make planning a first, separate stage in your writing process. You will feel freer to explore ideas and directions for your writing if you compose tentative outlines, take notes, and write journal entries before attending to matters of neatness, correctness, and final form.
2. Play with ideas while you draft, research, revise, and edit. Just as it's important for invention and discovery to be a first, discrete stage, it's also important to continue inventing and discovering as your draft moves toward its final shape.
3. When you begin writing, write out crazy as well as sane ideas. While the wild ones may not in themselves prove useful, they may suggest others that are.
4. When stuck for ideas, try to articulate, in writing or speech, how you are stuck, where you are stuck, and why you think you are stuck. Doing so may help you get unstuck.

5. When searching for direction, *read* to find new information, *talk* to find out how your ideas sound to others, *listen* to the responses you receive, and *keep writing* to test the directions you find.

↜ WRITING 2

Describe the strategies you commonly use when you plan papers. How much does your planning vary from time to time or assignment to assignment? Now use your favorite planning strategy for twenty minutes to plan one currently assigned paper.

↜ DRAFTING

At some point all writers need to move beyond thinking, talking, and planning and actually start writing. Many writers like to schedule a block of time, an hour or more, to draft their ideas, give them shape, see what they look like. One of the real secrets to good writing is simply learning to sit down and write. *Drafting* is the intentional production of language to convey information or ideas to an audience. First drafts are concerned with ideas, with getting the direction and concept of the piece of writing clear. Subsequent drafting, which includes revising and editing, is concerned with making the initial ideas ever sharper, more precise and clearer.

While most writers hope their first draft will be their final draft, it seldom is. Still, try to make your early drafts as complete as possible at the time—that is, give each draft your best shot: Compose in complete sentences, break into paragraphs where necessary, and aim at a satisfying form. At the same time, allow time for second and third drafts and maybe more.

Sometimes it's hard to separate drafting from planning, researching, revising, and editing. Many times in writing *The Working Writer,* I sat down to explore a possible idea in a notebook and found myself drafting part of a chapter instead. Other times, when trying to advance an idea in a clear and linear way, I kept returning instead to revise a section just completed. While it's useful to separate these phases of writing, don't worry too much if they refuse to stay separate. In most serious writing, every phase of the process is as much circular and haphazard as linear and direct as you move back and forth almost simultaneously from planning to revising to editing to drafting, back to planning, and so on. While Part Three will discuss the details of drafting specific papers, the following ideas may prove useful now.

Strategies for Drafting

1. Sit down and turn on your computer, or place paper in your typewriter, or open your writing notebook and pick up a pen. Once you have done any of these initial acts, your chances of starting your paper increase dramatically. Plan to sit still and write for one hour.

2. Start writing by writing. Do not sit and stare at the blinking cursor or the blank page. Instead, put words and sentences in front of you and see where they lead. Do this for at least fifteen minutes and then pause and see what you've got.

3. Plan to throw away your first page. This simple resolution will take off a lot of pressure, help you relax, and let the momentum of the writing take over. Later, you may even decide to keep some of this page—a clear bonus.

4. Compose in chunks. It's hard to write a whole term paper; it's fairly easy to write a section of it; it's easier still to write a paragraph; it's a breeze to write a sentence or two. In other words, even large projects start with single words, sentences, and paragraphs.

5. Allow time to revise and edit. Start drafting any writing assignment as soon as you can, not the night before it's due.

☞ WRITING 3

Describe the process you most commonly use to draft a paper. Is your way of starting consistent from paper to paper? Now write the first draft for the paper you planned in Writing 2. Sit down, and for half an hour compose as much of the paper as you can, noting in brackets as you go along where you need to return with more information or ideas.

☞ RESEARCHING

Unless writers are drafting completely from memory, they need ideas and information to make their writing interesting. However, even personal essays, experiential papers, and self-profiles benefit from additional factual information that substantiates and intensifies what the writer remembers. In other words, good working writers are researching writers.

Don't confuse using real and useful research in your writing with writing what are sometimes called *research papers*—school exercises meant to demonstrate how to find information in libraries, and how to include it in your papers, but that often focus more on the mechanics of collecting information than on writing with information about something important to you. Actually, as a college student you're researching every time you write an analysis or an interpretation of a text, comparing one text to another, tracking down the dates of historical events or conducting laboratory experiments, visiting museums, interviewing people in the college community, or surfing the World Wide Web. Research is an integral part of learning and learning to write well.

Consider this. Whenever you write about unfamiliar subjects, you have two choices: to research and find things out, or to bluff with unsupported generalizations. Which kind of paper would you prefer to read? Which kind of writing will you profit by doing? Part Four of *The Working Writer* explains what you need to know to write effectively with research in a college community. Meanwhile, the brief ideas listed below may prove useful.

Strategies for Writing with Research

1. Consider incorporating research information into every paper you write. For interpretive papers, revisit your texts; for argument and position papers, visit the library. For experiential papers, revisit places and people.
2. Research in the library. Visit the library, look around, hang around, ask questions, and take a tour. The library is the informational center of the university; using it well will make all of your writing and learning more substantial.
3. Research people. Interview experts to add a lively and local dimension to your papers. Consider who in your college community can provide current information, ideas, or insider stories to enhance your paper.
4. Research places. Visit settings in which you can find real, concrete, current information. Where appropriate, visit local sites—stores, institutions, streets, neighborhoods, farms, factories, and lakes—to connect local people with your topic.
5. Learn to document sources. Whenever you do research, write down who (the author) said what (the title), where (publication), and when (date). Then, as needed, look up the specific forms required in specific disciplines.

ஃ WRITING 4

Describe the kind of research assignments you have done in the past. See if you can add one piece of research information to the paper you began drafting in Writing 3, using any research method with which you are familiar.

ஃ REVISING

Somewhere in the midst of their writing, most writers revise the drafts they have planned, started, and researched. Revising involves rewriting to make the purpose clearer, the argument stronger, the details sharper, the evidence more convincing, the organization more logical, the opening more inviting, or the conclusion more satisfying.

I consider revising to be separate from editing, yet the two tasks may not always be separable. Essentially, revising occurs at the level of ideas, whereas editing occurs at the level of the expression. Revising means re-seeing the drafted paper and thinking again about its direction, focus, arguments, and evidence. In writing this third edition of *The Working Writer*, I revised, to some extent, every chapter to make it sharper, simpler, and more direct than it was in the first and second editions.

While it is tempting to edit individual words and sentences as you revise major ideas, try to ignore the small stuff and keep your focus on the big stuff—in the long run, revising before you edit saves time and energy. Revising to refocus or redirect often requires that you delete paragraphs, pages, and whole sections of your draft, actions that can be painful if you have already carefully edited them. Revising is discussed in greater depth in Part Five; meanwhile, consider the ideas listed below.

Strategies for Revising

1. Plan to revise from the beginning. Allow time to examine early drafts for main points, supporting evidence, and logical direction from first to last. (In addition, allow time later to edit and proofread.)
2. Revise by limiting your focus. Many first drafts are too ambitious. When you revise, make sure your topic is narrow enough for you to do it justice, given the time and space you have available. Often, this means omitting points that aren't really relevant to your main focus.
3. Revise by adding new material. An excellent time to do additional research, regardless of the kind of paper you are writing, is *after* you've written one draft and now see exactly where you need more information.
4. Revise by reconsidering how you tell your story. Consider the effect other points of view may have on your subject. Consider the effect of past tense versus present tense.
5. Revise for order, sequence, and form. Have you told your story in the only form you can, or are there alternative structures that would improve how you tell it?

ᴥ WRITING 5

Does your usual process for revising a paper include any of the ideas discussed in this section? Describe how your process is similar or different. Now revise the paper to which you added research information in Writing 4, using any revision techniques with which you are comfortable.

ᴥ EDITING

Whether writers have written three or thirteen drafts, they want the last one to be perfect—or as near perfect as time and skill allow. When editing, writers pay careful attention to the language they have used, striving for the most clarity and punch possible. Many writers edit partly to please themselves, so their writing sounds right to their own ear. At the same time, they edit hoping to please, satisfy, or convince their intended readers.

You edit to communicate as clearly as possible. After you've spent time drafting and revising your ideas, it would be a shame for readers to dismiss those ideas because they were poorly expressed. Check the clarity of your ideas, the logic and flow of paragraphs, the precision and power of your words, and the correctness and accuracy of everything, from facts and references to spelling and punctuation.

In finishing *The Working Writer,* I went over every word and phrase to make sure each one expressed exactly what I wanted to say. Then my editors did the same. They even sent the manuscript to other experts on writing, and they, too, went over the whole manuscript. Then I revised and edited once again. While editing is discussed in greater depth in Part Five, the ideas listed below may also be helpful:

Strategies for Editing

1. Read your draft out loud. Does it sound right? Your ear is often a trustworthy guide, alerting you to sentences that are clear or confused, formal or informal, grammatically correct or incorrect.
2. "Simplify. Simplify. Simplify." Henry David Thoreau offers this advice about both life and writing in his book *Walden*. I agree. When you edit, simplify—words, sentences, paragraphs, the whole paper—so that you make your point clearly and directly.
3. Delete unnecessary words. The easiest of all editing actions is to omit words that do not carry their own weight. Cut to improve clarity, simplicity, and directness as well as sentence rhythm.
4. Proofread by reading line by line with a ruler to mask out the following sentences. This forces your eyes to read word by word and allows you to find mistakes you might otherwise miss. This is important advice even if you use a spell checker on a computer, for a spell checker will not catch all mistakes (such as the use of *their* for *there*).

ᔑ WRITING 6

Do you edit using any of the ideas mentioned in this section? Describe your usual editing techniques. Now edit the paper you revised in Writing 5, referring to Part Five.

ᔑ WRITING WITH COMPUTERS

Computers are the greatest writing tools ever invented. Unlike typewriters, pens, and pencils, computers allow writers to change their writing infinitely and easily before the words are ever printed on paper. Writers are not committed to final copy until they print it out, and even then they can work on it again and again without retyping the whole thing over.

All word-processing programs work in pretty much the same way, so it doesn't matter if you're using a Macintosh, DOS, or a Windows-based system. You type the words on the computer screen, then store the file on your hard drive or on a portable disk, giving this file a brief descriptive name (paper.1). When you want to work on the document again, you call the file back to the screen and start all over, not needing to print it until you are ready. But the advantages of computers go far beyond paper-saving efficiency, giving you the freedom to play with ideas and sentences as well as add solid research without leaving your writing desk. The following suggestions may be useful:

1. **Planning.** Use the computer to invent and discover ideas by writing out lists of topics or tentative outlines. The computer's ability to add, delete, and rearrange makes these planning and organizing strategies easy.
2. **Freewriting.** Write rapidly on your computer whether you're exploring ideas or simply stuck. Don't worry about spelling, punctuation, grammar, or style.

Let your words trigger new thoughts and suggest new plans and directions. Save these entries on disk to create a computer journal.

3. **Drafting.** Use the computer to compose initial ideas, taking advantage of the ease with which words, sentences, and paragraphs can be modified and moved around as your ideas and direction become clearer. It's also easy to lift whole passages from computer-written freewrites or journal writing and incorporate them directly into your draft.

4. **Researching.** Networked computers allow you to gain access to either your campus library or the Internet at the stroke of a key. Instead of traveling physically to locate books, periodicals, and special collections in the library, you search for material and receive printouts right in your room. And for the most up-to-date, but sometimes questionable, information, the World Wide Web is loaded with information about every possible research topic.

5. **Revising.** Typing on a computer creates instant distance from your words and ideas, allowing you to view them more objectively. Whole paragraphs can be deleted, added, changed, and moved around—all useful activities when revising drafts. You can add new information or evidence in appropriate sections. Your computer will repaginate and reformat instantly. But remember that your paper won't be good simply because it looks good in an attractive font or after laser printing.

6. **Editing.** Computers allow you to try out numerous possibilities when editing sentences and paragraphs. The search-and-replace function can make each sentence start a new line so it can be judged on its own merits. Periodically, print out a hard copy to review your text; changes you make on paper can then be incorporated easily on screen for a new printout.

7. **Referencing.** With a keystroke you can consult CD or online dictionaries, encyclopedias, thesauruses, grammar books, and style manuals to check and change your text.

8. **Proofreading.** The built-in spell checker becomes your first line of spelling defense, as it will rapidly identify which words you've mistyped or misspelled. You must still proofread with your own eyes, since the computer will not identify misspelled words that spell other words. The grammar checker, likewise, identifies missing or misused grammatical components, though it may also mark long sentences that are otherwise grammatically correct.

9. **Formatting.** Word-processing programs provide type styles, fonts, graphic images, and page layouts that can produce professional-looking and visually exciting papers with improved readability and aesthetic appeal. Keep in mind, however, that an attractive presentation is no substitute for clear language, logic, and organization. You'll also find that the ways in which you use technology can benefit from their combination with more "traditional" methods— for example, printing hard copy for editing and for preliminary revisions. Also, visiting the library and hunting for information there bolsters Web-generated research sources.

10. **Saving.** When you write with a computer, save all versions of your papers on the hard drive or external disks so that you can always return to them. And be

sure to make duplicate or backup copies of all work on separate disks in case an accident destroys one disk or wipes out your hard drive. If you make radical revisions on one draft and don't like them, simply go back to the saved original and try again.

ᴄᴧ SUGGESTIONS FOR WRITING AND RESEARCH

Individual

Study your own writing process as you work on one whole paper from beginning to end, taking notes in your journal to document your habits and practices. Write an analytic sketch describing the way you write and speculating about the origins of your current habits.

Collaborative

With your classmates, form interview pairs and identify local professional writers or instructors who publish. Make an appointment with one of these practicing writers, interview him or her about the writing process he or she practices, and report back to the class. Write a collaborative report about writers in your community; make it available to other writing classes or interested instructors.

❧ 6 ❧

Sharing and Responding

Listening to other people's criticism is really helpful, especially when they
stop being too nice and really tell you what they think about your paper.
KELLY

All writing profits from help. Most published writing has been shared, explored, talked over, revised, and edited somewhere along the way to make it as readable, precise, and interesting as it is. The published writing you read in books, magazines, and newspapers that is signed by individual authors is seldom the result of either one-draft writing or one-person work. This is not to say that authors do not write their own work, for of course they do. But even the best of writers begin, draft, and revise better when they receive suggestions from friends, editors, reviewers, teachers, and critics. This chapter explores specific ways to ask for help with your own writing as well as to provide it to others.

❧ SHARING YOUR WRITING

Writers can ask for help at virtually all stages of the writing process. Sometimes they try out ideas on friends and colleagues while they are still planning or drafting. More often, however, writers ask for help while they are revising, as they try to make their ideas coherent and convincing, and while they are editing, as they try to make their language clear and precise. In addition, when a draft is nearly final, many writers ask for proofreading help since most writers are their own worst proofreaders. Here are some suggestions for getting good help as you revise your writing.

Specify what you want. When you share a draft with a reader, be sure to specify what kind of help you are looking for. If you consider your draft nearly finished and want only a quick proofreading, it can be very frustrating if your reader suggests major changes that you do not have time for or interest in. Likewise, if you share an early draft and want help organizing and clarifying ideas because you intend to do major rewriting, it is annoying to have your paper returned with every sentence edited for wordiness, misspellings, and typographical errors. You can usually head off such undesirable responses by being very clear about exactly what kind of help you want. If you do want a general reaction, say so, but be prepared to hear about everything and anything.

Ask specific questions. Tell your reader exactly what kinds of comments will help you most. If you wonder whether you've provided enough examples, ask about that. If you want to know whether your argument is airtight, ask about that. If you are concerned about style or tone, ask about that. Also mark in the margins your specific concerns about an idea, a phrase, a sentence, a conclusion, or even a title.

Ask global questions. If you are concerned about larger matters, make sure you identify what these are. Ask whether the reader understands and can identify your thesis. Ask whether the larger purpose is clear. Ask whether the paper seems right for its intended audience. Ask for general reactions about readability, style, evidence, and completeness. Ask whether your reader can anticipate any objections or problems other readers may have.

Don't be defensive. Whether you receive responses about your paper orally or in writing, pay close attention to them. You have asked somebody to spend time with your writing, so you should trust that that person is trying to be helpful, that he or she is commenting on your paper, not on you personally. While receiving oral comments, stay quiet, listen, and take notes about what you hear, interrupting only to ask for clarity, not to defend what your reader is commenting on. Remember, a first draft may contain information and ideas that are clear to you; what you want to hear is where they are less clear to someone else.

Maintain ownership. If you receive responses that you do not agree with or that you consider unhelpful, do not feel obliged to heed them. It is your paper; you are the ultimate judge of whether the ideas in it represent you. You will have to live with the results; you may, in fact, be judged by the results. Never include someone else's idea in your paper if you do not understand it or believe it.

᠅ WRITING 1

Describe the best response to a piece of your writing that you remember. How old were you? What were the circumstances? Who was the respondent? Explain whether you think the response was deserved or not.

᠅ GIVING HELPFUL RESPONSES

When you are asked to respond to other writers' work, keep these basic ideas in mind.

Follow the golden rule. The very best advice is to give the kind of response to others' writing that you would like to receive on your own. Remember how you feel being praised, criticized, or questioned. Remember what comments help advance your own papers as well as comments that only make you defensive. Keeping those in mind will help you help others.

Attend to the text, not the person. Word your comments so that the writer knows you are commenting on his or her writing and not his or her person. The writer is vulnerable, since he or she is sharing with you a product of individual thinking and reasoning. Writers, like all people, have egos that can be bruised easily with careless or cruel comments. Attending to the text itself helps you avoid these problems. Point out language constructions that create pleasure as well as those that create confusion, but avoid commenting on the personality or intelligence of the writer.

Praise what deserves praise. Tell the writer what is good about the paper as well as what is not good. *All* writers will more easily accept critical help with weaknesses if you also acknowledge strengths. But avoid praising language or ideas that do not, in your opinion, deserve it. Writers can usually sense praise that is not genuine.

Ask questions rather than give advice. Ask questions more often than you give answers. You need to respect that the writing is the writer's. If you ask questions, you give the writer room to solve problems on his or her own. Of course, sometimes it is very helpful to give advice and answers or to suggest alternatives when they occur to you. Use your judgment about when to ask questions and when to give advice.

Focus on major problems first. If you find a lot of problems with a draft, try to focus first on the major problems (which are usually conceptual), and let the minor ones (which are usually linguistic and stylistic) go until sometime later. Drafts that are too marked up with suggestions can overwhelm writers, making them reluctant to return to the job of rewriting.

ᴄᴈ WRITING 2

What kind of response do you usually give to a writer when you read his or her paper? How do you know what to comment on? How have your comments been received?

ᴄᴈ RESPONDING IN WRITING

The most common written responses that college students receive to their writing are those that instructors make in the margins or at the end of a paper, usually explaining how they graded the paper. Many of these comments—except the grade—are similar to those made by professional editors on manuscripts. In writing classes you will commonly be asked by classmates to read and write comments on their papers. Here are some suggestions to help you do that:

Use a pencil. Many writers have developed negative associations from teachers covering their writing in red ink, primarily to correct what's wrong rather than to praise what's right. If you comment with pencil, the message to the writer is more gentle—in fact, erasable—and suggests the comments of a colleague rather than the judgments of a grader.

Use clear symbols. If you like, you can use professional editing symbols to comment on a classmate's paper. Or you can use other symbols that any writer can figure out. For example, underline words or sentences that puzzle you and put a question mark next to them. Put brackets where a missing word or phrase belongs or around a word or phrase that could be deleted. Circle misspellings.

There are many advantages to written responses. First, writing your comments takes less time and is therefore more efficient than discussing your ideas orally. Second, written comments are usually very specific, identifying particular sentences, paragraphs, or examples that need further thought. Third, written comments leave a record to which the writer can refer later—after days, weeks, and even months—when he or she gets around to revising.

There are also disadvantages to writing comments directly on papers. First, written comments may invite misunderstandings that the respondent is not present to help clarify. Second, written comments that are too blunt may damage a writer's ego—and it's easier to unintentionally make such comments in writing than face to face. Third, written comments do not allow the writer and reader to clear up simple questions quickly and so risk allowing misinterpretations to persist.

↷ WRITING 3

Describe your most recent experience in receiving written comments from a reader. Were the comments helpful? Did the respondent use an approach similar to that detailed in this section or some other approach? In either case, were the reader's comments helpful?

↷ RESPONDING THROUGH CONFERENCES

Most writers and writing teachers believe that one-to-one conferences provide the best and most immediate help that writers can get. Sitting together, a reader and a writer can look at a paper together, read passages aloud, and ask both general and specific questions about the writing: "What do you want to leave me with at the end?" or "Read that again, there's something about that rhythm that's especially strong" or "Stop. Right there I could really use an example to see what you mean." Often an oral conference helps as a follow-up to written comments.

The suggestions for making effective written responses in the previous section also apply to oral conferences. In addition, here are a few other things to keep in mind:

Relax. Having your conference in a comfortable place can go a long way toward creating a friendly, satisfying discussion. Don't be afraid of digressions. Very often a discussion about a piece of writing branches into a discussion about the subject of the paper instead of the paper itself. When that happens, both writer and reader learn new things about the subject and about each other, some of which will certainly help the writer. Of course, if the paper is not discussed specifically, the writer may not be helped at all.

Ask questions. If you are the reader, ask follow-up questions to help the writer move farther faster in his or her revising. If you have written your responses first, the conference can be a series of follow-up questions, and together you can search for solutions.

Listen. If you are the writer, remember that the more you listen and the less you talk, the more you will learn about your writing. Listen attentively. When puzzled, ask questions; when uncertain, clarify misunderstanding. But keep in mind that your reader is not your enemy and that you and your work are not under attack, so you do not need to be defensive. If you prefer the battle metaphor, look at it this way: Good work will defend itself.

One advantage of one-to-one conferences is that they promote community, friendship, and understanding between writer and reader. Also, conferences can address both global and specific writing concerns at the same time. In addition, conferences allow both writer and reader to ask questions as they occur and to pursue any line of thought until both parties are satisfied with it. And finally, writer and reader can use their facial expressions, body language, and oral intonation to clarify misunderstandings as soon as they arise.

There are, however, a few disadvantages to one-on-one conferences. First, it is harder to make tough, critical comments face to face, so readers are often less candid than when they write comments. Second, conferring together in any depth about a piece of writing takes more time than communicating through written responses.

ふ **WRITING 4**

Confer with a writer about his or her paper, using some of the techniques suggested in this section. Describe in a journal entry how each technique worked.

ふ **RESPONDING IN WRITING GROUPS**

Writing groups provide a way for writers to both give and receive help. When the group considers a particular writer's work, that writer receives multiple responses; and the writer is also one respondent among several when another writer's work is considered.

All of the suggestions in previous sections about responding to writing apply, with appropriate modifications, to responding in writing groups. But writing groups involve more people, require more coordination, take more time, and, for many people, are less familiar. Here are some guidelines for organizing writing groups:

Form a group along common interests. Most commonly, writing groups are formed among classmates, often with the instructor's help, and everyone is working on the same or similar class assignments. Membership in a group may remain fixed over a semester, and members may meet every week or two. Or membership may change with every new assignment. Writing groups can also be created outside of class by interested people who get together regularly to share their writing.

Focus on the writing. The general idea for all writing groups is much the same: to improve one another's writing and encourage one another to do more of it. Writers pass out copies of their writing in advance or read it aloud during the group meeting. After members have read or heard the paper, they share, usually orally but sometimes in writing, their reactions to it.

Make your group the right size for your purpose. Writing groups can be as small as three or as large as a dozen. If all members are to participate, smaller groups need less time than larger groups and provide more attention to each member. Groups that meet outside of classroom constraints have more freedom to set size and time limits, but more than a dozen members will make it hard for each member to receive individual attention and will require several hours, which may be too long to sustain constructive group efforts.

Appoint a timekeeper. Sometimes group meetings are organized so that each member reads a paper or a portion of a paper. At other times a group meeting focuses on the work of only one member, and members thus take turns receiving responses. If papers are to be read aloud, keep in mind that it generally takes two minutes to read a typed, double-spaced page out loud. Discussion time should at least match the oral reading time for each paper. If group members are able to read the papers before the meeting, length is not as critical an issue because group time can be devoted strictly to discussion. Independently formed groups can experiment to determine how much they can read and discuss at each session, perhaps varying the schedule from meeting to meeting.

There are many advantages to discussing writing in groups. First, writing groups allow a single writer to hear multiple perspectives on his or her writing. Second, writing groups allow an interpretation or consensus to develop through the interplay of those perspectives; the result can be a cumulative response that existed in no single reader's mind before the session. Third, writing groups can give both writers and readers more confidence by providing each with a varied and supportive audience. Fourth, writing groups can develop friendships and a sense of community among writers that act as healthy stimuli for continuing to write.

One disadvantage is that groups meeting outside of class can be difficult to coordinate, set up, and operate, as they involve people with varied schedules. Also, at the outset, the multiple audiences provided by groups may be more intimidating and threatening to a writer than a single person responding.

ᔰ WRITING 5

Imagine a writing group you would like to belong to. What subjects would you write about? Whom would you invite to join your group? How often and where would you like to meet? Explain in a journal entry why you would or would not join a writing group voluntarily.

ᔰ RESPONDING ELECTRONICALLY

In the event that you respond to classmates' papers via e-mail or by using the Web, you usually have two choices for response: (1) to mark the text itself with internal comments (using boldface type, italics, capital letters, or colors to distinguish your comments from their language) and send it back, or (2) to send back a written response only, in which you generalize about the language in the text and your response. As an instructor, I have done both, depending on the time and circumstances. Here is what I might suggest:

- When you read classmates' discovery drafts, freewrites, and early drafts, send back summary responses with your reactions to the paper as a whole—what aspects are strong, where you have questions, and so on. Don't mark up the text itself to send back, since at the early stages, writers need to attend to the larger idea level of their texts and not so much to the specific language of sentences and paragraphs.

- When you read later drafts, it may be more helpful—so long as it is convenient and you have the time—to mark up the text itself with your questions and suggestions about specific paragraphs or sentences.

It may go without saying—but I'll say it anyway—that most of the preceding guidelines still apply: Try to ask questions rather than give advice, be specific rather than general, and so on. However, with electronic responses, since people see only your disembodied words and not accompanying facial expressions, hand gestures, or other cues that might moderate written language, the Golden Rule is more important than ever.

☞ SUGGESTIONS FOR WRITING AND RESEARCH

Individual

Recently a large body of literature has developed concerning the nature, types, and benefits of peer responses in writing. Go to the library and see what you can find about writing groups or peer response groups. Check, in particular, for work by Patricia Belanoff, Kenneth Bruffee, Peter Elbow, Anne Ruggles Gere, Thom Hawkins, and Tori Haring-Smith. Write a report to inform your classmates about your discoveries.

Collaborative

Form interview pairs and interview local published writers about the ways in which responses by friends, family, editors, or critics affect their writing. Share results orally or by publishing a short pamphlet.

Chapter

❧ *7* ❧

Strategies for Starting

Get something down! The hardest part of writing is starting. Forget the introduction, skip the outline, don't worry about a thesis—just blast your ideas down, see what you've got, then go back more slowly and work on them.

AARON

Good writing depends on good ideas. When ideas don't come easily or naturally, writers need techniques for finding or creating them. Writers need to invent new ideas or discover old ones at all phases of the writing process, from finding and developing a topic to narrowing an argument and searching for good evidence. And knowing how to invent and discover ideas when none seems apparent is also the best antidote for writer's block, helping you get going even when you think you have nothing to say.

The main premise behind the techniques discussed in this chapter is "the more you write, the more you think." Language begets more language, and more language begets ideas, and ideas beget still more ideas. Virtually all writers have had the experience of starting to write in one direction and ending up in another; as they wrote, their writing moved their thinking in new directions—a powerful, messy, but ultimately positive experience and a good demonstration that the act of writing itself generates and modifies ideas. This occurs because writing lets people see their own ideas, and doing that, in turn, allows them to change those ideas. This chapter suggests ways to harness the creative power of language and make it work for you.

❧ WRITING 1

Describe the procedures you usually use to start writing a paper. Where do you get the ideas—from speaking? listening? reading? writing? Do you do anything special to help them come? What do you do when ideas don't come?

☞ BRAINSTORMING

Brainstorming is systematic list making. You ask yourself a question and then list as many answers as you can think of. The point is to get lots of possible ideas on paper to examine and review. Sometimes you can do this best by setting goals for yourself: What are five possible topics for a paper on campus issues?

1.   Overcrowding in campus dormitories
2.   Prohibiting cars for first-year students
3.   Date rape
4.   Multiculturalism and the curriculum
5.   Attitudes toward alcohol on campus

Sometimes you can brainstorm best by leaving the question open-ended: What do you already know about multiculturalism and the curriculum that interests you?

> Racial diversity high among campus students
> Racial diversity low among faculty
> Old curriculum dominated by white male agenda
> New curriculum dominated by young feminist agenda
> How to avoid simplistic stereotypes such as those I've just written?

In making such lists, jotting down one item often triggers the next, as is seen above. Each item becomes a possible direction for your paper. By challenging yourself to generate a long list, you force yourself to find and record even vague ideas in concrete language, where you can examine them and decide whether or not they're worth further development.

☞ FREEWRITING

Freewriting is fast writing. You write rapidly, depending on one word to trigger the next, one idea to lead to another, without worrying about conventions or correctness. Freewriting helps you find a focus by writing nonstop and not censoring the words and ideas before you have a chance to look at them. Try the following suggestions for freewriting:

1.   Write as fast as you can about an idea for a fixed period of time, say five or ten minutes.
2.   Do not stop writing until the time is up.
3.   Don't worry about what your writing looks like or how it's organized; the only audience for this writing is yourself.

If you digress in your freewriting, fine. If you misspell a word or write something silly, fine. If you catch a fleeting thought that's especially interesting, good. If you think of something you've never thought of before, wonderful. And if nothing interesting comes out—well, maybe next time. The following five-minute freewrite shows John's attempt to find a topic for a local research project:

> I can't think of anything special just now, nothing really comes to mind, well maybe something about the downtown mall would be good because I wouldn't

mind spending time down there. Something about the mall . . . maybe the street vendors, the hot dog guy or the pretzel guy or that woman selling T and sweat-shirts, they're always there, even in lousy weather—do they like it that much? Actually, all winter. Do they need the money that bad? Why do people become street vendors—like maybe they graduated from college and couldn't get jobs? Or were these the guys who never wanted anything to do with college?

John's freewrite is typical: He starts with no ideas, but his writing soon leads to some. This kind of writing needs to be free, unstructured, and digressive to allow the writer to find thoughts wherever they occur. For John, this exercise turned out to be a useful one, since he ultimately wrote a paper about "the hot dog man," a street vendor.

✍ LOOP WRITING

Loop writing is a sequenced set of freewrites. Each freewrite focuses on one idea from the previous freewrite and expands it. To loop, follow this procedure:

1.   Freewrite for ten minutes to discover a topic or to advance the one you are working on.
2.   Review your freewrite and select one sentence closest to what you want to continue developing. Copy this sentence, and take off from it, freewriting for another ten minutes. (John might have selected "Why do people become street vendors?" for further freewriting.)
3.   Repeat step 2 for each successive freewrite to keep inventing and discovering.

✍ ASKING REPORTER'S QUESTIONS

Writers who train themselves to ask questions are training themselves to find information. Reporters ask six basic questions about every news story they write: Who? What? Where? When? Why? and How? Following this set of questions leads reporters to new information and more complete stories.

1.   Who or what is involved? (a person, character, or thesis)
2.   What happened? (an event, action, or assertion)
3.   Where did this happen? (a place, text, or context)
4.   When did it happen? (a date or relationship)
5.   Why did it happen? (a reason, cause, or explanation)
6.   How did it happen? (a method, procedure, or action)

While these questions seem especially appropriate for reporting an event, the questions can be modified to investigate any topic:

What is my central idea?
What happens to it?
Where do I make my main point? On what page?
Are my reasons ample and documented?
How does my strategy work?

❧ OUTLINING

Outlines are, essentially, organized lists. In fact, outlines grow out of lists, as writers determine which ideas go first, which later; which are main, which subordinate. Formal outlines use a system of Roman numerals, capital letters, Arabic numerals, and lowercase letters to create a hierarchy of ideas. Some writers prefer informal outlines, using indentations to indicate relationships between ideas.

When Carol set out to write a research essay on the effect of acid rain on the environment in New England, she first brainstormed a random list of areas that such an essay might cover.

> What is acid rain?
> What are its effects on the environment?
> What causes it?
> How can it be stopped?

After preliminary research, Carol produced this outline:

I. Definition of acid rain
II. The causes of acid rain
   A. Coal-burning power plants
   B. Automobile pollution
III. The effects of acid rain
   A. Deforestation in New England
      1. The White Mountain study
      2. Maple trees dying in Vermont
   B. Dead lakes

Note how Carol rearranged the second and third items in her original list to talk about causes before effects. The very act of making the outline encouraged her to invent a structure for her ideas. Moving entries around is especially easy if you are using a computer, because you can see many combinations before committing yourself to any one of them. The rules of formal outlining also cause you to search for ideas: If you have a Roman numeral I, you need a II; if you have an A, you need a B. Carol thought first of coal-burning power plants as a cause, then brainstormed to come up with an idea to pair with it.

Writing outlines is generative: In addition to recording your original thoughts, outlines actually generate new thoughts. Outlines are most useful if you modify them as you write in accordance with new thoughts or information.

❧ CLUSTERING

A *clustering diagram* is a method of listing ideas visually to reveal their relationships. Clustering is useful both for inventing and discovering a topic and for exploring a topic once you have done preliminary research. To use clustering, follow this procedure:

1. Write a word or phrase that seems to be the focus of what you want to write about. (Carol wrote down *acid rain.*)

2.   Write ideas related to your focus in a circle around the central phrase and connect them to the focus phrase. If one of the ideas suggests others related to it,
write those in a circle around it. (Carol did this with her idea *solutions*.)

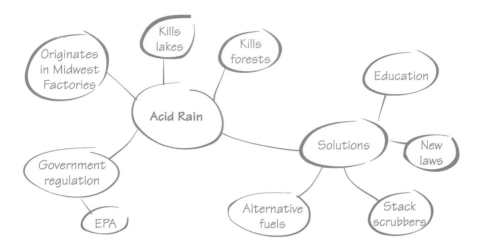

3.   If one idea (such as *solutions*) begins to accumulate related ideas, start a second
cluster with the new term in the center of your paper.

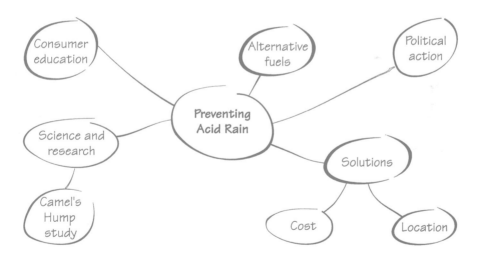

ᴈ STARTING A DIALOGUE

One of the most powerful invention techniques is talking to a partner with the deliberate intention of helping each other find ideas. The directions are simple: Sit across
from each other for five or ten minutes and talk about possible topics or approaches or

ways of finding sources. It doesn't matter who starts or finishes, since the principle at work here is that oral language, like written language, begets ideas. At some point it will be helpful to write down what you are talking about so that you have a record to return to.

You can also start a deliberate dialogue by writing back and forth with a classmate. Each of you starts by posing a problem to solve; the other responds by offering a solution. Continue to exchange ideas, each time pushing harder to solve your classmate's problem as well as your own.

Suggestions for Invention and Discovery

1. Brainstorm a list of five possible topics to write about.
2. Freewrite for ten minutes about the most interesting topic on your list.
3. Loop back in your freewriting, selecting the most interesting or useful point, and freewrite again with that point as the focus.
4. Ask the reporter's questions about the topic.
5. Make an outline of a possible structure for your paper.
6. Cluster ideas about your topic; then cluster on a related idea that occurs during the initial clustering.
7. Talk with a partner for seven minutes; take turns helping each other find or advance one idea, seeing how fast you can go.

↷ WRITING 2

Pose a writing problem and try to solve it using at least three of the invention strategies described in this chapter. Which seems most helpful? If you still have a problem to solve, try several of the other techniques and see if they help.

↷ SUGGESTIONS FOR WRITING AND RESEARCH

Individual

Explain your own most useful invention technique for finding ideas. Explain your technique and support it with samples from your earlier papers. Give clear directions to teach other writers how to use it.

Collaborative

Find a common writing topic by having each person in the group or class select one of the invention and discovery techniques described in this chapter and practice using it for ten minutes. Make a collective list of the topic ideas generated this way. Then ask each individual to select one topic and write for another five minutes. Again make a list of topics and the important ideas generated about them. Discuss the ideas together and try to arrive at a consensus on a common writing topic.

PART TWO

✤ ✤ ✤

WRITING AND REVISING ESSAYS

Source: *The Working Writer,* Third Edition, by Toby Fulwiler, published by Prentice-Hall.

Chapter

❧ **8** ❧

Exploring Identity

I am the son of a man who does not know who Mick Jagger is, but can recite the names of all the state capitals in alphabetical order.

JEREMY

How do you write about your own past, present, and future? How much does your current identity depend upon your past or anticipate your future? The four assignments explored here let you construct in writing a limited but substantial version of yourself. An *autobiography* asks you to explore how you became who you are today by reconstructing and reflecting on your past, while a *language autobiography* focuses on your specific development as a user of language. A *self-portrait* asks you to present a version of your present self to share with the world. And a *career profile* asks you to build upon both past and present to anticipate an interesting future.

❧ AUTOBIOGRAPHY

It is presumptuous, of course, for most people to write an autobiography while still in college, with so much life still ahead. However, it may be useful to use your enrollment in college as a life marker—a point of reflection—to examine how your precollege years have shaped the person you are today.

In order to write even a partial autobiography, it helps to remember and then examine the important influences that come to mind: family, home life, neighborhood environment, school, favorite activities (hobbies, sports, clubs), political and religious experiences, and so on. It also helps to research your past by interviewing those who have watched you grow up: parents, siblings, relatives, teachers, neighbors, and friends. And it helps to dig, too, among saved artifacts that offer clues to your development: journals, diaries, letters, report cards, photographs, letters, posters, toys, scrapbooks, and the like. Following are a number of approaches to experiment with or help you get started.

Locating Artifacts

Explore a dimension of your growing up based on something you once valued—a present from someone, something you saved up money to purchase, or an object that played an important role in the past. When you recall this artifact, describe it in as much concrete detail as you can so that others who did not grow up with you can see it. In the following example, Sara writes about a journal she kept as a child:

> When I was in fifth grade, I used to keep a journal that I would write in every day. Its shiny red cover was decorated with yellow sunflowers and it had my initials embossed in gold in the corner—SAH. It also had a lock and key so my older sisters couldn't read it. I would write freely in it about being happy or sad, or about adventures with my girlfriend, Molly, or sometimes I just wrote when I felt lonely. I stopped writing in it when I was in sixth grade, because then I started having boyfriends.

Describing Interests

Write a version of yourself based on what you care about most passionately. Think about old interests that carry through to the present as well as more recent interests (playing guitar, collecting sports cards, running, ballet) and describe them as well as explore the reason they fascinate you. In the following example, Rene focuses on so common an activity as playing cards:

> I have always been a card player. I have played with family, friends, boyfriends, and strangers. I have played by myself and with as many as ten or twelve people. Card playing is an exercise in skill and chance, a social event, and a creative act. I say creative because on more than one occasion I've invented my own game—though you won't find them in *The Complete Hoyle*. When I meet someone who doesn't play cards, I look at them with suspicion—what's wrong with you I think, not liking to play cards is not natural.

Using Quotations

Write a version of yourself based on what somebody has said about you. Sometimes when you overhear others talking about you, you gain insight into how others in the world perceive you. Think about overheard conversations, the way your parents characterize you, what friends have said, or what a teacher has written on a report card. In the following example, Joy seems rather pleased that she was often described as a handful when she was young:

> I was what some people would call a problem child. When I talk to my aunt or grandmother about my younger years, they just shake their heads and say, "You were a pisser, that's for sure." But they also smile when they say it, so it couldn't have been that bad.

Writing Snapshots

One of the most daunting aspects of writing an autobiography or self profile of any kind is our own complexity as human beings. While some of us may be said to have one clearly dominant characteristic that stands out above others, most of us see ourselves as more complicated than that, made up of multiple and even contradictory selves, making it especially difficult to write unified and coherent portraits of ourselves. One way to solve the coherence problem is to write in a form that allows you to celebrate multiplicity without pretending to unity and to portray contradictions without resolving them.

Writing prose snapshots is just such a form, allowing writers to compose their autobiographies through a collection of short prose pictures or verbal snapshots. Each individual snapshot focuses on one dimension of self the way a single photograph captures one particular scene. At the same time, a collection of such verbal episodes, carefully juxtaposed against others, tells a larger, more complete story the way a collection of photographs in an album or exhibit tells a larger story.

Consider a single prose snapshot as an autonomous paragraph of a few sentences or a few hundred words, but separated from preceding and following snapshots by white space rather than transitional phrases. Each snapshot tells its own small story, and each may be followed by another snapshot telling either a related or a quite different story. An accumulation of such snapshots allows writers to present complex versions of self in a brief amount of space and time. Here, for example, are three of thirteen snapshots from Becky's personal portrait:

- My mother grew up in Darien, Connecticut, a Presbyterian. When she was little, she gave the Children's Sermon at her church.
- My father grew up in Cleveland, Ohio, a Jew. When I went away to college, he gave me the Hebrew Bible he received at his Bar Mitzvah.
- The only similarity between my parents' families is freckles. They both have them, which means I get a double dose. Lucky me. My mother once told me that freckles are "angels' kisses." Lucky me.

Note that Becky explores her conflicting religious heritage as well as her common freckle inheritance by briefly but carefully juxtaposing mother against father. She covers a lot of ground with a few sentences, allowing the reader to figure out the transitions without writing them in herself. (Additional versions of snapshot writing will be presented later in this chapter. For the complete version of Becky's snapshot essay, see the end of this chapter.)

✑ WRITING 1

Make a list of five episodes in your life, each of which reveals something about who you are or what you value. Arrange these episodes in two different ways: first, chronologically, with earliest episode first, most recent last. Then arrange according to significance, with least important first, most important last. Which way would you prefer telling your story?

ᔥ LANGUAGE AUTOBIOGRAPHY

In many ways, getting a college education is getting a language education, learning course by course, new vocabulary, new meanings, and new ideas. Consequently, one of the most interesting types of autobiography to write is one that focuses on your growth and development as a user of language. Such "language autobiographies" focus on those moments when you learned something connected with language—reading, writing, speaking, listening. Such studies need not be limited to verbal languages, as other languages such as music, mathematics, visual, and body languages also have much to teach. You would go about constructing a language autobiography in the same way as any autobiography but now limiting your investigation to those experiences and episodes that shed light on you as a reader, writer, and speaker.

To construct a language autobiography, list all the possible places and episodes where you remember language making a special impact on you—home, neighborhood, school, hobbies, sports, clubs, and so forth. Also, list the books, films, television shows, and song lyrics that you remember most vividly as well as any stories, poems, and lyrics you may have written yourself.

Creating a Time Line

One way to begin a language autobiography is to create a time line. Draw a vertical line on a sheet of paper. On one side write a chronological list of all the books you remember reading in school, and on the other side, make a similar chronology of readings (including being read to) at home. Expand the entries on either side of the line by adding in other episodes of language learning—keeping a journal, writing letters, entering a short story contest, and so on, as Figure 9.1 illustrates. Include age or grade in parentheses next to each entry.

Adding Research

Research will add an element of persuasive authenticity to this project. First, plan to talk—in person, on the telephone, via e-mail—with your parents, aunts, uncles, and brothers or sisters in the event they remember something about the "young you" growing up that you do not. Next, browse among the books in your current bookshelf as well as among any childhood books still available, and make a list of the titles that most influenced you. Finally, dig—at home or in your own school files—among your own literate artifacts, and look again at old school reports, report cards, stories, poems, journals, or letters to the editor—any written documents that provide clues to early language influences or habits.

It makes good sense to write this paper in chronological order, beginning with earliest influences and working forward to watch yourself develop. However, consider reversing chronology or using flashbacks if that way of telling your story seems more interesting

Time Line

Personal	School
Read to: Dr. Seuss--lots (age 4?)	
The Giving Tree	
Good Night, Moon	
Winnie the Pooh	Learn to write a paragraph (2nd grade)
	Learn cursive (3rd)
The Jungle Book (9)	
Letters to Mike (10)	
	Where the Red Fern Grows (6th)
Write and perform play: *The Moon Man*	
(Summer Festival	
of the Arts)	
Write story about Mars (12)	
Catcher in the Rye (13)	*The Diary of Anne Frank* (8th)
	Presentation of moon study in biology class (10th)
Keep personal journal (15)	Paper on *Caged Bird* read aloud in class
Story of Michael Jordan	Keep basketball diary
Letter to editor published (17)	Two poems published in school paper (11th)
	Research paper on Ecuador (12th)
College entrance essay (successful!)	

Figure 9.1   Time line

to you. Megan, for example, began her language autobiography by recounting a trip home to rummage through the attic looking for artifacts:

> I took great pains to discover my first creative writing. Luckily, my mother has saved boxes of drawings, class pictures, and old stories from my kindergarten year on in our attic. I found two Big Chief writing tablets from first grade, a story about my summer vacation from second grade, and the complete manuscript of my first novel from fifth grade.

Including Artifacts

Once you've located a poem, letter, or journal entry from the past, you need to decide how to use it: If you simply mention it, you are suggesting it is notable but not very important. If you summarize it, you are suggesting the content is important, but there's no need to see the document itself. If you reproduce it, you are telling us the artifact is pretty interesting reading in and of itself. Keep in mind that the more space you devote to a single artifact in your essay, the more importance it assumes for your reader.

In the sample below, Susan includes a complete poem written in elementary school when she was seven years old.

My Special Tree

My special tree is very old.
It is large and green and in our yard.
It is a maple tree.
Birds fly in and out of its leaves.
It has a big curved branch.
I hang on tight and swing.

In fact, Susan's language autobiography is composed of fourteen artifacts solely from her elementary years, ages five through eleven. She prefaces the collection with this introduction:

The truth and honesty of my childhood writing is the centerpiece of my language autobiography. In rummaging through my essays, research papers, stories, poems, and even journal entries from later years, I realized my true voice was already shaped by the time I entered seventh grade. I am now fourteen years older than the earliest sample included here, but it speaks for me as well now as it did then.

As a reader I infer that the simplicity of childhood dreams and pleasures is still very much alive in this now more experienced college student. Because Susan's paper is made up almost entirely of her own early writing, neither edited nor explained, I must do most of the interpretive work, a method which works so long as the material is self-explanatory. However, many times when a writer refers to an old poem or mentions a book, we don't understand its importance unless the writer tells us. Here, for example, when Kate writes about her first encounter with classical literature, she is explicit about why it was so important:

When I was in sixth grade, we were assigned *The Odyssey*. It was the thickest book I'd ever tried to read, so it seemed like a big deal. How could I possibly read so many pages—here were at least 200? I trudged home with it in my backpack, feeling its weight, grumpily calculating how long it would take to read it. But I ended up reading it hungrily—Homer's beautiful writing drew me in to the most ghastly and majestic stories I'd ever experienced. Good literature had affected me for the first time.

Writing Snapshots

Snapshots prove to be an ideal way to represent a language autobiography, since each snapshot focuses on one specific literate event or idea, while the whole collection shows a broad range of influences. In the following series, Abbey gives a thematic title to each episode in her snapshot essay—four of twenty are included here.

> SILENCE. They say that girls who have had a bad relationship with their fathers will have bad relations with men later in life. One day my father went on a business trip and never came back. I have not spoken to him since I was six years old. I have no relationship with my father. This does not bode well for me.
>
> WRITING. "The Fire Bird," my dramatic sixth-grade entry into a national fable contest, tells the story of a pure white dove, a smoky gray pigeon, and their battle against the evil black raven and his destructive reign of fire. It is the first thing I have written that requires a title page. I do not win, but am honored to be nominated.
>
> READING. BAM! BAM! BAM! My mom has learned very quickly how to rouse me from reading. Lost in words, I am deaf to the world outside. The only sound I hear is the clicking of Nancy Drew's pumps on the hidden staircase or the tapping of chalk as Laura Ingalls finishes her homework. Mom bangs a pot on the kitchen wall, and finally I hear.
>
> SPEAKING. Twelve years old, dressed completely in white, I stand in front of a crowd of people, reciting Sylvia Plath from memory. I no longer remember the title or the words, just that she spoke of being broken, of being imprisoned in a white cast, and at twelve I knew how she felt.

☞ WRITING 2

List five artifacts from five different years that reveal something significant about your life as a language user. Write a paragraph about each one, describing it and explaining its significance. When you are able, retrieve these artifacts, study them closely, and expand your paragraphs accordingly.

☞ SELF-PORTRAIT

A different way to explore your identity is to focus primarily on the present, on who you are now rather than the way you were or even how you got here. Composing a profile of your current self is a hard assignment—maybe impossible, since full self-knowledge is difficult to obtain. But even attempting to profile yourself may prove to be instructive and rewarding, since the attempt asks you to reflect upon what you've learned to value and what next you hope to become.

To portray yourself in writing, you might start internally by constructing an idea you have of yourself. Conversely, you might start by looking around you, at your room or possessions, and jot down what they seem to say about you. You might start looking in your notebooks, journals, diaries, or letters to see how you represent yourself in writing. Or you might simply start by looking in a mirror and describing who or what you see there. Let's look at the opening paragraphs of several writers looking for ways to portray themselves.

Looking Inside

Alexis writes imaginatively, as if she were somewhere else, suggesting that there's an inner Alexis quite different and less wary than the person she normally appears to be.

> I linger beneath the surface, enjoying the prickly coldness of water against my forehead and eyelids. I am alone. I am naked. I cannot see, but I can feel, imagine, and remember. I am free to accept the moods of my conscience. They do not scare me here as they do in the real world. Down here, the solitude echoes as the water whirls around my body and I remember. . . .

Looking Outside

Doug opens his language autobiography by examining familiar objects in his room, looking for clues about how they might help define him:

> My life is plagued by half-completed projects. One glance at my room proves this. Nothing plays the role it was meant to because at some point I lost interest.
>
> Take my fish tank, for instance. A lovely fish tank. Twenty gallons of water-holding potential, not a leak in sight. The plan was to buy a few fish, toss them in the tank, and throw some food at the little guys every few days. That was last summer. For one reason or another, I never got around to buying the fish, never filled it with water, never made the aquarium I intended.
>
> As the months passed, the Plexiglas top of the tank became a place to put things—photos, newspapers, rolled-up Grateful Dead posters, guitar strings, loose change, dirty socks, poly-sci notebooks, more change . . . I never put anything in the tank, only on top, only because I had no place left in my cluttered room to store things.

Notice especially how casual specific details—guitar strings, posters, dirty socks—allow us to see other dimensions of Doug's life that he doesn't choose to dwell on but which, nevertheless, help fill our view of who he is.

Looking in the Mirror

Sandra starts her essay by methodically staring at herself in a mirror, describing precisely what she sees in the glass so we can see her too. She uses the mirror image to reflect inward on her origins, teaching us something of her past:

> I go stare into a mirror which stares back at me—white skin, dark hair, and deep brown eyes. Do I still see the little girl whose daddy called her *muy bonita?* Am I the little girl who struggled to follow her father's step to the salsa beat? Am I the little girl who stole his lemon slices when he was drinking? Am I the little girl who hated the smell of alcohol on her daddy's breath?
>
> I close and open my eyes, scrunch up my face, tug at my cheeks. Now I see images of a woman. I wear a black leather jacket, faded denim jeans, Steve Madden shoes with three-inch heels, and a shirt so short that when I move, you can see my belly button ring. I have hips and breasts, a feminine walk, and flirtatious eyes—I have filled out well.

In the first paragraph Sandra's questions teach us about growing up with an alcoholic father, suggesting a tough young life; in the second paragraph her clothing shows us that, mature now, she's become one tough woman.

Establishing Distance

Cathleen opens her portrait by writing from a third-person point of view, even calling herself by another name, creating distance between herself the writer and herself the subject:

> At this time the subject would like to be known as Kitten Junkie, but first she wants to clarify her pseudonym. She chose the name for pop culture and aesthetic reasons only. Kitten was raised in a liberal activist atmosphere where marijuana was treated as an hors d'oeuvre. As a child she remembers finger-painting in a Rainbow Coalition office, her eyes watering from thick clouds of marijuana smoke. However, other than aspirin, she does not use drugs of any kind. She is not a junkie. She can't remember the last time she smoked weed and has no plans to smoke it in the future—as she reminds her mother, she is every parents' dream.

Cathleen's stance here is ironic, sassy, and analytical all at the same time, so that her tone teaches us as much about who she is as the details of her liberal activist youth. We know she is serious; at the same time, we know she doesn't take herself too seriously.

Writing Snapshots

Snapshots are also a useful alternative to conventional paragraphs for presenting views of your present self. Even if you *limit* a self-profile to the approximate present—to glimpses or versions of you during only the past year or so—the choices are many. Snapshots allow you to show rapid glimpses of who you are and what you value, suggesting in a brief space the many dimensions of a single individual. Following are three such snapshots from three different writers, each covering a lot of material in a limited space, each also using deliberate rhetorical repetition to create memorable rhythms:

Jeremy:

I am the son of a man who does not know who Mick Jagger is, but who can recite the names of all of the state capitals in alphabetical order. I am the son of a woman whose only work experience prior to motherhood was cashiering at Sears, but who now runs her own business.

Sarah:

Mine, mine, mine. I am greedy. I love my stuff. I love Elizabeth, my faded and fuzz-worn-off teddy bear with the pink dress knitted by my aunt. I love the address book that I bought at Harrod's in London, the only souvenir I could afford, now filled with the names of my favorite people. I love my puffy white comforter—have you ever wondered what it feels like to sleep on a cloud? When I look at my stuff, I see parts of myself—the endurance of Elizabeth, the irony of Harrod's, the calmness of my comforter.

Marcianna:

I prefer summer to winter. I prefer hot to cold. I prefer dark chocolate to milk choco-late. I prefer writing by myself to talking in front of the class. I prefer dressing up to dressing down. I prefer "trick-or-treat" to buying candy. I prefer friends to enemies and laughing to worrying.

✑ WRITING 3

Write three different openings for a possible self-portrait: first, define yourself by de-scribing something in your room or apartment and speculating upon what it says about you. Second, describe yourself by standing in front of a full-length mirror and make inferences about what your clothes and facial expressions say about you. Third, give yourself a fictive name and then write about yourself from the third-person point of view (as he or she). Which of these portrait techniques captures you best?

✑ CAREER PROFILE

This identity assignment involves exploring who you intend to become next by ex-ploring either potential college majors or out-of-college careers. If you know what you want to pursue as life work, it makes the most sense to investigate and report on that; if you are undecided about either career or major, it makes good sense to explore those to-ward which you are leaning or most attracted. If you are more uncertain than that, uncer-tain even about why you are in college or what to major in, this assignment could be your chance to give voice to that confusion and look more closely at possible resolutions.

Whatever your college goals, you might start with a close look at your own past work experiences as well as at any other firsthand experience with what seem to be attrac-tive careers. You also might explore how you selected a college to attend as well as a disci-pline in which to major. Any of these initial investigations will be relevant to what you intend to do next with your life. For this paper, plan to include a substantial amount of research into possible careers or majors as well as to look closely at your own past experience and interests.

Mining the Past

Your past interests, hobbies, and successes often anticipate your college major as well as your life work. Even in those instances where you encounter whole new fields in college, from engineering to social work, the origins of your new interest are often evident in past activities. In the following example, Chris outlines a childhood dream.

> As far back as I can remember, I wanted to be a weather reporter. If I couldn't be a professional sailboat racer, I wanted to be a weatherman. I never had any desire to be the guy on TV, but I wanted to know what the guy on TV knows.

Early on in his paper, Chris also explores impediments to pursuing this dream.

> One day, when I was in eighth grade, my teacher told me I had to drop back from the regular math group to the slower math group. Math was not my strong suit. But when obtaining a degree in meteorology—the degree you need to be a weather reporter I got the same answer every time: "You need lots of math."

Researching the Present

If you're interested in finding out what certain jobs or professions are like, look in the phone book and find out where, in your community, people actually practice this work. If you want to research the global dimensions of this career, your local library or bookstore will have occupation guidebooks to read. And if you want to find out how your college or university could help prepare you, talk to professors in the disciplines that interest you as well as visit your career counselor or job placement service.

To find out firsthand whether or not even to attempt to major in meteorology, Chris set up an appointment with Paul Sisson of the National Weather Service in Burlington, Vermont, whom he interviewed in person:

> I asked several questions, eventually getting around to my fear of math. "Yes, you have to be pretty proficient in math to survive meteorology. If you can't survive calculus, you won't be able to survive the rest." I looked across at Paul in his blue oxford shirt, navy knit tie, pressed khakis, and boat shoes with a combination of respect, envy, and hopelessness.

But in spite of his difficulty with math, writing this paper became a way for Chris to explore his fascination with weather more deeply and resolve what next to do about it:

> In a way I'd never considered before, my desire to be a meteorologist stems from my desire to help people since the ability to predict severe weather can help everyone from airline pilots to farmers to flood victims. More than ever, I realize

that this is what I want to do with my education. I believe my desire to learn will help me overcome my difficulties with mathematics.

Writing Snapshots

Snapshots also work well to present your explorations of career choices. In the following excerpts from a ten-snapshot essay, Sonya explores her dual interest in the environment and in teaching, letting each snapshot reveal a stage on her way to selecting a college major:

1. What I care about is the environment, and what I want to do is teach younger children to care about it too. That's what brings me to college, and to this English class, writing about what I want to be when I grow up.

2. My first teaching was this past summer on the Caribbean island of South Caicos. In the classroom one morning, I tried to teach local teenagers about the fragility of their island environment, but they did not seem to hear me or attend to my lesson, and I left class very frustrated. Later on, we went to the beach, and they taught me back my morning lessons, and I felt so much better. I thought then I wanted to be a teacher. . . .

3. The School of Education scares me. A lady named Roberta and a professor named Merton gave me a list of classes I would need in order to major in education. "Environmental education is not a real field, yet," the professor said. I realized it would take four years and many courses and still I wouldn't be studying the environment or be sure of ever teaching about it in public schools.

4. The School of Natural Resources excites me. Professor Erickson is my advisor, and in one afternoon, she helped me plan a major in "Terrestrial Ecology." I now know, for the first time, exactly what I'm doing in college. I need to study natural resources first, later on decide whether I want to teach, work in the field or what.

Earlier drafts of Sonya's essay included a fair amount of complaining and editorializing, but when she switched to writing snapshots, she focused only on the highlights of her decision-making process and skipped most of the complaining that characterized earlier drafts.

✍ WRITING 4

Write about where you currently stand in terms of college major or career choice. Include the names of people you might talk to or places you might visit to gather more information. When you finish writing, plan to set up appointments with the most available prospects.

Shaping the Whole Essay

This short autobiographical essay (six hundred words) portrays Rebecca Rabin's mixed religious heritage, strong commitment to Protestantism, and current participation in Christian rituals. Each individual snapshot focuses on a single small event—a cross necklace, prayer, a church, and so forth. Each actually tells a small story, complete with beginning, middle, and punch line. At the same time, the cumulative effect of these thirteen snapshots reveals Becky's broad tolerance, education, and interest in a spirituality that goes well beyond separate religious creeds. This theme emerges as one experience is juxtaposed against another, past tense against present tense, without editorializing, allowing readers to supply the connective tissue by filling in the white spaces for themselves.

I Know Who I Am

Rebecca Rabin

- My mother grew up in Darien, Connecticut, a Presbyterian. When she was little, she gave the Children's Sermon at her church.
- My father grew up in Cleveland, Ohio, a Jew. When I went away to college, he gave me the Hebrew Bible he received at his Bar Mitzvah.
- The only similarity between my parents' families is freckles. They both have them, which means I get a double dose. Lucky me. My mother once told me that freckles are "angels' kisses." Lucky me.
- When my parents married and decided to have kids, they agreed to raise them Christian. Thus, I was brought up Presbyterian. According to Jewish tradition and law, Judaism is passed on via a person's mother. Thus I am not a Jew.
- I have attended First Presbyterian Church of Boulder, Colorado, for most of my life. When I was baptized, Reverend Allen said: "Becky is being baptized here today, brought by her believing mother and her unbelieving—but supportive—father."
- When I was little, I was terrified of the darkness. Sometimes, I would wake up in the night and scream. It was my mother who came in to comfort me, smoothing my hair, telling me to think of butterflies and angels.
- I once went through this stage in which I was quite certain I was meant to be Greek Orthodox. That was one my parents couldn't quite understand. My fascination came from watching a movie that had an Eastern Orthodox wedding with the bride wearing beautiful flowers.
- I have always said my prayers before going to bed. Lying silently in the dark, talking to God. Like the disciples in the Garden of Gethsemane, I have been known to fall asleep while praying. Now I pray on my knees, it is harder to doze off that way.
- My father's sister's family is Orthodox Jewish. Things in their house are very different from things in our house. They have two of everything: refrigerators, sinks, dish sets, and dishwashers. When I go there, though, I always feel comfortable in the most basic way—as if my heart says, Oh yes, this is where I belong.
- I am not afraid of the dark anymore. Except sometimes, when I wake up in a sweaty panic, certain there's an axe murderer in my room. My father, the Jewish psychiatrist, says that nightmares are from going to sleep before your brain has sufficiently wound down from a busy day. He says reading before sleeping will cure that.
- When I am in Vermont, I attend North Avenue Alliance Church. I chose it because it is big, like my church at home. The last two Sundays I have sung solos. The first

time, I sang "Amazing Grace." The second time, I sang "El Shaddai," which is partly in Hebrew. In church, my heart says, Oh yes, this is where I belong.

- I wear a cross around my neck. It is nothing spectacular to look at, but I love it because I bought it at the Vatican. Even though I am not a Catholic, I am glad I bought it at the Pope's home town. Sometimes, when I sit in Hebrew class, I wonder if people wonder, "What religion is she, anyway?"
- From a very early age I have always known exactly what I wanted: To live in a safe world. To worship freely. To sing. I know what I believe. I know who I am. I know where I'm going.

↷ SUGGESTIONS FOR WRITING AND RESEARCH

Individual

1. Explore your identity by selecting one of the four types of autobiographical writing discussed in this chapter—autobiography, language autobiography, self-portrait, or career profile. Write an impressionistic first draft based on remembered experiences. Write a researched second draft based on artifacts or interviews. Write a snapshot-shaped third draft, mixing memory and research in a structure that pleases you.
2. If you keep a journal or diary, compile an edited, annotated edition of it so that it profiles or portrays you in a way you are willing to share with the world. Edit or otherwise rewrite entries to protect privacy or improve clarity. Construct an introduction that explains the time period this document covers, and add notations as needed for those who do not know you to understand you better.

Collaborative

Compile a class book of autobiographical sketches that includes a contribution from each class member. Elect a team of editors who will collect, compile, introduce, and produce these essays. Ask your instructor to write an afterword explaining the assignment.

Chapter

⤳ **9** ⤳

Profiling People

When I met Lisa for coffee, it was like the meeting of two total strangers. But we're both from the South, so when she told me about growing up in Charleston, we got a lot closer. I still need to find what makes Lisa uniquely Lisa. We'll meet again.

REBECCA

Reading and writing profiles about people teach us not only about others, but also about ourselves. Newspaper and magazine writers commonly profile the rich, famous, and powerful people of the world. Some popular magazines, such as *Vanity Fair* and *Rolling Stone,* feature well-researched profiles in virtually every issue. Weekly newsmagazines, such as *Time, Newsweek,* and *Sports Illustrated,* use short profiles as regular features. And literary magazines, such as *The New Yorker, Atlantic,* and *Esquire,* are well-known for their lengthy, in-depth profiles. Profiles are not easy to write, but they are rewarding because the process of writing them inevitably brings the writer and subject closer together.

⤳ WRITING A PROFILE

The purpose of a profile is to capture a person's essence on paper. Good profiles generally focus on a single aspect of the subject's life or personality and make some sort of comment on it. In short, a good profile tells a story about its subject.

Profiles are usually about people other than the writer, but you, the writer, are ultimately in control. You decide what to include, what to omit, how to describe the subject and his or her surroundings, where to begin, and where to end. However, the ultimate purpose of a profile is to convey a sense of who your subject is. You must develop a portrait that is essentially true.

Profiles lie on a spectrum between two related forms, interviews and biographies. Interviews are conversations between a writer and a living person. They are commonly the result of a single visit, though some may be based on multiple visits. Published interviews often transcribe the interviewer's questions followed by the subject's responses.

Biographies are usually book-length studies of people, dead as well as living. A biographer's sources include letters from and to the subject; diaries and notebooks; stories by relatives and acquaintances; newspaper and magazine reports; previously published interviews; legal and medical records; and the subject's published writing or other work—all available resources that shed light on the life and character of the subject.

Like interviews, profiles include direct conversations with living people. Like biographies, they make use of other sources of information about the subject. Profiles are usually longer than interviews, but they are considerably shorter than biographies. Profiles are more tightly focused than both interviews, which may contain questions on a wide variety of subjects, and biographies, which attempt to convey information on all aspects of a subject's life. In contrast, a profile selectively presents information to create a unified portrait.

A common college assignment will ask you to profile a professor or staff member who works at your college or university, people who work in the local community, or other students. Profile writing requires, first, a willing subject; second, time to collect information about the subject; and third, the skill to focus on one aspect of the subject and develop a clear theme.

✺ WRITING 1

Describe any profiles that you recall reading in magazines or newspapers. What details do you remember about the person profiled? Why do you think these details remain in your memory?

✺ FINDING A SUBJECT

Profiles can be written about virtually any person willing to hold still long enough to reveal something about himself or herself. While a list of people you might profile is unlimited, some subjects are more accessible than others for students in a college writing class. The profile examples in this chapter are all taken from assignments to profile classmates. But you can select for your own profile subject anyone in whom you are especially interested.

Relatives make good profile subjects because they are usually more than willing to cooperate, and the knowledge resulting from the profile will contribute to your family history. However, some family members are not easily accessible for more than one visit. And family members such as parents, who are emotionally close to you, may be difficult to profile because you may lack the objectivity necessary to portray them realistically.

Members of the campus community are usually willing subjects: professors, librarians, cafeteria workers, resident assistants, alumni staff, and coaches, to name some of the obvious ones. In addition, the local community contains other potential subjects: shopkeepers, street vendors, police officers, city administrators, and various local characters of good and ill repute. The advantage of profiling members of your community is that you can learn about people in various occupations and social circumstances. The disadvantages include the unavailability of busy people for extended interviews and the extra time it takes to conduct off-campus interviews.

Your own classmates can also provide a wealth of characters with varied backgrounds and interests. The advantages of profiling your peers includes their willingness to be profiled, their availability, and the chance to get to know what they are like. The only disadvantage is that writing about a classmate may not expose you to a wider range of people, though this certainly depends on who is in your class. Note, too, that it is very difficult to profile objectively students with whom you're romantically involved.

❧ WRITING 2

Make a list of people in your family, campus community, and local community whom you might be interested in profiling. Make a similar list of classmates who might make good profile subjects. Talk with your instructor about which subjects would be best for a profile assignment.

❧ PROVIDING BACKGROUND INFORMATION

To write an effective profile, you need to learn as much about your subject as possible. You will eventually use some of this background information when you draft the profile itself, to provide a context for the subject's words and actions. However, much of it is useful primarily during your planning and invention stages, as you decide on a focus for the profile and a direction for more research.

Finding background information requires good research skills. You must take advantage of all the available sources of information and follow up on new leads wherever you find them.

Preliminary Interviews

Talking with your subject often is the best place to start. In addition to providing valuable background information, he or she can give you leads to further information. If you are profiling a classmate, interview him or her for ten or fifteen minutes to get started. For other subjects, call ahead and set up a time to meet.

Public Information

If your subject has a résumé, ask to see it. If your subject has published something—whether a letter to the editor or a book—get a copy. If your subject has made a speech or taken a public stand, find a record of it. If the person has been the subject of an interview or biography, read it to see what previous writers have found out.

Writing Portfolios

A rich source of recent background information is your subject's writings—especially if your subject is a student. Assigned papers or essay tests will tell you something of the person's intellectual interests, but journals or letters may reveal more personal information.

Friends and Acquaintances

An obvious source of background information is the people who know, live, and work with your subject. Each conversation you have with a friend or acquaintance of your subject is itself a small interview. It is a good idea to begin such a conversation with specific questions and to take notes. Good questions include the following: What is this person like? How did you come to know each other? What do you most often do together? Whom does this person admire? What does this person want to do or become next?

✎ WRITING 3

Locate a profile subject and find out as much about his or her background as you can. Take good notes. What further questions are suggested by the subject's responses? Set a time to meet again and probe your subject's history further.

✎ DESCRIBING PHYSICAL APPEARANCE

Often the first thing we notice about people we've just met is their appearance. Profiles, too, commonly introduce the subject through descriptions of how the person looks and acts. In the early stages of your writing process, you may want to take notes on every aspect of your subject's appearance. Later, you should select details that capture your subject's individuality and reveal his or her personality.

When describing your subject, use words that appeal to the senses, that express size, shape, color, texture, and sound. Be as specific as possible. You may want to describe physical appearance, clothing, and habits or gestures. Pam can capture Mari Anne's appearance by employing all three types of information:

> While sitting at her desk, Mari Anne keeps twirling her hair to help her think and relax. She is dressed in solid colors, black and red, and has a dozen bracelets on her right arm. She smiles as if nervous, but as I got to know her, I found that smile always on her face. She is five feet two inches tall, has naturally curly brown hair, a dark complexion, and dark brown eyes, and is always smiling. She is a second-generation American since both sets of grandparents came from Greece.

Pam's description tells readers much about Mari Anne's tastes (solid colors, lots of jewelry) and personality (friendly but perhaps a little high-strung). Pam also uses physical description (dark complexion, dark brown eyes) to lead directly to background information (her Greek heritage). It is important to realize how much you, the writer—either consciously or unconsciously—can shape such descriptions. By mentioning Mari Anne's nervous hair twisting at the beginning of the description and her nervous smile a bit later, Pam makes readers see the subject as nervous.

✍ WRITING 4

As an exercise, sit with a classmate and spend ten minutes taking detailed notes on what he or she looks like; pay attention to face, body, height, clothing, gestures, and expressions. Write one to two pages organizing these physical details to convey a dominant impression.

✍ DESCRIBING THE SETTING

Effective description of the setting contributes to realism in a profile and advances readers' understanding of your subject. As in all descriptions, you should note specific details of the physical environment, using sensory words that help readers experience what it was like to be there.

The setting you describe should be the one in which you and your subject met and talked. If this is where your subject lives, you have the opportunity to observe an environment that he or she created and that no doubt reflects much of his or her personality. Do your best to record the details that tell the most about your subject's special interests. If the interview takes place elsewhere, your description may be primarily a way of creating a realistic backdrop, but you may also reveal a great deal about your subject by the way he or she reacts to a less personal environment. Settings can be described on their own—usually near the beginning of the profile—or subtly and indirectly along with the action of the interview.

In the following example, Caleb meets Charles at Charles's favorite off-campus hangout in order to get to know him better. Before turning to his subject, Caleb describes the ambiance of their meeting place:

> Charles suggested we meet in the Other Place, a downtown bar commonly referred to as OP. Charles had basketball practice until seven or eight, so he'd meet me there around 9:30. The OP had a dive bar ambiance to it. In the far corner of the bar stood two outdated pinball machines being hugged respectively by a barefoot girl and a portly man wearing jeans and a leather vest. Both were shaking their hips to the noises of their machines. Above the actual bar a mute hockey game was taking place on television.

Caleb describes the "dive" with a good eye for detail, implying in his descriptions of its people that it's not a place he feels comfortable in. But he lets readers know that Charles is comfortable there.

Beth indirectly includes a description of the setting in her profile:

> Becky sits cross-legged at the foot of the bottom bunk on her pink and green homemade quilt. She leans up against the wall and runs her fingers through her brown shoulder-length hair. The sounds of James Taylor's "Carolina on My Mind" softly fill the room. Posters of John Lennon, James Dean, and Cher look down on us from the walls. Becky stares at the floor and scrunches her face as if she is thinking hard.

Beth includes a rich number of sight words about Becky's home away from home—describing bed, posture, person, posters, and room—letting the detail contribute to the portrait of the person. By including the James Taylor song as well as the three posters, she allows readers to make inferences about what these say about Becky's tastes. Beth slips in the setting details quietly so as not to detract attention from the subject herself.

When including details of setting, think about whether they should strongly reinforce your verbal portrait of the subject, provide a colorful platform for your interaction to take place, or stay quietly in the background.

✍ WRITING 5

If possible, arrange to visit the place where your profile subject lives, and record as much sensory information about that place as you can. Capture what is on the walls and floors, out the windows, on the desk, and on the bed and under it. Also note the brand names of things; their sizes, colors, smells; and the sounds from the CD player and from down the hall as well.

✍ GIVING SUBJECTS A VOICE

Interviews allow people to reveal information about themselves that contributes to a portrait. Interviews are the primary source of information about many profile subjects, especially classmates. You can conduct interviews in three ways.

First, you and your subject can have an informal conversation in which you get to know the subject, usually without notes. In an informal interview, ten prepared questions may be more intrusive than helpful. If you don't take notes, be sure to capture your recollections of the conversation within twenty-four hours, or you'll forget most of them.

The second method of interviewing is to take notes from the subject's responses to prepared questions. You'll need to write fast in a small notebook, catching the essence of your subject's responses and filling in the details later. Note taking is especially helpful during an interview because it lets you see what information you've got as you go along and sometimes helps you decide where to go next with your questions.

As a third method, tape-recording captures your subject's language *exactly* as it was spoken. If you plan to bring a tape recorder to the interview, be sure to secure your subject's permission in advance. While reconstructing dialogue from tape may sound easier than reconstructing it from notes, transcribing the conversation accurately and selecting which passages to use in the profile demand a great deal of time and patience. Plan to use especially those ways of speaking that seem most characteristic of your subject.

In all but the most informal interviews, you should come with prepared questions. In your first interview, ask a coherent set of questions to provide you with an overview of your subject. While questions might vary depending on the age, status, and occupation of your subject, the following is a good starting list:

1.   Where did you grow up? What was it like?
2.   What do your parents do for a living?
3.   Do you have any brothers or sisters? What are they like? How are you similar to or different from them?
4.   How do you spend your free time?
5.   What kinds of jobs have you held?
6.   What are your favorite books, movies, or recordings?
7.   How did you come to be where you are today?
8.   What do you intend to do next?

During subsequent interviews, narrow your questions to a more limited range of interests. For example, if your first interview revealed that photography is your subject's favorite hobby, in your second interview focus several questions on his or her involvement with photography. Your profile will succeed according to the amount of detailed information you get your subject to reveal through interviews. After the interview with Becky, Beth wrote the following narrative from her tape transcript:

> Finally, after minutes of silence she says, "I don't ever remember my father ever living in my house, really. He left when I was three and my sister was just a baby, about a year old. My mom took care of us all. Forever, it was just Mom, Kate, and me. I loved it, you know? Just the three of us together."

Beth is aware that if she can capture the small details of Becky's childhood along with her teenage conversational style (*like, you know*), Becky's story will be all the more plausible—which in turn will make Beth's profile more readable.

✌ WRITING 6

Interview your profile subject in a place that is convenient and comfortable to you both. If this is a first interview, start with informal, conversational questions like those presented in the text.

✌ SELECTING A POINT OF VIEW

Your profile will be written from either the first-person or the third-person point of view. The point of view you choose will do much to establish the tone and style of your profile. In the first-person point of view, the narrator (*I*) has a presence in the story. You can use this point of view to let readers know that you are presenting the subject through the filter and perhaps the bias of your own eyes, as Caleb does in the following passage:

> I walked in past the overfilled coat rack and scanned the room for Charles. The smell of smoke was overwhelming and it was hard to see. It surprised me that Charles would hang out in a joint like this, especially since he seemed to be such a disciplined athlete. I spotted him with a group of tall guys near the pinball machines. We made eye contact and he rose to greet me.

In the third-person point of view, *I* is never used, only proper names (*Joan, Sara*), nouns for persons (*athlete, grocer*), and the pronouns *he, she,* and *they.* You can use this point of view to keep yourself out of the narrative, focusing instead on the subject and on the words and actions that any observer might witness. Caleb does this in the following passage as he describes an exchange that takes place where he and Charles are sitting:

> Again the girls came over, accosting Charles. One of them gave him a Budweiser, which he gladly accepted.
> "You want to play tennis tomorrow?" the shorter girl asked.
> "Sure, what time?" Charles asked in a soft voice.
> "Whenever you're free."
> "How about three? I have a Saturday practice tomorrow morning."

Many profiles are actually written, as Caleb's is, in a combination of first person and third person. Although most of the focus is naturally on the subject, many writers find that since they select what to report and what to ignore, some acknowledgment of their presence is the most honest approach.

Write your first draft from whatever points of view seem comfortable to you. In the revising stages, you can experiment with increasing or decreasing your presence in the narrative, and in editing you will check that the point of view is consistent.

ꜱ WRITING 7

Write one page about your profile subject in the first-person point of view and then one page in the third person, using essentially the same information in each version. Which do you prefer? Why?

ꜱ DEVELOPING A THEME

Ultimately, profiles tell stories about people. Though you have read only a few examples of student profiles in this chapter, already you may have drawn some conclusions about what these people are like. Profile writers select the details and dialogue and background information that tell the story they want to tell about their subject. Most often, that story builds as the profile progresses so that the last page or paragraph focuses on the most important point the writer wants to make about the subject. This central theme can be revealed *explicitly,* with the writer telling readers what to think, or *implicitly,* with the evolution of the profile making the theme clear.

Explicit Theme

Pam concludes her profile, which focuses on Mari Anne's continued love of gymnastics, with her own summary, a small judgment on what the realities of college life have done to Mari Anne's passion.

> [Mari Anne says,] "I want to be able to judge [gymnastics] here at college, so I will still have to pass part two of the exam. I would especially like to judge creative matches that show each gymnast's unique ability." As of now Mari Anne has not had time to fit gymnastics into her schedule. She is too busy trying to keep up with her studies. But you can bet that next year will find her on the floor or behind the judge's table; Mari Anne has too much passion for the sport to stay out for very long.

Implicit Theme

Beth never suggests what readers should think of Becky. She lets her subject's words end the profile, allowing readers to make their own inferences about who Becky is and what she stands for.

> "I think that because I didn't have my dad, we're closer to my grandparents. Because Mom was so young and they helped us out all the time. They gave us property to build a house and everything. So we're a lot closer because she could always count on them. That's the most important thing, you know, being able to count on people."

๛ WRITING 8

In the profile you are developing, would you like your theme to emerge explicitly or implicitly? If implicitly, how would you conclude the profile so that readers would be most likely to understand the theme you intend?

๛ PROFILE OF A CLASSMATE AS A WRITER

An interesting variation on the profile assignment is studying, then profiling a classmate—or anybody else for that matter—as a writer. Such an assignment makes use of all the profiling strategies outlined above, but holds the focus on how a person developed as a writer. Such projects usually begin with classmates interviewing each other and asking questions such as the following:

- How did you learn to write?
- What kinds of writing have you done on your own?

- What was your experience as a writer in school?
- What's the best writing experience you ever had, in school or out?
- What's the worst writing experience you ever had, in school or out?
- What do you most enjoy about writing?
- Describe your writing habits.
- What causes you the most problems when you write?
- Describe your experience writing in college.
- Describe your experience writing in this class.

In the following example, Megan quotes her profile subject, Nicole, talking about the writing she has done on her own and plans to do in the future:

> "I've kept a journal—more of a diary—since I was twelve or thirteen. But that's private writing. In high school I used to write stories and poems occasionally, but I never showed these to anyone. I never felt confident in my creative writing." Nicole studies the edges of the quilt on her dormitory bed and rubs her chin. "I'm trying to change that. I think I have a lot of West Virginia stories to tell—that's where I grew up. My dad worked in a steel mill for thirty years. If you don't come from a town with a steel mill, you don't know what that's like. Those towns are dying off now—I'd like to capture that life in words."

Nicole, in turn, profiles Megan through a combination of close observation and interview, which she weaves together in the following paragraph:

> Megan tries to keep her own desk clean, but often finds it muddled with glasses and coffee mugs. She'll sit in front of her secondhand AT&T computer and compose on the screen, stopping every half an hour to get up and move around. Being a fast typist allows her to write fast, letting her thoughts flow rapidly, not worrying much about punctuation or capitalization—at least on early drafts. Her favorite pen is a black fine point Uniball Micro, which she uses to catch stray thoughts away from the computer. "I prefer to write almost everything on my computer, but I do love to write letters, lists, and journal entries with my Uniball—it's very inky and smooth and spidery."

In addition to paraphrasing and directly quoting interview subjects, plan to share with each other samples of past and current writing, including journals, letters, school assignments, and self-initiated writing. When you compose your final profile draft, weave together the several types of information you've collected—observations, interview material, and original sources. Before concluding this paper, share a version with your subject and ask for reactions, including corrections in fact or adjustments in tone.

Strategies for Writing Profiles

1. When interviewing a classmate, agree on guidelines beforehand: whether or not to use tape recorders; where, when, and for how long to exchange visits; where else to meet; what sources of background to share; and so on.
2. Use your own narration to summarize, to provide background and context, and to interpret. Try to strike a balance between writing about your subject and letting him or her speak.

3.   Quote interview material directly to reveal your subject's personality and be-
     liefs. Subjects who talk directly to readers characterize themselves and provide
     living proof to support your inferences about them.

4.   Share drafts with your profile subject. When subjects see early drafts, they may
     tell you important information that will improve your representations of them.

5.   You are the author of the profile you write: Take your subject's comments into
     account as much as you can, but maintain ownership of your interpretation
     and characterization.

☞ WRITING 9

Write a response to any of the questions above; then give this response to the classmate who is writing your profile to help him or her get started.

☞ SHAPING THE WHOLE PAPER

Beth Devino's finished draft of her profile "Becky" is presented here. Notice that Beth
chose to shape the profile as if it took place at one sitting in Becky's dormitory room; in
fact, she interviewed Becky at several different times and places over several weeks. Beth
removes herself almost completely from the profile, letting Becky's own words do most of
the characterizing—though at times she also presents information from the dormitory setting and her own summary of background information.

Notice the focus on trust and dependability, which develops early in the profile and
carries through to the concluding words that express Becky's attitudes toward men. The
final line makes a very strong ending, but be aware that the writer, not her subject, created
this ending. Over the course of several interviews, Becky talked about a wide range of subjects, including sports, teacher education, and college life. It was Beth who shaped these
many conversations into a coherent essay with a beginning, a middle, and an end.

Becky

Beth Devino

Becky sits cross-legged at the foot of the bottom bunk on her pink and green
homemade quilt. She leans up against the wall and runs her fingers through her
brown shoulder-length hair. The sound of James Taylor's "Carolina on My Mind"
softly fills the room. Posters of John Lennon, James Dean, and Cher look down on
us from the walls. Becky stares at the floor and scrunches her face as if she is thinking hard.

Finally, after minutes of silence she says, "I don't ever remember my father
ever living in my house, really. He left when I was three and my sister was just a
baby, about a year old. My mom took care of us all. Forever, it was just Mom, Kate,
and me. I loved it, you know? Just the three of us together."

Becky smiles and continues, "And I remember little things, you know, like we
would all sleep together in Mom's bed. We'd all climb in. Little things like, I remember one night there was a bat in the house and Mom is afraid of bats and I was

only, like, five, and Mom climbed under the covers with my little sister and I had to go down and call my grandmother to get the bat out of the house.

"But I'm really proud of my mother for bringing up my sister and me on her own. She had to work, sometimes two jobs, and she worked really hard. I don't remember a sad time then, ever. I had the happiest childhood. You know, some of my friends who have whole families complain about fights with their parents, but I have no complaints about anything. I never felt like I needed anything or that I lacked anything."

Becky pauses, hugging her knees close to her chest, rocking slightly. "Hmmm," she mumbles. She traces her lips with the back of her fingernail. "Oh, I always do this when I'm thinking or I'm upset—now I'm just thinking."

Becky Harris grew up in West Granville, a small town where people knew and supported each other. She came to the university to major in elementary education: "I really think those early years are so crucial, when children are first learning how to live in and trust the world."

On campus, she lives in Connors Hall, with Trish, a roommate from Maine who is fast becoming a best friend. Trish agrees, saying, "Outside of classes, we do everything together, share tapes, run on the weekends, borrow clothes, and talk late almost every night. The posters? She put those up. I really like them."

Becky offers me a cup of herbal tea, then makes a cup for herself and resumes her place on the bed. "Anyway, Mom and I have the strangest relationship. It's like we're friends—she's my mom, but we're friends more than she's my mom because, when my dad left, I kinda had to grow up overnight and take care of my sister 'cause my mom was working so much. I mean, she never left us alone or anything, but I had to do things. I had to learn to dress myself and all those little things really fast, earlier than lots of kids because she didn't have time for both of us.

"Oh! I have this watch bear. I put it over my bed, somewhere where it can watch me all the time." She gets up from the bed and slides across the linoleum floor to her desk to pick up the little white stuffed animal. "Two years ago, I lost Watch Bear. For almost three whole days, and I didn't have anybody watching over me. But I found him, he was under the bed. I brought him with me to college to sit on my desk to watch over me and to make sure I'm safe like he did when I was little."

Becky carefully places Watch Bear against the wall near her and continues, "Anyway, I hope that if I were ever in the same situation as my mom, I could be as strong as she. 'Cause that would scare me to have a car and this brand new house that they just built and have to take care of everything. 'Cause my dad never paid any money, never a cent of child support, ever in his life to us.

"I've seen him maybe three or four times in ten or twelve years. Once two years ago, at Thanksgiving, I saw him, and that was when he had just gotten remarried, and I met his wife. I really liked her a lot and I really liked their kids. I got along with them, but you know, I don't think of him as part of my family. I don't even really think of him as my father, really. I mean biologically, but that's all. I used to get really sad sometimes that I didn't have a dad. But I don't feel like I've missed anything in my life, ever. I'd rather have my mother happy than to have her live with someone just to make a whole family 'cause I think we had a whole family.

"My mother has never said a bad thing about my father, ever, in her life. And if it was me who got dumped with two children, I would just—would always be bad-talking, I'm sure. She never wanted us to hate him and wanted us to have the opportunity to get to know him if we wanted to when we could choose to. When he called and asked us to go to Thanksgiving with him a few years ago, I didn't want to, but Mom really encouraged us to 'cause she said maybe he's going to reach out and try to change his ways and be your dad. So we went. Kate, my sister, who was just a year when he left, never knew him at all. She was very uncomfortable there, but I talked to him a little bit."

Becky pauses and traces her lips again. "I used to have really bad feelings towards men in general. Like, I didn't trust them at all 'cause I thought that, you know, they were all sort of like him; you couldn't count on them for anything. I just don't think there's. . . . I get so mad that there's people that would just leave someone with children—especially their own, you know? I'm better now. I have a boyfriend and I trust him a lot, but I question everything he does. When he makes commitments I don't really think he's going to come through, you know? I wonder about that a lot because—I don't really have a reason to distrust all men but, you know?

"I think that because I didn't have my dad, we're closer to my grandparents. Because Mom was so young and they helped us out all the time. They gave us property to build a house and everything. So we're a lot closer because she could always count on them. That's the most important thing, you know, being able to count on people."

✏ SUGGESTIONS FOR WRITING AND RESEARCH

Individual

1. Write a profile of a classmate using the information you have collected in Writings 2–7. In doing this assignment, write several drafts. Share these with your subject, listen to his or her response to your profile, and take those comments into account when writing your final draft. Keep in mind the golden rule of profile writing: Do unto your subject as you would want him or her to do unto you.

2. Write a profile of somebody in the university community who is not a student: a professor, counselor, security officer, cafeteria staffperson. Be considerate in arranging interview times; focus on the work this person does; plan to share your resulting profile with the subject.

3. Write a profile of a family member. Interview this person and collect as much information about him or her as you can: letters, yearbooks, photographs. Plan to contribute your final draft to whoever in your family collects such records. (If nobody does, would you want to start collecting yourself?)

Collaborative

1. Pair up all students in the class—including the instructor if there is an uneven number of students. Within each pair, members will take turns being subject and writer, with each profiling the other to find out the details of his or her writing life. Each student should then compose a profile of the pair partner *as a writer.* As a class, plan to publish all such profiles in a class book. Elect a team of editors to collect, collate, introduce, and produce the class book.

2. Write a collaborative profile of your class. First discuss what a class profile might be like: Would it be a collection of individual profiles arranged in some order? Or would it consist of written bits and pieces about people, places, and events, arranged as a verbal collage? Would there be a place for visual components in this class profile? Would you want to challenge other writing classes to develop similar profiles and share them with one another?

Chapter

❧ **10** ❧

Explaining Things

When I give directions to somebody about how to find some place, it's much easier to draw a map than write it out in words. I mean, with words you have to be so precise but with a map you just draw lines.

JANE

To explain something is to make it clear to somebody else who wants to understand it. Explaining is fundamental to most acts of communication and to nearly every type of writing, from personal and reflective to argumentative and research writing. At the same time, explanatory writing is also a genre unto itself; for example, see a newspaper feature on baseball card collecting, a magazine article on why dinosaurs are extinct, a textbook on the French Revolution, a recipe for chili, or a laboratory report.

❧ **WRITING TO EXPLAIN**

Whether you write to explain something as part of a larger intention or write to report information, explanatory writing (also called expository or informational writing) answers questions such as these:

- What is it?
- What does it mean?
- What are the consequences?
- How does it work?
- How is it related to other things?
- How is it put together?
- How do you get there?
- Why did it happen?
- Why did it fail?

To write a successful explanation, you need to find out first what your readers want to know, then what they already know and what they don't know. If you are able to determine—or at least make educated guesses about—these audience conditions, your writing task becomes clear. When you begin to write, keep in mind three general principles that typify much explanatory writing: (1) It focuses on the idea or object being explained rather than on the writer's beliefs and feelings; (2) it often—not always—states its objective early in what might be called an informational thesis; and (3) it presents information systematically and logically.

In writing classes, explanation usually takes the form of research essays and reports that emphasize informing rather than arguing, interpreting, or reflecting. The assignment may be to describe how something works or to explain the causes and effects of a particular phenomenon. This chapter explains how to develop a topic, articulate your purpose, and use strategies appropriate for your audience.

☞ WRITING 1

How good are you at explaining things to people? What things do you most commonly find yourself explaining? What is the last thing you explained in writing? How did your audience receive your explanation?

☞ FINDING A TOPIC

Topics with a limited, or specific, scope are easier to explain carefully and in detail than topics that are vague, amorphous, or very broad. For example, it's hard to know where to start with subjects such as mountains, cities, automobiles, or sound systems: What, exactly, are you interested in writing about? EVERYTHING? If so, the task is daunting for even the world's foremost expert. However, a specific mountain range, city, or automobile would be a better place to start. But even then you would still need to know what it is about this subject that sparks your curiosity. For example, general subjects such as mountains, automobiles, or music sound systems are so broad that it's hard to know where to begin. However, a specific aspect of sound systems, such as compact discs (CD's), is easier. Within the subject of CD's, of course, there are several topics as well (design, manufacturing process, cost, marketing, sound quality, comparison to tape and vinyl recordings, and so on). If your central question focuses on how CD's are manufactured, you might address some of these other issues (cost, marketing, comparison) as well, but only insofar as they illuminate and advance your focus on manufacturing.

Once you have a focused topic on a central question, you need to assemble information. If you're not an expert yourself, you'll need to consult authorities on the topic. Even if you are already an expert, finding supporting information from other experts will help make your explanation clear and authoritative. Keep your audience in mind as you begin your research. You don't want to waste time researching and writing about things your audience already knows.

࿇ DEVELOPING A THESIS

A thesis is simply a writer's declaration of what the paper is about. Stating a thesis early in an explanatory work lets readers know what to expect and guides their understanding of the information to be presented. In explanatory writing, the thesis states the answer to the implied question your paper sets out to address: What is it? How does this work? Why is this so?

QUESTION   **Why do compact discs cost so much?**

THESIS   **CD's cost more than records because the laser technology required to manufacture them is so expensive.**

The advantage of stating a thesis in a single sentence is that it sums up the purpose of your paper in a single idea that lets readers predict what's ahead. Another way to state a single-sentence thesis is to convey an image, an analogy, or a metaphor that provides an ongoing reference point throughout the paper and gives unity and coherence to your explanation—a good image keeps both you and your readers focused.

QUESTION   **How are the offices of the city government connected?**

THESIS   **City government offices are like an octopus, with eight fairly independent bureaus as arms and a central brain in the mayor's office.**

The thesis you start with may evolve as you work on your paper—and that's okay. For example, suppose the more you learn about city government, the less like an octopus and the more like a centipede it seems. So, your first thesis is really a working thesis, and it needs to be tentative, flexible, and subject to change; its primary function is to keep your paper focused to guide further research.

࿇ WRITING 2

Find a topic that needs explaining to someone for some reason, and write out a working thesis. If you are addressing a *when?* or *how?* question, find an analogy to something familiar that will help your reader understand your explanation better.

࿇ USING STRATEGIES TO EXPLAIN

Good strategies that can be used to explain things include: defining, describing, classifying and dividing, analyzing causes and effects, and comparing and contrasting. Which strategy you select depends on the question you are answering as well as the audience to whom you are explaining. You could offer two very different explanations to the same question depending on who asked it: For example, if asked "Where is Westport Drive?" you would respond differently to a neighbor familiar with local reference points ("one block north of Burger King") than to a stranger, who would not know where Burger King was either. With this caution in mind on considering who is the receiver of the explanation, here is a brief overview of possible strategies, using CD's as a sample topic:

QUESTION	STRATEGY
What is it?	Define

A CD is a small plastic disc containing recorded music.

What does it mean?　　　　　　Define

Today, when you talk about a "recording," you mean a cassette tape or a CD, not a grooved vinyl disc.

What are its characteristics?　　Describe

A vinyl disc is round with tiny grooves covering its surface in which a needle travels to play sound.

What will its consequences be?　Analyze cause and effect

If you scratch a vinyl record with a knife, it will skip.

How does it work?　　　　　　Describe process

On a CD, a laser beam reads the tiny dots on the spinning disc and sends back sound.

How is it related to other things?　Compare and contrast

A CD transmits clearer sound than a cassette tape.

How is it put together?　　　　Classify and divide

A basic sound system includes an input (to generate sound), a processor (to amplify and transmit sound), and an output (to make sound audible).

To what group does it belong?　Classify and divide

CD players, along with tuners and tape cassette decks, are sources of music in a sound system.

Why did it happen?　　　　　　Analyze cause and effect

A CD skips either because its surface is dirty or because the player is broken.

If your paper is on a tightly focused topic and answers a narrow, simple question, you may need to use only one strategy. More often, however, you will have one primary strategy that shapes the paper as a whole and several secondary strategies that can vary from paragraph to paragraph or even sentence to sentence. For example, to explain why the government has raised income taxes, your primary strategy would be to analyze cause and effect, but you may also need to define terms such as *income tax*, to classify the various types of taxes, and to compare and contrast raising income taxes to other budgetary options. In fact, almost every explanatory strategy makes use of other strategies: How, for example, do you describe a process without first dividing it into steps? How can you compare and contrast without describing the things compared and contrasted?

Defining

To *define* something is to identify it, to set it apart so that it can be distinguished from similar things. Writers need to define any terms central for reader understanding in order to make points clearly, forcefully, and with authority.

Formal definitions are what you find in a dictionary. They usually combine a general term with specific characteristics.

> A computer is a programmable electronic device [general term] that can store, retrieve, and process data [specific characteristics].

Usually, defining something is a brief, preliminary step accomplished before you move on to a more important part of the explanation. When you need to define something complex or difficult or when your primary explanatory strategy is definition, you will need an extended definition consisting of a paragraph or more. This was the case with Mark's paper explaining computers, in which he defined each part of a typical computer system. After defining the central processing unit (CPU), he then defined computer memory:

> Computer storage space is measured in units called "kilobytes" (K). Each K equals 1,024 "bytes" or approximately 1,000 single typewriter characters. So one K equals about 180 English words, or a little less than half of a single-spaced typed page, or maybe three minutes of fast typing.
>
> Personal computers generally have their memories measured in "megabytes" (MB). One MB equals 1,048,567 bytes (or 1,000 K), which translates into approximately 400 pages of single-spaced type. One gigabyte (GB) equals 1,000 MB or 400,000 pages of single-spaced type!

Describing

To *describe* a person, place, or thing means to create a verbal image so that readers can see what you see; hear what you hear; or taste, smell, and feel what you taste, smell, and feel. In other words, effective descriptions appeal to the senses. Furthermore, good description contains enough sensory detail for readers to understand the subject, but not so much as to distract or bore them. Your job, then, is to include just the right amount of detail so that you put readers in your shoes.

To describe how processes work is more complicated than describing what something looks like: In addition to showing objects at rest, you need to show them in sequence and motion. You need to divide the process into discrete steps and present the steps in a logical order. This is easier to do with simple processes, such as making a peanut butter and jelly sandwich, than for complex processes, such as manufacturing an automobile.

Whenever you describe a process, show the steps in a logical sequence that will be easy for readers to follow. To help orient your readers, you may also want to number the steps, using transition words such as *first, second,* and *third.* In the following example, taken from an early draft of his paper, Keith describes the process of manufacturing compact discs:

> CD's start out as a refrigerator-sized box full of little plastic beads that you could sift your hands through. They are fed into a giant tapered corkscrew—a blown-up version of an old-fashioned meat grinder. As the beads pass down the corkscrew, they are slowly melted by the heated walls.

At the bottom of their descent is a "master recording plate" onto which the molten plastic is pressed. The plastic now resembles a vinyl record, except that the disc is transparent. The master now imprints "pits," rather than grooves, around the disc, the surface resembling a ball of Play-Doh after being thrown against a stucco wall—magnified 5,000 times.

Comparing and Contrasting

To *compare* two things is to find similarities between them; to *contrast* is to find differences. Comparing and contrasting at the same time helps people understand something two ways: first, by showing how it is related to similar things, and second, by showing how it differs. College assignments frequently ask you to compare and contrast one author, book, idea, and so on with another.

People usually compare and contrast things when they want to make a choice or judgment about them: books, food, bicycles, presidential candidates, political philosophies. For this reason, the two things compared and contrasted should be similar: You'll learn more to help you vote for president by comparing two presidential candidates than one presidential candidate and a Senate candidate; you'll learn more about which orange to buy by comparing it with other types of oranges (navel, mandarin) than with apples, plums, or pears. Likewise, it's easiest to see similarities and differences when you compare and contrast the same elements of each thing. If you describe one political candidate's stand on gun control, describe the other's as well; this way, voters will have a basis for choosing one over the other.

Comparison-and-contrast analysis can be organized in one of three ways. (1) A point-to-point analysis examines one feature at a time for both similarities and differences; (2) a whole-to-whole analysis presents first one object as a whole and then the other as a whole; (3) a similarity-and-difference analysis presents first the similarities between two things, then the differences, or vice versa.

Use a point-to-point or similarity-and-difference analysis for long explanations of complex things, such as manufacturing an automobile, in which you need to cover everything from materials and labor to assembly and inspection processes. But use a whole-to-whole analysis for simple objects that readers can more easily comprehend. In the following whole-to-whole example, a student explains the difference between Democrats and Republicans:

> Like most Americans, both Democrats and Republicans believe in the twin values of equality and freedom. However, Democrats place a greater emphasis on equality, believing equal opportunity for all people to be more important than the freedom of any single individual. Consequently, they stand for government intervention to guarantee equal treatment in matters of environmental protection, minimum wages, racial policies, and educational opportunities.
>
> In contrast, Republicans place greater emphasis on freedom, believing the specific rights of the individual to be more important than the vague collective rights of the masses. Consequently, they stand for less government control in matters of property ownership, wages and the right to work based strictly on merit and hard work, and local control of schools.

Note how the writer devotes equal space to each political party, uses neutral language to lend academic authority to his explanation, and emphasizes the differences by using parallel examples as well as parallel sentence structure. The careful use of several comparison-and-contrast strategies makes it difficult for readers to miss his point.

An *analogy* is an extended comparison that shows the extent to which one thing is similar in structure and/or process to another. Analogies are effective ways of explaining something new to readers, because you can compare something they are unfamiliar with to something they already know about. For example, most of us have learned to understand how a heart functions by comparing it to a water pump. Be sure to use objects and images in analogies that will be familiar to your readers.

Classifying and Dividing

People generally understand short more easily than long, simple more easily than complex. To help readers understand a complicated topic, it helps to classify and divide it into simpler pieces and to put the pieces in context.

To *classify* something, you put it in a category or class with other things that are like it:

Like whales and dolphins, sea lions are aquatic mammals.

To *divide* something, you break it into smaller parts or subcategories:

An insect's body is composed of a head, a thorax, and an abdomen.

Many complex systems need both classification and division to be clear. To explain a music sound system, for example, you might divide the whole into parts: headphones, graphic equalizer, tape deck, CD player, preamplifier, amplifier, tuner, and speakers. To better understand how these parts function, you might classify them into categories:

Inputs	Tuner
	Tape deck
	Compact disc player
Processors	Preamplifiers
	Amplifiers
	Graphic equalizers
Outputs	Speakers
	Headphones

Most readers have a difficult time remembering more than six or seven items at a time, so explaining is easier when you organize a long list into fewer logical groups, as in the preceding example. Also be sure that the categories you use are meaningful to your readers, not simply convenient for you as a writer.

Analyzing Causes and Effects

Few things happen all by themselves. Usually, one thing happens because something else happened; then it, in turn, makes something else happen. You sleep because you're tired, and once you've slept, you wake up because you're rested, and so on. In other words, you already know about cause and effect because it's a regular part of your daily life. A *cause* is something that makes something else happen; an *effect* is the thing that happens.

Cause-and-effect analyses are most often assigned for college papers to answer *why* questions: Why are the fish dying in the river? Why do CD's cost more than records? The most direct answer is a *because* statement.

> Fish are dying because of low oxygen levels in the lake.

Each answer, in other words, is a thesis, which the rest of the paper must both defend and support:

> There are three reasons for low oxygen levels . . . .

Cause-and-effect analyses also try to describe possible future effects:

> If nitrogen fertilizers were banned from farmland that drains into the lake, oxygen levels would rise, and fish populations would be restored.

Unless there is sound, widely accepted evidence to support the thesis, however, this sort of analysis may lead to more argumentative writing. In this example, for instance, farmers or fertilizer manufacturers might complicate the matter by pointing to other sources of lake pollution—outboard motors, paper mill effluents, urban sewage runoff—making comprehensive solutions harder to reach. Keep in mind that most complex situations have multiple causes. If you try to reduce a complex situation to an overly simple cause, you are making the logical mistake known as *oversimplification*.

✌ WRITING 3

Decide which of the five strategies described in this section best suits the primary purpose of the explanatory paper you are drafting. Which additional or secondary strategies will you also use?

✌ ORGANIZING WITH LOGIC

If you explain to your readers where you're taking them, they will follow more willingly; if you lead carefully, step by step, using a good road map, they will know where they are and will trust you.

Your method of organization should be simple, straightforward, and logical, and it should be appropriate for your subject and audience. For example, to explain how a sound system works, you have a number of logical options: (1) you could start by putting a CD in a player and end with the music coming out of the speakers; (2) you could describe the system technically, starting with the power source to explain how sound is made in the speakers; (3) you could describe it historically, starting with components that were developed earliest and work toward the most recent inventions. All of these options follow a clear logic that, once explained, will make sense to readers.

❧ WRITING 4

Outline three possible means of organizing the explanatory paper you are writing. List the advantages and disadvantages of each. Select the one that best suits your purpose and the needs of your audience.

❧ MAINTAINING A NEUTRAL PERSPECTIVE

First, you need to understand that absolute neutrality or objectivity is impossible when you write about anything. All writers bring with them assumptions and biases that cause them to view the world—including this explanatory project—in a particular way. Nevertheless, your explanations will usually be clearer and more accessible to others when you present them as fairly as possible, with as little bias as possible—even though doing this, too, will depend upon who your readers are and whether they agree or disagree with your biases. In general, it's more effective to emphasize the thing explained (the object) rather than your personal beliefs and feelings. This perspective allows you to get information to readers as quickly and efficiently as possible without you, the writer, getting in the way.

To adopt a neutral perspective, write from the third-person point of view, using the pronouns *he, she,* and *it.* Keep yourself in the background unless you have a good reason not to, such as explaining your personal experience with the subject. In some instances, adopting the second-person *you* adds a friendly, familiar tone that keeps readers interested.

Be fair; present all the relevant information about the topic, both things you like about it and things you dislike. Avoid emotional or biased language. Remember that your goal is not to win an argument, but to convey information.

❧ WRITING 5

For practice, write a one-paragraph explanation of your topic from a deliberately biased perspective (political, class, gender, etc.); then compare your version with those written by your classmates and decide on the strategies needed to avoid biases in your writing.

❧ SHAPING THE WHOLE PAPER (STUDENT ESSAY)

In the following essay, Keith Jordan asks the question "How is the music that our generation listens to and takes for granted actually made?" He says, in effect, read my essay ("Let me fill you in.") and I'll explain how CD players operate and how the discs are manufactured. His organization is simple as he starts with the playing of the disc and backtracks to how they are made. Keith's voice throughout is that of a knowledgeable tour guide. Although his personality is clear ("How much can you screw up a yes or no?"), his biases do not affect the report. Although the primary explanatory strategy in Keith's essay is cause and effect, he uses most of the other strategies discussed in this chapter as well: definition, process description, and comparison and contrast. His essay is most remarkable for its effective use of analogy. At various points, he asks his readers to think of radar, the game of telephone, jimmies on an ice cream cone, corkscrews, meat grinders, player pianos, and Play-Doh.

The Sound Is Better than the Music: The Making of Compact Discs
Keith Jordan

Our generation is the music generation. We buy and listen to more music more often than any generation before us, but few of us actually understand how this music is made. The purpose of your whole sound system, from recording to speaker, is to reproduce music that sounds as much like the original source as possible. The compact disc (CD) technology that we take for granted reproduces music better than previous recording systems because it's both simpler and more complicated than they were. Let me fill you in.

A CD player operates by sending out a laser beam of light that bounces off an object, like radar, and returns with a message, which becomes the music. On one CD there are hundreds of thousands of tiny pits that resemble those of a player piano scroll, telling the piano which keys to hit. The CD player reads either a simple "yes" or a "no"—a pit or no pit—from the disc. The laser in your CD player detects the distance to the disc to determine whether there's a pit, which will be farther away, or not.

What's the difference, you ask, in receiving music from tiny pits versus the grooves on vinyl records or magnetic deposits on tapes? The result is less interference between the message sent and the message received. Do you remember playing the "telephone game" in fifth grade? You know, the one where someone on one side of class whispers something in your ear and it gets passed along until it gets to the last person, who says what he or she was told? This is much the way in which your sound system works: a recording—either a disc or a tape—is like the first person, and your speakers are like the last. In the case of the vinyl records or magnetic tapes, I whisper some line in your ear and you pass it on, but by the time it reaches the last person, it's been touched and twisted and has a few more words attached. However, in the case of the CD, I whisper either a "yes" or a "no," and by the time it reaches the last person it should be exactly the same—this is where the term "digital" comes from, meaning either there is a signal ("yes") or there isn't one ("no"). How much can you screw up a yes or a no?

The CD manufacturing process, however, is not so simple. To guarantee that almost nothing will interfere with (scratch or break) the digital message encoded on the plastic, the disc is metallized, a process that deposits a thin film of metal, usually aluminum, on the surface; you see it as a rainbow under a light. Since light won't bounce back from transparent plastic, the coating acts as a mirror to bounce back the laser beam. The disc is mirrored by a precise spray-painting process called "sputtering." You couldn't just dip the thing because then the pits would fill in or melt. The clear disc is inserted into a chamber and placed opposite a piece of pure aluminum called a "target," which is bombarded with electricity, causing the aluminum atoms to jump off and embed themselves into the surface of the disc, like jimmies on an ice cream cone. Then the disc is "spin-coated" yet again with a fine film of resin, which becomes the outer coating on the CD.

Once the resin is cured by a brief exposure to ultraviolet light, your CD is pretty much idiot-proof. As long as you don't interrupt the light path in the film, your CD will perform perfectly, even with small scratches, so long as they don't diffract the laser beam—and even then you may be able to rub them smooth with a finger. No object, other than a ray of light, comes in contact with the recorded surface of a compact disc.

The CD is finished when it is stamped with the appropriate logo and allowed to dry. In other words, the way CD's are played and made eliminates the interference that caused distortion in earlier music systems. These steps, which have taken me several hours to explain on paper, take a mere seven seconds on the assembly line from materials that cost no more than a pack of gum. The technology behind CD systems guarantees a faithful sound recording and a disc that will last virtually forever—longer, perhaps, than some of the music we listen to.

᪣ SUGGESTIONS FOR WRITING AND RESEARCH

Individual

1. Write a paper explaining any thing, process, or concept. Use as a starting point an idea you discovered in Writing 2. When you have finished one draft of this essay, look back and see if there are places where your explanation could be improved through use of one of the explanatory strategies described in this chapter.
2. Select a writer of your choice, fiction or nonfiction, who explains things especially well. Read or reread his or her work and write an essay in which you analyze and explain the effectiveness of the explanation you find there.
3. Revise by directing your last draft to a less knowledgeable audience or one with more specialized expertise.

Collaborative

Form writing groups based on mutual interests; agree as a group to explain the same thing, process, or concept. Write your explanations separately and then share drafts, comparing and contrasting your different ways of explaining. For a final draft, either (1) rewrite your individual drafts, borrowing good ideas from others in your group, or (2) compose a collaborative single paper with contributions from each group member.

Chapter

❧ 11 ❧

Strategies for Revision

Writing. I'm more involved in it. But not as attached. I used to really cling to my writing and didn't want it to change. Now I can see the usefulness of change. I just really like my third draft, but I have to let it go. I can still enjoy my third draft and make an even better fourth.

KAREN

A first draft is a writer's first attempt to give shape to an idea, argument, or experience. Occasionally, this initial draft is just right and the writing is done. More often, however, the first draft shows a broad outline or general direction that needs further thinking and further revision. An unfocused first draft, in other words, is not a mistake but rather a start toward a next, more focused draft.

No matter how much prior thought writers give to complex composing tasks, once they begin writing, the draft begins to shift, change, and develop in unexpected ways. Each act of writing produces new questions and insights that must be dealt with and incorporated into the emerging piece of writing; it is during this process that active and aggressive revision strategies can help. Inexperienced writers often view revising as an alien activity that neither makes sense nor comes easy. However, most experienced writers view revising as the essence of writing, the primary way of developing thoughts to be shared with others.

❧ UNDERSTANDING REVISION

The terms *revising, editing,* and *proofreading* are sometimes used to mean the same thing, but there is good reason to understand each as a separate process, each in its own way contributing to good finished writing. *Revising* is reseeing, rereading, rethinking, and reconstructing your thoughts on paper until they match those in your mind. It's conceptual work, generally taking place beyond the sentence, at the level of the paragraph and higher.

In contrast, *editing* is changing language more than ideas. You edit to make precise what you want to say, testing each word or phrase to see that it is accurate, appropriate, necessary. Editing is stylistic and mechanical work, generally taking place at the level of the sentence or word.

Proofreading is checking a manuscript for accuracy and correctness. It is the last phase of the editing process, completed after conceptual and stylistic concerns have been addressed. When you proofread, you review spelling, punctuation, capitalization, and usage to make sure no careless mistakes have occurred that might confuse or distract readers.

There are two good reasons to revise before you edit. First, in revising you may cut out whole sections of a draft because they no longer suit your final purpose. If you have already edited those now-deleted sections, all that careful work goes for naught. Second, once you have invested time in carefully editing sentences, you become reluctant to cut them, even though these sections may no longer suit your purpose. Of course, writers are always circling back through the stages, editing when it makes more sense to revise, inventing when they mean to edit. Nonetheless, you will save time if you revise before editing, and edit before proofreading.

ॐ **WRITING 1**

Describe any experience you've had with revising papers: Was it for a school assignment or some writing on your own? Why did you revise? How many drafts did you do? Were you pleased? Was your audience?

ॐ **PLANNING TO REVISE**

You cannot revise if you haven't first written, so write early and leave time to revise later. Good college papers are seldom written in one draft the night before they are due. When you plan in advance to revise, the following tools and techniques will serve you well:

Keep a revision notebook. When you begin any substantial writing project, keep a notebook or journal in which to capture all ideas related to your paper, including invention, drafting, research, and revision ideas. Over the span of several days or weeks, your revision may profit from your returning to earlier information, ideas, or insights.

Impose due dates. Write the due date for a final draft on your calendar, then add earlier, self-imposed due dates for first, second, or third drafts. Your self-imposed or false due dates will guarantee you the time you need to revise well.

Write and rewrite with a computer. Computers make revising easier and more effective. Any kind of word-processing program allows you to change your text infinitely before ever calling it finished. The computer allows you to change words and sentences as well as move blocks of text from one part of your paper to another with ease—all essential acts of revising.

Read hard copy. When revising with a computer, print out hard copy of your drafts and see how they read on paper. Hard copy lets you scan several pages at a time and quickly flip pages in search of certain patterns or information.

Save draft copies. Make backup files of old drafts on floppy disks or on your hard drive; if you become unhappy with your revisions, you can always return to the earlier copy.

⊰ **WRITING 2**

Describe your approach to writing a paper from the time it's assigned to the time you hand it in. Do you do any of the prerevision work described above? Which of these general strategies makes sense in view of your current writing habits?

⊰ **ASKING REVISION QUESTIONS**

To begin revising, return to the basic questions of purpose, audience, and voice: Why am I writing? To whom? In what voice?

Questions of Purpose

It is often easier to see your purpose—or lack thereof—most clearly after you have written a draft or two. Ask the following questions:

1. Why am I writing this paper? (Review the assignment.)
2. Do all parts of the paper advance this purpose? (Outline by paragraph and make sure they do.)
3. What is my rhetorical strategy: to narrate, explain, interpret, argue, reflect, or something else? (Review appropriate chapters to fine-tune strategy.)
4. Have I stated the paper's theme or thesis clearly? (If not, do so, or have a good reason for not doing so.)

Questions of Audience

Make sure your paper is aimed accurately at your readers by asking the following questions:

1. What does my audience know about this subject? (Avoid repeating elementary information.)
2. What does my audience need to know to understand the point of my paper? (Provide full context and background for information your audience is not likely to know.)
3. What questions or objections do I anticipate my audience raising? (Try to answer them before they are asked.)

Questions of Voice

Make sure your paper satisfies you. Revise it as necessary so you say what you intend in the voice you intend by asking the following questions:

1. Do I believe everything I've written in this paper? (Eliminate nonsense and filler.)
2. What doubts do I have about my paper? (Address these; don't avoid them.)

3.   Which passages sound like me speaking and which don't? (Enjoy those that do; fix those that don't.)

∽ REVISING STRATEGIES

For many writers, revising seems to be an instinctive or even unconscious process—they just do it. However, even experienced writers might profit by pausing to think deliberately about what they do when they revise.

This section lists more than a dozen time-tested revision strategies that may be useful to you. While they won't all work for you all the time, some will be useful at one time or another. Notice that these suggestions start with larger concerns and progress toward smaller ones.

Four revising strategies—*limiting, adding, switching,* and *transforming*—are complicated enough that I'll treat them in detail in the next chapter. Limiting is focusing on a narrow portion of a paper or concept and eliminating extraneous material; adding is incorporating new details and dialogue to make writing more vivid and powerful. Switching and transforming are more innovative strategies for revision: by changing the tense, point of view, form, or genre of a piece of writing, writers can gain insights into their writing and present their ideas in a new light.

Establish Distance

Let your draft sit for a while, overnight if possible, then reread it to see if it still makes sense. A later reading provides useful distance from your first words, allowing you to see if there are places that need clarification, explanation, or development that you did not see when drafting. You can gain distance also by reading your draft aloud—hearing instead of seeing it—and by sharing it with others and listening to their reactions. No matter how you gain it, with distance you revise better.

Reconsider Everything

Reread the whole text from the beginning: Every time you change something of substance, reread again to see the effect of these changes on other parts of the text. If a classmate or instructor has made comments on some parts of the paper and not on others, do not assume that those are the only places where revision is needed.

Believe and Doubt

First, reread your draft as if you wanted to believe everything you wrote (imagine you are a supportive friend), putting checks in the margins next to passages that create the most belief—the assertions, the dialogue, the details, the evidence. Next, reread your draft as if you were suspicious and skeptical of all assertions (imagine your most critical teacher), putting question marks next to questionable passages. Be pleased with the check-marks, and answer the question marks.

Test Your Theme or Thesis

Most college papers are written to demonstrate a theme or thesis (to outlaw handguns; to legalize marijuana). However, revision generates other ideas, raises new questions, and sometimes reshapes your thesis (license handguns; legalize hemp as a cash crop). Make sure to modify all parts of your paper to keep up with your changing thesis.

Evaluate Your Evidence

To make any theme or thesis convincing, you need to support it with evidence. Do your facts, examples, and illustrations address the following questions?

1. Does the evidence support my thesis or advance my theme? (In states that license handgun ownership, crime rates have decreased.)
2. What objections can be raised about this evidence? (The decrease in crime rates has other causes.)
3. What additional evidence will answer these objections? (In states that do not license handguns, crime has not decreased.)

Make a Paragraph Outline

The most common unit of thought in a paper is the paragraph, a group of sentences set off from other groups of sentences because they focus on the same main idea. Make a paragraph outline to create a map of your whole paper and see whether the organization is effective: Number each paragraph and write a phrase describing its topic or focus. Does the subject of each paragraph lead logically to the next? If not, reorganize.

Rewrite Introductions and Conclusions

Once started, papers grow and evolve in unpredictable ways: An opening that seemed appropriate in an earlier draft may no longer fit. The closing that once ended the paper nicely may now fail to do so. Examine both introduction and conclusion to be sure they actually introduce and conclude. Sometimes it is more helpful to write fresh ones than to tinker with old ones.

Listen for Your Voice

In informal and semiformal papers, your language should sound like a real human being speaking. Read your paper out loud and see if the human being speaking sounds like you. If it doesn't, revise so that it does. In more formal papers, the language should sound less like you in conversation and more like you giving a presentation—fewer opinions, more objectivity, no contractions.

Let Go

View change as good, not bad. Many writers become overly attached to the first words they generate, proud to have found them in the first place, now reluctant to abandon them. Learn to let your words, sentences, and even paragraphs go. Trust that new and better ones will come.

Start Over

Sometimes revising means starting over completely. Review your first draft, then turn it face down and start fresh. Starting over generates your best writing, as you automatically delete dead-end ideas, making room for new and better ones to emerge. (Many writers have discovered this fact accidentally, by deleting a file on a computer and thus being forced to reconstruct, almost always writing a better draft in the process.)

☞ WRITING 4

Look over the suggestions for revision in this section. Which of them have you used in the past? Which seem most useful to you now? Which seem most far-fetched?

☞ A REVISION CHECKLIST

1. Reread the assignment and state it in your own words. Does your paper address it?
2. Restate your larger purpose. Has your paper fulfilled it?
3. Consider your audience. Have you told your readers what they want and need to know?
4. Read the text out loud and listen to your voice. Does the paper sound like something you would say?
5. Restate the paper's thesis or theme in a single sentence. Is it stated in the paper? Does the paper support it?

6.   List the specific evidence that supports this thesis or theme. Is it sufficient? Is it arranged effectively?

7.   Outline the paper paragraph by paragraph. Is the development of ideas clear and logical?

8.   Return to your introduction. Does it accurately introduce the revised paper?

9.   Return to your conclusion. Does it reflect your most recent thoughts on the subject?

10.   Return to your title and write five alternative titles. Which is the best one?

ঙ SUGGESTIONS FOR WRITING AND RESEARCH

Individual

Select any paper that you previously wrote in one draft but that you believe would profit from revision. Revise the paper by following some of the revision strategies and suggestions in this chapter.

Collaborative

Have each member of the class go to the library and research the revision habits of a favorite or famous writer. If you cannot find such information, interview a professor, teacher, or person in your community who is known to write and publish. Find out about the revision process he or she most often uses. Write a report in which you explain the concept of revision as understood and used by the writer you have researched, and publish all the reports in a class anthology.

Chapter

~ 12 ~

Arguing For and Against

When I argued against federal gun control laws with my roommates, it was pretty easy to convince them I was right, but when I wrote the same arguments in my English paper, my writing group challenged every point I made and kept asking for more evidence, more proof. Do you have to have evidence for everything you write?

WOODY

No, you don't *have* to have evidence for every paper you write, but if you want reasonable people—for example, the instructors and students of a college or university—to believe your assertions, interpretations, and arguments, you'd better have evidence—substantial, plentiful, convincing evidence.

Argument is deeply rooted in the American political and social system, in which free and open debate is the essence of the democratic process. Argument is also at the heart of the academic process, in which scholars investigate scientific, social, and cultural issues, hoping through the give-and-take of debate to find reasonable answers to complex questions. Argument in the academic world, however, is less likely to be about winning or losing—as it is in political and legal systems—than about changing minds or altering perceptions about knowledge and ideas.

Argument as rational disagreement, rather than as quarrels and contests, most often occurs in areas of genuine uncertainty about what is right, best, or most reasonable. In disciplines such as English, history, and philosophy, written argument commonly takes the form of interpretation, in which the meaning of an idea or text is disputed. In disciplines such as political science, engineering, and business, arguments commonly appear as position papers, in which a problem is examined and a solution proposed.

~ WRITING TO CHANGE PEOPLE'S MINDS

The reason for writing an argumentative paper in the first place is to persuade other people to agree with a particular point of view. Arguments focus on issues about which there is some debate; if there's no debate, there's no argument. College assignments commonly ask you to argue one side of an issue and defend your argument against attacks from skeptics.

In a basic position-paper assignment, you are asked to choose an issue, argue a position, and support it with evidence. Sometimes your investigation of the issue will lead you beyond polar positions toward compromise—a common result of real argument and debate in both the academic and political worlds. In other words, such a paper may reveal that the result of supporting one position (*thesis*) against another (*antithesis*) is to arrive at yet a third position (*synthesis*), which is possible now because both sides have been fully explored and a reasonable compromise presents itself. This chapter explains the elements that constitute a basic position paper: an arguable issue, a claim and counterclaim, a thesis, and evidence.

Issue

An *issue* is a controversy, something about which there is disagreement. For instance, mountain bikes and cultural diversity are things or concepts, not in themselves issues. However, they become the foundation for issues when questions are raised about them and controversy ensues.

ISSUE   **Do American colleges adequately represent the cultural diversity of the United States?**

ISSUE   **Should mountain bikes be allowed on wilderness hiking trails?**

These questions are issues because reasonable people could answer them in different ways; they can be argued about because more than one answer is plausible, possible, or realistic.

Position

Virtually all issues can be formulated, at least initially, as yes/no questions about which you will take one position or the other: pro (if the answer is yes) or con (if the answer is no).

ISSUE   **Should mountain bikes be allowed on trails in Riverside Park?**

PRO   **Yes, they should be allowed to share pedestrian trails.**

CON   **No, they should not be allowed to share trails with pedestrians.**

Claims and Counterclaims

A *claim* is a statement or assertion that something is true or should be done. In arguing one side of an issue, you make one or more claims in the hope of convincing an audience to believe you. For example, you could make a claim that calls into question the educational experience at Northfield College:

CLAIM   **Northfield College fails to provide good education because the faculty is not culturally diverse.**

Counterclaims are statements that oppose or refute claims. You need to examine an opponent's counterclaim carefully in order to refute it or, if you agree with the counterclaim, to argue that your claim is more important to making a decision. For example, the following counterclaim might be offered against your claim about the quality of Northfield College education:

COUNTERCLAIM The Northfield faculty are good scholars and teachers; therefore, their race is irrelevant.

You might agree that "Northfield faculty are good scholars and teachers" but still argue that the education is not as good as it would be with more diversity. In other words, the best arguments provide not only good reasons for accepting a position, but also good reasons for doubting the opposition. They are made by writers who know both sides of an issue and are prepared for the arguments of the opposition.

Thesis

The primary claim made in an argument is called a *thesis*. The thesis in an argumentative paper is the major claim the paper makes and defends.

THESIS Northfield College should enact a policy to make the faculty more culturally diverse by the year 2005.

In taking a position, you may make other claims as well, but they should all work to support this major claim or thesis.

CLAIM The faculty is not culturally diverse.

CLAIM A culturally diverse faculty is necessary to provide a good education for today's student.

CLAIM The goal of increased cultural diversity by the year 2005 is achievable and practical.

In arguing a position, you may state your thesis up front, with the remainder of the paper supporting it (thesis first), or you may state it later in the paper after weighing the pros and cons with your reader (delayed thesis). As a writer, you can decide which approach is the stronger rhetorical strategy after you fully examine each claim and the supporting evidence. Each strategy, thesis first or delayed, has its advantages and disadvantages.

Evidence

Evidence makes a claim believable. Evidence consists of facts, examples, or testimony that supports a claim. For example, to support a claim that Northfield College's faculty lacks cultural diversity, you might introduce the following evidence:

EVIDENCE According to the names in the college catalog, 69 of 79 faculty members are male.

EVIDENCE According to a recent faculty survey, 75 of 79 faculty members are Caucasian or white.

EVIDENCE According to Carmen Lopez, an unsuccessful candidate for a position in the English Department, 100 percent of the faculty hired in the last ten years have been white males.

Most arguments become more effective when they include documentable source material; however, shorter and more modest argument papers can be written without research and can profitably follow a process similar to that described here.

ᔆ WRITING 1

An issue debated by college faculty is whether or not a first-year writing course should be required of all college students. Make three claims and three counterclaims about this issue. Then select the claim you most believe in and write an argumentative thesis that could form the basis for a whole essay.

ᔆ FINDING AN ISSUE

You'll write better and have a more interesting time if you select an issue that interests you and about which you still have real questions. A good issue around which to write a position paper will meet the following criteria:

1. It is a real issue about which there is controversy and uncertainty.
2. It has at least two distinct and arguable positions.
3. Resources are available to support both sides.
4. Writing a position paper on the issue fits the time frame and scope of the assignment.

In selecting an issue to research and write about, consider both national and local issues. The advantage of selecting national issues is that you are likely to see them explained and argued on the national news programs—*CBS Evening News* or *All Things Considered* on NPR—or in national news publications such as *Time, Newsweek,* and the *New York Times.* In addition, you can count on your audience having some familiarity with the subject. The disadvantage is that it may be difficult to find local experts or a site where some dimension of the issue can be witnessed. These are examples of national issues:

Are SATs a fair measure of academic potential?
Should handgun ownership be outlawed in the United States?
Does acid rain kill forests?

Local issues are derived from the community in which you live. You will find issues like these argued about in local newspapers and on local news broadcasts:

Should a new mall be built on the beltway?
Should mountain bikes be allowed in Riverside Park?
Should Northfield College require a one-semester course introducing students to diverse American cultures?

The advantage of local issues is that you can often visit a place where the controversy occurs, interview people who are affected by it, and find generous coverage in local news media. The disadvantage is that the subject won't be covered in the national news.

Perhaps the best issue is a national issue (hikers versus mountain bikers) with a strong local dimension (this controversy in a local park). Such an issue will enable you to find both national press coverage and local experts, and you can be reasonably sure that both your instructor and your classmates will know something about it and will be interested in your position on it.

⟨ WRITING 2

Make a list of three national and three local issues about which you are concerned. Next, select the three issues that seem most important to you and write each as a question with a yes or no answer. Finally, note whether each issue meets the criteria for a good position paper topic.

⟨ ANALYZING AN ISSUE

The most demanding work in writing a position paper takes place after you have selected an issue but before you actually write the paper. To analyze an issue, you need to conduct enough research to explain it and identify the arguments of each side.

In this data-collecting stage, treat each side fairly, framing the opposition as positively as you frame the position. Research as if you are in an honest debate with yourself; doing so may even cause you to switch sides—one of the best indications of open-minded research. Furthermore, empathy for the opposition leads to the selection of qualified assertions and heads off overly simplistic right-versus-wrong arguments. Undecided readers who see merit in the opposing side respect writers who acknowledge an issue's complexity.

Establishing Context

Provide full context for the issue you are writing about, as if readers know virtually nothing about it. Providing context means answering these questions: What is this issue about? Where did the controversy begin? How long has it been debated? Who are the people involved? What is at stake? Use a neutral tone, as Issa does in discussing the mountain bike trail controversy:

> With all these new riders, there is a need for places to ride, and this is where the wilderness trail controversy begins. The mountain bike is designed to be ridden on dirt trails, logging roads, and fire trails in backwoods country. However, other trail users who have been around much longer than mountain bikers prefer to enjoy the woods at a slow, leisurely pace. They find the rapid and sometimes noisy two-wheel intruders unacceptable.

Claims For (Pro)

List the claims supporting the pro side of the issue. Make each claim a distinctly strong and separate point, and make the best possible case for this position, identifying by name the most important people or organizations that hold this view. Issa makes the following claims for opening up wilderness trails to mountain bikes:

1. All people should have the right to explore the wilderness so long as they do not damage it.
2. Knobby mountain bike tires do no more damage to hiking trails than Vibram-soled hiking boots.
3. Most mountain bike riders are respectful of the wilderness and courteous to other trail users.

Claims Against (Con)

List the claims supporting the con side of the issue—the counterclaims. It is not necessary to have an equal number of reasons for and against, but you do want an approximate balance.

1. Mountain bike riders ride fast, are sometimes reckless, and pose a threat to slower-moving hikers.
2. Mountain bike tires damage trails and cause erosion.

Annotated References

Make an alphabetical list on note cards or computer files of the references you consulted during research, briefly identifying each according to the kind of information it contains. The same article may present claims from both sides as well as provide context. Following are three of Issa's annotated references:

> Buchanan, Rob. "Birth of the Gearhead Nation." Rolling Stone 9 July 1992: 80-85. Marin Co. CA movement advocates more trails open to mountain bike use. Includes history. (pro)
>
> "Fearing for Desert, A City Restricts Mountain Bikes." New York Times 4 June 1995, A24. Controversy in Moab, Utah, over conservation damage by mountain bikes. (con)
>
> Schwartz, David M. "Over Hill, Over Dale on a Bicycle Built for . . . Goo." Smithsonian 25.3 (June 1992): 74-84. Discusses the hiker vs. biker issue, promotes peaceful coexistence, includes history. (pro/con)

Annotating your list of references allows you to check and rearrange your claims at any time during the writing process. In addition, if you write and organize your references now, your reference page will be ready to go when you've finished writing your paper.

✒ WRITING 3

Select one of the issues you are interested in, establish the necessary context, and make pro and con lists similar to those described in this section, including supporters of each position. Make the best possible case for each position.

◌ TAKING A POSITION

Once you have spread out the two positions fairly, determine which side is stronger. Select the position that you find most convincing and then write out the reasons that support this position, most compelling reasons last. This will be the position you will most likely defend; you need to state it as a thesis.

Start with a Thesis

Formulate your initial position as a *working thesis* early in your paper-writing process. A working thesis asserts your major claim; it is merely something to start with, not necessarily to stick with—which is why we're calling it "working": it's still in the process of being developed and made final. Even though it's tentative, it serves to focus your initial efforts in one direction, and it helps you articulate claims and assemble evidence to support it.

WORKING	**Hikers and mountain bikers should cooperate and support each other in**
THESIS	**using, preserving, and maintaining wilderness trails.**

Writers often revise their initial positions as they reshape their paper or find new evidence; however, do your best to make each assertion of a thesis as strong as possible—even if you're pretty sure it's not final. Your working thesis should meet the following criteria:

1.   It can be managed within your confines of time and space.
2.   It asserts something specific.
3.   It proposes a plan of action.

◌ WRITING 4

Take a position on the issue you have identified. Formulate a working thesis that you would like to support. Test your thesis against the criteria listed for good theses.

◌ DEVELOPING AN ARGUMENT

Your *argument* is the case you will make for your position; it is the means by which you will try to persuade your readers that your position is correct. Good arguments, as Woody discovered at the beginning of this chapter, need solid and credible evidence and clear and logical reasoning.

Assembling Evidence

A claim is meaningless without evidence to support it, and good evidence can come from a variety of sources: *facts, examples, inferences, informed opinion,* and *personal experience* all provide believable evidence.

Facts and Examples

Facts are verifiable and agreed upon by everyone involved regardless of personal beliefs or values. Facts are often numerical or statistical, and they are recorded in some place where anybody can look them up—a dictionary, an almanac, a public report, or a college catalog.

Water boils at 212 degrees Fahrenheit.

Northfield College employed 79 full-time faculty and enrolled 1,143 full-time students in 1996.

Five hundred Japanese-made "Stumpjumper" mountain bikes were sold in the United States in 1981.

Examples can be used to illustrate a claim or clarify an issue. If you claim that many wilderness trails have been closed to mountain biking, you can mention examples you know about:

The New Jersey trails at South Mountain, Eagle Rock, and Mills Park have all been closed to mountain bikes.

Facts and examples can, of course, be misleading and even wrong. For hundreds of years malaria was believed to be caused by "bad air" rather than, as we know today, by a parasite transmitted through mosquito bites; however, for the people who believed the bad-air theory, it was fact.

The accumulation of a certain number of facts and examples should lead to an interpretation of what those facts mean—an *inference* or a generalization. For example, if you attend five different classes at Northfield College and in each class you find no minority students, you may infer that there are no minority students on campus. However, while your inference is reasonable, it is not a fact, since your experience does not allow for your meeting all the possible students at the college.

Facts are not necessarily better or more important than inferences; they serve different purposes. Facts provide information, and inferences give that information meaning.

Sometimes inference is all that's available. For example, statistics describing what "Americans" believe or do are only inferences about these groups based on information collected from a relatively small number of individuals. To be credible, however, inferences must be reasonable and based on factual evidence.

Expert Opinion

Expert opinion makes powerful evidence. When a forest ranger testifies about trail damage caused by mountain bikes or lug-soled hiking boots, his training and experience make him an expert. A casual hiker making the same observation is less believable. To use expert opinion in writing arguments, be sure to cite the credentials or training that makes this person's testimony "expert."

Personal Testimony

A useful kind of evidence is testimony based on *personal experience*. When someone has experienced something firsthand, his or her knowledge cannot easily be discounted. If you have been present at the mistreatment of a minority student, your eyewitness testimony will carry weight, even though you are not a certified expert of any kind. To use personal testimony effectively, provide details that confirm for readers that you were there and know what you are talking about.

Demonstrating Reasoning

To build an effective argument, consider the audience you must persuade. In writing about the mountain bike controversy, for example, ask yourself these questions:

- Who will read this paper: members of an environmentally conscious hiking club, members of a mountain bike club, or your instructor?
- Where do I think they stand on the issue? (Hikers are often opposed to mountain bikes, mountain bikers are not, but you would need more information to predict your instructor's position.)
- How are their personal interests involved? (Hikers want the trails quiet and peaceful, bikers want to ride in the wilderness, and your instructor may or may not care.)
- What evidence would they consider convincing? (A hiker would need to see convincing examples of trails being improved by mountain bike use, bikers would accept anecdotal testimony of good intentions, and you're still not sure about your instructor.)

The more you know about the audience you're trying to sway, the easier it will be to present your case. If your audience is your instructor, you'll need to make inferences about his or her beliefs based on syllabus language, class discussion, assigned readings, or personal habits. For example, if your instructor rides a mountain bike to work, you may begin to infer one thing; if he or she assigns Sierra Club readings in the course, you infer something else; and if the instructor rides a mountain bike and reads *Sierra Club,* well, you've got more homework ahead. Remember that inferences based on a single piece of evidence are often wrong; find out more before you make simple assumptions about your audience. And sometimes audience analysis doesn't work very well when an instructor assumes a deliberately skeptical role in reading a set of papers. It's best to assume you will have a critical reader and to use the best logic and evidence available. Following are some ways to marshal careful and substantial evidence.

First, establish your credibility. Demonstrate to your audience that you are fair and can be trusted. Do this by writing in neutral, not obviously biased language—avoid name-calling. Also do this by citing current sources by respected experts, and don't quote them out of context. Identify elements that serve as common ground between you and the audience; be up front and admit when the opposite side makes a good point.

CREDIBLE   Northfield College offers excellent instruction in many areas; however, its offerings in multicultural education would be enhanced by a more diverse faculty.

LESS CREDIBLE Education at Northfield College sucks.

Second, use logic. Demonstrate that you understand the principles of reasoning that operate in the academic world: Make each claim clearly, carefully, and in neutral language. Make sure you have substantial, credible evidence to support each claim. Make inferences from your evidence with care; don't exaggerate or argue positions that are not supported by the evidence.

LOGICAL   Since 75 of 79 faculty members are white or Caucasian, and 69 of 79 are male, it would make good sense to seek to hire more black, Hispanic, and Native American women faculty when they are available.

ILLOGICAL   Since all Northfield faculty members are racists, they should all be fired.

Third, appeal to your audience's emotions. It's fair to use means of persuasion other than logic to win arguments. Write with vivid details, concrete language, and compelling examples to show your audience a situation that needs addressing. It is often helpful, as well, to adopt a personal tone and write in friendly language to reach readers' hearts as well as minds.

EMOTIONAL   When Bridget Jones, the only black student in Philosophy 1, sits down,
APPEAL   the desks on either side of her remain empty. When her classmates choose partners for debate, Bridget is always the last one chosen.

ॐ WRITING 5

Develop an informal profile of the audience for your position paper by answering the questions posed in this section. Make a list of the kinds of evidence most likely to persuade this audience.

ॐ ORGANIZING THE PAPER

To organize your paper, you need to know your position on the issue: What is the main point of your argument? In other words, move from a working thesis to a final thesis: Confirm the working thesis that's been guiding your research so far, or modify it, or scrap it altogether and assert a different one. You should be able to articulate this thesis in a single sentence as the answer to the yes/no question you've been investigating.

THESIS   Wilderness trails should be open to both mountain bikers and hikers.

THESIS   Wilderness trails should be closed to mountain bikes.

Your next decision is where in this paper should you reveal your thesis to the reader—openly up front or strategically delayed until later? Neither strategy is necessarily right or wrong, but the decision is important because each one has a different psychological effect on your reader.

Thesis-First Organization

When you lead with a thesis, you tell readers from the beginning where you stand on the issue. The remainder of the essay supports your claim and defends it against counterclaims. Following is one good way to organize a thesis-first argument:

1. Introduce and explain the issue. Make sure there are at least two debatable sides. Pose the question that you see arising from this issue; if you can frame it as a yes/no, for/against construction, both you and your reader will have the advantage throughout your answer of knowing where you stand.

    Minority students, supported by many majority students at Northfield College, have staged a weeklong sit-in to urge the hiring of more minority faculty across the curriculum. Is this a reasonable position? Should Northfield hire more minority faculty members?

2. Assert your thesis. Your thesis states the answer to the question you have posed and establishes the position from which you will argue. Think of your thesis as the major claim the paper will make.

    Northfield College should enact a policy to make the faculty more culturally diverse as soon as is reasonably possible.

    Writers commonly state their thesis early in the paper, at the conclusion of the paragraph that introduces the issue.

3. Summarize the counterclaims. Explain the opposition's "counterclaims" before elaborating upon your own claims, because doing that gives your own argument something to focus on—and refute—throughout the rest of the paper. Squeezing the counterclaims between the thesis (2) and the evidence (5) reserves the strongest places—the opening and closing—for your position.

    COUNTERCLAIM 1 Northfield college is located in a white middle-class community, so its faculty should be white and middle class also.

    COUNTERCLAIM 2 The Northfield faculty are good scholars and teachers; therefore, their race is irrelevant.

4. Refute the counterclaims. Look for weak spots in the opposition's argument, and point them out. Use your opponent's language to show you have read closely but still find problems with the claim. To refute counterclaim 1:

    If the community in which the college is located is "white middle class," there is all the more reason to offer that diversity in the college.

    Your reputation is often stronger when you acknowledge the truth of some of the opposition's claims (demonstrating your fairness) but point out the limitations as well. To refute counterclaim 2:

Although Northfield College offers excellent instruction in many areas, its instruction in multicultural education would be enhanced by a more diverse faculty.

5.   Support your claims with evidence. Spell out your own claims clearly and precisely, enumerating them or being sure to give each its own full-paragraph explanation, and citing supporting evidence. This section will constitute the longest and most carefully documented part of your essay. The following evidence supports the thesis that Northfield needs more cultural diversity.

According to the names in the college catalog, 69 of 79 faculty members are male.

According to a recent faculty survey, 75 of 79 faculty members are Caucasian or white.

According to Carmen Lopez, an unsuccessful job candidate for a position in the English Department, all faculty hired in the last ten years have been white males.

6.   Restate your position as a conclusion. Near the end of your paper, synthesize your accumulated evidence into a broad general position, and restate your original thesis in slightly different language.

While Northfield College offers a strong liberal arts education, the addition of more culturally diverse faculty members will make it even stronger.

There are several advantages to leading with a thesis. First, your audience knows where you stand from the first paragraph. Second, your thesis occupies both the first and last position in the essay. In addition, this is the most common form of academic argument.

Delayed-Thesis Organization

Using the delayed-thesis type of organization, you introduce the issue, discuss the arguments for and against, but do not obviously take a side until late in the essay. Near the end of the paper, you explain that after listening carefully to both pros and cons, you have now arrived at the most reasonable position. Concluding with your own position gives it more emphasis. The following delayed-thesis argument is derived from the sample student essay at the end of this chapter:

1.   Introduce the issue and pose a question. Both thesis-first and delayed-thesis papers begin by establishing context and posing a question. Following is the question for the mountain bike position paper:

Should mountain bikes be allowed on wilderness trails?

2.   Summarize the claims for one position. Before stating which side you support, explain how the opposition views the issue:

To traditional trail users, the new breed of bicycle [is] alien and dangerous, esthetically offensive, and physically menacing.

3.   Refute these claims. Still not stating your own position, point out your difficulties with believing this side:

Whether a bicycle—or a car or horse for that matter—is "alien . . . and esthetically offensive" depends on your personal taste, judgment, and familiarity. And whether it is "dangerous" depends on how you use it.

In addition, you can actually strengthen your position by admitting that in some cases the counterclaims might be true.

While it's true that some mountain bikers—like some hikers—are too loud, mountain biking at its best respects the environment and promotes peace and conservation, not noise and destruction.

4. Summarize the counterclaims. You are supporting these claims, and so they should occupy the most emphatic position in your essay, the last:

Most mountain bikers respect the wilderness and should be allowed to use wilderness trails.

5. Support your counterclaims. Now give your best evidence; this should be the longest and most carefully documented part of the paper:

Studies show that bicycle tires cause no more erosion or trail damage than the boots of hikers, and far less than horses' hooves.

6. State your thesis as your conclusion. Your rhetorical stance or strategy is this: You have listened carefully to both the claims and counterclaims, and after giving each side a fair hearing, you have arrived at the most reasonable conclusion.

It's clear that mountain bikers don't want to destroy trails any more than hikers do. The surest way to preserve America's wilderness areas is to establish strong cooperative bonds among the hikers and bikers, as well as those who fish, hunt, camp, canoe, and bird-watch, and encourage all to maintain the trails and respect the environment.

There are many advantages to delayed-thesis arguments. First, the audience is drawn into your struggle by being asked to weigh the evidence and arrive at a thesis. Second, readers are kept in suspense about your position; their curiosity is aroused. Finally, readers understand your difficulty in making a decision.

✍ WRITING 6

Make two outlines for organizing your position paper, one with the thesis first, the other with a delayed thesis. Share your outlines with your classmates and discuss which seems more appropriate for the issue you have chosen.

✍ SHAPING THE WHOLE PAPER

In the following paper, Issa Sawabini explores whether or not mountain bikers should be allowed to share wilderness trails with hikers. In the first part of the paper he establishes the context and background of the conflict; then he introduces the question his paper will address: "Is any resolution in sight?" Note his substantial use of sources, including the Internet and interviews, cited in the MLA documentation style. Issa selects a delayed-thesis strategy, which allows him to air both sides of the argument fully before revealing his solution, a compromise position: So long as mountain bikers follow environmentally sound guidelines, they should be allowed to use the trails.

On the Trail: Can the Hikers Share with the Bikers?
Issa Sawabini

The narrow, hard-packed dirt trail winding up the mountain under the spreading oaks and maples doesn't look like the source of a major environmental conflict, but it is. On the one side are hikers, environmentalists, and horseback riders who have traditionally used these wilderness trails. On the other side, looking back, are the mountain bike riders sitting atop their modern steeds wanting to use them too. But the hikers don't want the bikers, so trouble is brewing.

The debate over mountain bike use has gained momentum recently because of the increased popularity of this form of bicycling. Technology has made it easier for everyone to ride these go-anywhere bikes. These high-tech wonders incorporate exotic components, including quick gear-shifting derailleurs, good brakes, and a more comfortable upright seating position—and they can cost up to $2,000 each (Kelly 104). Mountain bikes have turned what were once grueling hill climbs into casual trips, and more people are taking notice.

Mountain bikes have taken over the bicycle industry, and with more bikes come more people wanting to ride in the mountains. The first mass-produced mountain bikes date to 1981, when five hundred Japanese "Stumpjumpers" were sold; by 1983 annual sales reached 200,000; today the figure is 8.5 million. In fact, mountain biking is second only to in-line skating as the fastest growing sport in the nation: "For a sport to go from zero to warp speed so quickly is unprecedented," says Brian Stickel, director of competition for the National Off Road Bicycle Association (Schwartz 75).

With all these new riders, there is a need for places to ride, and this is where the wilderness trail controversy begins. The mountain bike is designed to be ridden on dirt trails, logging roads, and fire trails in backwoods country. However, other trail users who have been around much longer than mountain bikers prefer to enjoy the woods at a slow, leisurely pace. They find the rapid and sometimes noisy two-wheel intruders unacceptable: "To traditional trail users, the new breed of bicycle [is] alien and dangerous, esthetically offensive and physically menacing" (Schwartz 74).

"The problem arises when people want to use an area of public land for their own personal purpose," says Carl Newton, forestry professor at the University of Vermont. "Eventually, after everyone has taken their small bit of the area, the results can be devastating. People believe that because they pay taxes for the land, they can use it as they please. This makes sense to the individual, but not to the whole community." Newton is both a hiker and a mountain biker.

When mountain bikes first came on the scene, hikers and environmentalists convinced state and local officials to ban the bikes from wilderness trails (Buchanan 81; Kelly 104). The result was the closing of many trails to mountain bike use: "Many state park systems have banned bicycles from narrow trails. National Parks prohibit them, in most cases, from leaving the pavement" (Schwartz 81). These trail closings have separated the outdoor community into the hikers and the bikers. Each group is well organized, and each group believes it is right. Is any resolution in sight?

The hikers and other passive trail users have a number of organizations, from conservation groups to public park planning committees, who argue against allowing mountain bikes onto narrow trails traditionally traveled only by foot and horse in the past. They believe that the wide, deeply treaded tires of the mountain bikes cause erosion and that the high speeds of the bikers startle and upset both hikers and horses (Hanley B4; Schwartz 76).

The arrival of mountain bikes during the 1980s was resisted by established hiker groups, such as the Sierra Club, which won debate after debate in favor of closing wilderness trails to mountain bike activities. The younger and less well organized biking groups proposed compromise, offering to help repair and maintain trails in return for riding rights, but their offers were ignored. "Peace was not given a chance. Foes of the bicycle onslaught, older and better connected, won most of the battles, and signs picturing a bicycle crossed with a red slash began to appear on trail heads all over the country" (Schwartz 74).

In Millburn, New Jersey, trails at South Mountain, Eagle Rock, and Mills Park have all been closed. Anyone caught riding a bike on the trails can be arrested and fined up to $100. Local riders offered an amendment calling for trails to be open Thursday through Sunday, with the riders helping maintain the trails on the other days. The amendment was rejected. According to hiker Donald Meserlain, the bikes "ruin the tranquillity of the woodlands and drive out hikers, bird watchers, and strollers. It's like weeds taking over the grass. Pretty soon we'll have all weeds" (Hanley).

Many areas in western New York, such as Hunter's Creek, have also been closed to mountain bike use. Anti-biking signs posted on trails frequently used by bicyclists caused a loud public debate as bike riding was again blamed for trail erosion.

Until more public lands are opened to trail riding, mountain bikers must pay fees to ride on private land, a situation beneficial to ski resorts in the off season: "Ski areas are happy to open trails to cyclists for a little summer and fall income" (Sneyd). For example, in Vermont, bike trails can be found at the Catamount Family Center in Williston, Vermont, as well as at Mount Snow, Killington, Stratton, and Bolton Valley. At major resorts, such as Mount Snow and Killington, ski lifts have actually been modified to the top of the mountains, and each resort offers a full-service bike shop at its base.

However, the real solution to the conflict between hikers and bikers is education, not separation. In response to the bad publicity and many trail closings, mountain bikers have banded together at local and national levels to educate both their own member bike riders and the non-riding public about the potential alliance between these two groups (Buchanan 81).

The largest group, the International Mountain Bike Association (IMBA), sponsors supervised rides and trail conservation classes and stresses that mountain bikers are friends, not enemies of the natural environment. "The IMBA wants to change the attitude of both the young gonzo rider bombing downhill on knobby tires, and the mature outdoorsman bristling at the thought of tire tracks where boot soles alone did tread" (Schwartz 76). IMBA published guidelines it hopes all mountain bikers will learn to follow:

1. Ride on open trails only.
2. Leave no trace.
3. Control your bicycle.
4. Always yield trail.
5. Never spook animals.
6. Plan ahead. (JTYL)

The New England Mountain Bike Association (NEMBA), one of the largest East Coast organizations, publishes a home page on the Internet outlining goals: "NEMBA is a not-for-profit organization dedicated to promoting land access, maintaining trails that are open to mountain bicyclists, and educating riders to use those trails sensitively and responsibly. We are also devoted to having fun" (Koellner).

At the local level, the Western New York Mountain Bike Association (WNYMBA) educates members on proper trail maintenance and urges its members to cooperate with local environmentalists whenever possible. For instance, when angry cyclists continued to use the closed trail at Hunter's Creek, New York, WNYMBA used the Internet to warn cyclists against continued trail use: "As WNYMBA wishes to cooperate with Erie County Parks Department to the greatest extent possible on the use of trails in open parks, WNYMBA cannot recommend ignoring posted signs. The first IMBA rule of trail is 'ride on open trails only'" (JTYL).

Educated mountain biking, like hiking and horseback riding, respects the environment and promotes peace and conservation, not noise and destruction. Making this case has begun to pay off, and the battle over who walks and who rides the trails should now shift in favor of peaceful coexistence. "Buoyed by studies showing that bicycle tires cause no more erosion or trail damage than the boots of hikers, and far less than horses' hooves, mountain bike advocates are starting to find receptive ears among environmental organizations" (Schwartz 78).

Even in the Millburn, New Jersey, area, bikers have begun to win some battles, as new trails have recently been funded specifically for mountain bike use: "After all," according to an unnamed legislator, "the bikers or their parents are taxpayers" (Hanley).

The Wilderness Society now officially supports limited use of mountain bikes, while the Sierra Club also supports careful use of trails by riders so long as no damage to the land results and riders ride responsibly on the path. "In pursuit of happy trails, bicycling organizations around the country are bending backward over their chain stays to dispel the hell-on-wheels view of them" (Schwartz 83).

Education and compromise are the sensible solutions to the hiker/biker standoff. Increased public awareness as well as increasingly responsible riding will open still more wilderness trails to bikers in the future. It's clear that mountain bikers don't want to destroy trails any more than hikers do. The surest way to preserve America's wilderness areas is to establish strong cooperative bonds among the hikers and bikers, as well as those who fish, hunt, camp, canoe, and bird-watch, and to encourage all to maintain the trails and respect the environment.

Works Cited

Buchanan, Rob. "Birth of the Gearhead Nation." Rolling Stone 9 July 1992: 80-85.

"Fearing for Desert, A City Restricts Mountain Bikes." New York Times 4 June 1995: A24.

Hanley, Robert. "Essex County Mountain Bike Troubles." New York Times 30 May 1995: B4.

JTYL (editor). Western New York Mountain Bike Association Home Page. Western New York Mountain Bike Association. <http://128.205.166.43/public/wnymba/wnymba.html>. (4 Oct. 1995).

Kelly, Charles. "Evolution of an Issue." Bicycling 31 (May 1990): 104-105.

Koellner, Ken (editor). New England Mountain Bike Association Home Page. 19 Aug. 1995. New England Mountain Bike Association. <http://www.ultranet.com/~kvk/nemba.html>. (30 Sep. 1995).

Newton, Carlton. Personal interview. 13 Nov. 1995.

Schwartz, David M. "Over Hill, Over Dale on a Bicycle Built for . . . Goo." Smithsonian 25.3 (June 1992): 74-84.

Sneyd, Ross. "Mount Snow Teaching Mountain Biking." Burlington Free Press 4 Oct. 1992: E1.

⌇ SUGGESTIONS FOR WRITING AND RESEARCH

Individual

1. Write a position paper on the issue you have been working with in Writings 2–6. Follow the guidelines suggested in this chapter, using as much research as you deem appropriate.
2. Write a position paper on an issue of particular interest to your writing class. Consider topics such as (a) student voice in writing topics, (b) the seating plan, (c) the value of writing groups versus instructor conferences, or (d) the number of writing assignments.
3. Revise your argumentative paper to submit to your student newspaper, either as a special feature or as an opinion piece for the editorial page. Consider carefully any special appeal, argument, or word choice that would make this paper more convincing to your college audience.

Collaborative

1. In teams of two or three, select an issue; divide up the work so that each group member contributes some work to (a) the context, (b) the pro argument, and (c) the con argument (to guarantee that you do not take sides prematurely). Share your analysis of the issue with another group and receive feedback. Finally, write your position papers individually.
2. Follow the procedure for the first collaborative assignment, but write your final position paper collaboratively.

Chapter

❧ 13 ❧

Focused Revision

I never realized before that in revising you can do drafts from totally different
perspectives and keep experimenting with your ideas. When you write the final draft,
it could be totally different from how you expected it to come out in the beginning.

GARY

I want my audience to feel like they're actually attending the game, that they're sitting just behind
the bench, overhearing Coach telling us how to defend against the in-bounds pass, and I can do this
if I just close my eyes while I write and remember being there—I can put you at the game.

KAREN

Have you ever found yourself running out of ideas, energy, or creativity on what seemed to be a perfectly good topic for a paper? Have you ever been told to rewrite, revise, review, redo, rethink a paper, but didn't know exactly what those suggestions meant? Have you ever written a paper you thought was carefully focused and well researched but also was dull and lifeless?

Odds are you're not alone. When anyone writes a first draft—especially on an assigned topic to which he or she has given little prior thought—it's easy to summarize rather than analyze, to produce generalities and ignore specifics, to settle for clichés rather than invent fresh images, to cover too much territory in too little time. In fact, most first drafts contain more than their share of summary, generalization, superficiality, and cliché, since most first-draft writers are feeling their way and still discovering their topic. In other words, it's seldom a problem if your first draft is off the track, wanders a bit, and needs refocusing. However, it *is* a problem if, for your second draft, you don't know what to do about it.

The best way to shape a wandering piece of writing is to return to it, reread it, slow it down, take it apart, and build it back up again, this time attending more carefully to purpose, audience, and voice. Celebrate first-draft writing for what it is—a warm-up, a scouting trip—but plan next to get on with your journey in a more deliberate and organized fashion. Sometimes you already know—or your readers tell you—exactly where to go.

Other times, you're not sure and need some strategies to get you moving again. This chapter offers four specific strategies for restarting, reconceiving, and refocusing a stuck paper.

❧ LIMITING

Broad topics lead to superficial writing. It's difficult to recount a four-week camping trip, to explain the meaning of *Hamlet,* or to solve the problems of poverty, crime, or violence in a few double-spaced pages. You'll almost always do better to cover less ground in more pages. Instead, can you *limit* your focus to one pivotal day on the trip? Can you explain and interpret one crucial scene? Can you research and portray one real social problem in your own backyard?

Limit Time, Place, and Action

When a first draft attempts to describe and explain actions that took place over many days, weeks, or months, try limiting the second draft to actions that took place on one day, on one afternoon, or in one hour. Limiting the amount of time you write about automatically limits the action (what happened) and place (where it happened) as well. For example, in the first draft of a paper investigating the homeless in downtown Burlington, Vermont, Dan began with a broad sweep:

> In this land of opportunity, freedom takes on different meaning for different people. Some people are born to wealth, others obtain it by the sweat of their brows, while average Americans always manage to get by. But others, not so fortunate or talented, never have enough food or shelter to make even the ends of their daily lives meet.

While there is nothing inherently wrong with this start, neither is there anything new, interesting, or exciting. The generalizations about wealth and poverty tell us only what we already know; there are no new facts, information, or images to catch our attention and hold it for the pages still to come.

Before writing his second draft, Dan visited the downtown area, met some homeless people, and observed firsthand the habits of a single homeless man named Brian; then he limited his focus and described what he witnessed on one morning:

> Dressed in soiled blue jeans and a ragged red flannel shirt, Brian digs curiously through an evergreen bush beside a house on Loomis Street. His yellow mesh baseball cap bears no emblem or logo to mark him a member of any team. He wears it low, concealing any expression his eyes might disclose. After a short struggle, he emerges from the bush, a Budweiser can in hand, a grin across his face. Pouring out the remaining liquid, he tosses the can into his shopping cart among other aluminum, glass, and plastic containers. He pauses, slides a Marlboro out of the crumpled pack in his breast pocket, lights it, and resumes his expedition.

While only one small act happens in this revised first paragraph—the retrieving of a single beer can—that act anticipates Dan's story of how unemployed homeless people earn money. By starting with a single detailed—and therefore convincing—scene, Dan writes more about less; in the process, he teaches his readers specific things about people he originally labeled "not so fortunate or talented." By describing instead of evaluating or interpreting this scene, he invites readers to make their own inferences about what it means. In other words, writing one specific, accurate, nonjudgmental scene asks readers to interpret and therefore engage more deeply in the text.

Limit Scope

In the process of Dan's researching and writing, the scope of his paper became progressively more restricted: In draft one, he focused on the homeless in America; in draft two, he focused on the homeless in downtown Burlington; in draft three, he focused on those homeless people who collect cans for income. From his initial limitation in time came a consequent limitation in scope, and a distinct gain in specificity, detail, and reader interest.

One technique for limiting the scope of any type of paper is to identify the topic of any one page, paragraph, or sentence in which something important or interesting is introduced. Begin your next paper with that specific topic, focusing close now and limiting the whole draft to only that topic. For example, in a paper arguing against the clear-cutting of forests, focus on one page describing the cutting of Western red cedar in one specific place; limit the next whole draft to that single subject. In a paper examining the exploitation of women in television advertising, focus on one paragraph describing a single soda ad; limit the next whole draft to that single subject. In a paper examining your high school soccer career, focus on one sentence describing the locker room after the loss of an important game. When you limit scope, you gain depth.

ᔓ WRITING 1

Devote a portion of your journal or class notebook exclusively to exploring the revision possibilities of one paper. For your first entry, reread the paper you intend to revise, and limit either the time or scope that you intend to cover in the second draft.

ᔓ ADDING

A sure way to increase reader interest in a paper, and your own interest as well, is to *add* new and specific material to that overly general first draft. Whether you are arguing about the effects of mountain bikes on the wilderness, explaining the situation of the homeless people downtown, or interpreting the poems of Gwendolyn Brooks, it is your job to become the most informed expert on this subject in your writing class. It's your job to read the necessary articles, visit the appropriate places, interview the relevant people who will make you the authority to write the paper. On first drafts, neither your instructor nor classmates expect you to be this authority; on subsequent drafts, their expectations increase.

Add Expert Voices

The surest way to locate new information to add to next drafts is to read widely and listen carefully. Get to the library and locate sources that supplement and substantiate your own knowledge. Enlist the support of experts by citing them in your paper, identifying who they are and why they should be listened to. Also get out into the field and talk to people who are the local experts on your subject. Quote these experts, too, and include their voices in your next draft.

Although textual quotations are helpful and expected in academic papers, they are seldom so locally specific or lively as interview quotations from local people. In many instances where little may have been published on local issues, the only way to get up-to-date local information is from talking to people. Quoting people directly not only adds new and credible information to your paper, it invariably adds a sense of life as well. For example, as Dan continued his story of Burlington's homeless people, he interviewed a number of people, such as police officer Pat Hardy, who had firsthand knowledge of the homeless can collectors:

> "They provide a real service to the community," he explains. "You'd see a lot more cans and bottles littering the streets if they weren't out here working hard each day. I've never had a problem with any of them. They are a real value."

While Dan himself could have made the same observation, it has greater authority and life coming from a cop on the beat.

In another instance, a team of first-year students collaborated to write a profile of the local Ronald McDonald House, a nonprofit organization providing free room and board for the families of hospital patients. In their first draft, they researched the local newspaper for introductory information on the origins of this institution. It was useful information, but without much life:

> The McDonald's corporation actually provided less than 5 percent of the total cost of starting the Ronald McDonald House. The other 95 percent of the money came from local businesses and special-interest groups.

For their second draft, the group interviewed the director of the Ronald McDonald House and used her as an additional and more current source of information. In fact, they devoted the entire second draft to material collected through interviews with the director and staff at the house. In the following sample, the director substantiates the information from the initial newspaper story but adds more specific, local, and lively details.

> "Our biggest problem is that people think we're supported by the McDonald's corporation. We have to get people to understand that anything we get from McDonald's is just from the particular franchise's generosity—and may be no more than is donated by other local merchants. Martins, Hood, and Ben and Jerry's provide much of the food. McDonald's is not obligated to give us anything. The only reason we use their name is because of its child appeal."

The final profile of the Ronald McDonald House included information ranging from newspaper and newsletter stories to site descriptions and interviews with staff, volunteers, and family.

Add Details

If you quickly review this chapter's samples of revision by *limiting* and *adding,* you will notice the increase in specific detail. Focusing close, interviewing people, and re-searching texts all produce specific information, which adds both energy and evidence to whatever paper you are writing. In the can-collecting paper, the visual details make Brian come alive—*soiled blue jeans, red flannel shirt, yellow mesh baseball cap, Budweiser can, Marlboro.* In the Ronald McDonald revisions, the newspaper statistics add authority (*5 percent of the total cost*) while the interview information adds specificity (*Martins, Hood, and Ben and Jerry's*), both of which help explain the funding of this nonprofit organization.

⌁ WRITING 2

Identify texts, places, or people that contain information relevant to your paper topic and go collect it. If you are writing a paper strictly from memory, close your eyes and visit this place in your imagination: Describe the details and re-create the dialogue you find there.

⌁ SWITCHING

Another strategy for focusing a second or third draft is to deliberately alter your customary way of viewing and thinking about this topic. One sure way to change how you see a problem, experience, story, issue, or idea is to *switch* the perspective from which you view it (the point of view), the language in which you portray it (the verb tense), or the audience for whom you are writing.

Switch Point of View

Switching the point of view from which a story, essay, or report is written means changing the perspective from which it is told. For example, in recounting personal experience, the most natural point of view is the first person (*I, we*) as we relate what happened to us. Here Karen writes in the first person in reporting her experience participating in the Eastern Massachusetts women's basketball tournament.

> We lost badly to Walpole in what turned out to be our final game. I sat on the bench most of the time.

However, Karen opened the final draft of her personal experience basketball narrative with a switch in point of view, writing as if she were the play-by-play announcer broadcasting the game at the moment, in this case moving to third person *and* adopting a new persona as well:

> Well folks, it looks as if Belmont has given up; the coach is preparing to send in his subs. It has been a rough game for Belmont. They stayed in it during the first

quarter, but Walpole has run away with it since then. Down by twenty with only six minutes left, Belmont's first sub is now approaching the table.

In her final draft, Karen opened from the announcer's point of view for one page, then switched for the remainder of the paper to her own first-person perspective, separating the two by white space. Karen's switch to announcer is credible (she *sounds* like an announcer); if she chose to narrate the same story from the perspective of the bouncing basketball, it might seem silly.

In research writing, as opposed to personal narrative, the customary point of view for reporting research results is third person (*he, she, it*) to emphasize the information and de-emphasize the writer. For example, the profile of the Ronald McDonald House begins, as you might expect, with no reference to the writers of the report:

> The Ronald McDonald House provides a home away from home for out-of-town families of hospital patients who need to visit patients for extended periods of time but cannot afford to stay in hotels or motels.

However, in one of their drafts, the writers switched to first person and wrote a more personal and impressionistic account explaining their feelings about reporting on this situation. While the impressionistic draft did not play a large part in the final profile, some of it remained purposefully in their final draft as they reported where they had had difficulties.

> In this documentary, we had a few problems with getting certain interviews and information. Since the house is a refuge for parents in distress, we limited the kinds of questions we asked. We didn't want to pry.

Switch Tense

Switching verb tense means switching the time frame in which a story or experience occurs. While the present tense is a natural tense for explaining information (see the Ronald McDonald example above), the most natural tense for recounting personal experience is the past tense, as we retell occurrences that happened sometime before the present moment—the same tense Karen adopted in the first draft of her basketball essay. However, her final draft is written entirely in the present tense, beginning with the announcer and continuing through to the end of her own narrative.

> It's over now, and I've stopped crying, and I'm very happy. In the end I have to thank—not my coach, not my team—but Walpole for beating us so badly that I got to play.

The advantage of switching to the present tense is that it lets you reexperience an event, and doing that, in turn, allows you to reexamine, reconsider, and reinterpret it—all essential activities for successful revision. At the same time, readers participate in the drama of the moment, waiting along with you to find out what will happen next. The disadvantage is that the present tense is associated with fiction—it's difficult or impossible to write while you're doing something else, like playing basketball. It's also difficult to reflect on experience if you're pretending it's occurring as you write.

Switch Sides

Another way to gain a new revision perspective is to switch sides in arguing a position: Write your first draft supporting the "pro" side, then write a second draft supporting the "con" side. For example, Issa, a dedicated mountain bike enthusiast, planned to write in favor of opening up more wilderness trails for use by mountain bikers. However, before writing his final draft, he researched the arguments against his position and wrote from that point of view:

> The hikers and other passive trail users argue against allowing mountain bikes onto narrow trails traditionally traveled only by foot and horse. They point out that the wide, deeply treaded tires of the mountain bikes cause erosion and that the high speeds of the bikers startle and upset both hikers and horses. According to hiker Donald Meserlain, the bikes "ruin the tranquillity of the woodlands and drive out hikers, bird watchers, and strollers" (Hanley 4).

For the writer, the main advantage of switching sides for a draft may be a better understanding of the opposition's point of view, making for a more effective argument against it in the final draft.

For his final draft, Issa argues his original position in favor of mountain bikes, but he does so with more understanding, empathy, and effectiveness because he spent a draft with the opposition. His final draft makes it clear where he stands on the issue:

> Educated mountain biking, like hiking and horseback riding, respects the environment and promotes peace and conservation, not noise and destruction. Making this case has begun to pay off, and the battle over who walks and who rides the trails should now shift in favor of peaceful coexistence. Buoyed by studies showing that bicycle tires cause no more erosion or trail damage than the boots of hikers, and far less than horses' hooves, mountain bike advocates are starting to find receptive ears among environmental organizations (Schwartz 78).

The tone of the mountain bike essay is now less strident and more thoughtful—an approach apparently brought about by his spending time seriously considering the objections of the opposition.

Another switch that pays good dividends for the writer is changing the audience to whom the paper is being written. In college writing situations, the final audience always includes the instructor, so such a change may simply be a temporary but useful fiction. Had a draft of the mountain bike essay been aimed at the different constituencies mentioned in the essay—the Sierra Club, mountain bicycle manufacturers, property owners, or local newspapers—the writer might have gained a useful perspective in attempting to switch language and arguments to best address this more limited readership. Likewise,

---

ᴈᴖ **WRITING 3**

Write in your journal about a past experience, using the present tense and/or third-person point of view. Then reread the passage and describe its effect on you as both writer and reader.

drafts of various papers written to young children, empathetic classmates, skeptical professors, or sarcastic friends may also provide useful variations in writer perspective.

ᔐ TRANSFORMING

To *transform* a text is to change its form by casting it into a new form or genre. In early drafts, writers often attend closely to the content of their stories, arguments, or reports but pay little attention to the form in which these are presented, accepting the genre as "school paper" only. However, recasting ideas and information into different and more public genres presents them in a different light. The possibilities for representing information in different genres are endless, since anything can become anything else. Consequently, keep in mind that some transformations are useful primarily to help you achieve a fresh perspective during the revision process, while others are more appropriate for presenting the information to readers.

In the world outside of college, it is actually common for research information to be reported in different genres to different audiences. For example, in a business or corporate setting, the same research information may be conveyed as a report to a manager, a letter to a vice president, a pamphlet for the stockholders, and a news release for public media—and show up still later in a feature article in a trade publication or newspaper. As in the working world, so in college: Information researched and collected for any paper can be presented in a variety of forms and formats.

Transform Personal Experience from Essay to Journal

The journal form encourages informal and conversational language, creates a sense of chronological suspense, is an ideal form for personal reflection, substitutes dates for more complex transitions, and proves especially useful for conveying experience over a long period of time. For example, after several essay-like narratives written from a past-tense perspective, Jeff used the journal format to tell the story of his month-long camping trip with the organization Outward Bound. Following is an excerpt, edited for brevity, in which he describes his reactions to camping alone for one week, using a mix of past and present tenses:

Day 14   I find myself thinking a lot about food. When I haven't eaten in the morning, I tend to lose my body heat faster than when I don't. . . . At this point, in solo, good firewood is surprisingly tough to come by. . . .

Day 15   Before I write about my fifth day of solo, I just want to say that it was damn cold last night. I have a –20 degree bag, and I froze. It was the coldest night so far, about –25. . . .

Day 17   I haven't seen a single person for an entire week. I have never done this before, and I really don't want to do it again—not having anyone to talk to. Instead of talking, I write to myself. . . . If I didn't have this journal, I think I would have gone crazy.

Transform to Letters

An issue might be illuminated in a lively and interesting way by being cast as a series or exchange of letters. Each letter allows a different character or point of view to be expressed. For example, Issa's argumentative paper on mountain bike use in wilderness areas could be represented as a series of letters to the editor of a local paper arguing different sides of the controversy: from the perspective of a hiker, a horseback rider, a mountain bike rider, a forest ranger, a landowner, among others.

Transform to a Documentary

Radio, film, and television documentaries are common vehicles for hearing news and information. Virtually any research paper could be made livelier by being cast as a documentary film or investigative feature story. Full research and documentation would be required, as for formal academic papers; however, writers would use the style of the popular press rather than the MLA or APA. In fact, the final form of the profile of the Ronald McDonald House was written as a script for *Sixty Minutes* and opened with a Mike Wallace–type of reporter speaking into a microphone:

> Smith: Hello, this is John Smith reporting for Sixty Minutes. Our topic this week is the Ronald McDonald House. Here I am, in front of the house in Burlington, Vermont, but before I go inside, let me fill you in on the history of this and many other houses like it.

The final paper included sections with the fictional Smith interviewing actual staff members as well as some sections presented neutrally from the camera's point of view:

> Toward the back of the house, three cars and one camper are parked in an oval-shaped gravel driveway. Up three steps onto a small porch are four black plastic chairs and a small coffee table containing a black ashtray filled with cigarette butts.

Transform to a Book with Chapters

Teams of student writers can collaborate on writing short books with "chapters" exploring issues of common interest. Such a form could include a table of contents, preface, foreword, afterword, introduction, and so on. For example, Dan's report on the life of a can collector could become one chapter in a collaborative "book" investigating how the homeless live:

1. Housing for the Homeless
2. Dinner at the Salvation Army
3. Shopping at Goodwill
4. Brian: Case Study of a Can Collector
5. Winter Prospects

Transform to a Magazine Article

If you are investigating consumer products, such as mountain bikes and CD's, consider writing the final draft as a report for *Consumer Reports*. If you are investigating an issue such as homelessness, write it as an article for *Time* or *Newsweek*. Likewise, a campus story on the Greek system could be aimed at the campus newspaper or the profile of a classmate in the style of *People* magazine or *The New Yorker*. Before writing the final draft, be sure to study the form and conventions of the periodical for which you are writing.

Transform to a Talk-Show Debate

An especially good genre for interpretive or argumentative papers would be a debate, conversation, or panel discussion. For example, students recently wrote a paper as a debate on the advantages versus disadvantages of clear-cutting timber: On one side were the environmentalists and tourist industry, on the other side the paper companies and landowners; each side had valid points in its favor. The debate format was real, as it echoed very closely a similar debate in Congress.

Transform to Any Medium of Expression

The possibilities for reshaping college papers are endless: song, play, poem, editorial, science fiction story, laboratory report, bulletin, brochure, television or radio commercial, public address, political speech, telephone conversation, e-mail exchange, World Wide Web page, poster, "Talk of the Town" for *The New Yorker,* sound bite, environmental impact statement, conference paper, video game, philosophical debate, or bar stool argument.

> ### ᧢ WRITING 4
>
> Propose a transformation for a paper you are writing or have recently written. List the advantages and disadvantages of this transformation. Recast your paper (or a part of it) in the new genre and describe the effect.

᧢ EXPERIMENTATION VERSUS CONVENTION

Standard *academic conventions* are accepted ways of doing certain things, such as using an objective voice in research reports and placing the thesis first in position papers. These conventions have evolved over time for good reasons. When carefully done, they transmit ideas and information clearly and predictably, thereby avoiding confusion and misunderstanding. Although in many cases these conventions work well, successful writers sometimes invent unorthodox strategies and experiment with new or alternative forms to better express new or complicated ideas. In order to decide whether a conventional or experimental form is preferable in any part of your paper, try both to see which more appropriately presents your ideas in their best light. Sometimes an act as simple as changing time, tense, point of view, or genre can effectively change the impact of a piece of writing.

The strategies described in this chapter are useful revising tools because they force writers to resee the events in different languages and from different perspectives. Writing in new forms is also intriguing, exciting, and fun—which is often what writers need after working long and hard to put together a first draft.

When and under what circumstances should you limit, add, switch, or transform? While there are no rules, you might try using these strategies whenever you feel stuck or in need of new energy or insight. But be sure to weigh gains and losses whenever you use new focusing techniques.

Disregarding academic conventions in early drafts should seldom be a problem; however, disregarding them in final drafts could be if it violates the assignment, so check with your instructor. Be sure that in gaining reader attention in this way, you do not lose credibility or cause confusion.

↝ SUGGESTIONS FOR WRITING AND RESEARCH

Individual

1. Write the first draft of a personal experience paper as a broad overview of the whole experience. Write the second draft by limiting the story to one day or less of this experience. Write the third draft using one of the other techniques described in this chapter: adding, switching, or transforming. Write the final draft in any way that pleases you.

2. Write the first draft of a research-based paper as an overview of the whole issue with which you intend to deal. In the second draft, limit the scope to something you now cover in one page, paragraph, or sentence. In the third draft, adopt one of the focused revision strategies described in this chapter: adding, switching, or transforming. For your final draft, revise in any way that pleases you.

Collaborative

1. For a class research project, interview college instructors in different departments concerning their thoughts about transforming academic papers into other genres. Write up the results in any form that seems useful.

2. As a class, compile a catalog in which you list and describe as many alternative forms for college papers as you can.

Chapter
❧ 14 ❧
Openings and Closings

I could start this essay just about anywhere at all, by telling you about the background, by stating the thesis, by telling a funny story, or even by rambling, which is what I usually do. Where do you think I should start?

WENDY

My advice, Wendy, is to lead with your best punch. Make your opening so strong your reader feels compelled to continue. Make your closing so memorable that your reader can't forget it.

Readers pay special attention to openings and closings, so make them work for you. Start with titles and lead paragraphs that grab readers' attention and alert them to what is to come; end with closings that sum up and reinforce where they've been. This chapter looks closely at how these special paragraphs function and how you can make these paragraphs stronger through skillful editing.

❧ OPENINGS

Openings are first impressions. Your first paragraph—in fact, your whole first page—sets readers up for the rest of the paper. Here you provide the first clues about your subject, purpose, and voice and invite your audience to keep reading.

Good opening paragraphs are seldom written in first drafts. Often, it's not until you've finished a draft or two that you know exactly what your paper says and does. So when your paper is nearly finished, return to your first page, read it again, and edit carefully. The following examples of effective openings are taken from the student papers reproduced earlier in this textbook; all of them were rewritten at the editing stage.

Open with a Conflict

If your paper is about conflict, sometimes it's best to open by directly spelling out what that conflict is. Identifying a conflict captures attention by creating a kind of suspense: Will the conflict be resolved? How will it be resolved? Issa's exploration of the conflict between hikers and mountain bikers opens this way:

The narrow, hard-packed dirt trail winding up the mountain under the spreading oaks and maples doesn't look like the source of a major environmental conflict, but it is. On the one side are hikers, environmentalists, and horseback riders who have traditionally used these wilderness trails. On the other side, looking back, are the mountain bike riders sitting atop their modern steeds who want to use them too. But the hikers don't want the bikers, so trouble is brewing.

This essay argues, ultimately, in favor of opening wilderness trails to mountain biking; however, Issa uses a delayed-thesis organizational pattern, exploring both sides of the conflict without giving away his own position on the conflict—the opening tells us that *trouble is brewing*, but we don't know how it will be resolved.

Open with a Thesis

Argumentative and interpretive papers commonly open with a clear thesis statement that the rest of the paper will support. Opening with your thesis is the most direct way of telling your reader what the paper will be about. The reader may agree with you and want to see how you support your case, or the reader may disagree and want to find holes in your argument, or the reader may start off neutral and read to see whether or not your paper is believable and persuasive. Following is the first paragraph from Kelly's essay interpreting a poem by Gwendolyn Brooks:

Gwendolyn Brooks writes "We Real Cool" (1963) from the point of view of the members of a street gang who have dropped out of school to live their lives hanging around pool halls—in this case "The Golden Shovel." These guys are semiliterate and speak in slangy street lingo that reveals their need for mutual support in their mutually rebellious attitude toward life. The speakers in the poem, "We," celebrate what adults would call adolescent hedonism—but they make a conscious choice for a short, intense life over a long, safe, and dull existence.

While you will need to read Brooks's short poem to fully understand Kelly's argument, this opening passage states Kelly's position about the subjects—who are also the narrators—of the poem: "they make conscious choices for a short intense life over a long, safe, and dull existence."

Thesis stating, like summary writing, is among the most difficult of all writing tasks and for that reason is most easily and clearly written only when you are thoroughly familiar with your subject, which is seldom the case with early drafts. Consequently, openings such as Kelly's above are commonly written after the rest of the paper is completed.

Open with a Story

Most readers enjoy stories. Professional writers often open articles with anecdotes to catch readers' attention. The following first paragraph is from Judith's reflective essay about finding a safe place to study in the library. Only in her last draft did she decide to start at the door, in present tense, locking up as she leaves to walk to the library:

> It is already afternoon. I fiddle with the key to lock the apartment door after me. I am not accustomed to locking doors. Except for the six months I spent in Boston, I have never lived in a place where I did not trust my neighbors. When I was little, we couldn't lock our farmhouse door; the wood had swollen, and the bolt no longer lined up properly with the hole, and nobody ever bothered to fix it. I still remember the time our babysitter, Rosie, hammered the bolt closed and we had to take the door off the hinges to get it open.

Stories not only need to catch attention; they need to set up or foreshadow the paper to follow. In Judith's case, the theme and content of her paper emerged through several drafts, so it was only in the final draft that she discovered a personal story about locked doors to anticipate the theme of safety in the rest of the paper.

Open with a Specific Detail

Specific details appeal to readers' visual sense and help them see situations and settings. In early drafts, Beth opened her profile of Becky with Becky speaking; only in this latest version did she decide to set the physical scene first, letting Becky's manner and surroundings characterize her right from the start:

> Becky sits cross-legged at the foot of the bottom bunk on her pink and green homemade quilt. She leans up against the wall and runs her fingers through her brown shoulder-length hair. The sound of James Taylor's "Carolina on My Mind" softly fills the room. Posters of John Lennon, James Dean, and Cher look down on us from her walls. Becky stares at the floor and scrunches her face as if she were thinking hard.

Details need to be specific and interesting, but they also need to be purposeful and to advance the paper one way or another. It turns out that Becky is a nineties college student living in a room dominated by musical and visual icons from the fifties and sixties. The details anticipate an important theme in this profile—the subject's closeness to her mother and her mother's values, which are rooted in decades past rather than present.

Open with a Quotation

Although Beth decided not to open with her subject talking, an opening quotation can be an effective hook. Readers enjoy hearing the voices of people on the subject of the piece. The following paragraph was Beth's original opening; she moved it to the second paragraph, adding the transitional first sentence to link the two paragraphs. (It would work equally well as her opening, since it introduces the reader to Becky's lively and interesting human voice, after which we expect more talk about her early years growing up "forever" with her mother and sister.)

> Finally, after minutes of silence [Becky] says, "I don't ever remember my father ever living in my house, really. He left when I was three and my sister was just a

baby, about a year old. My mom took care of us all. Forever, it was just Mom, Kate, and me. I loved it, you know. Just the three of us together."

Sometimes it's just a matter of personal preference in deciding where to start. That, of course, is what editing is all about: trying one thing, then another, looking at options, in the end selecting the one that you think is best.

Open with Statistics

Statistics that tell a clear story are another form of opening that suggests immediately that the writer has done his or her homework. Statistics catch attention when they assert something surprising or answer in numbers something the reader has been wondering about. The more dramatic your statistics are, the more useful they are to open your paper. In the following example, Elizabeth opens a research essay about unethical marketing practices with statistics more reassuring than dramatic.

> A recent Gallup poll reported that 75% of Americans consider themselves to be environmentalists (Smith & Quelch, 1993). In the same study, nearly half of the respondents said they would be more likely to purchase a product if they perceived it to be environmentally friendly or "green." According to Smith and Quelch (1993), since green sells, many companies have begun to promote themselves as marketing products that are either environmentally friendly or manufactured from recycled material. Unfortunately, many of these companies care more about appearance than reality.

Statistics are used here to establish a norm—that most Americans care about the environment—and then to examine the way in which clever, but not necessarily truthful, advertisers exploit that norm.

Open with a Question

Questions alert readers to the writer's subject and imply that the answer will be forthcoming in the paper. Every paper is an answer to some implicit or explicit question. Look at the examples above: Issa's mountain bike essay asks, "Can mountain bikes peacefully coexist with hikers on wilderness trails?" Kelly's interpretative paper asks, "What is the meaning of the poem 'We Real Cool'?" Judith's reflection on the comfort of libraries asks, "What has scholarship to do with safety?" Beth's profile asks, "What is Becky like?" And Elizabeth's research essay asks, "How do advertisers exploit the environmental movement?" In other words, the question that drives the paper is implicit, not directly stated.

In contrast, sometimes it's most effective to pose your question explicitly in the title or first paragraph so that readers know exactly what the report is about or where the essay is going, as Gabe did by titling his paper "What Is Slam Poetry, Anyway?"

Open at the Beginning

In narrative writing, sometimes the best opening is where you think things started. In the following autobiographical snapshot, Rebecca opens a portrait of herself with brief portraits of her parents:

> My mother grew up in Darien, Connecticut, a Presbyterian. When she was little, she gave the Children's Sermon at her church. My father grew up in Cleveland, Ohio, a Jew. When I went away to college, he gave me the Hebrew Bible he received at his Bar Mitzvah.

Since the theme of Rebecca's self-profile is her devotion to an eclectic blend of religion, it seems right that she begin by focusing on the mixed religious heritage derived from her parents.

We have just looked at eight different openings from eight effective essays, each effective in its own way. All eight strategies are good ones, fairly commonly used. None is necessarily better or worse than another, as each reflects a different intention. If we examine eight more essays, we might find still another set of opening strategies. Keep in mind that the first opening you write is just that, an initial opening to get you started. If it's effective, you may decide to keep it, but don't be afraid to return to that opening once the essay is complete and see if a new approach might better suit the direction your essay has finally taken.

> ### ﾠWRITING 1
>
> Recast the opening of a paper you are currently working on, using one or more of the suggestions in this section: a conflict, a thesis, a story, a specific detail, a quotation, an interesting statistic, or a provocative question. For your final draft, use the opening that pleases you most.

ﾠCLOSINGS

Closings are final impressions. Your concluding sentences, paragraphs, or the entire last page are your final chance to make the point of your paper stick in readers' minds. The closing can summarize your main point, draw a logical conclusion, speculate about the issues you've raised, make a recommendation for some further action, or leave your reader with yet another question to ponder.

After writing and revising your paper, attend once more to the conclusion, and consider whether the final impression is the one you want. You may discover that an earlier paragraph makes a more suitable ending, or you may need to write a new one to conclude what you've started. The following examples of effective closings are from student papers reproduced earlier in this textbook.

Close with an Answer

If your paper began by asking a question, and the rest of the paper worked at answering that question, it makes good sense to close with an answer—or at least the summary of your answer, reminding readers where they started some pages ago. For example, consider Gabe's opening question, which is also the title of his paper: "What is slam poetry, anyway?" Following that question, Gabe explored answers by attending a slam poetry reading, interviewing people about what it meant, and searching the Internet for both its history and definitions. After digesting several different answers, Gabe concluded with this summary sentence:

> So, in the end, slam poetry proves to be simply another kind of poetry reading, with this difference: the audience and the performer are one and the same.

This conclusion closes the frame of Gabe's paper, satisfying the reader (and writer) by answering the paper's central question. Of course, the real exploration of the meaning of slam poetry occurs on the way to this one-sentence answer, the whole paper providing a more carefully detailed answer than any single sentence could provide.

Close by Completing a Frame

An effective way to end some papers is to return deliberately to the issue or situation with which you began—to frame the body of your paper with an opening and a closing that mirror each other. Keith's CD paper used as a frame a customer considering the cost of a CD. Judith uses a frame in her paper about personal safety, returning in the closing to the setting of the opening—her front door:

> Hours later—my paper started, my exam studied for, my eyes tired—I retrace the path to my apartment. It is dark now, and I listen closely when I hear footsteps behind, stepping to the sidewalk's edge to let a man walk briskly past. At my door, I again fumble for the now familiar key, insert it in the lock, open the door, turn on the hall light, and step inside. Here, too, I am safe, ready to eat, read a bit, and finish my reflective essay.

Close with a Resolution

Many argumentative papers present first one side of an issue and then the other side, then conclude by agreeing with one side or the other. This is the case in Issa's essay about the conflict between hikers and mountain bikers, where he concludes by suggesting that more education is the only sensible resolution to the problem:

> Education and compromise are the sensible solutions to the hiker/biker stand-off. Increased public awareness as well as increasingly responsible riding will open still more wilderness trails to bikers in the future. It's clear that mountain bikers don't want to destroy trails any more than hikers do. The surest way to preserve

America's wilderness areas is to establish strong cooperative bonds among the hikers and bikers, as well as those who fish, hunt, camp, canoe, and bird-watch, and to encourage all to maintain the trails and respect the environment.

The most successful resolution to many conflicts is not an either/or conclusion but an enlightened compromise where both sides gain. Issa manages to accomplish this by siding with mountain bikers but, at the same time, suggesting they need to change some of their actions to gain further acceptance by the opposition. In any case, it is especially important to edit carefully at the very end of your paper so that your last words make your best case.

Close with a Recommendation

Sometimes writers conclude by inviting their readers to do something—to support some cause, for example, or take some action. This strategy is especially common in papers that argue a position or make a case for or against something. Such papers seek not only to persuade readers to believe the writer but to act on that belief. In the following closing, Elizabeth asks consumers to be more careful:

> Consumers who are genuinely interested in buying environmentally safe products and supporting environmentally responsible companies need to look beyond the images projected by commercial advertising in magazines, on billboards, and on television. Organizations such as Earth First! attempt to educate consumers to the realities by writing about false advertising and exposing the hypocrisy of such ads ("Do people allow," 1994), while the Ecology Channel is committed to sharing "impartial, unbiased, multiperspective environmental information" with consumers on the Internet (Ecology, 1996). Meanwhile the Federal Trade Commission is in the process of continually upgrading truth-in-advertising regulations (Carlson et al., 1993). Americans who are truly environmentally conscious must remain skeptical of simplistic and misleading commercial advertisements while continuing to educate themselves about the genuine needs of the environment.

Along with asking consumers to be more careful in the future, this closing reveals that further action is being taken by watchdog groups, suggesting those who are careful will have powerful allies on their side.

Close with a Speculation

In papers relating personal experience, reflection, or speculation, the issues you raise have no clear-cut conclusions or demonstrated theses. In these papers, then, the most effective conclusion is often one in which you admit some uncertainty, as Zoe does at the end of her investigation of becoming a photographer's assistant:

> So I'll keep sitting around hoping for a break. I can't guarantee that this research method for landing an internship will work; it still remains to be tried and tested. To my knowledge, there is no foolproof formula for a successful start. Like everybody else before me, I'm creating my own method as I go along.

The casualness in such a paragraph, as if it were written off the cuff, is often deceptive. While that is the effect Zoe wanted to create, this paragraph emerged only late in her drafting process, and when it did, she edited and reedited it to achieve just the effect she wanted.

Close by Restating Your Thesis

In thesis-driven papers, it's often a good idea to close by reminding readers where you began, what you were trying to demonstrate in the first place. In Andrew's literary research paper, he concludes by restating the power of Thoreau's concept of freedom:

> Practical or not, Thoreau's writings about freedom from government and society have inspired countless people to reassess how they live their lives. Though unable to live as he advocated, readers everywhere remain inspired by his ideal, that one must live as freely as possible.

Restating a thesis is especially important in longer research-based papers where a lot of information has to be digested along the way.

Close with a Question

Closing with a question, real or rhetorical, suggests that things are not finished, final, or complete. Concluding by admitting there are things you, the author, still do not know creates belief because most of us live with more questions than answers. In the following example, Rebecca ends with a question that is both tongue-in-cheek and serious at the same time:

> I wear a cross around my neck. It is nothing spectacular to look at, but I love it because I bought it at the Vatican. Even though I am not a Catholic, I am glad I bought it at the Pope's home town. Sometimes, when I sit in Hebrew class, I wonder if people wonder, "What religion is she, anyway?"

Throughout her essay, Rebecca has presented herself and her commitment to religion in cryptic terms, suggesting perhaps that she herself is still not sure what she is or where her mixed religious heritage will take her. Closing with the bemused question above seems appropriate to her intentions.

As with openings, so with closings—there are no formulas to follow, just a variety of possibilities that you'll need to weigh with your audience and purpose in mind. Since closing is a last impression, be willing to revise and edit carefully, and be willing to try more than once to get it just right.

ॐ WRITING 2

Recast the closing of a current draft using one or more of the suggestions in this section: a summary, a logical conclusion, a real or a rhetorical question, a speculation, a recommendation, or the completion of a frame. In the final draft, use the closing that pleases you most.

ॐ FINDING THE TITLE

Finally, after revising and editing to your satisfaction, return to your title and ask, "Does it work?" You want to make sure it sets up the essay to follow in the best possible way, both catching readers' attention and providing a clue for the content to follow. One good strategy for deciding on a title is to create a list of five or ten possibilities and then select the most suitable one. Play with words, arranging and rearranging them until they strike you as just right. Many writers spend a great deal of concentrated time on this task because titles are so important.

In my own case, when I was casting about for a title for this book, I happened to be riding my motorcycle late one chilly October night on the interstate highway between Binghamton and Albany, New York. I was cold and knew I had a good hour before arriving at my destination, so to forget the cold, I set about brainstorming titles and came up with "Writing to Discover" or "The Discovering Writer." As I thought about them, I decided to keep the word *writing* but to move away from *discover* toward *work,* and so I played with "The Writer Working," "Working Writers," "The Writer at Work," "Work and the Writer," and finally *The Working Writer.* Work hard to find the words that seem about right, and play with them until they form a construction that pleases you.

The following suggestions may help you find titles:

- Use one good sentence from your paper that captures the essence of your subject.
- Ask a question that your paper answers.
- Use a strong sense word or image from your paper.
- Locate a famous line or saying that relates to your paper.
- Write a one-word title (a two-word, a three-word title, and so on).
- Make a title from a gerund (an *-ing* word, such as *working*).
- Make a title starting with the word *on* and the name of your topic.
- Remain open at all times to little voices in your head that make crazy suggestions and copy these down.

ॐ WRITING 3

Using some of the strategies described in this section, write five titles for a paper you are currently working on. For the final draft, use the title that pleases you most.

Chapter

❧ 15 ❧

Working Paragraphs

Paragraphs tell readers how writers want to be read.

WILLIAM BLAKE

While there are no hard-and-fast rules for editing, there are important points to keep in mind as your essay nears completion. Once you are satisfied with the general shape, scope, and content of your paper, it's time to stop making larger conceptual changes—to stop revising—and start attending to smaller changes in paragraphs, sentences, and words—to begin editing. When you edit, you shape these three elements (paragraphs, sentences, and words) so that they fulfill the purpose of the paper, address the audience, and speak in the voice you have determined is appropriate for the paper.

❧ THE WORK OF PARAGRAPHS

Most texts of a page or more in length are subdivided by indentations or breaks—paragraphs—that serve as guideposts, or as Blake puts it, "that tell readers how writers want to be read." Readers expect paragraph breaks to signal new ideas or directions; they expect each paragraph to have a single focus as well and to be organized in a sensible way; and they expect clear transition markers to link one paragraph to the next.

In truth, however, there are no hard-and-fast rules for what makes a paragraph, how it needs to be organized, what it should contain, or how long it should be.

I could, for instance, start a new paragraph here (as I have just done), leaving the previous sentence to stand as a single-sentence paragraph and so call a little extra attention to it. Or I could connect both that sentence and these to the previous paragraph and have a single five-sentence paragraph to open this section.

Most experienced writers paragraph intuitively rather than analytically; that is, they indent almost unconsciously, without thinking deliberately about it, as they develop or emphasize ideas. Sometimes their paragraphs fulfill conventional expectations, presenting a single well-organized and -developed idea, and sometimes they serve other purposes—for example, creating pauses or breathing spaces or points of emphasis.

The following paragraphs, many of which are excerpts from student papers that have already appeared in previous chapters, do different kinds of work, and although each is a good example, none is perfect. As you study them, bear in mind that each is *illustrative* of various purposes and organization, not *definitive*.

ॐ WRITING WELL-ORGANIZED PARAGRAPHS

Unity: Stick to a Single Idea

Paragraphs are easiest to write and easiest to read when each one presents a single idea, as most of the paragraphs in this textbook do. The following paragraph opens Kelly's interpretive essay:

> Gwendolyn Brooks writes "We Real Cool" (1963) from the point of view of the members of a street gang who have dropped out of school to spend their lives hanging around pool halls—in this case "The Golden Shovel." These guys are semiliterate and speak in slangy street lingo that reveals their need for mutual support in their mutually rebellious attitude toward life. The speakers in the poem, "We," celebrate what adults would call adolescent hedonism—but they make a conscious choice for a short, intense life over a long, safe, and dull existence.

The opening sentence focuses on "the point of view of the members of a street gang" and the sentences that follow continue that focus on "these guys" and "the speakers."

Focus: Write a Topic Sentence

One of the easiest ways to keep each paragraph focused on a single idea is to include a *topic sentence* in it, announcing or summarizing the topic of the paragraph, with the rest of the sentences supporting that main idea. Sometimes topic sentences conclude a paragraph, as in the previous example, where the topic sentence is also the thesis statement for the whole essay. More commonly, however, the topic sentence introduces the paragraph, as in the next example from Issa's essay on mountain biking:

> Mountain bikes have taken over the bicycle industry, and with more bikes come more people wanting to ride in the mountains. The first mass-produced mountain bikes date to 1981, when five hundred Japanese "Stumpjumpers" were sold; by 1983 annual sales reached 200,000; today the figure is 8.5 million. In fact, mountain biking is second only to in-line skating as the fastest growing sport in the nation: "For a sport to go from zero to warp speed so quickly is unprecedented," says Brian Stickel, director of competition for the National Off Road Bicycle Association (Schwartz 75).

The sentences after the first one support and amplify the topic sentence, explaining the rapid growth of mountain bikes, from *five hundred Japanese "Stumpjumpers"* to *8.5 million* today.

Most of the following examples have topic sentences, and all focus on single subjects. Note, however, that not all paragraphs need topic sentences. For example, if a complicated idea is being explained, a new paragraph in the middle of the explanation will create a pause point. Sometimes paragraph breaks are inserted to emphasize an idea, like my own one-sentence paragraph earlier, which is a topic and a support sentence all in one. Additionally, paragraphs in a personal experience essay seldom have a deliberate topic sentence since these sorts of essays are seldom broken into neat topics (see, for example, Judith's paragraph below). Nevertheless, in academic writing, there is great reverence for topic sentences because they point to clear organization and your ability to perform as an organized and logical thinker within the discipline. Thus, when you write academic papers, attend to topic sentences.

✒ WRITING 1

Examine the paragraphs in a recent draft, and pencil in brackets around those that stick well to a single idea. Put an *X* next to any sentences that deviate from the main idea in a paragraph, and note whether you want to delete that sentence or use it to start a new paragraph. Finally, underline each topic sentence. If a paragraph does not have one, should it? If so, write it.

Order: Follow a Recognizable Logic

On first drafts, most of us write sentences rapidly and paragraph intuitively. However, when we revise and edit, it pays to make certain that paragraphs work according to a recognizable logic. There are dozens of organizational patterns that make sense. Here we look at five of them: free association, rank order, spatial, chronological, and general to specific.

When ideas are organized according to *free association,* one idea triggers the next because it is a related one. Free association is especially common in advancing a narrative, as in a personal experience essay. It is quite fluid and suggestive and seldom includes topic sentences. In the following paragraph, Judith allows the first act of locking a door to trigger memories related to other locked doors.

> It is already afternoon. I fiddle with the key to lock the apartment door after me. I am not accustomed to locking doors. Except for the six months I spent in Boston, I have never lived in a place where I did not trust my neighbors. When I was little, we couldn't lock our farmhouse door; the wood had swollen, and the bolt no longer lined up properly with the hole, and nobody ever bothered to fix it. I still remember the time our babysitter, Rosie, hammered the bolt closed and we had to take the door off the hinges to get it open.

Notice that Judith uses a reverse chronological arrangement to order her associations; that is, she moves backward from the present—first to Boston, then to childhood—thereby using one pattern to strengthen another, helping us still further to follow her.

When ideas are arranged by *rank order,* that is, order of importance, the most significant idea is reserved for the end of the paragraph. The writer leads with the idea to be emphasized least, then the next most important, and so on. This paragraph is commonly introduced by a topic sentence alerting readers that an orderly list is to follow. Here is a paragraph from Kelly's essay interpreting "We Real Cool" where he explains the values of the narrators of the poem:

> However, the most important element of their lives is being "cool." They live and love to be cool. Part of being cool is playing pool, singing, drinking, fighting, and messing around with women whenever they can. Being cool is the code of action that unites them, that they celebrate, for which they are willing to die.

Kelly explains three dimensions of being cool, making sure he concludes the paragraph with his most important point: first, being cool includes "[living] and [loving] to be cool," second, that it includes "playing pool, singing, drinking," and so on; and third, that it is their "code of action . . . for which they are willing to die."

When ideas are arranged *spatially,* each is linked to the next. Thus, the reader's eye is drawn through the paragraph as if through physical space. For example, a writer might describe a landscape by looking first at the field, then the forest, then the mountain, then the sky. In the following paragraph, Beth begins by showing Becky in the spatial context of her dormitory room; her description moves from bed to walls to floor:

> Becky sits cross-legged at the foot of the bottom bunk on her pink and green homemade quilt. She leans up against the wall and runs her fingers through her brown shoulder-length hair. The sound of James Taylor's "Carolina on My Mind" softly fills the room. Posters of John Lennon, James Dean, and Cher look down on us from her walls. Becky stares at the floor and scrunches her face as if she were thinking hard.

Becky's subtle, silent actions carry readers through the paragraph as Beth describes her sitting, leaning, listening, and staring—actions that set up the next paragraph in her paper in which Becky speaks.

When ideas or facts are arranged *chronologically,* they are presented in the order in which they happened, with the earliest first. Sometimes it makes sense to use *reverse chronology,* listing the most recent first and working backward in time. The following paragraph from a collaborative research paper illustrates forward chronology; it begins with the first microbrewery and then moves to a full-fledged brewers' festival five years later.

> According to Shaw (1990) the home brewing revolution did not begin in Vermont until February 1987 when Stephan Mason and Alan Davis opened Catamount Brewery, which offered golden lager, an amber ale, and a dark porter as well as several seasonal brews. This was only the beginning. In September 1992, the first Vermont Brewers Festival was held at Sugarbush Resort. Sixteen breweries participated and the forty-plus beers present ranged from American light lagers to German-style bock and everything in between. The beers included such colorful names as Tall Tale Pale Ale, Black Fly Stout, Slopbucket Brown Ale, Summer Wheat Ale, Avid Barley Wee Heavy, and Hickory Switch Smoked Amber Ale.

Notice that starting in the middle of the paragraph, another supportive pattern is at work here: the pattern of general to specific. It is unlikely that the first draft of this paragraph contained these mutually supportive organizational patterns; careful editing made sure the final draft did.

A *general to specific pattern* begins with an overall description or general statement and moves toward a description of smaller, more specific details. In the preceding paragraph, the general idea is "all breweries"; the specific idea is "Catamount beer." Notice, too, the pattern in Elizabeth's essay on questionable environmental advertising:

> Some companies court the public by mentioning environmental problems and pointing out that they do not contribute to those problems. For example, the natural gas industry describes natural gas as an alternative to the use of ozone-depleting CFC's ("Don't you wish," 1994). However, according to Fogel (1985), the manufacture of natural gas creates a host of other environmental problems from land reclamation to the carbon-dioxide pollution, a major cause of global warming. By mentioning problems they don't cause, while ignoring ones they do, companies present a favorable environmental image that is at best a half truth, at worst an outright lie.

The opening sentence introduces the general category, "environmental problems," and the following sentences provide a particular example, "the natural gas industry."

Note, too, that *specific to general,* the reverse of the previous pattern, is also common and has a recognizable logic. For example, the environmental paragraph could have opened with the description of a specific abuse by a specific company and closed by mentioning the general problem illustrated by the specific example. The point here, as it is in all writing, is to edit carefully for a pattern that's recognizable and logical so that you lead your readers through the paper in ways that match their expectations.

ᕦ WRITING 2

Review a near-final draft of a paper you are working on, and identify the organizational pattern in each paragraph. Do you find a pattern to your paragraphing? Identify paragraphs that contain a single idea carefully developed and paragraphs that need to be broken into smaller paragraphs. What editing changes would you now make in light of this review?

ᕦ HELPING THE READER

So far, most of this discussion has focused on structures within paragraphs. When editing, it's important to know how to rewrite paragraphs to improve essay readability. However, you can improve readability in other ways as well. One of them is to break up lengthy paragraphs.

Paragraph breaks help readers pause and take a break while reading, allowing them, for example, to imagine or remember something sparked by the text and yet find their place again with ease. Breaking into a new paragraph can also recapture flagging attention, especially important in long essays, reports, or articles where detail sometimes overwhelms readers. And you can emphasize points with paragraph breaks, calling a little extra attention to what follows.

༈ TRANSITIONS BETWEEN PARAGRAPHS

Your editing is not finished until you have linked the paragraphs, so that readers know where they have been and where they are going. In early drafts, you undoubtedly focused on getting your ideas down and paid less attention to clarifying relationships between ideas. Now, as you edit your final draft, consider the elements that herald transitions: words and phrases, subheads, and white spaces.

Words and Phrases

Writers often use transitional expressions without consciously thinking about them. For example, in writing a narrative, you may naturally use sequential transition words to indicate a chronology: *first, second, third; this happened, next this happened, finally this happened;* or *last week, this week, yesterday, today.* Here are some other transitional words and phrases and their functions in paragraphs:

- Contrast or change in direction: *but, yet, however, nevertheless, still, at the same time, on the other hand*
- Comparison or similarity: *likewise, similarly*
- Addition: *and, also, then, next, in addition, furthermore, finally*
- Summary: *finally, in conclusion, in short, in other words, thus*
- Example: *for example, for instance, to illustrate, specifically, thus*
- Concession or agreement: *of course, certainly, to be sure, granted*
- Time sequence: *first, second, third; (1), (2), (3); next, then, finally, soon, meanwhile, later, currently, eventually, at last*
- Spatial relation: *here, there, in the background, in the foreground, to the left, to the right, nearby, in the distance, above, below*

There is no need to memorize these functions or words; you already know and have used all of them and usually employ them quite naturally. When reworking your final draft, though, be sure you have provided transitions. If you haven't, work these words in to alert your readers to what's coming next.

Alternative Transitional Devices

Other common devices that signal transitions include subheadings, lines, alternative typefaces, and white spaces. The first two are more common in textbooks and technical reports; the latter two may appear in any text, including literary-style essays. When you edit your final draft, consider whether using any of these techniques would make your ideas clearer.

Subheads

To call extra attention to material or to indicate logical divisions of ideas, some writers use subheads. They are more common in long research papers, technical reports, and laboratory analyses and less common in narrative essays. They are essential in textbooks, such as this one, for indicating divisions of complex material.

Lines

Blocks of text can be separated by either continuous or broken dashes (————) or asterisks (*****), which signify material clearly to be set off from other material. In technical writing, for example, material may even be boxed in by continuous lines to call special attention to itself. In a *New Yorker* research essay or short story, a broken line of asterisks may suggest a switch in time, place, or point of view.

Alternative Typefaces

Writers who use computers can change fonts with ease. When they use alternative typefaces, they are indicating a transition or a change. In a narrative or essay, *italics* may suggest someone talking or the narrator thinking. A switch to a smaller or larger typeface may signal information of less or more importance.

White Space

You can indicate a sharp break in thought between one paragraph and the next by leaving an extra line of space between them (although the space break does not tell the reader what to expect next). When I use a space break, I am almost always suggesting a change in direction more substantial than a mere paragraph indentation; I want readers to notice the break and be prepared to make a larger jump than a paragraph break signals. In a narrative essay, I may use the space to suggest a jump in time (the next day, week, or year); in argumentative writing, to begin a presentation of an opposing point of view; in an essay, to introduce another voice. White space, in other words, substitutes for clear transition words and subheadings but does not explicitly explain the shift.

When I work on early drafts, I may use some of these transition or separation devices to help me keep straight the different parts of what I'm writing. In final drafts, I decide which devices will help my readers as much as they have helped me, and I eliminate those that no longer work. In other words, paragraphs and transitions are as useful for me when I'm drafting as they will be later for my readers.

⌁ WRITING 3

When you edit a final draft, look carefully at your use of transitional devices. Identify those that are doing their work well; add new ones where appropriate.

Chapter

❧ 16 ❧

Working Sentences

Teachers are always nitpicking about little things, but I think writing is for communicating, not nitpicking. I mean, if you can read it and it makes sense, what else do you want?

OMAR

Omar, editing is about nitpicking. It's about making your text read well, with the most possible sense. After the ideas are in order and well supported, your job is to polish the paragraphs, sentences, and individual words so that they shine. Then you correct to get rid of all the "nitpicky" errors in punctuation, spelling, and grammar. In other words, you attend to editing *after* your ideas are conceptually sound, carefully supported, skillfully organized, and fairly well aimed at your readers. (Even now, it doesn't hurt to review it once more to make sure it represents your voice and ideas in the best way possible.)

As in editing paragraphs, there is no one best way to go about editing sentences. You edit in such a way that you remain, as much as possible, in control of your text. (As you probably know by now, texts have a way of getting away from all of us at times. Editing is how we try to get control back!) At the same time you're wrestling for final control of a text for yourself, you're also anticipating reader needs. In this sense, sentence editing is your final balancing act, as you work to please yourself and your readers.

❧ EDITING FOR CLARITY, STYLE, AND GRACE

To effect maximum communication, you should edit your sentences first for clarity, making sure each sentence clearly reflects your purpose. You also must edit to convey an appropriate style for the occasion, that is, the formality or informality of the language. And at perhaps the highest level, you must edit to convey grace—some sense that this text is not only clearly written, by you, but that it is also particularly well written—what we might call elegant or graceful.

While I can explain this loose hierarchy as if these several levels are easily distinguished, in fact, they are not, and they mix and overlap easily. For instance, in writing the chapters for this text I have tried to edit each chapter, paragraph, and sentence with all three goals in mind, demanding that all my language be clear, hoping that my style is friendly and that my sentences are also graceful—knowing that, in many cases, grace has proved beyond my reach. The remainder of this chapter will examine the fine tuning of words and phrases that make clear, stylistically appropriate, and sometimes graceful sentences.

> ## ஃ WRITING 1
>
> Reread a near-final draft of one of your papers, and draw a straight vertical line next to places where your text seems especially clear. Draw a wavy line next to passages where the style sounds especially like you. And put an asterisk next to any passages that you think are especially graceful. Exchange drafts with a classmate and see if you agree with each other's assessment.

ஃ THE WORK OF SENTENCES

Sentences are written in relation to other sentences, so most of our attention thus far has been on larger units of composition, from whole texts on down to individual paragraphs. This chapter focuses on strategies for strengthening sentences. In editing, you should first look at the effect of particular words within sentences, especially nouns, verbs, and modifiers. Second, you should consider the importance of rhythm and emphasis in whole sentences. And finally, you should learn to identify and avoid the common problems of wordiness, clichés, jargon, passive constructions, and biased language.

ஃ WRITE WITH CONCRETE NOUNS

Nouns label or identify persons (*man, Gregory*), animals (*dog, golden retriever*), places (*city, Boston*), things (*book,* The Working Writer), or ideas (*conservation, Greater Yellowstone Coalition*). General nouns name general classes or categories of things (*man, dog, city*); concrete nouns refer to particular things (*Gregory, golden retriever, Boston*). Notice that concrete nouns (not just any dog, but a golden retriever) appeal more strongly to a reader's senses (I can see the dog!) than abstract nouns do and create a more vivid and lively reading experience.

Here is an example of a paragraph composed primarily of general nouns (underlined in the passage):

> Approaching the library, I see lots of <u>people</u> and <u>dogs</u> milling about, but no sub-
> jects to write about. I'm tired from my walk and go inside.

When Judith described a similar scene for her essay on personal safety, she used specific nouns (which are underlined) to let us see her story sharply:

> Approaching the library, I see <u>skateboarders</u> and <u>bikers</u> weaving through stu-
> dents who talk in clusters on the library steps. A <u>friendly black dog</u> is tied to a

bench watching for its master to return. Subjects to write about? Nothing strikes me as especially interesting and, besides, my heart is still pounding from the walk up the hill. I wipe my damp forehead and go inside.

Judith could have gone even further (writers always can) in using concrete nouns. She could have named the library, described some individual students, identified the dog, and described the bench. None of these modifications would have changed the essential meaning of the sentences, but each would have added a dimension of specific reality—one of the key ways writers convince readers that what they are writing about is true or really happened.

∿ WRITE WITH ACTION VERBS

Action verbs *do* something in your sentences; they make something happen. *Walk, stride, run, jump, fly, hum, sing, sail, swim, lean, fall, stop, look, listen, sit, state, decide, choose,* and *conclude*—all these words and hundreds more are action verbs. Static verbs, in contrast, simply *appear* to describe how something *is*—like the verb *is* in this sentence. Action verbs, like concrete nouns, appeal to the senses, letting readers see, hear, touch, taste, or smell what is happening. They create more vivid images for readers, drawing them more deeply into the essay.

In the following passage, the conclusion to Judith's reflective essay, notice how action verbs (underlined) help you see clearly what is going on:

> Hours later—my paper started, my exam studied for, my eyes tired—I retrace the path to my apartment. It is dark now, and I listen closely when I hear footsteps behind, stepping to the sidewalk's edge to let a man walk briskly past. At my door, I again fumble for the now familiar key, insert it in the lock, open the door, turn on the hall light, and step inside. Here, too, I am safe, ready to eat, read a bit, and finish my reflective essay.

Judith also uses several static verbs (*is, am*) in other places; these verbs describe necessary states of being, carrying a different kind of weight. When they are used among action verbs, they do good work. But the paragraph gets its life and strength from the verbs that show action.

Editing for action verbs is one of the chief ways to cut unneeded words, thus increasing readability and vitality. Whenever you find one of the following noun phrases (in the first column) consider substituting an action verb (in the second column):

reach a decision	decide
make a choice	choose
hold a meeting	meet
formulate a plan	plan
arrive at a conclusion	conclude
have a discussion	discuss
go for a run	run

☞ USE MODIFIERS CAREFULLY AND SELECTIVELY

Well-chosen modifiers can make both nouns and verbs more concrete and appealing to readers' senses. Words that modify—describe, identify, or limit—nouns are called *adjectives* (*damp* forehead); words that amplify verbs are called *adverbs* (listen *closely*). Modifiers convey useful clarifying information and make sentences vivid and realistic.

In the previous example paragraph, Judith could have added several more modifiers to nouns such as *man* (*tall, thin, sinister*) and *door* (*red, heavy wooden*). And she could have used modifiers with verbs such as *retrace* (*wearily, slowly*) and *fumble* (*nervously, expectantly*). Judith's writing would not necessarily benefit by these additions, but they are further possibilities for her to examine as she edits her near-final sentences. Sometimes adding modifiers to sentences distracts from rather than enhances a paragraph's purpose. And that's what editing is all about: looking carefully, trying out new possibilities, settling for the effect that pleases you most.

Not all modifiers are created equal. Specific modifiers that add descriptive information about size, shape, color, texture, speed, and so on appeal to the senses and usually make writing more realistic and vivid. General modifiers such as the adjectives *pretty, beautiful, good, bad, ugly, young,* or *old* can weaken sentences by adding extra words that do not convey specific or vital information. And the adverbs *very, really,* and *truly* can have the same weakening effect because they provide no specific clarifying information.

☞ WRITING 2

Review a near-final draft, and mark all concrete nouns (underline once), action verbs (underline twice), and modifiers (circle). Then place parentheses around the general nouns, static verbs, and general modifiers. Reconsider these words, and edit appropriately.

☞ FIND A PLEASING RHYTHM

Rhythm is the pattern of sound sentences make when you read them out loud. Some rhythms sound natural—like a person in a conversation. Such sentences are easy to follow and understand and are usually pleasing to the ear. Others sound awkward and forced, make comprehension difficult, and offend the ear. It pays to read your sentences out loud and see if they sound like a real human being talking. To make sentence clusters sound better, use varied sentence patterns and parallel construction.

Varied sentence patterns make sentence clusters clear and enjoyable for readers. Judith effectively varied her sentences—some long, some short, some simple, some complex. For example, note the dramatic effect of following a lengthy compound sentence with a short simple sentence (made up of short words) to end the paragraph above: "Nothing strikes me as especially interesting and, besides, my heart is still pounding from the walk up the hill. I wipe my damp forehead and go inside."

Parallelism, the repetition of a word or grammatical construction within a sentence, creates symmetry and balance, makes an idea easier to remember, and is pleasing to the ear. The following sentence from Brendan's essay demonstrates the pleasing rhythmic effect of parallel construction: "A battle is being waged between environmental conservationists, who support the reintroduction of wolves, and sheep and cattle farmers and Western hunters, who oppose it." The parallelism is established by repetition of the word *who* plus a verb; the verbs, opposite in meaning, provide additional dramatic effect.

In the following example, the repetition of the word *twice* establishes a rhythm and contributes as well to the writer's point about costs: "A CD may be twice as expensive as a cassette tape, but the sound is twice as clear and the disc will last forever."

➷ PLACE THE MOST IMPORTANT POINT LAST

As in paragraphs, the most emphatic place in sentences is last. You achieve the best effect by placing information that is contextual, introductory, or less essential earlier in the sentence and end with the idea you most want readers to remember. Sometimes you write first-draft sentences with emphatic endings, but often such emphasis needs to be edited in. Notice the difference in emphasis in the following version of the same idea:

Angel needs to start now if he wants to have an impact on his sister's life.

If Angel wants to have an impact on his sister's life, he has to start now.

The second sentence is much more dramatic, emphasizing the need for action on Angel's part.

The next two sentences also illustrate the power of placing what you consider important at the end of the sentence:

Becky stares at the floor and scrunches her face as if she were thinking hard.

As if she is thinking hard, Becky stares at the floor and scrunches up her face.

The first sentence emphasizes Becky's concentration. To end with Becky's scrunching up her face diminishes the emphasis on her thinking.

In the following sentence, Judith uses end-of-sentence emphasis for a transitional purpose: "I wipe my damp forehead and go inside." The ending forecasts the next paragraph—in which Judith goes inside the library. To reverse the actions would emphasize the damp forehead instead of Judith's entrance into the library.

One more example from Judith's essay suggests how emphasis at the end can increase and then resolve suspense: "It is dark now, and I listen closely when I hear footsteps behind, stepping to the sidewalk's edge to let a man walk briskly past." At first we are alarmed that footsteps are coming up behind the writer—as Judith wants us to be. Then we are relieved that a man passes harmlessly by—as Judith also wants us to be. The end of the sentence relieves the tension and resolves the suspense.

Examine the sentences in a recent draft for rhythm and end-of-sentence emphasis by reading the draft out loud, listening for awkward or weak spots. Edit for sentence variety and emphasis as necessary.

☙ EDIT WORDY SENTENCES

Cut out words that do not pull their weight or add meaning, rhythm, or emphasis. Sentences clogged with unnecessary words cause readers to lose interest, patience, and comprehension. Editing sentences for concrete nouns, action verbs, and well-chosen modifiers will help you weed out unnecessary words. Writing varied and emphatic sentences helps with this task too. Look at the following sentences, which all say essentially the same thing:

- In almost every situation that I can think of, with few exceptions, it will make good sense for you to look for as many places as possible to cut out needless, redundant, and repetitive words from the papers and reports, paragraphs and sentences you write for college assignments. (48 words)
- In most situations it makes good sense to cut out needless words from your college papers. (16 words)
- Whenever possible, omit needless words from your writing. (8 words)
- Omit needless words. (3 words)

The forty-eight-word-long first sentence is full of early-draft language; you can almost see the writer finding his or her way while writing. The sixteen-word sentence says much the same thing, with only one-third the number of words. Most of this editing simply cut out unnecessary words. Only at the end were several wordy phrases condensed: "from the papers and reports, paragraphs and sentences you write for college assignments" was reduced to "from your college papers."

That sixteen-word sentence was reduced by half by rephrasing and dropping the emphasis on college writing. And that sentence was whittled down by nearly two-thirds, to arrive at the core three-word sentence, "Omit needless words."

The first sentence was long-winded by any standard or in any context; each of the next three might serve well in different situations. Thus, when you edit to make language more concise, you need to think about the overall effect you intend to create. Sometimes the briefest construction is not the best one for your purpose. For example, the three-word sentence is more suited to a brief list than to a sentence of advice for this book. To fit the purposes of this book, in fact, I might write a fifth version on needless words, one including more of my own voice:

> **I prefer to read carefully edited papers, where every word works purposefully and pretty much pulls its own weight. (19 words)**

In this sentence, I chose to include *I* to emphasize my own preference as a teacher and reader and to add the qualifying phrase *pretty much* to impart a conversational tone to the sentence.

In the following example, one of Judith's effective paragraphs has been deliberately padded with extra words, some of which might have existed in earlier drafts:

> It is now several hours later, almost midnight, in fact. I have finally managed to get my paper started and probably overstudied for my exam. My eyes are very tired. I get up and leave my comfortable chair and walk out of the library, through the glass doors again, and retrace the path to my apartment. Since it is midnight, it is dark, and I nervously listen to footsteps coming up behind me. When they get too close for comfort, I step to the sidewalk's edge, scared out of my wits, to let a man walk briskly past. When I am finally at my door, I again fumble for the now familiar key, insert it in the lock, open the door, turn on the hall light, and step inside. Here, too, I am safe, ready to eat leftover pizza, study some more for my exam, and finish my reflective essay.

Now compare this with Judith's final version for simplicity, brevity, smoothness, and power.

> Hours later—my paper started, my exam studied for, my eyes tired—I retrace the path to my apartment. It is dark now, and I listen closely when I hear footsteps behind, stepping to the sidewalk's edge to let a man walk briskly past. At my door, I again fumble for the now familiar key, insert it in the lock, open the door, turn on the hall light, and step inside. Here, too, I am safe, ready to eat, read a bit, and finish my reflective essay.

The best test of whether words are pulling their own weight and providing rhythm, balance, and emphasis is to read the passage out loud and let your ear tell you what is sharp and clear and what could be sharper and clearer.

∽ EDIT CLICHÉS

Clichés are phrases we've heard so often before that they no longer convey an original or individual thought. In the wordy paragraph above, the phrase "scared out of my wits" is a cliché. As you edit, note whether you remember hearing the same exact words before, especially more than once. If so, look for fresher language that is your own. Common clichés to avoid including the following:

throwing the baby out with the bath water
a needle in a haystack
the last straw
better late than never
without further ado
the handwriting on the wall
tried and true

last but not least
lay the cards on the table
jump-start the economy

Each of these phrases was once new and original and attracted attention when it was used; now when we read or hear these phrases, we pay them no conscious mind and may even note that the writer or speaker using them is not very thoughtful or original.

EDIT PASSIVE CONSTRUCTIONS

A construction is passive when something is done to the subject rather than the subject's doing something. *The ball was hit by John* is passive. *John hit the ball* is active. Not only is the first sentence needlessly longer by two words, it takes readers a second or two longer to understand since it is a roundabout way to make an assertion. Writing that is larded up with such passive construction lacks vitality and is tiresome to read.

Most of the example paragraphs in this book contain good examples of active constructions: *I retrace . . . I get up . . . Becky sits . . . Greg attributes. . . .*

EDIT BIASED LANGUAGE

Your writing should not hurt people. As you edit, make sure your language doesn't discriminate against categories of people based on gender, race, ethnicity, or social class.

Eliminate Sexism

Language is sexist when it includes only one gender. The most common occurrence of sexist language is the use of the word *man* or *men* to stand for *human being* or *people*—which seems to omit *women* from participation in the species. Americans have been sensitized to the not-so-subtle bias against woman embedded in our use of language.

It is important to remember that many thoughtful and powerful English-language works from the past took masculine words for granted, using *man, men, he, him,* and *his* to stand for all members of the human race. Consider Thomas Jefferson's "All men are created equal" and Tom Paine's "These are the times that try men's souls." Today we would write "All people are created equal" or "These are the times that try our souls"—two of several possible fixes for this gender nearsightedness. When you read older texts, recognize that the composing rules were different then, and the writers are no more at fault than the culture in which they lived.

As you edit to avoid sexist language, you will notice that the English language does not have a gender-neutral third-person singular pronoun to match the gender-neutral third-person plural (*they, their, them*). We use *he* (*him, his*) for men and *she* (*her, hers*) for women. In the sentence "Everybody has his own opinion," the indefinite pronoun *everybody* needs a singular pronoun to refer to it. While it is grammatically correct to say

"Everybody has *his* own opinion," the sentence seems to exclude women. But it is grammatically incorrect to write "Everybody has *their* own opinion," although *their* is gender neutral. In editing, be alert to such constructions and consider several ways to fix them:

- Make the sentence plural so it reads *"People* have *their* own opinions."
- Include both pronouns: "Everybody has *his* or *her* own opinion."
- Eliminate the pronoun: "Everybody has *an* opinion."
- Alternate masculine and feminine pronouns throughout your sentences or paragraphs, using *she* in one paragraph and *he* in the next.

In my own writing, I have used all of these solutions at one time or another. The rule I most commonly follow is to use the strategy that makes for the clearest, most graceful writing.

Avoid Stereotypes

Stereotypes lump individuals into oversimplified and usually negative categories based on race, ethnicity, class, gender, sexual preference, religion, or age. You know many of these terms. The kindest are perhaps "Get out of the way, old man" and "Don't behave like a baby." I am willing to set these down in this book since we've all been babies and we're all growing older. The other terms offend me too much to write.

The mission of all institutions of higher learning is to teach students to read, write, speak, and think critically, which means treating each situation, case, problem, or person individually on its own merits and not prejudging it by rumor, innuendo, or hearsay unsupported by evidence or reason. To use stereotypes in academic writing will label you as someone who has yet to learn critical literacy. To write with stereotypes in any setting not only reveals your ignorance but hurts people.

✌ PROOFREAD

The last act of editing is *proofreading,* the process of reading your manuscript word for word to make sure it is correct in every way. Here are some tips to help you in this process:

- Proofread for typing and spelling errors first by using a spelling checker on your computer, if you have one. But be aware that computers will *not* catch certain errors, such as omitted words or mistyping (for example, *if* for *of*). So you must also proofread the old-fashioned way—by reading slowly, line by line, word by word.
- Proofread for punctuation by reading your essay out loud and looking for places where your voice pauses, comes to a full stop, questions, or exclaims. Let your verbal inflections suggest appropriate punctuation (commas, periods, question marks, and exclamation points, respectively). Also review Writer's Reference 5, the punctuation reference at the end of this book, paying special attention to the use of commas, the most common source of punctuation errors.

- Proofread the work of others, and ask others to proofread for you. It's easy when reading your own writing to fill in missing words and read through small errors; you're much more likely to catch such errors in someone else's writing. We are all our own worst proofreaders; ask somebody you trust to help you.
- Proofread as a whole class: Tape final drafts on the wall, and roam the class with pencils reading one another's final drafts, for both pleasure and correctness.

℘ WRITING 4

Examine a recent draft for wordiness, clichés, passive constructions, and biased language. Edit as necessary according to the suggestions in this section. Proofread before you hand in or publish the paper.

PART THREE

THE RESEARCH PROCESS

Source: *The College Writer's Reference,* Third Edition, by Toby Fulwiler and Alan R. Hayakawa.

17 | BEGINNING THE RESEARCH PROCESS

Although doing a research paper is demanding, it also can be rewarding if the subject interests you and if you have the time and resources necessary for the job. The real secret is to start early, work steadily, and locate a personal interest. Following are some suggestions for how to do that.

Keeping a research log   17a

The best way to manage a complex research project is to log in a notebook every aspect of it from start to finish. That way, you'll always know where you are, what your questions are, how they've changed, what you've done, how much information you have, what it's worth, and where you need to go next. A **research log** is essentially a journal dedicated to thinking methodically about a research project. Your log helps you keep track of the whole research project from beginning to end—to write about your curiosity, to pose questions, to brainstorm where

RESEARCH STRATEGIES

◆   **Ask questions.** Begin by asking questions about a subject, both of yourself and of others. Preliminary questions lead to more specific inquiries.

◆   **Read extensively.** Texts of all kinds—books, journal and magazine articles, and studies—are the raw material from which you will build your research paper.

◆   **Question knowledgeable people.** Start with people you know. If they can't help, ask who can. Then broaden that circle to include people with specialized knowledge.

◆   **Seek firsthand information and experience.** No matter how many answers other people offer you, seek out information yourself.

◆   **Evaluate your sources.** And double-check the information you find. Sources vary in their accuracy and objectivity. Try to confirm the information you gather by checking more than one reliable source.

◆   **Write at every stage.** The notes you take on your reading, the field notes you write, and the research log you keep all help you gain control of your subject.

answers might be found, to keep track of sources found (and not found), and to explore modifications of research questions as new information leads your thinking in new directions. Use the log to answer questions such as these.

- What subject do I want to research?

- Am I starting with a working thesis or looking for one?

- What evidence best supports my working thesis?

- What evidence challenges my working thesis?

- What information do I still need to find?

- Where am I likely to find it?

Writing out answers to these questions in your research log clarifies your tasks as you go along. It forces you to articulate ideas and examine supporting evidence critically. This, in turn, helps you focus your research activities. When you keep notes in a research log, record each as a separate note card. Here is a sample from a research log for an investigation of ozone holes in the atmosphere.

> 11/12 Checked the subject headings--found no books on ozone depletion. Ref. librarian suggests looking at magazines because books take much longer to get published. Found twenty articles in the General Science Index--got printouts on about half. Start obtaining the sources and reading them tomorrow.

> 11/17 Conference today with professor about the ozone-hole thesis--said I didn't really have much of a thesis yet, just a lot of notes on the same subject. I should look at what I've got, then step back and decide what question it answers—that will probably point to my thesis.

17b Finding a topic

The first step in any assigned research project is to understand its purpose. What are the course goals? How does this research project advance them? How do your own interests intersect with the assignment? What sources are available? How extensive should the project be? How long do you have?

Choosing a topic

Many instructors let students choose their own research topics as long as they are consistent with course goals. Try using some invention techniques to brainstorm about topics. Whether your topic is assigned or created, keep in mind that it's better to do more with less than less with more: limit your topic to a manageable scope and size.

BROAD TOPIC   The fiction of Alice Walker

NARROW TOPIC   Historical reality in novel *The Color Purple.*

Owning the topic

When you conduct research, you enter into a conversation with a select community of people who are knowledgeable about a subject. As you collect information, you too become an author, an authority who can teach your classmates—and your instructor—something they didn't know before.

The best way to exercise your newfound authority is to put the facts and ideas you collect into your own words at every chance—in your research log, on your note cards, in your drafts. Finding your own language to express an idea guarantees that you understand the idea and, at the same time, increases your chances of saying something useful, interesting, or provocative.

Developing a research question   17c

Research projects are designed to answer questions, so spend some time formulating a good **research question** about your subject. By isolating a particular aspect of the subject, the research question helps you tighten and maintain the focus you want.

What makes a good research question?

- It encourages you to focus on a topic in which you are interested.

- It asks you to explore a topic that is reasonably complex, with plenty of gray areas for investigation and argument.

- It can probably be answered by investigation using your school's resources.

If source materials are not available, adapt your question to fit the materials at hand. Ask your instructor to check your research question before you invest a lot of time in it. He or she can help you hone the question and save you time on a project too large to manage.

17d Formulating a working thesis

When an answer to your research question starts to take shape, it's time to construct a working thesis. Your **working thesis** is a preliminary answer that helps you investigate further. If more research leads you in a different direction, be ready to redirect your investigation and revise your working thesis.

If you don't yet know the answer to your research question, begin to do informational research. Start with an open mind and focus on your research question. This may lead to an opinion you can argue in greater detail with more research, or it may turn up explanatory material for later use. Either way, you need to answer your research question. Informational research, then, is *thesis-finding*. In contrast, in an argumentative paper, you begin by knowing the answer to your question (which side you support) and looking for evidence to support and strengthen your position. Such research is *thesis-driven*.

17e Using the writing process

Research writing, like all important writing, goes through all the stages of the writing process: planning, researching, drafting, revising, and editing. In research writing, however, managing information and incorporating sources present special problems.

Planning

The technical requirements of research writing—length, format, the nature and number of the sources you need, and the special documentation system required—take extra time and attention.

When you have an idea of what information is available, plan schedules for trips to the library, online research, and interviews. Most important, allow enough time for writing, revising, and editing your paper. Whenever you fall behind in your schedule, revise your plan.

Researching

To evaluate sources, you first need to understand how different kinds of sources work as evidence. **Primary sources** contain original material and/or raw information. **Secondary sources** report on, describe, interpret, or analyze someone else's work. If you explore the development of a novelist's style, for example, the novels themselves are primary sources. Other people's reviews and interpretations of the novels are secondary sources. Many research essays use both primary and secondary sources. Primary sources ground a paper in firsthand observations and facts; secondary sources supply context and support for your own analysis and argument.

Drafting

Write your first draft early so you will have time for further research in case you find yourself creating a new working thesis or discover gaps in your coverage. The tentative answer to your research question has been your working thesis. As you gather material and begin drafting, however, this answer crystallizes into a more definite **thesis statement.**

In an informational paper—one that defines, describes, or explains—your thesis makes a statement about the information presented in the paper but does not advance one position over another. For example, if you are asked to report on holes in the ozone layer, your paper will define, describe, or explain ozone holes but will not argue any point about them. Your research question (*What are ozone holes?*) becomes the thesis statement: *Huge gaps in the earth's stratospheric ozone layer are caused by chlorofluorocarbons and other chemicals that react with and destroy ozone.*

In an argumentative paper—one that interprets, argues, or assesses—your thesis states your position on an issue. You begin research by looking for information to substantiate your point, with a research question such as *Should Congress regulate handgun ownership?* After conducting research that supports a particular side, you refine the thesis statement to *The ownership of handguns in the United States should/should not be strictly regulated by the federal government.*

Many research essays present the thesis statement at the beginning, in the first or second paragraph, where it establishes what will follow. Some research papers delay the thesis statement until the end, where it acts as a conclusion or a summary. If you take the delayed-thesis approach, be sure that the topic and scope of your paper are clear to your readers in the beginning paragraphs.

Revising

In a research paper, revising entails not only modifying the writing of the paper but also doing the research that underlies it. Once you begin conducting research, your questions and answers multiply and change. Be prepared to find new questions more interesting to you than your original question. The research process must remain flexible if it is to be vital and exciting. Keep an open mind, but also keep an eye on your topic.

In writing a research paper, it's a good idea to be writing even as you're still researching; the act of writing will help you focus and refocus and make sense of your topic. However, new information found late in the research project may well change questions or assertions written early in the paper, so be sure to review your whole paper each time you revise.

Editing

Editing and proofreading a research paper require extra time. Not only should you check your own writing; you should also pay special attention to where and how you document sources, making sure you use the correct documentation format. The editing stage is a good time to assess your use of quotation, paraphrase, and summary to make sure you have not misquoted or used a source without crediting it.

18 CONDUCTING LIBRARY RESEARCH

The college library is the heart of the academic community and the most reliable source of credible information in all academic subjects. Many informative resources are also available on the Internet and in the field, though their reliability varies immensely. In contrast, resources screened by professional librarians for authenticity and credibility are likely to be reliable. Librarians can save you precious time by showing you the most helpful resources. If you are not sure how to begin, follow this research plan.

SUGGESTIONS FOR TALKING WITH LIBRARIANS

◆   Before you ask for help, try to answer your questions yourself.

◆   Bring with you a copy of the research assignment.

◆   Be ready to explain the assignment in your own words: purpose, format, length, number of sources, and due date.

◆   Identify any special requirements about sources. Should information come from government documents? Rare books? Films?

◆   Describe the particular topic you are researching and the tentative question you have framed to address the topic.

◆   Describe any work you have done so far: Web sites, books, or periodicals looked at; log entries written; people interviewed; and so on.

Reference room   18a

Start in the reference room to discuss a research plan with a reference librarian. Here you can also locate background information, definitions, and basic facts about your topic. Search appropriate dictionaries, encyclopedias, bibliographies, indexes, and databases (online or in texts) to find summaries, overviews, and definitions that will help you decide whether or not to pursue a topic further and where to turn next for more specific information. General reference works help begin—but not complete—serious academic investigations.

Bibliographies list books alphabetically by title, by author, or by subject. Many books include bibliographies of the works the author consulted while writing the book. When you find a useful book, follow up on the items in its bibliography. Many other bibliographies are published separately as reference tools.

Indexes are guides to material published sometimes in books but more often in periodicals. Each index covers a particular group of periodicals, alphabetically by author or by subject, so be sure to look in the index that deals with your subject. To do a subject search, use the keywords associated with your topic and check these against the *Library of Congress Subject Headings*, the official guide identifying the terms used to catalog subjects within the Library of Congress system.

Computerized sources—CD-ROMs, online databases, and networks—contain many types of information, ranging from previously published books and periodicals to online reports, journals, and conferences. Your librarian should have guides and lists of these materials as well. The database most commonly found in college libraries is

DIALOG, which tracks more than a million sources of information. It is divided into nearly a thousand specialized databases listed in the DIALOG Blue Sheets, so you must find out which database you need before you begin your search.

18b Periodicals

Search periodicals (magazines and journals) to locate more up-to-date information than books can supply. General periodical indexes list articles in magazines, journals, and newspapers that are of interest to the general public. Specialized periodical indexes list articles of interest to people in specific academic disciplines or professional fields. Both kinds of indexes are useful, but you need to know what each does and which you need. As with books, the quickest and most efficient way to find periodicals is by computer. You search for articles in these databases the same way you look for books: by author, title, or subject headings and keywords.

To find journal articles on your topic, being with an online index such as *Expanded Academic ASAP*, which provides access to citations in both scholarly journals and general-interest magazines on a variety of topics. If you are not sure how or where to start, tell your reference librarian what you are looking for and inquire about the best method to access the most recent periodical information. In most campus libraries you should be able to search indexes such as InfoTrac, *Reader's Guide to Periodical Literature,* Lexus-Nexus, and others—many of which allow you to reprint full-text articles directly from your computer station.

18c Online catalog

Move to your library's catalog to locate library books by author, title, subject, or keyword. Searching by subject is generally the most useful method of finding sources. By entering subject headings or keywords alone or in combination, you can locate books you might never have found otherwise. Finding these books can help you make connections that can move your research in new directions, or it can simply help you narrow your search for sources and so focus your research topic.

To do a keyword search, use the words you've identified as describing your topic, linked by *and* or *or.* The computer will present you with a list of works that fit that description. As with all computer searches, the more specific your request, the more useful your list will be.

Most online catalogs allow searching with partial information; if you know only the first two words of a title, the computer will generate a list of all works beginning with those words. The computer search can identify other related works and other titles by the same author.

Once you identify the book you want, the online catalog provides complete information on it, including where to locate the book and whether or not it is checked out. To find the book, use the book's call number to locate it in the stacks. The first letters or numbers in a call number indicate its general subject area, and this tells you, in turn, where in the library to find the book.

Alternative resources   18d

Check other sources. Many libraries own materials other than books and periodicals that often do not circulate. Ask a librarian about your library's holdings.

Government documents   The U.S. government publishes numerous reports, pamphlets, catalogs, and newsletters on most issues of national concern. Reference books that can lead you to these sources include the *Monthly Catalog of United States Government Publications* and the *United States Government Publication Index,* both available on CD-ROM and online.

Nonprint media   Records, audio CDs, audiocassettes, videotapes, slides, photographs, and other media are generally cataloged separately from book and periodical collections.

Pamphlets   Pamphlets and brochures published by government agencies and private organizations are generally stored in a library's vertical file. The *Vertical File Index: A Subject and Title Index to Selected Pamphlet Material* (1932/35–present) lists many of the available titles.

Special collections   Rare books, manuscripts, and items of local interest are commonly found in a special room or section of the library.

Bibliography   18e

Develop a **working bibliography.** Make an alphabetical list of all the works you have consulted (or plan to consult), using 3″ × 5″ index cards or a computer file (especially if you use a database manager). Both methods allow for easy alphabetizing, useful when you create a reference page for your paper. For each source, record the following information.

BOOKS

1. Call number or other location information
2. Full name(s) of author(s)
3. Full title and subtitle
4. Editor or translator
5. Place of publication
6. Publisher
7. Date of publication

PERIODICALS

1. Full name(s) of author(s)
2. Full title and subtitle of article
3. Periodical title
4. Periodical volume and number
5. Periodical date
6. Page numbers
7. Location

18f Notes

Take good notes from the texts you locate. Use note cards or computer files separate from your bibliography cards, putting only one bit of information or one idea on a card or page—a strategy that will help you locate, shuffle, and rearrange ideas as you shape your paper. If using a laptop computer, dedicate a file to your topic, insert topic subheads alphabetically, and file each note in the topic area where it belongs. (Make backup copies of all such stored information.) Each note should contain the following information.

1. Author and title of the source (These can be abbreviated.)
2. Page numbers
3. Brief statement of the source topic
4. Information quoted, paraphrased, or summarized from the source
5. Notes, in brackets or parentheses, on how you might use the material or cross-reference to other material

19 CONDUCTING INTERNET RESEARCH

The Internet and World Wide Web (WWW) provide a variety of information unavailable either in the library or in the field. Within the past decade, businesses and individuals have gained widespread access to the Internet, especially to that portion known as the World Wide Web. Although academic and scientific use of the Internet continues, commercial applications drive most Web development—making it a messy, crowded, but ever-so-useful place in which to conduct research, academic or otherwise. Many Web sites are secondary sources, written by people describing, analyzing, or interpreting the work of others. Less easy to find are primary sources, the original words and accounts of people describing their own experiences or findings.

HOW TO READ AN INTERNET ADDRESS

Every site on the Internet has a unique electronic address or *URL* ("universal resource locator") that specifies the name of the organization and a domain suffix that identifies the type of organization sponsoring the site. The following domain suffixes are currently in use.

- **.aero** aviation groups
- **.biz** businesses
- **.com** commercial/business
- **.coop** credit unions and rural coops
- **.edu** educational
- **.gov** government institutions
- **.info** information, open to public
- **.museum** accredited museums worldwide
- **.mil** military
- **.name** second-level names .name
- **.net** news & other networks
- **.org** non-profit agency
- **.pro** professionals
- ~ personal home page

Each URL abbreviation suggests the potential bias of the site: **.com** and **.biz** sites are usually selling something; **.coop,** and **.pro** may be selling something, but may have a stronger interest in promoting the public welfare; **.mil, .org** are non-profit, but each has an agenda to promote and defend; **.edu, .gov, .museum,** or **.net** should be more neutral; and **.info, .name** or ~ could be anyone with any idea.

A URL may also specify an individual file within the main site such as htm or .html for Web pages written in hypertext markup language or .jpg for digitally stored photographs. Knowing sponsorship and file type may suggest which addresses to check first, which to ignore. Careful researchers scrutinize all sources of information with a critical eye.

Much of the difficulty and delight of the Internet stems from the fact that no one is in charge. No single agency or company is responsible for organizing or policing the Internet. And no one knows exactly what is on it, nor is there a central card catalog or index showing what's available, from whom, or where it's located. The unscreened nature of the Internet makes it essential that you supplement Internet information with other sources. If you are unfamiliar with Web searching for non-commercial information, the following suggestions will help.

19a Select a search engine

To begin an online search from off campus, log on to the Internet via your service provider. From on campus, use the campus network to arrive at the same place. If your computer logs on to a university home page first, find the Internet link or type in the **URL** (universal resource locator, or electronic address) of a search engine in the home page locator box. Search engines help you locate information; any of the following are useful for academic searches.

- **Alta Vista** <http://www.altavista.digital.com>: A powerful and comprehensive site. Allows restricted searches; full texts often available.

- **Excite** <http://www.excite.com>: Good for first and general searches. Ranks sites by frequency of keywords; suggests related sites.

- **Hotbot** <http://www.hotbot.com>: Powerful; good for customized searches by date, media, specific subject areas. Includes newsgroups, classified ads, Yellow Pages, e-mail directories.

- **Infoseek** <http://infoseek.go.com>: Identifies sites by frequency of keywords. Allows searching by title, URL, directory, and newsgroup databases.

- **Lycos** <http://www.lycos.com>: Allows advanced and previous-search searches; directory covers 90 percent of the Web; includes newsgroups, Reuters news service.

- **Net Search** <http://netscape.com>: Located on the Netscape task bar; powerful, easy to use, and connected to other Web search engines.

- **Northern Light** <http://www.northernlight.com>: Sorts search results into customized folders. Special collections of abstracts (free) and periodical articles (small charge to download).

◆   **Yahoo!** <http://www.yahoo.com>: The most comprehensive sub-
    ject directory. Good for browsing; allows restricted searches;
    includes full-text downloads.

In addition, check out search engines that search other ones: All
in One <http://www.albany.net/allinone/>, Dogpile <http://www.dogpile
.com>, MetaCrawler <http://metacrawler.com>, and 37.com
<http://37.com>. However, these collective search engines sometimes
provide too many sites with too few restrictions, making it difficult to
limit your search to relevant information.

Limit the search   19b

First searches often provide too much information—sometimes several
thousand (or million!) sites—making it hard to locate those you can
use. For example, a broad search term such as "Vietnam" may locate
everything from travel information to news articles to geography and
language—thousands of sites, too many to explore.

If your subject is the Vietnam War, most search engines will
retrieve a list of sites whose titles, Web addresses, or text contain only one
of the two search words. Thus, some will be about Vietnam, but not the
war; others about war, but not Vietnam. To help you find two or more
terms at the same time, most search engines offer logical tools called
Boolean operators.

◆   Use double quotation marks to limit a search to a specific phrase,
    title, or name: "Vietnam War," "The Best and the Brightest," or
    "David Halberstam." The search engine will select only sites that
    include all the words within the quotation marks.

◆   Use *and* between words to limit the search to sources that include
    both terms (not already combined in a phrase). Typing "crime *and*
    punishment" will return any documents that include both the
    word *crime* and the word *punishment,* while using quotation
    marks will get you *Crime and Punishment,* the novel by
    Dostoevsky. (Some sites, such as Excite and Alta Vista, use a plus
    sign instead of *and.* Try both *and* and + to be sure you're getting
    the information you want.)

◆   Use *or* between words to retrieve documents that include any, rather
    than most, of the search words. Type "puma *or* mountain lion *or*
    cougar *or* panther"—all different names for the same animal.

◆ Use *not* after a term to exclude a word that must not appear in the documents. Example: you want dolphin, the fish, so you type "dolphin *not* mammal *or* NFL."

◆ Use an asterisk * to substitute for letters or word endings that might vary: "universit*" could stand for *university* or *universities.*

◆ Use parentheses ( ) to group and combine search expressions: "(treaty *or* armistice *or* police action) *and* Korean War." (The Korean War was technically called a police action, and no side won). There is no limit to the levels of nesting that you can use in a query: "(treaty *or* armistice) *and* Korean (war *or* police action) *and* Joseph McCarthy." The more you limit up front, the more specific your information will be.

19c Search strategies

Type keywords that describe or name your topic, click the search button, and wait for a list of sites to examine one by one. Try searching several different ways, using related terms in combination or alone. Narrow your search by using other, more specific terms, such as "Vietnam *and* war *and* infantry" or "(Tet Offensive) *or* (Ho Chi Minh Trail)." These may return shorter, more useful lists.

Try several different search engines and directories. (See 13a.) No search engine or directory catalogs the entire Web, and no two engines search exactly the same way. Depending on your topic, you may find one search engine much more useful than the others. The law of the Web is trial and error. If you are still not getting what you expect, click on the help or advanced search option included on every site, read it, and try again.

If you type in a URL (Web address) but cannot locate the site, or if you get an error message saying "Object not found," check your typing very carefully and try again. If you still get an error message, try a simplified version of the URL to take you to the site's home page, and then click on a link for more information. Even if the specific file you were seeking has been moved, chances are you can find related or updated information you can use.

Also try searching several different sites. Web sites with similar-sounding names can provide remarkably different information, so be sure to check all sites. For example, one site may be more recent than another, one more comprehensive, while another may be trying to sell you something.

Surf strategies   19d

Research profits from curiosity and exploration. No place on Earth takes you faster to more information than the Internet. To explore it, log on and type one of the following URLs into the command line of your browser, and hit the enter key to see what you find.

♦   **Amazon.com** <http://www.amazon.com>: Lists books in print along with out-of-print titles. Useful to locate or buy books; includes all relevant publishing data and reviews.

♦   **Argus Clearinghouse** <http://www.clearinghouse.net>: Selects, describes, and evaluates Internet resources; a good site to begin any research project.

♦   **Biographical Dictionary** <http://www.s9.com/biography/>: Searchable by name, birth and death years, profession, works, and other terms.

♦   **E.span** <http://www.espan.com/doot/doot.html>: Job hunting and the *Occupational Outlook Handbook.*

♦   **Encyclopaedia Britannica** <http://www.britannica.com>: Information on any subject under the sun.

♦   **Frequently Asked Questions (FAQ) about the Web** <http://www.boutell.com/openfaq/browsers/>

♦   **Information Please** <http://www.infoplease.com>: A searchable online almanac; topics from architecture to biography to historical statistics to weather.

♦   **Learn the Net Inc.** <http://www.learnthenet.com/english/index.html>: Web tours and training.

♦   **Peterson's Education Center** <http://www.petersons.com:8080/>: Information on colleges.

♦   **Research-It** <http://www.iTools.com/research-it/research-it.html>: A reference toolkit of online dictionaries, with a thesaurus.

♦   **Shakespeare Web** <http://www.shakespeare.com>: Links to sites for searching the works of Shakespeare.

♦   **Statistical Abstract of the United States** <http://www.census.gov/stat_abstract/>: From the Census Bureau.

♦   **ABC News** <http://www.abcnews.com/>

- ◆ **MSNBC**   NBC News <http://www.msnbc.com>
- ◆ **ESPN** <http://espn.sportszone.com>: Cable sports news.

When you locate a useful site, you need to remember how you got there. Retracing steps is sometimes difficult, so keep a notebook listing which search engines and keywords you use so that you can reproduce a search easily. When you find a useful Web page, print a copy for your records. If your browser doesn't automatically do so, write the URL of the page on your printout along with the date and time you accessed the page. These notes will help to document your paper and "freeze" the contents of a site that changes between visits. If you find a site that you expect to use again, identify it as a "bookmark" or "favorite" if you will be using the same computer again.

19e Check e-mail and newsgroups

Once you have an electronic address, you can correspond electronically with any of millions of people around the world who can, in turn, write to you. Of course, you need your correspondent's e-mail address. Try using an e-mail address search site such as Search.com <http://www.search.com>. Enter a name and check the search results against other information you already have. For example, if you were looking for Toby Fulwiler's address and found one ending with *uvm.edu,* you could be fairly sure you had found the co-author of this book, who works at the University of Vermont (UVM), an educational institution.

E-mail can make a good interview tool. If you have questions for the author of an article you're citing in your research, you may be able to e-mail your questions and get quick answers. If you write to someone in search of information, be sure to identify yourself and describe your research project. In addition to your specific questions, don't forget to ask a general question such as *Can you think of other important issues I should be aware of?*

Another kind of continuing discussion group on the Internet is the newsgroup or Usenet group. A newsgroup consists of a collection of postings on a single topic. As with mailing lists, there are thousands of newsgroups. Most Internet service providers include newsgroup access as part of basic service. Rather than browse through lists of newsgroups, you can instruct some Web sites to search through newsgroups' current and archived postings. Two sites that specialize in finding newsgroups are Reference.COM at <http://www.reference.com> and Deja News at <http://www.dejanews.com>. Many academically oriented newsgroups contain abbreviations such as *lit* for literature, *sci* for science, or *soc* for sociology. You can pick the groups you wish to read by subscribing to each one, then see the messages by selecting the group name.

 CONDUCTING FIELD RESEARCH

Depending on your research question, you may need to conduct research outside the library and away from computers. **Field research** simply means visiting places (a lakeshore, a downtown, a factory, a museum) or people (a biologist, a police officer, a farm worker, a professor) and taking careful notes. Field research gets you fresh, local information about people, places, events, or objects that you cannot find in books or cyberspace. Your observation and interview notes provide you with original data to incorporate into research papers.

Observing places   20a

Unlike a library, which bundles millions of bits of every kind of information in a single location, fields are everywhere. A college campus is an ideal place in which to conduct field research since there are many potential sites for investigation: academic departments, administrative offices, labs, libraries, dining and sports facilities, and dormitories. In the neighborhood beyond the campus, sites for field research include theaters, malls, parks, playgrounds, business offices, homes, and so on. Furthermore, accessing the Internet opens up the possibility of field research in cyberspace, from e-mail on your own campus to contact with a site halfway around the world. Field information is not cataloged, organized, indexed, or shelved for your convenience. Obtaining it requires diligence, energy, and careful planning.

The following suggestions will increase your chances of successful site visits.

- ◆ **Select relevant sites.** When doing research at local sites, visit places that will be the primary focus of your paper or offer supplementary details to support your major points.

- ◆ **Do homework.** To observe with understanding and use on-site time efficiently, consult reference-room or online sources such as encyclopedias, dictionaries, and atlases to inform yourself about the places you will visit.

◆ **Call ahead.** Find out directions and convenient times to visit and let people at the site know you are coming; also let them know if you need to cancel.

◆ **Bring a notebook with a stiff cover.** It will help you write while walking or standing. Record both general impressions and specific details. Double-entry notebooks record facts in one column and your reactions in the other.

◆ **Use a hand-held tape recorder** for on-site dictation to supplement or replace written notes.

◆ **Review, transcribe, and rewrite** both written and dictated notes within twenty-four hours after your visit. Both your memory and the completeness of your records will benefit.

◆ **Sketch, photograph, map, or videotape** useful visual information. Supplement visual records with measurements or notes as appropriate.

ELECTRONIC RESEARCH TOOLS

Use electronic media to capture interview data when conversations in person are difficult or impossible to arrange.

◆ **Telephone** Use your telephone to interview people you cannot talk to in person. Even a ten-minute phone conversation can give you insights and quotable nuggets to enliven your paper. Keep a pen handy and take good notes.

◆ **Telephone answering machine** Pose simple questions to interview subjects and ask them to call back to record their answers on your answering machine (when you know you won't be home). You can transcribe the recording later.

◆ **E-mail** Send queries by e-mail to interview subjects with a limited number of questions, and allow them to e-mail their responses. This technique is convenient for subjects as it allows them to answer you when they have time; it also provides you with a written record for quotations.

◆ **Home page** Ask interview subjects to visit your Web home page on which you've described situations or posed questions as well as provided a means to record responses (e-mail or listserv, chat box). You will spend time setting up the page to serve research purposes, but you will save time later if many people access your questions and respond in writing.

Interviewing people   20b

A good interview provides the researcher with timely, original, and useful information that often cannot be obtained by other means. Getting such information is part instinct, part skill, and part luck. If you find talking to strangers easy, then you have a head start on being a good interviewer; in many respects, a good interview is simply a good conversation. If you do not, you can still learn how to ask good interview questions that will elicit the answers you need. Your chances of obtaining good interview material increase when you've carefully selected your interview subject and thought about what questions you want to pose ahead of time.

Keep in mind that people differ in both the amount and the kind of knowledge they have. Not everyone who knows something about your research topic will be available to be interviewed. In other words, before you make an appointment with a local expert, consider whether this is the best person to talk to. The following guidelines should help you conduct good interviews.

- **Select relevant people.** Determine what information you need, who is likely to have it, and how to approach them. To find such people, start by asking people you know. Use the Yellow Pages and the Internet to locate experts.

- **Call ahead for an appointment.** Let your subject know when you are coming or when an appointment needs to be changed or canceled.

- **Do homework.** Consult library or Internet sources for background information on your interview subject. Experts will say more and provide greater depth if you know more; they will say less if you seem ignorant and settle for superficial answers.

- **Prepare questions in advance.** Plan to ask general questions early to establish context; plan to ask more specific questions as you become more informed. Write these out in a small notebook so that you remember to ask them.

- **Ask open questions** to elicit general information and to set the context for further questions: *How did that situation develop? What are your plans for the future?* Open questions allow your interviewee to add new information, insights, and direction that you may not have thought of but that might prove crucial for your paper.

◆ **Ask closed questions** when you need facts or concrete details to support a point or to focus the direction an interview is taking: *On what date did that policy take effect? What is the name of the district manager?*

◆ **Ask follow-up questions** if answers are incomplete or confusing. It's often the follow-up question that allows your interviewee to provide you with more depth and detail: *How many gallons does it hold? How long ago was that?* Get all the information possible at one sitting.

◆ **Use silence.** Often when people don't answer immediately it's because they are thinking or formulating an answer. If your subject does not respond right away, allow time for him or her to think, recall, or reflect before you fill the silence with another question.

◆ **Read body language.** Notice how your subject acts: Does the person look you in the eyes? Fidget? Look bored? Smile? Pace around the room? Each of these actions suggests whether someone is speaking honestly, avoiding your question, or tiring fast. In your notes, describe body language along with conversation to add color, context, or extra meaning to recorded words.

◆ **Use a tape recorder.** Ask permission in advance and make sure your equipment works. Continue to make written notes of conversation highlights to help you remember questions that occur while your subject is talking and to describe the subject's appearance and manner.

◆ **Confirm important assertions.** Read back important or controversial statements to check for accuracy and allow for further explanation.

20c Conducting surveys

A type of field research commonly used in the social sciences is the **survey,** a structured interview in which respondents, representative of a larger group, are all asked the same questions. Their answers are then tabulated and interpreted. Researchers usually conduct surveys to discover attitudes, beliefs, or habits of the general public or segments of the population. They may try to predict how soccer moms will vote in an election, determine the popularity of a new movie with teenage audiences, compare the eating habits of students who live off campus to those of students who eat in college dining halls—the possible topics are infinite.

Respondents to surveys can be treated like experts for research purposes because they are being asked for their own opinions or information about their own behavior. However, you must ask your questions skillfully to get useful answers. Instead of collecting candid responses, wording that suggests a right or wrong answer reveals the researcher's biases and preconceived ideas. Furthermore, questions should be easy to understand and answer, and they should be reviewed to make sure they are relevant to the research topic or hypothesis. The format for questioning and the way the research is conducted also have an influence on the responses. For example, to get complete and honest answers about a sensitive or highly personal issue, the researcher would probably use anonymous written surveys to ensure confidentiality. Other survey techniques involve oral interviews, in person or by phone, in which the researcher records each subject's responses on a written form.

Surveys are usually brief to gain the cooperation of a sufficiently large number of respondents. And to enable the researcher to compare answers, the questions are usually closed, although open-ended questions may be used to gain additional information or insights.

21 | EVALUATING RESEARCH SOURCES

Good sources inform your papers and make them believable. For a source to be "good," it needs to meet two criteria: Is the source itself credible? Is it useful in your paper? This chapter provides guidelines for evaluating the credibility and usefulness of sources found in the library, on the Internet, and in the field.

Evaluating library sources   21a

The sources you find in a college library are generally credible because experts have already screened them. The books, periodicals, documents, special collections, and electronic sources have been recommended for acquisition by scholars, researchers, and librarians with special expertise in the subject areas the library catalogs. Consequently, library resources have been prejudged credible, at some level, before you locate them.

However, just because *some* authorities judged a source to be credible *at one time* does not necessarily mean it still is, or that it's the best available, or that it's not contested, or that it's especially useful to the paper you are writing. Two of the main reasons for distrusting a source found in the library have to do with *time* (when was it judged true?) and *perspective* (who said it was true and for what reason?).

Identifying dated sources   Most library documents include a date of publication inside the cover, and in most cases this will be a fact that you can rely on. In some cases, such as articles first published in one place and then reprinted in an anthology, you may have to dig harder for the original date, but it's usually there (check the permissions or credits page).

One of the main reasons any source may become unreliable—and incredible—is the passage of time. For example, any geographical, political, or statistical information true for 1950 or even 1999 will be more or less changed by the time you examine it—in many cases, radically so. (See atlas or encyclopedia entries for Africa or Asia from 1950!) Yet at one time this source was judged to be accurate.

Check the critical reception of books when they were published by reading reviews in *The Book Review Digest* (also online); often you can tell whether the critical argument over the book twenty years ago is still relevant or has been superseded by other events and publications.

At the same time, dated information has all sorts of uses. In spite of being "dated," works such as the Bible, the I Ching, the novels of Virginia Woolf, and the beliefs of Malcolm X are invaluable for many reasons. In studying change over time, old statistical information is crucial. Knowing the source date lets you decide whether to use it and how.

Identifying perspective   Who created the source and with what purpose or agenda? Why has someone or some organization written, constructed, compiled, recorded, or otherwise created this source in the first place? This second critical question is difficult to answer by reviewing the source itself. While most library texts include the dates they were published, few accurately advertise their purpose or the author's point of view—and when they do, this information cannot always be believed.

To evaluate the usefulness of a text, ask questions about the assumptions it makes, the evidence it presents, and the reasoning that holds it together. Finding answers to these critical questions reveals an author's bias.

- What is the writer's purpose—scholarly analysis, political advocacy, entertainment, or something else?

◆ Can you classify the author's point of view (liberal, conservative, radical) and differentiate it from other points of view?

◆ What does the writer assume about the subject or about the audience? (What does unexplained jargon tell you?)

◆ How persuasive is the evidence? Which statements are facts, which inferences drawn from facts, which matters of opinion?

◆ Are you aware of relevant points that the writer *doesn't* mention? What does this tell you?

◆ How compelling is the logic? Are there places where it doesn't make sense? How many?

Your answers to these questions should reveal the degree to which you accept the author's conclusions.

Cross-referencing sources   At first it may seem daunting to answer all these questions, but have patience and give the research process the time it needs. On a relatively new subject, you won't know many answers; however, the more you learn, the more you learn! As you read further, you begin to compare one source to another and to notice differences, especially if you read carefully and take notes to keep track of each source's timeliness and perspective. The more differences you note, the more answers to the above questions you find, and the more you know whether a source might be useful.

Evaluating electronic sources   21b

You need to apply the same critical scrutiny to Internet sources as to library sources, only more so. With no editor, librarian, or review board to screen for accuracy, reliability, or integrity, anyone with a computer and a modem can publish personal opinions, commercial pitches, bogus claims, bomb-making instructions, or smut on the World Wide Web. Although the Internet is a marvelous source of research information, it's also a trap for unwary researchers. So, in addition to timeliness and perspective, what do you need to look out for? First, look at the electronic address (URL) to identify the type of organization sponsoring the site. Each abbreviation suggests the potential bias in sites: .com sites are selling something; .mil or .org sponsors have their own policies to promote and defend; .edu, .gov, and .net sites should be most neutral and unbiased but should also be checked if a position on a debatable issue is advocated; and ~ could be sponsored by anyone with any idea.

Second, ask as many critical questions as you would of a library source. An easy way to do this is to ask the reporter's standard questions—*who, what, where, when, why,* and *how?*—and see what the answers reveal to you.

WHO IS THE SITE AUTHOR?

- Look for an individual's name: check the beginning or end of the URL.

- Look for expert credentials: scholar, scientist, doctor, college degrees, experience?

- Look for the author's connection to an organization or agency: university, government, NRA, Sierra Club?

- If no individual's name is provided, look for the sponsoring organization: what causes or positions does it stand for?

- Look for links to the author's or agency's home page.

- Look for a way to contact the author or agency by e-mail, phone, or mail to ask further questions.

- If you cannot tell who created the site or cannot contact its sponsors, expect the site credibility to be low. Don't rely on this site's information.

WHAT IDEAS OR INFORMATION DOES THE SITE PRESENT?

- Look for concepts and terminology you know.

- Summarize the claim or central idea in your own language. How does this site meet your research needs?

- Look for facts versus inferences versus opinions versus speculations—be wary of opinion and speculation.

- Look for balanced versus biased points of view. What tips you off? Which would you trust more?

- Look for missing information. Why is it not there?

- Look for advertising. Is it openly identified and separated from factual material?

◆ Look for a "hit count" to suggest the popularity of the site—a sign that others may have found it useful.

HOW IS THE INFORMATION PRESENTED?

◆ Look at the care with which the site is constructed, an indication of the educational level of the author. If the site contains spelling and grammar errors or is loaded with unexplained jargon, do you trust it? Will your readers?

◆ Look at the clarity of the graphics and/or sound features. Do they contribute to the content of the site?

◆ Look for links to other sites that suggest a connected, comprehensive knowledge base.

WHERE DOES THE INFORMATION COME FROM?

◆ Identify the source of the site: .edu, .gov, .com, and so on.

◆ Identify the source of the site's facts. Do you trust it?

◆ Look for prior appearance as a print source. Are you familiar with it? Is it reputable?

◆ Look for evidence that the information has been refereed. If so, where?

WHEN WAS THE SITE CREATED?

◆ Look for a creation date; a date more than a year old suggests a site not regularly updated.

◆ Look for absence of a creation date. Would lack of a date affect the reliability of the information?

◆ Look at whether or not the site is complete or still under construction. If incomplete, note that.

WHY IS THE INFORMATION PRESENTED?

◆ Look for clues to agenda of the site. Is it to inform? Persuade? Entertain? Sell? Are you buying?

◆ Does getting information from the site cost money? (You should not have to pay for general reference material or information for a college paper.)

IDENTIFYING ANONYMOUS INTERNET SOURCES

You can find out who owns an Internet domain name—and often get addresses for owners or officers of a Web site—by contacting InterNIC WHOIS at <http://rs.internic.net/>, a site run by Network Solutions Inc., the company responsible for administering most domain names. But a site that makes you search for such information, rather than providing it for you, should not inspire confidence.

Welcome to the *InterNIC* Website!

This website has been established to provide the public information regarding Internet domain name registration services and will be updated frequently.

For a list of ICANN-accredited registrars that are currently taking registrations in the .com, .net and .org domains, please go to The Accredited Registrar Directory.

To view a list of frequently asked questions (FAQs) regarding domain name registration, please go to The InterNIC FAQ.

To access information regarding registered domains, please go to the Registry WHOIS

Thank you for visiting the InterNIC website!

It is expected that the InterNIC website will be updated and revised frequently, so please check back often for new information. An e-mail address will be posted soon for the submission of comments.

InterNIC is a registered service mark of the U.S. Department of Commerce. This site is being hosted by Network Solutions, Inc. on behalf of the U.S. Department of Commerce.

This page last updated 1/5/2000

Evaluating field sources   21c

People and places are, by their nature, not as carefully documented, reviewed, cataloged, and permanent as library sources or as widely available as Internet sources. The reliability and credibility of field sources is problematic because it is often more difficult for readers of your paper to track down field sources than textual sources. An interview is usually a single event, so a subject available one day may not be there the next day for follow-up questions or confirmation of responses. A location providing information one day may change or become off-limits the next. To critically examine field sources, you need to "freeze" them and make them hold still. Here's what to do.

Interviews   To freeze an interview, use a tape recorder and transcribe the whole session. Once an interview is taped, apply to it the critical questions you would a written source. If you cannot tape-record, be sure to take careful notes, review main points with your subject before the interview ends, and apply these same critical questions.

Site observations   To freeze a site, make photographic or video records of what it looked like and what you found, in addition to taking copious notes about time and details of location, size, shape, color, number, and so forth. If you cannot make photo records, then sketch, draw, or diagram what you find. Pictures and careful verbal descriptions add credibility to papers by providing specific details that would be difficult to invent had the writer not been present. Even if you don't use them directly in your paper, visual notes will jog your memory of other important site events.

Personal bias   Evaluating personal observations is complicated since you are both the creator and the evaluator of the material at the same time. The world is out there, and in and of itself, it has no meaning or value until you, the recorder, assign it. This material has not been filtered through the lens of another writer. You are the interpreter of what you witness, and when you introduce field evidence, it's your own bias that will show up in the way you use language; you will lead your reader one way or another depending on the words you select to convey what you saw: Was the lake water *cloudy, murky,* or *filthy?* Was the electric car *slow, relaxed, hesitant,* or *a dog?* You also shape interview material by the questions you ask, the manner in which you conduct the interview, and the language of your notes. In other words, in field research, the manner in which you collect, record, and present information is most likely to introduce the bias that is the most difficult to control—your own.

22 USING SOURCES

As you prepare to draft, you need to assess all the information you've found and decide which sources to use and how. In other words, you need to synthesize unorganized raw material into an original, coherent paper. To synthesize notes in preparation for writing: (1) Look for connections among similar statements made by several sources. (2) Look for contradictions between and among sources. (3) Marshal the evidence that furthers your paper's goal and set aside that which doesn't—everything you've collected cannot possibly fit, and shouldn't.

Beware of constructing a source-driven paper, one whose direction is dictated by what you've found rather than what you are curious about and want to explore and examine. In other words, don't quit pursuing an interesting question because your first few sources don't answer it: if you need more evidence, go get it rather than faking it or settling for answers to a question you haven't asked. Source-driven papers are obvious and odious to practiced instructors in every discipline.

Most research notes exist in three basic formats: direct quotation, paraphrase, and summary. Field notes may be more rambling. Whenever you quote, paraphrase, or summarize, be sure to document the source to the best of your ability.

22a Direct quotations

Reproduce authors' or speakers' exact words to examine their ideas or to add credibility to your own ideas. However, using too many quotations reduces your own authority, suggesting too much reliance on others' thoughts. Using too many quotations can also be distracting; if you have more than two or three per page, you may not have introduced, explained, or interpreted them well. In addition, long quotations slow readers down and invite skim reading. Use only as much of a quotation as you need to support your point.

Using brief quotations gains space and readability. You can't change what a source says, but you can control how much of it you use. When you shorten a quotation, be careful not to change or distort its meaning. If you omit words within quotations, indicate the missing words with an ellipsis (. . .). Any changes or additions must be indicated by including the new words in brackets ([ ]).

Original

The human communication environment has acquired biological complexity and planetary scale, but there are no scientists or activists monitoring it, theorizing about its health, or mounting campaigns to protect its resilience.

—Stewart Brand, *The Media Lab,* 258

Inaccurate Quotation (Changed Meaning)

In *The Media Lab,* Stewart Brand describes "biological complexity" as a hazard to scientists.

Accurate Quotation

In *The Media Lab,* Stewart Brand notes the growth and complexity of the modern telecommunications environment. But nobody is "monitoring it . . . to protect its resilience" (258).

Integrating quotations into your paper

Integrate direct quotations smoothly into your paper by providing an explanatory tag *at the beginning* to explain the quotation and show its relevance. Brief quotations (four or fewer typed lines) should be embedded in the main body of your paper and enclosed in quotation marks. The short quotation in the following passage is from a personal interview.

```
Photo editor Tom Brennan took ten minutes to sort
through my images and then told me, "Most photography
editors wouldn't take more than two minutes to look at
a portfolio."
```

Set off quotations of five lines or longer in block format, indented ten spaces. Do not use quotation marks. The end punctuation precedes parenthetical documentation.

```
Kelly focuses on Americans' peculiarly negative chau-
vinism, in this case, that of New York residents:
            New Yorkers are a provincial lot. They wear
            their city's accomplishments like blue rib-
            bons. To anyone who will listen, they boast
            of leading the world in everything from
            street vendors to porno movie houses. (89)
```

Introducing quotations

Specify who is speaking, what the quotation refers to, and where it is from. If the author is well known, be sure to mention his or her name as part of the signal phrase introducing the quotation.

```
In Walden, Henry David Thoreau claims, "The mass of
men lead lives of quiet desperation" (5).
```

If the title of your written work is well known, you can introduce a quotation with the title rather than the author's name as long as the reference is clear.

```
Walden sets forth one individual's antidote against
the "lives of quiet desperation" led by the working
class in mid-nineteenth-century America (Thoreau 5).
```

If neither the author nor the title is well known, introduce the quotation with a brief explanation to provide a context.

```
Mary Catherine Bateson, daughter of anthropologist
Margaret Mead, has become a close observer of modern
civilization. In Composing a Life, she writes, "The
twentieth century has been called the century of the
refugee because of the vast numbers of people uprooted
by war and politics from their homes" (8).
```

Signal phrases

When you use a signal phrase to introduce a quotation, make sure it accurately reflects the intention of the source. Unless the context requires a past-tense verb, use the present. You can vary the verb in your signal phrase by using the following synonyms.

admits	disputes	refutes
agrees	emphasizes	reports
argues	endorses	reveals
asserts	finds	says
believes	grants	shows
claims	illustrates	speculates
comments	implies	states
concedes	insists	suggests
declares	invites	thinks
denies	observes	wonders
disagrees	points out	writes

Explaining quotations

Sometimes a quotation needs to be explained to assure clarity, as in the final sentence below.

> In *A Sand County Almanac*, Aldo Leopold invites urban readers to confront what they lose by living in the city: "There are two spiritual dangers in not owning a farm. One is the danger of supposing that breakfast comes from the grocery, and the other that heat comes from the furnace" (6). In other words, Leopold sees city dwellers as dangerously ignorant of how their basic needs are met.

You may also need to clarify what a word or reference means. Do this by using square brackets. In the passage below, it's unclear *who* will shrink.

Unclear

> Observing the remains of earwigs, sow bugs, moths, and spiders, Dillard reminds us that everything is changing, even in death: "Next week, if the other bodies are any indication, he will be shrunken and gray, webbed to the floor with dust."

Clear

> Observing the remains of earwigs, sow bugs, moths, and spiders, Dillard reminds us that everything is changing, even in death: "Next week, if the other bodies are any indication, [the earwig] will be shrunken and gray, webbed to the floor with dust."

Adjusting grammar in quoted passages

A passage containing a quotation must follow all the rules of grammatical sentence structure: tenses should be consistent, verbs and subjects should agree, and so on. If the form of the passage doesn't fit the grammar of your own sentences, change your sentences, or slightly alter the quotation. Use this last option sparingly, and always indicate any changes with brackets.

Grammatically Incompatible

> If Thoreau thought that in his day, "The mass of men *lead* lives of quiet desperation" (*Walden* 5), what would he say of the masses today?

Grammatically Compatible

If Thoreau thought that in his day the masses *led* "lives of quiet desperation" (*Walden* 5), what would he say of the masses today?

Grammatically Compatible

In the nineteenth century, Thoreau stated, "The mass of men lead lives of quiet desperation" (*Walden* 5). What would he say of the masses today?

Grammatically Compatible

If Thoreau thought that in his day the "mass of men [led] lives of quiet desperation" (*Walden* 5), what would he say of the masses today?

- Quote directly when you cannot express the ideas better yourself.

- Quote directly when the original words are especially clear, powerful, or vivid.

- Quote directly when you want an authority's exact words to back you up.

22b Paraphrasing

To paraphrase, you restate an author's ideas in your own words to make the ideas clearer or better suited to your purpose. Paraphrases should generally re-create the original source's order and emphasis and should include most details. A paraphrase should be clearer, but not necessarily briefer, than the original.

A paraphrase should neither distort meaning nor reproduce too closely the sentence patterns of the original, a practice called plagiarism. To paraphrase, follow these guidelines.

- Check all word definitions you don't know.

- Recast ideas in your own words (avoid plagiarism).

- Don't paraphrase one sentence at a time—go for whole-passage meaning.

- Include any context necessary to explain the passage.

Original

The human communication environment has acquired biological complexity and planetary scale, but there are no scientists or activists monitoring it, theorizing about its health, or mounting campaigns to protect its resilience.

—Stewart Brand, *The Media Lab,* 258

Accurate Paraphrase

Our "communication environment" is as complex and vast as any ecosystem on the planet. Yet no one monitors this environment to keep track of its growth and warn us if something is about to go wrong (258).

Summarizing 22c

To summarize is to condense the main ideas of a passage in your own words. A summary includes only the essentials of the original, not the specific details. You may summarize a paragraph, a chapter, or even a book in a few sentences. In other words, a summary is always shorter than the original source. The more material summarized, however, the more general and abstract it becomes, so be careful not to distort the meaning of the original.

Original

The human communication environment has acquired biological complexity and planetary scale, but there are no scientists or activists monitoring it, theorizing about its health, or mounting campaigns to protect its resilience.

—Stewart Brand, *The Media Lab*

Inaccurate Summary

The current telecommunications networks compose a nasty, unchangeable, and inescapable environment (Brand 258).

Accurate Summary

The telecommunications networks have expanded so rapidly that monitoring and controlling them is difficult (258).

- Summarize to show the main points from an original source but not the supporting details.

- Summarize to provide an overview or an interesting aside without digressing from your paper's focus.

- Summarize to condense lengthy notes into tight sentences.

22d Plagiarism

You need to give credit to other people when you use their ideas and words in your own writing. If you don't, you are guilty of **plagiarism**—passing off someone else's insights or words as your own. Plagiarism is grounds for dismissal from reputable academic institutions. If, to the best of your knowledge, an idea or the language used to express it originates with another person, you must document that source. Several styles of documentation for academic writing are presented in Part VIII. To avoid plagiarizing, be aware of what you need to document and what you do not.

The common knowledge rule You do not need to document common historical knowledge or geographical information that an educated person can be expected to know. This includes factual information that appears in multiple sources, such as the dates of historical events (the fall of Rome in A.D. 410), the names and locations of states and cities, the general laws of science (gravity, motion), and statements of well-known philosophies (feminism, liberalism).

AVOIDING PLAGIARISM

- Place all quoted passages, even a single brief phrase, in quotation marks, and always provide source information.
- Identify the source from which you have paraphrased or summarized ideas, just as you do when you quote directly.
- Give credit for any creative ideas you borrow from an original source. For example, if you use an author's anecdote to illustrate a point, acknowledge it.
- Replace unimportant language with your own, and use different sentence structures when you paraphrase or summarize.
- Acknowledge the source if you borrow any organizational structure or headings from an author. (For example, don't use the same subheading as your original source.)
- Use quotation marks with any words or phrases you borrow, especially when you reproduce an author's unique way of saying something.

You don't need to document ideas or terms that are common current knowledge and in widespread use in your culture (*politically correct, World Wide Web*).

You don't need to document ideas that are commonly known in the field or discipline in which you are writing and that can be found in several sources. For example, don't document the term *libido* (associated with Sigmund Freud) in a psychology paper, *means of production* (associated with Karl Marx) in a political science paper, or *postmodern* in an English, history, art, or philosophy paper.

However, if an author offers unique opinions or interpretations about any type of common knowledge, these should be credited, using the proper documentation style.

The plagiarism problem   *Intentional plagiarism* is simply cheating, which honest students avoid. *Unintentional plagiarism*, a far more common problem, occurs when a writer paraphrases or summarizes another author but stays too close to the wording or sentence structure of the original. The following examples will help you avoid unintentional plagiarism.

Original

Notwithstanding the widely different opinions about Machiavelli's work and his personality, there is at least one point in which we find a complete unanimity. All authors emphasize that Machiavelli is a child of his age, that he is a typical witness to the Renaissance.
—Ernst Cassirer, *The Myth of the State*

Plagiarized Paraphrase

Despite the widely different opinions about Machiavelli's work and personality, everyone agrees that he was a representative witness to the Renaissance (Cassirer 43).

Even though Cassirer is credited with the idea, the writer does not credit him with the wording.

Acceptable Paraphrase

Although views on the work and personality of Machiavelli vary, everyone agrees that he was "a typical witness to the Renaissance" (Cassirer 43).

216

PLAGIARISM IN AMERICAN ENGLISH

In many countries, it is customary to use another writer's words in your writing. This is done to demonstrate knowledge; to honor intellectuals, writers or philosophers; or to rely on the words of an authority to add credibility to your writing. Although there is nothing wrong with this practice, if you are not extremely careful about diligently acknowledging each time you use the words, thoughts, or teachings of someone else, you will be accused of plagiarism. It is not enough to rearrange the words or to replace them with synonyms; even if you completely rewrite the words of the original, you are still borrowing the ideas of another person. U.S. schools treat the idea of plagiarism very seriously, and you could find yourself in serious trouble if ever accused of plagiarizing. Talk to your instructors to make sure you really understand what they mean by quoting, paraphrasing, and summarizing another writer's words.

PART FOUR

EDITING: CLARITY

Source: *The College Writer's Reference*, Third Edition by Toby Fulwiler and Alan R. Hayakawa.

23 PARAGRAPH STRUCTURE

Editing involves reshaping paragraphs so that they flow logically one to the next, sharpening sentences to clarify ideas, and finding the most precise words to express meaning.

When you begin to edit your work, consider these questions. Refer to the chapter in parentheses for tips on how to create and choose alternatives.

- Does each paragraph advance my paper's point?

- Does my introduction catch the reader's attention?

- Does my conclusion produce the effect I intended?

- Do I control the language and structure of my sentences?

- Do I write with strong verbs, concrete nouns, and precise modifiers?

- Do I use language appropriate for my audience?

- Have I proofread for errors in typing, spelling, punctuation, and grammar?

Good paragraphing helps readers follow an author's ideas throughout a piece of writing by providing markers (indents) that catch the eye. When a new paragraph begins, readers expect a new idea or direction to begin. They expect that within a paragraph, each sentence will help develop or advance a main idea—that the paragraph will be **unified.** Readers also expect that each paragraph will present its ideas in an order that makes sense—that it will be **organized.** And they expect that each sentence within a paragraph will relate clearly to the sentences around it—that it will be **coherent.**

Paragraphs also give readers a chance to pause, start over, and regain their place when reading difficult material or lengthy explanations of a single idea. Writers often break into new paragraphs intuitively at places where they leave one thought and begin another or where a break seems needed. So, while there are no hard and fast rules that cover every reason to paragraph, it's a good idea to review your intuitive paragraphing to see that it helps rather than confuses readers. The following basic principles will help you paragraph effectively.

23a Unity

To edit a paragraph for unity, first determine the paragraph's main idea or topic. Keep words or sentences that support or clarify that main idea, and delete or move those that do not. In actual practice, how you determine the unifying principle for any given paragraph depends on the amount of your information, your larger organizing principle, and what point you want to make, but all things being equal, keep things together that you believe your audience expects to be together.

Writing a **topic sentence** at the beginning or end of a paragraph can state the unifying principle in one clear sentence. This strategy is especially helpful for readers looking for information or trying to follow an argument. In experiential or reflective writing, paragraph topics are more often implied than stated.

In the following passage, the writer identified the first sentence as her topic sentence. When she read the other sentences, she realized that her fourth sentence did not illustrate the topic sentence, so she moved it to the next paragraph, where it fit better.

♦ For various reasons, some unhappy couples remain married. Some are forbidden to divorce by religion, others by social custom. Still others stay together "for the sake of the children." In recent years, psychologists and sociologists have studied families to determine whether more harm is done to children by divorce or by parents who stay together despite conflict. ~~But by staying together, such parents feel~~ believing they are sparing their children the pain of divorce.

In his study of family conflict, Robert S. Weiss found that children in such families were often happiest "when Daddy is at work."

23b Standard patterns of organization

Ideas presented in no apparent organizational pattern confuse readers. To organize information within paragraphs, a topic sentence helps, but so do predictable patterns of organization; which strategy you choose depends on what you are trying to do. The following patterns are well known, so readers will follow them easily, but many other organizing ideas would work as well.

General to specific

This common paragraph pattern begins with a general statement of the main idea. Subsequent sentences contain examples that support, explain, and expand that statement.

GENERAL
STATEMENT

SPECIFIC
EXAMPLES

The evolution of the horse can be inferred from fossil evidence of related animals with progressively more sophist-cated leg structure. The earliest horse, *eohippus,* ran on four toes like many mammals. A later species, *mesohippus,* or middle horse, ran on three toes. The modern horse runs on one toe; its hoof is the toenail of the digit that corresponds to a middle finger. Vestiges of the second and fourth toes can be found above the hoof.

Specific to general

This pattern begins with a series of details or examples and culmi-nates in a general statement. Placing your general statement, or topic sentence, at the end of the paragraph allows you to build toward and emphasize your conclusion.

SPECIFIC
EXAMPLES

GENERAL
STATEMENT

As early horse species changed, so did their environ-ment, from forest to open grasslands. The tougher hooves were better on hard ground. Longer legs provided speed where there was nowhere to hide. Along with the changes in the feet came changes in teeth to shift from chewing leaves to grinding grasses and grain. *The fossil record shows the horse's ancestors adapting to their changing habitat.*

Chronological order

Events are sometimes best presented in the order in which they happened. The topic sentence, or general statement, can appear at the beginning or the end of the paragraph.

EVENT 1
EVENT 2

EVENT 3

EVENT 4

GENERAL
STATEMENT

Before the arrival of Europeans, Haiti was populated by the Arawak tribes. Within fifty years after Columbus set foot on the island in 1492, the Arawaks had nearly died out, victims of disease and enslavement. The Spanish colonists imported blacks from Africa to replace the natives as slaves on their plantations. Late in the seven-teenth century, the island was ceded to France but was the subject of dispute among England, Spain, and France for decades before achieving independence. *The population of Haiti today, predominantly black and French-speaking, reflects that history.*

Consider using reverse chronological order—moving backward from the most recent events to the most distant. This can be an effective way to reflect on the past.

Climatic order

To draw readers in and build toward a conclusion, begin with a general statement, present specific details in order of increasing importance, and end with a dramatic statement or prediction.

GENERAL STATEMENT

SPECIFICS OF INCREASING IMPORTANCE

CLIMAX

Consider the potential effect of just a small increase in the earth's atmospheric temperature. A rise of only a few degrees would melt the polar ice caps. Rainfall patterns would change. Some deserts might bloom, but lands now fertile might turn to desert. Many hot climates could become uninhabitable. *If the sea level rose only a few feet, dozens of coastal cities would be destroyed, and life as we know it would be changed utterly.*

Spatial order

The details in a descriptive paragraph can be ordered so that the mind's eye moves from one concrete object to another. The topic sentence, here a general statement summarizing and interpreting the details, can appear at the beginning or the end.

SPECIFICS ARRANGED SPATIALLY

GENERAL STATEMENT

Above the mantelpiece hung an ancient wheel-lock musket that gave every indication of being in working order. A small collection of pewter, most of it dating from the colonial period, was arrayed across the mantel. To the left of the hearth stood a collection of wrought-iron fireplace tools. At the right, a brass hopper held several cut limbs of an apple tree. On an iron hook in the fireplace hung a copper kettle, blackened with age and smoke. *The fireplace looked as if it had changed little since the Revolution.*

23c Coherent paragraphs

Paragraphs are coherent—literally, they "stick together"—when each sentence relates appropriately to the surrounding ones. Your writing will be more coherent if you join choppy paragraphs by using transitional expressions, shorten overly long paragraphs, and deliberately repeat key words.

Transitional expressions

Many words and phrases can indicate that one idea expands, exemplifies, qualifies, specifies, summarizes, implies, causes, or results from another. Other terms can compare or contrast ideas or show relationships in time and space. **Transitions** smooth out shifts in ideas. Without its transitional expressions, the following paragraph would be a string of seemingly unrelated facts.

> Newspaper and magazine publishing is not usually regarded as cyclic, *but* the recent recession cut deeply into advertising revenue. As the economy gathers steam, classified-ad buyers should return, *although* display advertising will lag. *Meanwhile,* publications that have already sharply cut their costs should see profits taking a strong upturn as advertisers return. *For them,* the coming year looks rosy.

The changes you make when restructuring paragraphs for unity, organization, or length often mean adding new transitional expressions. In this paper on divorce, the writer added two new transitional sentences.

◆ During a divorce, parents have the ability to shield a child from potential harm. Many couples who stay together believe that the two-parent structure is crucial to the child's well-being. This, however, appears not to be the case. A child's security is based on his or her relationship with each parent individually, according to studies by Judith Wallerstein, who found that a stable, caring relationship between a child and each parent is the most significant ingredient in a child's emotional health. Maintaining even one stable relationship appears to reduce the effect of divorce on a child's emotions. The issue during a divorce, then, is how well a child can maintain at least one secure relationship. During the early stages of a breakup, both parents are often distracted by other issues. The child may suffer as a result.

Revising paragraph length

A very long paragraph may strain readers' attention. A string of very short paragraphs, on the other hand, can seem choppy and make ideas appear disconnected. Look for places where several small paragraphs develop what is really one idea, and join them together.

Deliberate repetition

Words or phrases, repeated sparingly, link sentences and help your ideas stick together. Deliberately repeating key words keeps the writing focused, making it easier for readers to follow your thoughts. Notice how the key words, in italics, echo the topic of this paragraph.

The *controversy* over the proposed Northgate Mall has continued for at least five years. The *dispute* has divided the city into two camps. A small group seems *opposed* to the mall, but its members are vocal and energetic. The *opponents* maintain that the mall would rob trade from existing businesses downtown and contribute to traffic congestion. *Proponents* say that the growth it would bring would be easily manageable.

Substituting similar words (*dispute* for *controversy*) prevents the repetition from becoming monotonous.

A deliberate repetition can also create a rhythmic effect.

◆ When ~~s~~he read to me, I ~~could see~~ *and* *saw* faraway islands fringed with coconut palms. ~~With~~ *She read to me, and with* Jim Hawkins, I shivered in the apple barrel while the pirates plotted. *She read to me, and* I ran with Maori warriors to raid the villages of neighboring tribes. *She read to me, and* I heard Ahab's peg leg thumping on the deck overhead, and I marveled at the whiteness of the whale.

Make sure that any element you repeat deserves the emphasis you give it and that any rhythmic effect you create is appropriate to your subject and your audience.

TRANSITIONAL EXPRESSIONS

TO EXPAND

also, and, besides, finally, further, in addition, moreover, then

TO EXEMPLIFY

as an illustration, for example, for instance, in fact, specifically, thus

TO QUALIFY

but, certainly, however, to be sure

TO SUMMARIZE OR CONCLUDE

and so, finally, in conclusion, in short, in sum, therefore, this shows, thus we see

TO SHOW LOGICAL RELATIONSHIPS

as a result, because, by implication, for this reason, if, since, so, thus, therefore, this shows that

TO COMPARE

also, as well, likewise, similarly

TO CONTRAST

although, but, despite, even though, nevertheless, on the other hand, yet

TO SHOW RELATIONSHIPS IN TIME

after, before, between, earlier, formerly, later, longer than, meanwhile, since

TO SHOW RELATIONSHIPS IN SPACE

above, adjacent to, behind, below, beyond, in front of, nearby, next to, north (south, east, west) of, opposite to, over, through, within

226

SUGGESTIONS FOR USING TRANSITIONAL EXPRESSIONS

Here are some guidelines for deciding when to use a transitional expression.

◆ Use transitions to warn readers of shifts in thought that they may not expect. For example, a contrast or contradiction is often unexpected and needs a transition.

> The film's plot is very predictable, and the characters are not especially likable. *Nevertheless,* the movie is worth seeing.

Other relationships, such as those in time and space, are often obvious from the context and do not need a transitional phrase.

> The main character of the film moves to Brazil. He *then* finds a job in a large corporation and settles into a routine.

> The *then in the second sentence signals the passage of time, but the reader can infer the sequence from the context without it.*

◆ If you use a series of transitional expressions to mark a sequence or to list points, make them parallel in form. For example, use *first, second,* and *last* to introduce three points, but not *first, in the second place,* and *the last.*

◆ Avoid beginning a series of sentences with one-word transitions. Consider omitting some transitions, or put some of the transitional expressions in the middle of sentences.

> Keeping a journal is helpful, in addition, because . . .

◆ Incorporate a variety of transitional expressions. Instead of always using *first, second,* and *third* to list sequences, for example, vary the fare with *for example, also,* and *finally.*

24 | STRONG OPENINGS

The first words of your paper may be the most important. Your **opening** must engage your readers, introduce your topic and your main idea, and point toward what you intend to say. In a short two- or three-page essay, one paragraph may suffice to open; in longer papers, you may have a page or two to play with.

Techniques for openings   24a

The following techniques, along with many others, make openings more engaging.

Opening with a thesis statement

Many opening paragraphs in college papers start with a broad general statement, narrow the focus, and end by stating the thesis, as in the following paragraph (thesis statement in italics).

> Anxiety, stress, and tension exist in us all. At worst, too much stress can cost us our lives. At the very least, it jeopardizes our health. *The most effective way to control stress and live more comfortable lives is to use techniques for relaxation.*

Opening with a striking assertion

Make a statement so improbable or far-reaching that the reader will demand to see how you support such an assertion.

> John Milton was a failure. In writing *Paradise Lost*, his stated aim was to "justify the ways of God to men." Inevitably, he fell short of accomplishing that and only wrote a monumental poem. Beethoven, whose music was conceived to transcend Fate, was a failure, as was Socrates, whose ambition was to make people happy by making them reasonable and just. The inescapable conclusion seems to be that the surest, noblest way to fail is to set one's own standards titanically high.
> —Lawrence Shanies, "The Sweet Smell of Success Isn't All That Sweet"

Opening with an anecdote

Try telling a brief story, no more than a paragraph or two, about someone or something that introduces, sets up, and illustrates the thesis of the whole paper.

> Once I met a woman who grew up in the small North Carolina town to which Chang and Eng, the original Siamese twins, retired after their circus careers. When I asked her how the town reacted to the twins marrying local girls and setting up adjacent households, she laughed and said: "Honey, that was nothing compared to what happened before the twins got there." Get the good gossip on any little mountain town, scratch the surface and you'll find a snake pit!
> —Francine Prose, "Gossip"

Opening with an interesting detail, statistic, or quotation

Plunge readers into an unfamiliar but provocative situation to pique their curiosity.

> "Mrs. Tolstoy is your basic L.O.L. in N.A.D., admitted for a soft rule-out M.I.," the intern announces. I scribble that on my patient list. In other words, Mrs. Tolstoy is a Little Old Lady in No Apparent Distress who is in the hospital to make sure she hasn't had a heart attack (rule out a myocardial infarction). And we think it's unlikely that she has had a heart attack (a soft rule-out).
>
> If I had learned nothing else during my first three months of working in the hospital as a medical student, I learned endless jargon and abbreviations.
>
> —Perri Klass, "She's Your Basic L.O.L. in N.A.D."

Opening with a provocative question

Introduce your paper with a question. After a few sentences of background information, pose the question that you will later answer, explore, or reflect upon.

> Many children spend more than five hours a day watching television when they could be reading or playing outside. What effect does television have on these kids? At what levels do those effects appear? In other words, how much TV is too much?

24b Edit opening paragraphs with special care

Because your introduction gives readers their first impression, pay special attention to every sentence in your opening paragraphs. Rewrite to eliminate unnecessary words (*it is a fact that, it is interesting to note that*), empty phrases (*first and foremost, last but not least*), and clichés (*the early bird gets the worm; if you don't like the weather, wait five minutes*)—all of which make for dull reading. Avoid broad generalizations you've heard too often, which put readers to sleep (*society is a rat race; the liberal arts provide a well-rounded education*).

WRITING STRONGER OPENINGS

Examine your opening paragraphs for unnecessary words, over-generalizations, or clichés that may distract your readers. The following advice will help you strengthen your openings.

◆   **Be direct.** Get to the point without rambling. Phrases like *it is a fact that, it appears that,* and *it has come to my attention that* keep the reader from engaging with your essay. During editing, pare away loose or empty phrases and clauses that don't serve your writing goals.

◆   **Sharpen your focus.** Opening statements that are too broad or obvious may fail to engage readers. Opening statements can be general, but they should also help readers know immediately what you are talking about. When editing, limit generalizations carefully, and use the strongest as a springboard to your thesis.

◆   **Emphasize the main idea.** Your opening should quickly establish your main idea. Anything that leads away from this idea confuses readers about the goals of your paper. When editing, place your thesis statement in a prominent position in the paragraph, and include only those points that appear later as crucial supporting details.

THOUGHTFUL CLOSINGS

An effective concluding paragraph leaves readers satisfied with the discussion and gives them something to think about or act upon. It also reminds readers of your main idea or thesis. You can develop a statement or restatement of the main idea in one of several ways.

Closing with a rhetorical question   25a

A **rhetorical question** is not really a question at all, but an answer framed as if it were a question. In posing such a question, the writer believes all reasonable readers will arrive at the same answer—which, of course, the paper has outlined in full. It's a strong persuasive strategy, pretending to let the reader answer a question to which there's only one answer.

Drug violence will continue as long as citizens tolerate the easy availability of guns on the streets; as long as the public shells out money for violence glorified in television and film; as long as drug users, deprived of effective treatment, pour money into disadvantaged neighborhoods. *How can society sit by and do nothing?*

25b Closing with a genuine question

In papers that pose real problems or ask difficult questions, it's fair to end realistically by stating honestly that you don't have all the answers.

Drug addition and the violence it creates seem almost impossible to stop. As soon as one dealer is put away, two come to take his (or her) place. Why do so many young people risk their lives in this dirty business? Because there's so much money to be made and because making it seems so easy. *So, do we solve this problem with better enforcement of existing laws? Do we spend more on education? Or do we give in and simply make the stuff legal and regulate it that way?*

25c Closing with a concise summary

Repeat the important points in the paper.

The tasks are urgent and difficult. Realistically, we know we cannot abolish crime. But we can abolish—as a nation, not just state by state—capital punishment. We can accept the fact that prisoners, convicted criminals, are hostages to our own human failures to develop and support a decent way of living. And we can accept the fact that we are responsible to them, as to all living beings, for the protection of society, and especially responsible for those among us who need protection for the sake of society.
—Margaret Mead, "A Life for a Life"

25d Closing with a call to action

Use your powers of persuasion to mobilize readers to action.

Until the SAT is reformed or abolished, those students who score low on the test will suffer. They will have a hard time getting into many colleges, even though they may have what it takes to succeed. The emphasis on the test distracts high school students from things that are also important to admission decisions, such as writing ability, grades, course load, and extracurricular activities. *It is time for those who care about justice to see that this system is fixed.*

Closing with speculation 25e

Imagine the future if the action you propose is—or is not—taken.

> Someday, perhaps, a democratic account of the physiology of sex will be written, an account that will stress both the functional and organic aspects of reproduction.

WRITING STRONGER CONCLUSIONS

An effective conclusion summarizes, but it should do something more. This is your last chance to speak to your readers. What do you most want them to remember? When editing, focus on the single most important idea and try to take it a step further.

◆ **Be direct.** Wordiness can undermine the authority of your final sentences and weaken your message. Use transitional phrases—*in conclusion, all in all,* or *to sum up*—sparingly, if at all; your readers should recognize your conclusion without them. Many qualifying phrases—*I think* or *I believe,* for example—are also unnecessary because readers assume the ideas in your paper are your own. Use such phrases when you need to distinguish your conclusions from someone else's.

◆ **Focus.** When editing, check to see that your concluding statements or questions do, in fact, fulfill the promises you made at the beginning of your paper. Also make sure you have not asked or answered a question your paper didn't pose in the first place.

◆ **Review.** If you have revised parts of your paper by adding new research or branching out in directions that differ from your first draft, make sure the conclusion you may have written earlier still holds. New beginning or middle material usually means a new conclusion is in order, too.

26 | POWERFUL SENTENCES

Reading a paper in which all the sentences are the same kind and length, and in which each does not clearly relate to the next, is tedious. Early drafts sometimes come out this way as writers concentrate on what they're saying, but not how effectively they're saying it. However, if you understand how sentences are constructed, it's easy to edit them into patterns more likely to please readers than bore them. This chapter introduces the basic **sentence types** (simple, compound, complex). Then it examines how those types emphasize the equality of ideas (**coordination**), or a hierarchy of ideas (**subordination**), or a similarity of ideas (**parallel structure**).

26a Types of sentences

Do you remember learning sometime in seventh grade to identify sentences by type: simple, compound, complex, and combinations of compound complex? Just knowing these labels doesn't help you write any better, but learning which type creates what effect does indeed.

A typical **simple sentence** is short. It contains few words. It is direct. It doesn't allow for any wandering around. It is simple. It contains a single thought. Technically, a **simple sentence** has a single independent clause (at least a subject and a verb; more commonly a subject, a verb, and an object).

subject verb

John ran.

subject verb   object

John hit a home run.

Simple sentences are especially easy to follow, so they are especially effective for young children's books and for technical writing (*Insert tab A into slot B*). However, they are tedious to read, one after the other (see the paragraph above). Short simple sentences are effective for emphasis following a series of longer sentences.

Thankfully, most northern trees aren't dead in winter. They still burn energy, maintaining life, but little goes on in the way of growth. It's just too cold.

A **compound sentence** contains two or more simple sentences (or independent clauses) combined within one sentence by joining words such as *and, but,* and *or.* Technically, compound sentences contain two or more independent clauses joined either by a comma and a coordinating conjunction (see the box on page 217) or by a semicolon.

independent clause   independent clause

~~John ran far, but he didn't run very fast.~~

   independent clause   independent clause

~~Pollution is a problem; however, it won't go away soon.~~

Compound sentences speed up reading and imply a close relationship between or among the ideas contained within the sentence.

A **complex sentence** also contains at least one simple sentence, hence, at least one simple thought. But it contains additional language that, to some extent, complicates that thought, making it deeper or broader or more tentative or comprehensive. Technically, a complex sentence has one independent clause and one or more dependent clauses.

independent clause   dependent clause

~~John ran as if he were dreaming or lost in thought.~~

A complex sentence, allowing as it does for more variety, depth, and qualification of expression, is the predominant medium of academic thought, so its many forms need to be studied, practiced, and mastered. (Most of the sentences in this book are complex in one way or another).

A **compound-complex sentence** is usually a long sentence including both compound and complex clauses in the same sentence.

John ran as if he were dreaming or lost in thought, his pace hardly faster than a brisk walk, <u>but</u> actually he was carefully counting the number of cracks in the sidewalk.

Few writers consciously worry about the type of sentences that express their ideas, especially in early drafts. However, when editing, they often modify their sentences one way or another to best reach their readers.

26b Coordinating equal ideas

Use the principle of **coordination** to suggest that ideas are roughly equal. Joining separate simple sentences into compound sentences is a way of showing that several related ideas are equally important and the reader must pay attention to both (or all).

To join two or more thoughts together in a compound sentence, use one of the following techniques.

Coordinating conjunctions

The most common method of joining independent clauses uses a **coordinating conjunction**—*and, or, nor, for, but, yet, so*—and a comma. Each coordinating conjunction expresses a different relationship, so be sure to choose the right one for the meaning you intend.

◆ Incoming students must pass a placement examination to meet the

foreign language requirement. ~~Those who fail the test~~ *, or they* must register

for an introductory language course.

Correlative conjunctions

Another way to coordinate two independent clauses is by using a pair of **correlative conjunctions** such as *both . . . and, either . . . or,* or *not only . . . but also.*

◆ *not only* Lavar won high honors in mathematics and physics. ~~He~~ *, but he* was also

recognized for his achievement in biology.

Conjunctive adverbs

A **conjunctive adverb** such as *however, moreover,* or *nevertheless* used with a semicolon can also join two independent clauses.

◆   An Advanced Placement Test score will be accepted/~~However,~~ the
                                                           ; however,

test must have been taken within the last year.

COORDINATING CONJUNCTIONS, CORRELATIVE CONJUNCTIONS, AND CONJUNCTIVE ADVERBS

RELATIONSHIP	COORDINATING CONJUNCTIONS	CONJUNCTIVE ADVERBS
addition	and	also, besides,
contrast	but, yet	furthermore,
choice	or, nor	moreover, however,
effect	so	instead, nevertheless,
causation	for	otherwise, likewise,
		similarly,
		accordingly,
RELATIONSHIP	CORRELATIVE CONJUNCTIONS	consequently,
addition	both . . . and	therefore, thus, finally,
choice	not only . . . but also	meanwhile, next, then,
substitution	either . . . or	certainly, indeed
negation	not . . . but	
	neither . . . nor	

Coordinating related ideas   26c

Skillful coordination can connect ideas and enhance readability. When you edit, look for places where your use of coordination sends a confusing message to your readers.

Illogical coordination

Because coordination implies equal relationships, avoid using coordination where the ideas are not equally important or the meaning of the two sentences is not related closely enough to warrant joining them.

> I made eggs for breakfast, and I missed the bus.
>
> *Is a cause-and-effect relationship intended? If so, the coordinating conjunction* and *does not make this relationship clear. If the breakfast preparations did not cause the writer to miss the bus, the two sentences are not related; in that case they should not be joined.*

Faulty coordination can connect ideas in a way that is not only confusing but inaccurate.

♦ The project was a huge undertaking, ~~yet~~ *so* I was exhausted at the end.

The conjunction yet *implies contrast, but that is not what the sentence means. The conjunction* so *states the proper cause-and-effect relationship.*

When the relationship between two ideas is apparent, a semicolon alone can join two independent clauses.

♦ Taking an introductory language course will fulfill the foreign language requirement. ~~The~~ *; the* courses are offered during the fall semester.

Overused coordination

Too much coordination begins to sound like baby talk. How much is too much? If a sentence with several coordinate structures seems weak, decide which elements belong together and which should stand alone. The following paragraph, for example, could be edited like this.

♦ Coordination can be overdone, ~~and when~~ *. When* it is used too much, it begins to sound repetitive, ~~and readers~~ *. Readers* may begin to imagine the voice of a child speaking in sentences that go on and on, strung together with *and*, ~~and soon~~ *; soon* they may get confused or bored, ~~so as~~ *. As* a writer you should try to prevent that.

26d Hierarchy of ideas (subordination)

Use the principle of **subordination** to emphasize one idea and de-emphasize (subordinate) another (or others) within a single sentence. Place the most important idea in a sentence last, for that is the place of greatest emphasis. To illustrate, look at these two ideas presented as separate simple sentences, neither given more weight than the other.

John Playford collected seventeenth-century music. He was an English musician.

To emphasize Playford's activity as a collector (first sentence), subordinate his nationality (second sentence) by embedding it in the middle of the sentence in a phrase set off by commas.

> John Playford, an English musician, collected seventeenth-century music.

To emphasize Playford's nationality, subordinate his activity by placing it in the middle of the sentence in a phrase set off by commas.

> John Playford, who collected seventeenth-century music, was an English musician.

When editing, if you find two related sentences with one more important than the other, put the less important sentence into a subordinate structure.

NO SUBORDINATION   John Playford was an English musician. He collected seventeenth-century music and descriptions of popular dances in a book called *The English Dancing Master.*

SUBORDINATION   John Playford was an English musician who collected seventeenth-century music and descriptions of popular dances in a book called *The English Dancing Master.*
Emphasizes the identification of Playford.

SUBORDINATION   John Playford, an English musician, collected seventeenth-century music and descriptions of popular dances in a book called *The English Dancing Master.*
Emphasizes what Playford did.

A subordinate element may appear as a clause, a phrase, or a single word. The less important the element is grammatically, the less attention the reader pays to it.

NO SUBORDINATION   The campaign manager wrote a plan. It seemed to cover every major contingency.

238

CLAUSE	The plan *that the campaign manager wrote* seemed to cover every major contingency.
PHRASE	The plan *written by the campaign manager* seemed to cover every major contingency.
WORD	The *campaign manager's* plan seemed to cover every major contingency.

A **dependent** or **subordinate clause,** one that contains a subject and a verb but cannot stand alone as a full sentence, is usually introduced by a **relative pronoun** such as *who, whom, which, what,* or *that* or a **subordinating conjunction** such as *although, because, if, since, whether,* or *while.*

Relative pronouns

Common relative pronouns include *that, what, which, who,* and *whom.* The clauses they introduce usually modify nouns or pronouns, so they are called **adjective clauses.**

◆ The gap between rich and poor _^ *, which has been widening for twenty years,* has caused great concern among social thinkers. ~~The gap has been widening for over twenty years.~~

You can also subordinate a sentence by using it as a subject or as an object. Such **noun clauses** can be introduced by *why, what, that, where, whether,* or *how.*

◆ *What we know today* ~~There are a few basic facts~~ about AIDS ~~we know today. They are~~ *is* the result of years of painstaking research.

SUBORDINATING CONJUNCTIONS

RELATIONSHP	SUBORDINATING CONJUNCTIONS
cause/effect	as, because, since, so, so that, in order that
condition	if, even if, if only, unless
contrast	although, even though, though
comparison	as if, as though, than, whereas, while
choice	rather than, than, whether
sequence	after, as, as long as, as soon as, before, once, since, until, when, whenever, while
space	where, wherever, whence

Subordinating conjunctions

Using a subordinating conjunction makes the dependent clause an **adverb clause.**

USING SUBORDINATING CONJUNCTIONS

◆   As the name suggests, subordinating conjunctions introduce subordinate, or dependent, clauses. In formal writing, a clause that begins with a subordinating conjunction should not stand alone because it would be considered a sentence fragment. Be sure to connect the clause beginning with a subordinating conjunction to a main or independent clause.

◆   When you use *whereas, while, although, though,* or *even though* in a dependent clause to contrast or concede something, do not use *but* before the independent clause.

> *Although* a smile shows happiness in most cultures, ~~but~~ in some it may be a sign of embarrassment.

◆   When you use *because* or *since* in a dependent clause to describe a reason or cause, do not use *so* in the independent clause.

> *Because* Rudolf Nureyev defected from Russia, ~~so~~ for many years he could not return to dance in his native country.

◆   *Because* and *because of* are not interchangeable. *Because* is a subordinating conjunction. Use it when your subordinate idea is expressed as a clause, with a subject and a verb.

> subject   verb
> *Because* snow peas die in hot weather, you should plant them in early spring.

> *Because of* is a two-word preposition. Use it when your subordinate idea is expressed as a *phrase,* with no verb.

> phrase
> *Because of* the hot weather, the snow peas did not grow well.

◆   Used by itself, *even* is not a subordinating conjunction. *Even though* is a subordinating conjunction meaning "despite the fact that."

> though
> *Even* I don't play well, I still enjoy taking piano lessons.

Even if is a subordinating conjunction meaning "whether or not."

> if
> Even it rains tomorrow, the race will be held.

◆ The campaign plan has a chance of success. ~~It needs~~ careful execution by many people.

if it receives

The clause introduced by if *modifies* has.

26e Effective subordination

Choose the subordination strategy that best expresses the relationship you intend between two ideas.

Illogical subordination

Subordinating the wrong element in a sentence changes the meaning of what you want to say. Watch for illogical subordination that may confuse readers.

INDEPENDENT SENTENCES	Scientists have carefully examined this theory. Some have criticized it.
INCORRECT SUBORDINATION	Some scientists who have criticized this theory have carefully examined it.
	This sentence inadvertently implies that some opponents have not been so careful.
CORRECT SUBORDINATION	Some of the scientists who have carefully examined this theory have criticized it.

Look also for subordination that suggests causal relationships you do not intend.

◆ The nation was plunged into a deep recession ~~when~~ Ronald Reagan took office in 1981.

that began shortly after

The writer did not mean to imply that Reagan's election caused the recession.

Overused subordination

If you believe you have subordinated too much, first find the ideas that are most closely related and leave the subordination you have there. Then edit the more distantly related ideas into independent sentences.

◆ Sometimes you may create passages that rely too much on subordi- *. This makes* nation, ~~which can make~~ them sound insipid ~~because every~~ *. Every* point seems to be qualified, while nothing is said directly.

SENTENCE FLOW

If every idea goes in a separate simple sentence, your writing will be choppy and disjointed. Carefully choosing coordination or sub-ordination can make your ideas flow better.

COORDINATION TO COMBINE SENTENCES
Use coordination to connect equally important ideas and to give your sentences weight and balance.

and
To generate electricity, utilities burn tremendous quantities of coal. ~~Another~~
, but many
~~fuel widely used is oil.~~ ~~Many~~ utilities also operate hydroelectric dams.

SUBORDINATION TO COMBINE SENTENCES
Use subordination to emphasize central ideas.
Although they are quite different restaurants,
Zoë and Match have both become popular within the past year. ~~They are quite different restaurants.~~ To succeed in New York, a restaurant should
Customers will respond best if it sets *excels*
not emulate a certain style. ~~It must set~~ its own style and ~~excel~~ at it.
~~Customers will respond best to that.~~ Zoë and Match accomplish this goal.
even though they
~~They~~ do it in different ways.

Parallel structures   26f

Parallelism is essentially the repetition of a grammatical structure within a sentence or paragraph to highlight a comparison or to emphasize a main point: words paired with words, phrases with phrases, clauses with clauses. Parallel constructions are powerful because of their repetitious rhythm and because they are easy to remember. In the following examples, notice how the parallelism creates a pleasing rhythm when you say the sentence aloud.

WORDS   We saw the frogs swimming, jumping, and splashing.

PHRASES   Of the people, by the people, for the people

CLAUSES   Where there's smoke, there's fire.

Compound elements

Compound elements can be joined by a coordinating conjunction (*and, or, nor, for, but, yet,* or *so*). Such elements should be grammatically parallel to avoid confusing readers.

- They spent their time praying and ~~work~~ working with the poor.

Compound elements can also be joined by correlative conjunctions (*either . . . or, neither . . . nor, not only . . . but also, both . . . and, whether . . . or*).

- Wind-generated electric power is not only difficult to capture, but also ~~it must be stored at great expense.~~ expensive to store.

Comparisons

When you use *than* or *as* in comparisons, set up equivalent alternatives that are parallel in grammatical form.

- Laura likes painting as much as ~~to read.~~ reading.

- He always believed that effective communication was more a matter of thinking clearly than ~~to try to write~~ writing well.

Lists

Elements presented in a series or list joined with *and* or *or* are also parallel in grammatical form.

- Her favorite activities were painting, walking, and ~~she liked to visit~~ visiting museums.

26g Effective parallelism

Few devices achieve greater power, gravity, and impact than the formal, rhythmic, and forceful words of parallel constructions. Use such constructions to highlight a comparison or to emphasize a main point.

♦   With local leaders afraid of the "no growth" label, the quality of local

decision making has clearly declined. The question facing towns like

Abilene is ~~whether they will do enough planning to avoid uncontrolled~~

~~development.~~

(handwritten annotation: not whether they will plan to have no growth but whether they will face growth with no plan.*)*

> *The addition of* not whether . . . but whether *and,* no growth . . . no plan *makes the conclusion more resonant.*

Many writers repeat parallel structures to create a rhythmic effect.

> To die, to sleep. To sleep, perchance to dream.
> —William Shakespeare, *Hamlet*

Good parallelism helps make comparisons clear. Edit ambiguous parallel structures in which the elements are not similar in form.

Also watch for words omitted from parallel structures: prepositions (*to, for, at*), subordinating conjunctions (*although, since, because*), and relative pronouns (*who, which, what*).

♦   The researchers tried to ensure that interviewees were representative

of the campus population and their opinions reflected those of the

whole student body.

(handwritten annotation: that*)*

> *Without the additional* that, *it is unclear whether the clause beginning with* their opinions *refers to the researchers or the interviewees.*

 ## 27 | CONCISE SENTENCES

Most academic, business, and technical writing should convey information clearly and efficiently, to help the reader understand without undue effort. Edit near-final drafts to express ideas plainly with no wasted words. Write directly and concisely, and you'll avoid being imprecise, wordy, obscure, or confusing. Writing concisely takes careful editing. Some writers call this process "boiling down," the way a cook turns large quantities of thin broth into a smaller quantity of hearty soup.

27a Vague generalities

Generalizations are broad statements without specific detail that express large concepts and abstractions—components especially necessary to academic writing. Sometimes, however, writers make too many general unsupported statements that have been repeated so often they pack no power: *It is our duty to take responsibility for our actions.* (How many times have you been told that?)

Other times the generality is so widely accepted that stating it seems silly: *Shakespeare is a great writer.* (Yes?)

Some generalities indulge in circular reasoning: *During the harsh winters of the 1870s, the weather was very cold.* (*Harsh* implies that.)

Others announce that a point is going to be made but don't make it: *Many factors played a part in the Bush victory.* (What factors?)

Although generalities can occur anywhere, look particularly at your openings and conclusions, where you may be trying hard to impress. Look for the obvious and edit it out.

◆ Fetal alcohol syndrome affects one of every 750 newborn babies. ~~It is clearly not good for them,~~ causing coordination difficulties, malformed organs, small brains, short attention spans, and behavioral problems.

27b Idle words

People use many extra and unnecessary words when they talk, the idle and empty words masking the speaker's search for meaningful words to say next. So, too, with writers of first drafts, who digress and explore in loose language on their way to finding out what they really want to say, more precisely, in a subsequent draft. After reading the previous two sentences, do you need further evidence of the effects of idle words? What can you do to rid your writing of this problem?

◆ To edit ~~very~~ wordy drafts, test each ~~and every~~ word to see if eliminating it tightens the expression ~~and makes it more concise~~ or changes its meaning. If the meaning is ~~ultimately~~ unchanged, ~~consider~~ cutting it. *the unneeded words.*

Automatic phrases   27c

Phrases like *in my opinion, it has come to my attention that,* and *due to the fact that* contribute nothing to a discussion. They are a writer's "throat-clearing." These automatic phrases often appear at the beginnings of sentences, but look for them anywhere. When you find an automatic phrase, remove it and reread the passage. If no meaning is lost, leave it out. If some meaning seems to be missing, try condensing the phrase.

◆   ~~In this day and age~~ children ~~in many instances~~ know more about

     Today,   *often*

    black holes than they do about Black Beauty.

Wordy phrases   27d

Vague, abstract nouns—*area, aspect, factor, kind, manner, nature, tendency, thing,* and *type*—may signal that wordiness is afoot. Often you can delete imprecise phrases, condense them, or find more concrete substitutes. If you ever write a sentence like *One of the factors that gave them problems in the lab was the tendency toward contamination,* change it swiftly to something more direct: *Contamination was a problem in the lab* or *The lab was contaminated.*

Useless modifiers   27e

Writers often use modifiers such as *clearly, obviously, interestingly, undoubtedly, absolutely, fortunately, hopefully, really, totally,* and *very* to make a sentence sound forceful or authoritative. In truth, a sentence usually sounds more direct and stronger if these adverbs are taken out and the verb stands by itself.

◆   These intensifiers ~~clearly~~ add ~~very~~ little, and they can ~~hopefully~~ be

    deleted.

Redundancy   27f

Public speakers are often advised, "Tell them what you're going to say; say it; then tell them what you said." In speaking, repetition helps listeners understand. In writing, however, where readers are able to reread, slow down, and pause as they please, repetition is redundant unless it serves other purposes—to create emphasis and rhythm, for instance. As you edit, evaluate each instance of repetition. Ask whether the repetition links ideas, sustains an established rhythm, or prevents confusion. If not, cut it.

◆ The general consensus ~~of opinion~~ among students was that the chancellor had exceeded her authority.

Consensus *means a generally held opinion.*

If you find yourself repeating the same word or using a similar one, look for ways to eliminate one of them.

◆ About ninety percent
~~A very high percentage~~ of the prison's inmates take advantage of the special education program ~~about ninety percent.~~

CHECKLIST OF REDUNDANT PHRASES

first ever	refer back
first and foremost	basic fundamentals
full and complete	initial preparation
past history	terrible tragedy
round in shape	final result
red in color	free gift
general consensus of opinion	true facts
a faulty miscalculation	completely destroyed

Elliptical constructions   27g

By omitting words that readers can be expected to supply for themselves, an elliptical construction helps avoid unneeded repetition. Such constructions are usually used in the second part of a parallel construction, where the first verb is implied for the second as well.

◆   Her words suggested one thing, her actions ~~suggested~~ another.

Pretentious language   27h

It is tempting, when you want to sound authoritative, to use technical, obscure, or ornate language. When such language is needlessly complicated or overinflated, it is called **pretentious.** Pretentious language uses two or three words where one would do, relies on the third-person point of view, and uses the passive voice. Edit such constructions to find concrete subjects for your verbs and address your readers more directly; rewriting is usually in order as crossing out existing language is seldom enough.

ORIGINAL   The range of diagnostic audiovisual services provided includes examinations to determine optical or auditory impairment.

EDITED   We offer eye and ear examinations.

248

> **CHECKLIST OF PRETENTIOUS LANGUAGE**
>
> Look for constructions such as these, and when you find them, change them accordingly.
>
> | PRETENTIOUS | MORE CONCISE |
> | --- | --- |
> | incarcerated offenders | prisoners |
> | client populations | people served |
> | voiced concern that | said, worried |
> | range of selections | choices |
> | minimizes expenditures | saves money |
> | of crucial importance | important, crucial |
> | institution of higher learning | college, university |

27i Euphemisms

A **euphemism** is an inoffensive word or phrase deliberately substituted for one considered harsh or indelicate. Our conversations are full of euphemisms, especially those that deal with money, death, sex, and body functions. Workers are fired in massive layoffs, but the company calls it *downsizing.* People whose grandmother has died say, "*I lost my grandmother*" or *She has passed away,*" and so on.

In academic writing, you strive to inform, not to obscure, but you must balance directness with your audience's comfort. If in doubt, ask a peer or an instructor to check your choices.

28 STRONG VERBS

Verbs make things happen. They make the subjects (nouns) of sentences *race, run, erupt, scoot, shoot, dive, fly, climb, sprawl, meander, wonder,* and *ponder* toward one end or another and, in the process, make your writing come alive. Write with strong verbs, and readers will stay with you.

Replace static verbs with action verbs   28a

Verbs drive sentences the way an engine powers a car. **Action verbs**—verbs that denote specific actions—add horsepower to your writing. **Static verbs** that show no action—*be, appear, become, seem, exist*—can leave your sentences underpowered. As you edit, replace static verbs with action verbs when you can.

◆   The outer suburbs of Los Angeles ~~are in~~ *sprawl onto* the hills beyond the San Fernando Valley.

◆   This problem will soon ~~become evident.~~ *erupt.*

A form of *be* preceding a phrase or a clause often signals a stronger verb coming up. For a stronger, more emphatic sentence, make this verb the main verb of the sentence.

◆   The most effective writers ~~are those who~~ write as though they are simply talking.

Stronger verbs are often hidden in parts of sentences beginning with constructions such as *there are, there is,* and *it is.* In these cases, turn the verb of the clause into the main verb of the sentence. This can often be done simply by deleting words, not adding new ones.

◆   ~~There are many~~ *Many* people ~~who~~ believe that Elvis Presley is still alive, even though ~~it is~~ only the tabloids ~~that~~ take such "news" seriously.

Avoid weak action verbs   28b

Not all verbs that describe action spark clear images. Verbs such as *do, get, go, have, make,* and *think* are more general than specific and so do not create mental pictures. As you edit, watch for weak action verbs and substitute stronger verbs where possible.

◆   He ~~makes~~ *bakes* good sourdough bread.

◆   She ~~has a wonderful singing voice.~~ *sings wonderfully.*

250

Often a verb that relies on other words for its descriptive power can be replaced with a more effective one.

- He ~~walked quickly~~ *scurried* from the room.

28c Change nouns back to verbs

Many English verbs have been changed into useful nouns with the help of a suffix—*announce* to *announcement* or *tempt* to *temptation*, for example. Nouns made from verbs (called **nominalizations**) often bury the real action of a sentence. To make matters worse, these nouns usually require a static verb—*have, do, make,* or *be.* As you edit, dig up the buried verbs to resurrect your point.

- Few biographies of FDR ~~have given a satisfactory explanation of~~ *satisfactorily explained* the Yalta conference.

To enliven your writing, replace these common expressions with the action verbs buried within them, making your sentences both more direct and concise.

CHANGING NOUNS TO VERBS

NOMINALIZATION	BURIED VERB
put forth a proposal	propose
hold a discussion	discuss
formulate a plan	plan
reach a decision	decide
arrive at a conclusion	conclude
hammer out an agreement	agree
hold a meeting	meet
call a strike	strike
make a choice	choose

28d Change passive voice to active

A person or thing (subject) acting (verb) on something (object) is the most natural, economical, and direct form of English expression:

subject, verb, object. The person or thing performing the action is the subject; the action word is the verb; the receiver of the action is the object. In this kind of sentence, the verb is said to be in the **active voice**.

Actor/subject   active-voice verb   direct object (recipient of action)

Juana   collects   the tickets.

When a verb is in the passive voice, the recipient of the action becomes the subject. Passive-voice sentences are less economical and less direct and take longer for readers to understand.

subject of action   passive-voice verb   agent of action

The tickets   are taken   by Juana.

Advantages of the active voice

By focusing on the actor, the active voice helps readers visualize what happens and who does it. Active-voice sentences usually use fewer words and have a more direct effect than passive-voice sentences. (The sentences in this paragraph and the majority throughout this book are in the active voice.)

Advantages of the passive voice

The passive voice de-emphasizes the actor and highlights the recipient of the verb's action—an effect you may choose for selected occasions.

To stress results

A $500 million reduction in the national debt was approved by Congress.

To leave the agent unstated

The city's first homeless shelter was established in a vacant warehouse.

To create the impression of objectivity

The samples were tested for bacteria.

29 SPECIFIC NOUNS AND MODIFIERS

Compare the mental pictures you get from the phrases *an old car* versus *a dented, badly rusted metallic blue Dodge minivan.* The first phrase evokes the abstract category *cars* but supplies no specific image; the second phrase shows a specific, concrete car for readers to visualize and identify. When sentences contain specific identifiable "characters" such as the *blue Dodge minivan,* they tell small stories that readers recognize and enter into.

Abstract words refer to ideas and concepts that cannot be perceived by the senses: *transportation, wealth, childhood, nutrition.* **Concrete words** name things that can be seen, felt, heard, tasted, or smelled: *dime, child, broccoli, cement.*

General words refer to categories and groups: *pets, stores, teachers, cars.* **Specific words** identify objects or people: *Rover, hardware store, history teacher, sport utility vehicle, 1959 Buick.*

29a Concrete, specific nouns

We would be unable to think, speak, or write about literature, constitutionality, or music without terms to name these abstract ideas. However, writing that relies exclusively on abstractions seems to have no substance. To give form, shape, and life to abstract and general ideas, look for specific details and examples to support them.

◆ The party ~~was awesome.~~

Halloween featured carving pumpkins and dipping apples in hot caramel.

29b Specific modifiers

Choose **modifiers** (words and phrases that describe nouns and verbs) that are specific and concrete. Choose modifiers that appeal to the any of the reader's five senses: *red peppers, whispered words, hot stove, sweet peaches, oily skin.*

However, some descriptive modifiers have become empty and meaningless through overuse. Be wary of writing any of these too often: *pretty, dull, dumb, nice, beautiful, good, bad, young, old, great, fantastic, terrible, awesome, awful.* The intensifier *very* can be one of the worst offenders.

◆ Madeline was a ~~very pretty~~ girl with ~~nice~~ brown eyes.

smooth-skinned laughing

30 | THE RIGHT WORD

The English language has a particularly rich vocabulary. The place you live, for instance, might be your *house, home, residence, abode, dwelling, domicile, habitation, quarters, lodging, apartment, pad, place, shack, spot,* or *digs.* It's your job as a writer to find the right word to convey your meaning.

The dictionary and the thesaurus   30a

All writers rely on dictionaries and thesauruses to supplement their internal vocabulary and to guide them in their use of language. If you consult these books regularly, your word skills and your writing will improve. The following tips are useful for all writers.

The dictionary

An **unabridged dictionary** offers the most comprehensive listing of words in American English plus information on word origins, definitions, and usage. Examples include *Webster's Third New International Dictionary,* with 470,000 entries, and the 615,000-word *Oxford English Dictionary* (commonly called the *OED*). A searchable edition of the *OED* is now available on CD-ROM.

An **abridged dictionary** omits less frequently used words and some obsolete or archaic definitions. The *American Heritage Dictionary* (2nd college ed.), *Merriam-Webster's Collegiate Dictionary* (10th ed.), and the *Random House Webster's College Dictionary* are good for everyday use.

The thesaurus

A **thesaurus** (the word comes from the Greek for "treasure") lists synonyms for each entry. Many thesauruses list antonyms as well. A thesaurus can help you find the right word for a particular context or level of formality. *Roget's Thesaurus of English Words and Phrases* lists words by concept. *Roget's 21st Century Thesaurus* lists words alphabetically, with a concept index.

To find the word that best expresses the meaning you wish to convey, place each word in the context of your sentence and assess it. When the thesaurus suggests a word you are unfamiliar with, be sure to look it up in the dictionary as well.

254

WHAT'S IN A DICTIONARY ENTRY?

Most dictionaries follow the format found in the tenth edition of *Merriam-Webster's Collegiate Dictionary.*

```
① ENTRY WORD   ② PRONUNCIATION        ③ PART OF SPEECH LABEL
                                       ④ INFLECTED FORMS
```

com•mu•ni•cate \ kə-'myü-nə-,kāt \ *vb* **-cat•ed; -cat•ing** [L *com-munications*, pp. of *communicare* to impart, participate, fr. *communis* common — more at MEAN] *vt* (1526) **1** *archaic* : SHARE **2 a** : to convey knowledge of or information about : make known ⟨ ~ a story⟩ **b** : to reveal by clear signs ⟨his fear *communicated* itself to his friends⟩ **3** : to cause to pass from one to another ⟨some diseases are easily *com-municated*⟩ ~ *vi* **1** : to receive Communion **2** : to transmit infor-mation, thought, or feeling so that it is satisfactorily received or under-stood **3** : to open into each other : CONNECT ⟨the rooms ~⟩ — **com•mu•ni•ca•tee** \ -,myü-ni-kə-'tē \ *n* — **com•mu•ni•ca•tor** \ -'myü-nə-,kā-tər \ *n*

⑤ DERIVATION

⑥ DEFINITIONS

1. The **entry word** appears in bold type. Bars, spaces, or dots between syllables show where the word can be hyphenated. If two spellings are shown, the first is more common, although both are acceptable. If two spellings are dissimilar, entries are cross-referenced: **gaol** (jal) *n Brit. sp. of* JAIL. A superscript numeral before an entry indicates that two or more words have identical spellings.

2. **Pronunciation** is spelled phonetically, set in parentheses or between slashes. (The phonetic key is at the bottom of the page.) If two pronuncia-tions are given, the first is more common, although both are acceptable.

3. **Parts-of-speech labels** are set in italic type. The abbreviations are *n* for noun, *vb* for verb, *vt* for transitive verb, and so forth.

4. **Inflected forms** are shown, including plurals for nouns and pro-nouns, comparatives and superlatives, and principal parts for verbs. Irregular spellings also appear here.

5. The **derivation** of a word that has roots in other languages is set between brackets or slashes (*OE* and *ME* = Old English and Middle English, *L* = Latin, *Gr* = Greek, *OFr* = Old French, *Fr* = French, *G* = German, and so on).

6. **Definitions** appear with major meanings numbered and arranged from the oldest to the most recent or from the most common to the least common. An example using the word may be enclosed in brackets.

◆ **Synonyms** or **antonyms** may be listed, often with comments on how the words are similar or different.

(continued)

◆   **Usage labels** are used for nonstandard words or meanings.

archaic: from a historic period; now used rarely if at all

colloquial (coll.): used informally in speech or writing.

dialect (dial.): used only in some geographical areas

obsolete (obs.): no longer used, but may appear in old writings

slang: highly informal, or an unusual usage

substandard (substand.): widely used but not accepted in formal usage

British (Brit.), Irish, Scottish (Scot.), and so on: a word used primarily in an area other than the United States. Some dictionaries use an asterisk to mark Americanisms.

◆   **Usage notes** may follow definitions. They may also comment on acceptability or unacceptability.

Roots, prefixes, and suffixes   30b

Roots, prefixes, and suffixes provide substantial clues to a word's meaning. A **root** is a base word, or part of a word, from which other words are formed: *mile* in the word *mileage*.

A **prefix** is a group of letters attached to the beginning of a root that changes its meaning: *un-* in *unfinished*. The word prefix itself consists of a root, *-fix*, which means "attach," and a prefix, *pre-*, meaning "before." A **suffix** is a group of letters attached to the end of a root: *-age* in *mileage*.

Both prefixes and suffixes change the meaning of the root to which they are attached. For example, the words *antebellum, bellicose,* and *belligerent* share the root *bellum*, Latin for "war." If you already know that belligerent means "warlike or at war," you might guess that antebellum means "before war."

Denotations and connotations   30c

The **denotation** of a word is its direct, literal meaning. *Fragrance, odor, smell,* and *stench* denote the same thing: a perception detected by your olfactory sense. But the associations, or connotations, of the words differ. *You have a distinct fragrance* suggests a pleasant smell while *You have a distinct odor* suggests an unpleasant one.

The associated or indirect meaning of a word is its **connotation.** The connotations of your words affect the meaning you convey, so consider them when you edit. You might say that the filmmaker Ingmar Bergman is *concerned* or *fascinated* with childhood, but you might not want to say that he is *obsessed* with it. Edit carefully to eliminate unintended connotations.

30d Idiomatic expressions

Why do we ride *in* a car but *on* a train? Why do we *take* a picture but *make* a recording? Such conventional—that is, widely accepted—speech patterns are called **idioms,** patterns that may not follow rules of logic or grammar.

Prepositions—*at, by, for, in, on, out, to,* and so on—show a relationship between a noun or a pronoun and other words in the sentence. The only guide to the correct use of prepositions with nouns and verbs and in standard expressions about time and space is to trust your ear—what expressions do you most often hear?—and learn that common idioms sometimes differ from the conventional rules of grammar.

This novel shows a great similarity *to* that one. The similarity *of* [or *between*] the stories is remarkable.

I will meet *with* you in the evening, *at* sunset.

Particles—such as *up, down, out, in, off,* and *on*—look like prepositions, but they combine with verbs to form **phrasal verbs,** or two-word verbs. Both the verb and the particle are needed to convey the meaning of a phrasal verb, which may be quite different from the meaning of the verb alone. The meanings of these phrasal verbs moved away from the original meaning of the verb *to come.*

How did this *come about?* (*happen*)

When did the question *come up?* (*When was it raised?*)

Of course, I expected things to *come out* all right. (*end*)

I was unconscious for a moment, but I soon *came to.* (*revived*)

When editing, check your use of idiomatic expressions, and whenever you are in doubt, consult a dictionary.

COMMON PHRASAL VERBS AND THEIR MORE FORMAL ALTERNATIVES

Remember, while informal spoken English may utilize phrasal (verb plus prepositions) forms, academic writing is more formal and therefore should utilize the single verb when possible.

VERB	MEANING
bring up	raise or educate someone
build up	make stronger
call off	cancel
catch up (with)	meet someone at a prearranged place *or* exchange news and/or gossip
check out	do research *or* appraise someone's looks
come up with	create
cut down	reduce
figure out	discover or determine something
find out	discover
get away	leave (suggests difficulty or obstacles)
get back	return
get in	arrive *or* enter
get out	leave
get over	recover from
get rid of	eliminate
get up	arise *or* stand
give up	quit, stop *or* discontinue
go up and down	fluctuate
gone up	increased
grow up	become an adult
help out	assist
keep up	continue *or* stay in pace with someone
let down	disappoint *or* break a promise
look into	investigate
look up	find facts (for example, a phone number) *or* plan to visit someone when on a trip or in a different place

(continued)

make up	pretend or invent *or* apologize after a fight *or* offer a rain check for plans canceled or changed
pick up	get or collect *or* meet someone at a party or bar
point out	tell *or* inform
run out	come to the end
set up	establish
settle down	relax
show off	look for attention *or* admiration
show up	appear
sign up	register
slow down	relax *or* become slower
take off	start *or* make free time
try out	test something *or* audition (for example, for a role in a play)
turn down	refuse a suggestion or invitation *or* decrease (for example, the volume on a radio or television)
turn off	disgust *or* stop from working (relax)
turn on	attract or arouse someone
turn up	increase (for example, volume on a radio or television) *or* to visit unexpectedly
work out	exercise *or* solve a problem

30e Slang, regionalisms, and colloquialisms

Everyone uses **slang,** informal language that originates in and is unique to small groups such as students, musicians, athletes, or politicians. Some slang words eventually enter the mainstream and become part of standard English. A *jeep* was originally slang for a *general purpose (g. p.)* military vehicle used in World War II. Now it is the brand name of a four-wheel-drive vehicle driven by many Americans.

Regionalisms are expressions used in one part of the country but not common elsewhere. The name for a carbonated beverage, for example, varies by region from *pop* to *soda* to *soft drink* to *seltzer.* Some bits of regional dialect are regarded as **nonstandard,** that is, not widely used in academic writing.

A **colloquialism** is an expression common to spoken language but seldom used in formal writing. For example, the noun *pot* can mean "a cooking vessel," "marijuana," "the amount of money bet on a hand of cards," and "ruination" (as in "go to pot").

Use slang words, regionalisms, and colloquialisms sparingly in academic writing. They may not be understood, and their informality may imply a lack of rigor, discrimination, or care on your part. They can, however, convey immediacy and authenticity in descriptions and dialogue.

PRESCRIPTIVE VERSUS DESCRIPTIVE GRAMMAR

Much of the grammar you have studied reflects the *prescriptive* approach to language, that is, a set of rules that prescribes or tells a speaker or writer how to use the language correctly. However, there is a large gap between the prescriptive grammar that you know and the language as you hear it used around you, called *descriptive* grammar—grammar that describes the way people actually interact and use the language.

Thus, you will hear people saying things like *There's* some *donuts on the table* instead of *There are* some donuts on the table. This discrepancy simply reflects the difference between the way people speak (informal and colloquial language) and the way they write (more formal and careful wording).

Focus on keeping your writing more formal even as you try to learn some of the more informal uses of language so that you can sound more like a native speaker when you talk.

Jargon   30f

Every profession or field develops terms to express its special ideas. Such specialized or technical language is called **jargon.**

As you edit, decide whether all your terminology will be understood by your audience. Using fewer technical terms helps you communicate better with a general audience, but a specialized audience expects you to use technical language appropriately. For example, for what kind of audience would you substitute *femur* for *thigh bone* or vice versa? Avoid jargon added merely to make your writing sound important.

JARGON   It is incumbent on us to challenge the prevailing proposition that theoretical approaches are the most enlightened ways of introducing students to literary experience.

EDITED   Students learn to appreciate literature better by reading it for themselves than by reading about how to read it.

30g Figurative language

Figurative language, which likens one thing to another in imaginative ways, brings freshness and resonance to writing. When well done, figurative language, often in the form of comparisons and analogies, can help readers gain insight better than any other language.

One of the most common problems writers have is inadvertently juxtaposing incongruous images. A **mixed metaphor** combines two or more unrelated images, often with unintended effects. When you find a mixed metaphor in your writing, eliminate the weaker one and extend the more appropriate one.

◆   We must swim against the tide of cynicism that threatens to ~~cloud~~ *drown* ~~our vision~~ *our hope* of a world without hunger.

Swim/tide/drown/hope make a more consistent metaphor of water images and, therefore, a clearer image than the mixed images of *swim/tide/cloud/vision.*

30h Clichés

Our language is full of overused, worn-out expressions called **clichés.** The word itself, interestingly, is a metaphor. *Cliché* is a French word for the sound a stamping press makes in a process of making multiple, identical images. In other words, something has become a cliché if it no longer causes the audience to think about it.

the last straw	needle in a haystack
as strong as an ox	handwriting on the wall
better late than never	tried and true
lay your cards on the table	hit the nail on the head
a drop in the bucket	best thing since sliced bread

To edit a cliché, try improving on it. Go back to the original image and describe it in new words or add fresh details.

◆   Outside, the wind ~~howled~~. *keened as though it had lost a child.*

If you can't revive it, replace the cliché with a direct statement of what you are trying to say.

◆   It was ~~dark as night~~ inside the cave. *so dark that we waited in vain for our eyes to adjust.*

SOME COMMON FIGURES OF SPEECH

Examine these examples of figurative language, and consider using some of these strategies in your own writing.

◆   A **simile** is a comparison that explicitly expresses a resemblance between two essentially unlike things, using *like, than,* or *as.*

German submarines swam the seas *like* sharks, suddenly seizing their prey without warning.

◆   A **metaphor** implicitly equates one thing with another.

Her life *became a whirlwind* of design meetings, client conferences, production huddles, and last-minute decisions.

◆   An **analogy** uses an extended comparison to show similarities in structure or process.

The course catalog at a large university *resembles a smorgasbord.* Courses range from differential calculus to American film, from Confucianism to liberation theology. Students receive little advice as to which classes are the salads, which the desserts, and which the entrees of a college education. Even amid this feast, a student risks malnutrition.

◆   **Personification** is the technique of attributing human qualities or behavior to a nonhuman event or phenomenon.

The ship sailed into the *teeth* of the hurricane.

◆   Deliberate exaggeration is called **hyperbole.**

No book in the world is more difficult than this economics text. Reading it is *absolute torture.*

◆   The opposite of hyperbole is deliberate **understatement.**

With temperatures remaining below zero all day, it will seem *just a bit chilly* outside tomorrow.

(continued)

262

- **Irony** is the use of words to mean the opposite of what they seem to mean on the surface.

  "Houseguests for three weeks? *Terrific.*"

- A **paradox** contains a deliberately created contradiction.

  For a moment after she spoke, the *silence was deafening.* Then the audience erupted in cheers.

31 | UNBIASED LANGUAGE

Nothing reveals ignorance and prejudice more quickly than people's spoken and written language. Using a generalization about a group of people to predict, describe, or interpret the behavior or characteristics of an individual in that group is both insensitive and illogical. Careless generalizations based on race, ethnicity, gender, cultural background, age, physical characteristics, or lifestyles are called **stereotypes.**

Whether they refer to gender, race, ethnicity, or sexual preference, stereotypes are oversimplified generalizations. Positive or negative, they substitute a simplistic formula for an appreciation of individual differences and the richness of human variation.

31a Recognizing stereotypes

Many stereotypes stem from ignorance and from fear of people who are perceived as "different." These stereotypes often penetrate our language both in descriptions of people (*liberal politician*) and in descriptive images (*sleepy Southern town*). Calling a doctor or a lawyer *he* reinforces the stereotype that all doctors and lawyers are men.

Edit your writing to eliminate stereotypes. Qualify broad generalizations, and support or replace sweeping statements with specific factual evidence. In some cases, drop the stereotypical observation altogether.

- Like most ~~teenage~~ *inexperienced* drivers, he was reckless.

- ~~Like so many of his race,~~ Michael Johnson is a superbly gifted athlete.

- Frank Peters, now in his late seventies, ~~but still alert,~~ remembers the dry, hot summer of the big forest fire.

ELIMINATING STEREOTYPES

As you edit, ask these four questions.

1. Have I relied more on stereotypes than on evidence to make my point? Are all "African Americans good dancers"?

2. Do my generalizations follow logically from factual evidence? Is it true that "students these days can't write"? (You know the truth of this one.)

3. Do my generalizations about a group improperly label individuals? Can I assume that my Canadian classmate "must be a soccer fan" simply because soccer is a popular sport in Canada?

4. Have I used euphemism to mask a stereotype? Is a wife "a wonderful asset to her husband" or something more in her own right?

Choosing group labels   31b

People often label themselves in terms of the groups to which they belong. However, labels inevitably emphasize a single feature of a person's identity, ignoring other characteristics. They may also offend people who do not want to be so characterized. Furthermore, many labels go beyond simple identification and become explicitly or implicitly derogatory. As you edit, examine any labels you have used; try to use only those acceptable to the members of the group themselves, and avoid labels with negative connotations.

Using a group's own labels

Even though members of a particular group may not agree on what they should be called, whenever possible, refer to such a group by the label most of its members prefer. Labels sometimes move quickly into or out of favor as they acquire unintended connotations, so be sure to check current practice.

Designations of race, ethnicity, and nationality

The terms *black* and *African American* refer to those people who used to be called *Negro* or *colored.* Some spokespeople and many of the media have adopted the term *African American* as both an adjective and a noun. *People of color* is another widely accepted term for this group, but it is sometimes used more broadly to include all non-Caucasians.

The terms *Asian* and *Asian American* have begun to replace *Oriental* for people of Asian ancestry, although some individuals and groups prefer to use a specific country of origin: *Japanese, Korean, Malaysian, Chinese.* To refer to national origin or ancestry, using a specific country is always correct.

Today some Americans of Spanish-speaking heritage refer to themselves as *Hispanics* while others prefer *Latino* and *Latina,* and some Mexican Americans, *Chicano* and *Chicana.* Some *Native Americans* prefer that term to *Indian,* but using the name of the tribe or nation is often a better choice: *Navajo, Lakota Sioux, Seneca.* Some *Inuit* prefer that term to *Eskimo.*

If the religion of a particular group has relevance in your writing, use the preferred terms; for example, a follower of Islam is a *Muslim.*

Designations of gender and sexual orientation

Most adult women prefer to be called *women* rather than *girls* or *ladies. Girls* is particularly inappropriate in reference to salespeople, administrative staff, or those in service jobs.

When writing about sexual orientation, keep in mind that people have widely different views about the role of sexuality in our personal and public lives. Be aware that not everyone may share your perspective, and consider using a group's own chosen term. *Heterosexual, homosexual, bisexual,* and *transgendered* are descriptive rather than evaluative words that are generally accepted.

Designations of ability

People with physical limitations often prefer *disabled* to *handicapped;* others prefer different labels.

Designations of age

Modern American culture does not extol old age, and even accepted terms can describe it bluntly or condescendingly. Think about using *senior citizens* rather than *the elderly.* If a person's age is critical to what you want to say, cite the person's actual age: *68-year-old.*

Checking labels for negative connotations

Some labels that on the surface seem neutral hide negative connotations. For example, the term *AIDS victims* implies that such people are blameless, which you may intend, but also that they are helpless, which you may not. As you edit, watch for such unnecessary or unintended negative connotations, and substitute more neutral alternatives. Because neutral phrases can be cumbersome, they are easily mocked as too "politically correct"—implying that you are using the term only because it's expedient rather than a strong personal belief. Here are two general rules to follow.

- Focus on people's strengths: people *live with* cancer, or they are cancer *survivors* rather than *suffering* from the disease.

- Focus on the person first and the characteristic or condition second: *a woman who is quadriplegic,* not *a quadriplegic.*

Using nonsexist language   31c

When you use words that embody sexual stereotypes, you run the risk of alienating half—or more—of your potential audience. Gender bias can arise from unexamined habits of thought and language.

Pronoun choice

Until recently, *he, him,* and *his* were used generically to refer to singular nouns or pronouns when the gender of the antecedent was unknown, unstated, or irrelevant: *Anyone who believes those promises should have his head examined.* Such usage is disappearing because many people believe that the general *he* excludes women.

However, English does not have a singular personal pronoun of indefinite gender to match the gender-neutral plural pronoun *they.* In speaking, people often use plural pronouns to avoid the masculine forms: *Everybody had fun on their vacations.* But in a sentence with a singular subject (*everybody*), any pronoun you use later in the sentence should be singular, so you have to choose between *his* and *her.*

If you know the gender of the first reference, match it with the pronoun of the same gender: *Each nun makes her own bed.*

If you don't know the gender, choose one of these strategies.

- Make the antecedent plural and adjust other agreement problems: *All the residents make their own beds.*

◆ Use *his or her* or *he or she*: *Each resident makes his or her own bed.* Use this strategy sparingly to avoid distracting repetition.

◆ Eliminate the pronoun by restructuring the surrounding sentence or sentences: instead of *Everyone has done his part,* write *Everyone has helped.*

Universal terms

The use of *man* and *mankind* to refer to the whole of humanity seems to ignore the female half of the species. As you edit, substitute more inclusive terms such as *humanity, the human race, humankind,* or *people.*

Occupational terms

In choosing terms for an occupation, focus on the occupation, not the gender of the person who holds it. There are almost no jobs that are "naturally" held by either men or women. Avoid language that implicitly identifies an occupation with gender, that assumes all flight attendants, nurses, secretaries, or teachers to be female or all airline pilots, business executives, streetcar conductors, or bronco busters to be male.

Avoid using occupational terms with feminine suffixes: *actor/actress, author/authoress, poet/poetess, executor/executrix.* Such feminine forms have become obsolete, and the formerly male form has become neutral: *author, poet, actor,* and *executor.* Others, such as *waitress,* are changing to more inclusive terms: *server.*

Occupational terms that end in *-man* imply that everyone who does that job is male. Sex-neutral substitutes for many occupations are readily available.

CHECKLIST OF NEUTRAL OCCUPATIONAL LABELS

SEXIST	NEUTRAL
statesman	diplomat
congressman	representative in Congress, congressional representative, representative
mailman	letter carrier, mail carrier
policeman	police officer
fireman	firefighter
businessman	executive, businessperson
salesman	sales representative, salesperson

32 PROOFREADING

Proofreading is the process of finding and correcting errors before submitting your final manuscript for publication or grading. The key to proofreading is to see what is actually on the page, not what you meant to put there. Plan to proofread twice: once on the edited draft from which you will prepare your final copy and once on the final copy itself, where small pencil corrections will be acceptable.

The main business of proofreading is correcting typographical errors and errors in spelling, punctuation, and mechanics. If you often make the same kinds of errors, list them in your journal or notebook, and check for them when you do subsequent papers. The following guidelines should ensure accurate proofreading:

- ◆ **Proofread on hard copy.** If you have been composing on a computer, print out a hard (paper) copy to proofread more effectively. Errors and awkward passages are much easier to see in print on paper. Then make your corrections immediately on the computer, or enter them all at once when you finish, whichever works better for you.

- ◆ **Read your paper aloud.** Reading aloud will give you a fresh perspective and the chance to hear anything that isn't clear and natural. It will also help you to find dropped words and incorrect punctuation.

- ◆ **Ask someone else to read your paper.** A friend who is knowledgeable about English language conventions will often spot errors of omission that you, because you're so close to the writing, might overlook. If that person also reads your work aloud, you may hear problems in rhythm, construction, and meaning.

- ◆ **Read your paper backward.** Most readers become distracted by meaning when they read and thus miss their technical or mechanical mistakes. One way around this problem is to start with the last word on each page and work back toward the beginning of the page, one word at a time. Use a ruler to help you focus on a single line, or point a pencil at each word.

- ◆ **Use your computer's spelling checker.** Automatic spelling checkers, sometimes turned off as a distraction while writers are composing, will tell you when you have misspelled a conventional word by underlining (usually in red) the misspelling. But the spelling checker won't reveal a misspelling or mistyping that creates another legitimate word—such as typing *of* when you meant to type *off* or *on.* It may alert you unnecessarily when you deliberately use unconventional spelling (*ain't, gotta*), unusual plurals (*underlinings*), or foreign words. Nor will the spelling checker provide the correct spelling of proper nouns or catch errors in numbers. Therefore, proofread again *after* your computer has checked for spelling. Make sure that you have typed the words you intended, and use a dictionary to check questionable spellings.

◆ **Use your computer's grammar checker.** Grammar checkers underline (often in green) errors in grammar, punctuation, and usage. They are sometimes turned off while writers are composing, but turning them on at the final draft makes good sense. While the green underlinings will identify all sorts of unconventional errors, they also identify minor ones (extra spaces) and items that are not errors (very long sentences). Their value is in alerting you that something may be amiss, so double-check the green underlinings.

◆ **Use standard proofreading symbols.** (See the box below.) Standard symbols provide a quick and efficient way to mark up your paper for correction later. If you have more than two corrections on a page, however, redo the page.

PROOFREADING MARKS

⌒	cl⌒ose up space between two letters
#	add#space between words
∧	insert ∧these words at this point
— or ℓ	delete this unneeded material
⌐ or ℐ	delete and clo⌐se up
⌐∧ or ∧ℓ	make a cha⌐n∧ge
∼	tran∼pose letters ⌒words⌒ or⌒
≡	capitalize
/	⧸owercase
___	italicize
¶	¶ start a new paragraph

Insert missing punctuation directly following the word where it should appear. All handwritten changes to a final manuscript should be made neatly.

PART FIVE

EDITING: PUNCTUATION

Source: *The College Writer's Reference,* Third Edition, by Toby Fulwiler and Alan R. Hayakawa.

33 COMMAS

Certain forms for punctuation are conventional in written English. Using the conventions for commas, semicolons, colons, dashes, quotation marks, brackets, and periods and other end punctuation—and using them correctly—shows that you know what you're doing when you write. It also shows that you have your readers' needs in mind. Punctuation varies according to purpose, with slight differences in the conventions for academic papers, research citations, business correspondence, journalism, and advertising. The chapters in this section follow the academic conventions of the MLA (Modern Language Association), the authority for papers written in English classes.

Commas are the most frequently used punctuation in English because they signal the many different ways in which sentences are divided into parts and how those parts are related, often within the same sentence. Sometimes commas are meant to reflect pauses, but not full stops, in spoken language. Just as frequently, however, commas specify how to read, connect, and separate textual information.

Commas that connect independent clauses   33a

Use a comma between two or more **independent clauses** (clauses that could stand alone as complete sentences) when they are joined by words such as *and, or, nor, for, but, yet* or *so* (**coordinating conjunctions**) to form a compound sentence.

> We must act quickly, *or* the problem will get worse.

> The farmers ate lunch at 10:00, *and* they rested in the shade whenever they got too hot.

The comma before the conjunction may be omitted when the two sentences are very short and closely related.

> The sun rose *and* the fog lifted.

Do not use a comma without a coordinating conjunction to join independent clauses. This error is called a **comma splice.**

◆   His hobby is raising geese, *and* he proudly displays blue ribbons his gander won at the fair.

33b Commas after introductory elements

Word groups such as clauses, phrases, and expressions that introduce the main sentence (see 44b) require pauses, so a comma is in order.

> *When Elizabeth I assumed the throne of England in 1558,* the country was in turmoil.
>
> *The comma signals the end of a dependent clause explaining* when *the country was in turmoil.*

> *In every taste test,* the subjects chose the new flavor over the old.
>
> *The comma signals the end of a prepositional phrase qualifying the main sentence.*

> *His dream of glory destroyed,* the boxer died an embittered man.
>
> *The comma signals the end of the absolute phrase adding information about the boxer.*

> *Yes,* we need to improve our parks.

> *Angered,* the bull charged once more.
>
> *The comma signals a pause following brief interjections or expressions.*

> *As a matter of fact,* John knows the answer.
>
> *The comma signals the end of a transition from a previous sentence.*

However, the comma is optional when a phrase is brief and when its absence will not cause confusion.

> *In 1963* an assassin's bullet shocked the world.

> *Unfortunately* Jane will be late.

Commas that set off supplementary information 33c

A pause is in order when you include information in a sentence that is not essential (**nonrestrictive**) to its meaning. That is, if you subtracted this extra or optional information, the sentence would still make perfect sense.

> I need a lot of supplies, *including groceries and gasoline,* to get through a week in the country.
>
> *The information set off by commas (nonrestrictive) adds details to the sentence; however, if the details were omitted, the sentence would still make good sense.*

Do not use commas when the information is essential (**restrictive**) to the meaning of the sentence.

> The students *who stayed up all night* missed the exam.
>
> *This sentence implies that only the students who stayed up all night missed the exam; other students, who did not stay up all night, attended the exam.*

The meaning of a sentence changes when a modifying phrase is set off by commas, making it nonrestrictive and therefore nonessential to the meaning of the sentence.

> The students, *who stayed up all night,* missed the exam.
>
> *All the students stayed up all night and so they all missed the exam.*

If you are not sure whether a modifier is essential to your meaning, rewrite the sentence, leaving out the modifier. If the meaning does not change, the modifier is not necessary but a comma is.

Adjective clauses

Clauses that begin with *that, where, which, who, whom,* or *whose* (**adjective clauses**) can be either restrictive or nonrestrictive. *That* is used only in restrictive clauses. *Which* may be used for either nonrestrictive or restrictive clauses.

Restrictive (necessary)

> The team *that scores the most points* will receive a bronze trophy.
>
> *No options, hence no commas: only the team scoring the most points gets the trophy.*

Nonrestrictive (not necessary)

The dinner party, *which had been carefully planned,* went smoothly.
Commas are needed since the careful planning is optional information.

A clause that modifies a proper noun is almost always nonrestrictive (optional), so commas are needed.

John Glenn, *who was one of the first astronauts,* was elected to the United States Senate from Ohio.

Phrases

Phrases can be either restrictive or nonrestrictive. Once again, if the phrase restricts the meaning, do not use a comma; if it does not (is not essential), use commas.

Restrictive phrase

◆ A house destroyed by fire can smolder for days.

Nonrestrictive phrase

◆ This book, written by an authority on camping, contains valuable information.

Appositives

A noun or phrase that immediately follows a noun and renames it is called an **appositive.** It can be essential to meaning (restrictive) or not (nonrestrictive). Do not use a comma when the noun following restricts the meaning of the sentence.

Restrictive appositive

Former president *Theodore Roosevelt* was an avid big-game hunter.
There are many former presidents; the appositive Theodore Roosevelt *restricts the statement to one.*

Nonrestrictive appositive

Former president Theodore Roosevelt, *commander in chief during the Spanish-American War,* was an avid big-game hunter.

The additional identity of Roosevelt as commander in chief is not essential to the meaning of the sentence, so commas are needed.

Commas that set off parenthetical elements 33d

A **parenthetical element** is a word, phrase, or clause that interrupts a sentence but does not affect its meaning, so it is nonrestrictive and requires a comma. It may appear anywhere in the sentence and can be moved from one place to another without changing the meaning.

Surprisingly enough, none of the bicycles was stolen.

None of the bicycles, *surprisingly enough,* was stolen.

None of the bicycles was stolen, *surprisingly enough.*

Commas between items in a series 33e

A **series** consists of three or more words, phrases, or clauses that are equal in importance and grammatical form. A coordinating conjunction—*and, or, nor, for, but, yet, so*—usually precedes the final element.

Use a comma after each element in a series, including the one that precedes the conjunction.

WORDS   He studied all the notes, memos, and reports.

PHRASES   To accelerate smoothly, to stop without jerking, and to make correct turns requires skill.

CLAUSES   He reported that some economists believed the recession was over, that some believed it continued, but that most agreed a slow recovery was under way.

Although some writers, such as journalists, omit the comma between the last two items in a series, the comma is preferred in academic writing to avoid confusion.

33f Commas that separate equal modifiers

Commas separate two or more adjectives of equal weight (coordinate adjectives) that modify the same noun—*a warm, sunny day.* To test, try inserting *and* between them or reversing their order. If the resulting sentence still makes sense, you need a comma.

Commas Required

He put on a *clean, pressed* shirt.

He put on a *pressed, clean* shirt.

Commas Not Required

I found *five copper* coins.

33g Commas that set off contrast elements, tag sentences, and direct address

Use commas in all these instances where a pause would seem natural in spoken English.

Use commas around **elements of contrast,** which are words, phrases, or clauses that describe something by emphasizing what it is not or by citing some opposite condition.

The experience was illuminating, *but unnerving,* for everyone.

Jeremiah was a bullfrog, *not a toad.*

Use a comma before **tag sentences,** which are short statements or questions at the ends of sentences that express or elicit an opinion.

You received my application in time, *I hope.*

They meet every Monday, *don't they?*

Use commas to set off words of **direct address** that name the person or group to whom a sentence is directed. Such words can appear at the beginning, middle, or end of a sentence.

Lilith, I hope you are well.

That, *my friends,* is not the end of the story.

Commas with quotations   33h

Use commas to set off direct quotations from the words that identify speakers. The comma appears inside the closing quotation mark if the speaker's identity follows and before the opening quotation mark if the speaker is identified first.

◆   **"When I went to kindergarten and had to speak English for the first**

     time," writes Maxine Hong Kingston, "I became silent."

Use a question mark or an exclamation point alone, without any comma, at the end of a quoted question or exclamation.

"What does the latest survey show?" Marion asked.

Do not use commas when a quotation is preceded by *that* or when the quotation is worked naturally into the sentence.

He closed by saying that time "will prove us right."

Time "will prove us right."

Do not use commas with *indirect* discourse that uses no quotation marks.

Emerson wrote that we should trust ourselves.

Commas with numbers, dates, names, and places   33i

Counting from the right, use a comma after every three digits in numbers with five or more digits. The comma is optional in four-digit numbers.

     2700 (or 2,700)   79,087   467,391

Do not use a comma in page numbers, street numbers, zip codes, or years.

21001 Southern Boulevard

Use commas before and after the year when a date giving month, day, and year is part of a sentence.

Sachmo always said he was born on July 4, 1900, in New Orleans.

When only the month and year are given or when the day precedes the month, do not use a comma.

The war broke out in August 1914 and ended on 11 November 1918.

Commas set off a title or abbreviation following a name.

Joyce B. Wong, M.D., supervised the CPR training.

Commas separate the state from the city.

She was born in Dayton, Ohio, and stayed there.

Commas separate each element of a full address given in a sentence. The zip code does not have a comma before or after it.

Please note that my address will be 169 Elm Street, Apartment 4, Boston, MA 02116 as of July 6.

33j Commas to prevent misreading

Even when no specific rule requires one, a comma is sometimes added to guarantee a cue or pause to prevent a misreading.

A stitch in time, saves nine.

We will all pitch in, in the event of a problem.

GUIDELINES FOR USING COMMAS

As you edit, make sure you have used commas in the following places.

◆   Before conjunctions that join independent clauses.

◆   After introductory elements at the beginning of sentences

◆   To set off unneeded modifiers

◆   To set off parenthetical elements

◆   Between all items in a series

◆   Between adjectives of roughly equal weight

◆   To set off elements of contrast, tag sentences, and words of direct address

◆   With quotations

◆   To separate numbers, dates, names, and addresses

◆   To prevent misreading

EDITING MISUSED COMMAS

Commas are the most frequently used mark of punctuation and therefore the most frequently misused. As you edit, keep the following points in mind.

Eliminate single commas between subjects and verbs, between verbs and their objects, between linking verbs and their complements, or between objects and their complements. [See complements, 44b.]

◆   A season of drought,/worried the farmers.

◆   The agreement entails,/training the part-time staff.

◆   The laid-off workers seem,/surprisingly calm.

◆   The extra pay made him,/quite happy.

(continued)

Eliminate commas between the parts of compound elements.

COMPOUND SUBJECT

◆ The members of the senior class/ and their parents were invited.

COMPOUND VERB

◆ Maria quickly turned off the lights/ and locked the door.

COMPOUND OBJECT

◆ Shawan put the books on the shelf/ and the pens in the drawer.

COMPOUND COMPLEMENT

◆ The weather was unbearably hot/ and much too humid.

COMPOUND OBJECT

◆ Gina tried to save more/ and spend less.

COMPOUND COMPLEMENT

◆ The rule applies to students who have maintained their grades/ and who have paid all their fees.

Eliminate commas after an introductory phrase when the word order of the sentence is inverted.

◆ With the changing colors of fall/ comes the time for cider.

Eliminate commas after an introductory phrase that functions as the subject of the sentence.

◆ Hearing that song/ evokes warm memories.

Eliminate commas before and after restrictive modifiers or appositives.

◆ The information/ that we requested/ has arrived.

Make sure to use two commas where necessary to set off nonrestrictive modifiers; parenthetical elements, words of direct address; attributory words; elements of contrast; and dates, states, titles, and abbreviations in the middle of a sentence.

◆ This book ˄ which he has read three times ˄ is slightly tattered.

(continued)

- ◆ Carla on the other hand is always on time.

- ◆ Do you think Alex that you could hurry a bit?

Eliminate commas that separate relative pronouns or subordinating conjunctions from the dependent clauses they introduce.

- ◆ He wrote that/ home accidents are the cause of most childhood injuries.

- ◆ Our legislators have no idea how to proceed because/ we have not come to a consensus.

Eliminate commas before the first element or after the last element in a series unless another rule requires one.

- ◆ The primary colors/ are red, yellow, and blue.

- ◆ They went to London, Paris, and Rome/ on their last trip.

Eliminate commas between a final coordinate adjective and the noun it modifies and between adjectives that are not coordinate.

- ◆ His old/ blue/ boat was finally ready for the water.

- ◆ Andy bought a new/ black/ leather motorcycle jacket.

 34 SEMICOLONS

Semicolons help the reader in two ways: first, they divide one closely related independent clause from another; second, they substitute for commas in a series in which some items contain commas. Semicolons are common in formal academic writing, less common in informal writing.

34a Semicolons between clauses

Use a semicolon to join two closely related independent clauses, especially when the thought following the first clause qualifies, complements, or contradicts it. In such cases, a semicolon substitutes for a period but suggests a stronger relationship between the two thoughts.

It rained in August; the leaves turned bright red in September.

Most dogs aim to please their owners; cats don't behave that way.

If you connect related sentences with a coordinating conjunction (*and, or, nor, for, but, yet, so*) use a comma instead of a semicolon.

Most dogs aim to please their owners, but cats don't behave that way.

A semicolon may be used with a coordinating conjunction when the sentences connected are complex and contain comas.

If the weather clears, we'll leave at dawn; but if it doesn't, we won't leave at all.

34b Semicolons following transitional expressions to join two independent clauses

Use a semicolon between independent clauses joined by **transitional expressions** (*indeed, for example, on the other hand*) or **conjunctive adverbs** (*however, furthermore, therefore*).

The cat jumped out of the hat; indeed, it was an amazing leap.

Many in the community were angry; however, they lacked a strong leader.

When the transitional expression appears in the middle or at the end of the second independent clause, place the semicolon between the clauses, not following the transitional expression.

Many in the community were angry; they lacked, however, a strong leader.

Semicolons between items in a series containing commas

Use semicolons between elements in a series when at least one element of the series includes a comma.

> The candidates for the award are Darnell, who won the essay competition; Elaine, the top debater; and Kiesha, the theater director.

SEMICOLON GUIDELINES

◆   Semicolons substitute for periods, implying that two sentences are closely related.

◆   Semicolons substitute for commas when too many commas would cause confusion.

EDITING MISUSED SEMICOLONS

A few semicolons go a long way, so save them for places where they are most effective.

Eliminate semicolons that come between an independent clause and a dependent clause.

◆   Even though my head continued to hurt; we sat in the emergency room for an hour.

◆   He ran down the block to the old mailbox; where he dropped his letter into the slot.

Eliminate semicolons that come between an independent clause and a phrase.

◆   Having failed in my exasperating search of the old files and dusty records; I longed for a simpler research assignment.

Do not use a semicolon to introduce a list. Use a colon instead.

◆   It was a fine old house, but it needed work; plaster repairs, wallpaper, rewiring, paint, and a thorough cleaning.

35 | COLONS

A colon is a more forceful stop within a sentence than a semicolon. As a mark of introduction, a colon alerts the reader that the information following it will provide further explanation. The colon also has specialized uses, as explained below. The colon is a powerful and somewhat formal mark of punctuation, so use it carefully.

35a Colons as marks of introduction

Use a colon to introduce an explanation, an example, a list, or a quotation. What precedes the colon must be an independent clause (full sentence). The explanation or example that follows the colon can be a single word, a phrase, or a clause.

> He has but one objective: success.

> He has three objectives: fame, money, and power.

Do not use a colon when the list is preceded by a phrase that is not an independent clause.

◆   **His three objectives are: fame, money, and power.**

Do not use a colon when the list is preceded by the phrase *for example, such as,* or *include.*

◆   **He believes in profitable objectives, such as: fame, money, and power.**

A colon may be used in place of a period or semicolon between two independent clauses to imply that the first clause helps make sense of the one that follows.

> The budget agreement erected a wall between the mayor and the school board: the mayor controlled the money, and the board controlled policy.

Capitalization after a colon may vary. Some writers capitalize the first word after the colon when that word begins an independent clause. However, a lowercase letter after a colon is always correct.

> This year's team is surprisingly inexperienced: seven of the players are juniors and six are sophomores.

If a list introduced with a colon is set off with each item on a separate line, it is optional whether or not you capitalize the first line of each item.

> The following issues need to be taken into account before the building site is selected:
> Climate variations
> Geographical context
> Site access
> Procedure for securing building permits
> Cost of building supplies

> In packing for the camping trip I made sure to include the following:
> down sleeping bag & air mattress
> tent, ground cloth, & rope
> one pr. extra blue jeans
> shorts & swimsuit
> sneakers & sandals.

Commas are generally used to introduce quotations and identify speakers.

> As the song from *South Pacific* puts it, "You've got to be carefully taught."

However, when an independent clause precedes and introduces a quotation, use a colon.

> The song from *South Pacific* puts it well: "You've got to be carefully taught."

Use a colon to introduce a long quotation (five lines or more according to MLA) set off from the main text in block format.

35b Colons between divisions of time, biblical chapters and verses, titles and subtitles, and in business communication

Use a colon to separate the numerals expressing hours, minutes, and seconds; to separate the numerals indicating chapter and verse in biblical citations; to separate main titles from subtitles; and after salutations and memo headings in business communications.

Hours, minutes, and seconds

Court convened promptly at 9:00 a.m.

The official elapsed time for the race was 2:45:56.

Biblical citations

Isaiah 14:10

In MLA style, use a period.

Main titles and subtitles

Blue Highways: A Journey into America

Salutations and memo headings in formal correspondence

Dear Mr. Nader:

To: Doris DiGiovanni

From: Paul Nkwami

Subject: 1996 budget

EDITING MISUSED COLONS

The colon is a powerful and somewhat formal mark of punctuation, so use it carefully.

Eliminate a colon that comes between a verb and its object or complement.

◆   The menu included: fruit, salads, and soups.

Eliminate a colon that comes between a preposition and its object.

◆   This trip took her to: New Orleans, San Francisco, and Chicago.

Eliminate a colon that follows introductory or transitional expressions: *for example, such as, like, especially* and *so on*.

◆   The show included a number of unusual pets, such as: iguanas, rac-

coons, a civet, and a black widow spider.

---

36 | APOSTROPHES

The apostrophe is used primarily to show the possessive form of a noun or pronoun, to mark certain plural forms, and to indicate where a letter has been dropped in contractions.

Apostrophes to show possession or ownership   36a

To form the possessive case, add either an apostrophe and *-s* or just an apostrophe to nouns and some indefinite pronouns.

Singular nouns

Use an apostrophe and *-s* to form the possessive of any singular noun that does not end in *-s*.

Brad Pitt's new movie is his best yet.

Use an apostrophe and *-s* to form the possessive of a singular noun ending in *-s*. (If pronouncing the additional syllable is awkward, you may use the apostrophe alone.)

Don't waste the *class's* time.

The company produced *Yeats'* cycle of plays.

Plural nouns

Use an apostrophe alone to form the possessive of a plural noun ending in *-s*.

They owe her several *months'* pay.

Use an apostrophe and *-s* to form the possessive of any plural noun that does not end in *-s*.

She has long been an advocate for *children's* rights.

Compound nouns

To form the possessive of a compound noun, use an apostrophe and *-s* on only the last word.

He borrowed his *mother-in-law's* car.

The *secretary of state's* office certified the results.

Joint possession

When nouns joined by *and* form a unit that has joint possession, use an apostrophe and *-s* on only the last noun.

◆   My aunt's and uncle's party was a disaster.

However, when nouns joined by *and* are individuals with separate possession, add an apostrophe and *-s* to each noun.

◆   The documentary compared Aretha ~~Franklin~~ Franklin's and Diana Ross's early

careers

Possessive apostrophes with indefinite pronouns

Use an apostrophe to show possession with the pronouns that refer to people in general (*someone, anybody, no one, one,* and *another*). Each of these anonymous categories is capable of possessing something.

Someone's umbrella was left at the bank.

That is *no one's* business but my own.

However, do not use an apostrophe and -*s* with the indefinite pronouns that commonly refer to objects as well as people (*all, any, both, each, few, many, most, much, none, several, some,* and *such*). Use the preposition *of* to show possession with these pronouns, or use a pronoun that has a possessive form.

We will read the works *of* both.

Apostrophes to form plurals of words used as words, letters, numbers, and symbols 36b

Use an apostrophe and -*s* to form the plural of a word discussed as a word or term and to form the plural of letters, numbers, and symbols.

There are two *perhaps*'s in that sentence.

The word *occurrence* is spelled with two *r*'s.

Some children have difficulty learning to write *8*'s.

A row of ***'s marks the spot where I'm having trouble.

Note that words, numbers, and letters referred to as themselves are italicized (or underlined). The apostrophe and the final *s*, however, are not italicized.

You may use an apostrophe and -*s* for the plural of centuries and decades expressed in figures; however, the Modern Language Association recommends the letter -*s* with no apostrophe. Do not use an apostrophe when the century or decade is expressed in words.

the 60s (or the 60's)   the 1800s (or the 1800's)   the sixties

Use an apostrophe and *-s* for plurals of abbreviations ending with periods. Use *-s* alone for abbreviations without periods.

My science professor has earned two *Ph.D.'s.*

Like all politicians, she has some *IOUs* to call in.

36c Apostrophes to form contractions

A **contraction** is a word in which one or more letters are intentionally omitted and replaced by an apostrophe, such as *can't, it's, they're, 'bye.* An apostrophe can also be used to show that digits have been dropped from a number, especially a year: *the class of '99.*

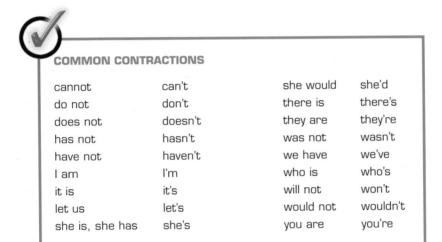

COMMON CONTRACTIONS

cannot	can't	she would	she'd
do not	don't	there is	there's
does not	doesn't	they are	they're
has not	hasn't	was not	wasn't
have not	haven't	we have	we've
I am	I'm	who is	who's
it is	it's	will not	won't
let us	let's	would not	wouldn't
she is, she has	she's	you are	you're

EDITING MISUSED APOSTROPHES

Possessives and contractions often sound alike—*whose* and *who's, its* and *it's, your* and *you're*. So do plurals and plural possessives. As you edit, be especially careful to check the placement and appropriateness of the apostrophes you use.

Eliminate apostrophes you may have used to make the possessive forms of plurals.

◆   Theirs̸ is the glory, theirs̸ the fame.

Eliminate apostrophes you may have used in forming the plural of a noun.

◆   Although they seemed like a happy family, the ~~Simpson's~~ *Simpsons* did not

always behave that way.

Make sure you have not confused a possessive with a contraction or a contraction with a possessive.

◆   ~~Your~~ *You're* late.

> *When you see a word with an apostrophe, spell out the contraction. If it is a true contraction, the sentence will still make sense:* You are late.

◆   ~~You're~~ *Your* hat looks like a biscuit box.

> *Spell out the contraction.* You are hat *is nonsense.*

◆   The accused are innocent until proven guilty, ~~its~~ *it's* aid.

> *When you see a pronoun such as* its, your, *or* their, *substitute the prepositional phrase* of it, of you, *or* of them. *If the possessive is correct, the sentence will make sense.* Of it said *doesn't make sense.*

◆   Can you hear ~~it's~~ *its* heartbeat?

> *The heartbeat* of it *does make sense.*

37 QUOTATION MARKS

Quotation marks indicate that certain words you have used in your writing are not your own. In quoting another person's exact words, either written or spoken, you must enclose those words in quotation marks and, in academic writing, indicate your source of information.

In written texts, quotation marks also distinguish certain titles, foreign expressions, and special terms from the main body of the work. American English uses double quotation marks (" ") for quotations and titles, but single quotation marks (' ')—apostrophes on most computer keyboards—for quotations within quotations (or titles within titles).

37a Quotation marks for direct quotations

When quoting another person's exact words directly, keep in mind the following two conventions for quoting short or long passages.

Short passages

Use quotation marks to enclose brief direct quotations of up to four typed lines of prose or up to three lines of poetry. Any parenthetical citation of a source goes after the closing quotation marks but before the period.

> In *Lives under Siege,* Ratzenburger argues that "most adolescents are far too worried about the next six months and far too unconcerned about the next sixty years" (84).

Use single quotation marks for a quotation within a quotation.

> After the election, the incumbent said, "My opponent will soon learn, as someone once said, 'you can't fool all of the people all of the time.'"

When quoting poetry within the body of your essay, use a slash preceded and followed by a single space to indicate line breaks.

Shakespeare concludes Sonnet 18 with this couplet: "So long as men can breathe or eyes can see, / So long lives this, and this gives life to thee."

Long passages

Set off longer quotations from the main text in **block format.** Start a new line for the quotation, indent all lines of the quotation ten spaces, and *do not use quotation marks.* If the words that introduce a block quotation are a complete sentence, use a colon or a period after them. If they are not a complete sentence, use either a comma or no punctuation, depending on the structure. Place a source in parentheses one space after the end punctuation of the quotation. Here is an example of a block quotation.

A recent editorial describes the problem:

> In countries like the United States, breast-feeding, though always desirable, doesn't mean the difference between good and poor nutrition—or life and death. But it does in developing countries, where for decades infant food manufacturers have been distributing free samples of infant formulas to hospitals and birthing centers. (*Daily Times* 17)

The editorial goes on to argue that the samples last only long enough for the mother's own milk to dry up; then the mothers find they cannot afford to buy the formula.

Use double quotation marks for a quotation within a block quotation, since the outer quotation has none.

Note that paragraph indents are not used for quoting single paragraphs or parts of paragraphs. For two or more paragraphs, indent the first line of each new paragraph after the first (use three additional spaces).

For poetry, copy as precisely as possible the line breaks, indents, spacing, and capitalization of the original, but do not use quotation marks, as the indentation signals quoted material.

In *Patience,* W. S. Gilbert has the character Reginald Bunthorne proclaim,

> This air severe
>   Is but a mere
>   Veneer!
>
> This cynic smile
>   Is but a wile
>   Of guile! (5–10)

37b Quotation marks for dialogue

Use quotation marks to set off dialogue. Using a new paragraph every time the speaker changes indicates who is speaking even without attributory words.

> "Early parole is not the solution to overcrowding," the prosecutor said. "We need a new jail."
> The chairman of the county commission looked startled and asked, "How do you propose we pay for it?"
> "Increase taxes if you must, but act quickly."

If one speaker's words continue for more than a single paragraph, use quotation marks at the beginning of each new paragraph but at the end of only the last paragraph.

37c Quotation marks for certain titles

Use quotation marks for the titles of brief poems, book chapters and parts, magazine and journal articles, episodes of television series, and songs. (Use italics or underlining for titles of longer works, such as books, magazines and journals, recordings, films, plays, and television series.)

"Araby" is the third story in James Joyce's book *Dubliners.*

This chart appeared with the article "Will Your Telephone Last?" in November's <u>Consumer Reports.</u>

In my favorite episode of *I Love Lucy,* "Job Switching," Lucy and Ethel work in a chocolate factory.

The Beatles' <u>Sgt. Pepper's Lonely Hearts Club Band</u> includes one of the most famous songs of the twentieth century, "A Day in the Life."

Do *not* use quotation marks or italics for the following.

GENERIC TITLES OF PARTS OF A WORK OR SERIES

    Chapter 6   Part II   Episode 43

TITLES OF SACRED WORKS AND ANCIENT MANUSCRIPTS

    the Talmud   the Bible

DOCUMENTS

    the Constitution   the Gettysburg Address

Use single quotation marks for quoted material that is part of a title enclosed in double quotation marks.

    We read "'This Is the End of the World': The Black Death" by historian Barbara Tuchman.

TITLES WITHIN TITLES

Use the following models when presenting titles within titles. These guidelines also apply to other words normally indicated by quotation marks or by italics, such as quotations and foreign words, when they appear in titles.

1. A title enclosed in quotation marks within an italicized (or underscored) title

    "A Curtain of Green" and Other Stories

2. An italicized title within a title enclosed in quotation marks

    "Morality in *Death of a Salesman*"

3. A title enclosed in quotation marks within another title enclosed in quotation marks

    "Symbolism in 'Everyday Use' "

4. A published title within another published title (italics for first title, underline for second title)

    Modern Critics on <u>Hamlet</u> *and Other Plays*

37d Quotation marks for special purposes

Translations

Use quotation marks around the translation of a foreign word or phrase into English. The foreign word or phrase itself is italicized.

> I've always called Antonio *fratellino,* or "little brother," because he is six years younger than I.

Special terms

Use quotation marks around specialized terms when they are first introduced and defined.

> The ecology of this "cryocore"—a region of perpetual ice and snow—has been studied very little.

> He called the new vegetable a "broccoflower," a yellow-green cross between broccoli and cauliflower.

Irony

Quotation marks may be used around a word or phrase used ironically—that is, with a meaning opposed to its literal one.

> Jonathan Swift's essay "A Modest Proposal" offers a quick "solution" to Ireland's poverty and overpopulation: eat the children.

Unusual nicknames

Use quotation marks around unusual nicknames at first mention.

> When I joined the firm, the president was a man named Garnett E. "Ding" Cannon.

37e Quotation marks with other punctuation

Which punctuation mark comes first when a word is followed by a quotation mark and another mark of punctuation? Both logic and convention govern the order.

Periods and commas

Put periods and commas inside quotation marks.

After Gina finished singing "Memories," Joe began to hum "The Way We Were."

"Denver is usually warm in the spring," he said, "but this year it's positively hot."

Colons and semicolons

Put colons and semicolons outside quotation marks.

The sign read "Closed": there would be no soda today.

In 1982, Bobbie Ann Mason wrote "Shiloh"; it is considered one of her finest works.

Question marks, exclamation points, and dashes

Put question marks, exclamation points, and dashes inside the quotation marks if they are part of the quotation, outside the quotation marks if they are not.

She asked, "Have you read 'The Tiger'?"

Was it you who asked, "Who's there?"

He began singing "Oklahoma!" and dancing.

I can't believe you've never read "The Lottery"!

"Hold on a minute. I can't hear—"

Emma's first word—"Dada"—caused Tom to beam.

298

EDITING MISUSED QUOTATION MARKS

Quotation marks are used frequently in academic writing, and they can be tricky. Examining some of their common misuses can help you as you edit your own papers.

Quotation marks are like shoes: use them in pairs. (The only exception is in extended dialogue.)

◆ "There are always a few students who boycott the assembly," he said,

"but that's no reason for us to call it off."

When quoting passages, make sure the material enclosed within the quotation marks is only quoted words. (For modifying quoted material, see uses of brackets.)

If the logic of a sentence dictates that a quotation end with a question mark or an exclamation point but sentence grammar calls for a period or comma as well, use the stronger mark (the question mark or exclamation point) and delete the weaker one (the period or comma).

◆ As soon as we heard someone shout "Fire!," we began to run for the

exit.

Do not use quotation marks to indicate emphasis. Emphasis is achieved through rhythm and sentence structure, although you may use italics for emphasis when necessary.

◆ He was guilty of a "felony," not a misdemeanor.

Do not use quotation marks for slang or for terms you think are overused. Instead, consider substituting another word or phrase.

◆ Several of these companies should go into a "hall of shame" for their

employment practices.

38 | PARENTHESES AND BRACKETS

Parentheses and brackets are marks that enclose, set aside, and remove the writer's language from the normal flow of thought within a sentence.

Parentheses   38a

Enclose elements that would otherwise interrupt a sentence: explanations, examples, asides, digressions, and supplementary information. (Since parentheses de-emphasize the material they enclose, use them carefully.)

Explanations, examples, and asides

Enclose explanations, examples, and asides within sentences or paragraphs.

> Relatives of famous people now famous themselves include Angelica Huston (daughter of John) and Michael Douglas (son of Kirk).

> Some vegetables resist light frost (pumpkins, squash) while others do not (tomatoes, peppers).

> Please define the term *postmodern*? (Good luck!)

Enclose the translation of a specialized term or foreign word.

> English also borrowed the Dutch word *koekje* ("cookie").

Dates, cross-references, and citations

Set off the date of an event or the dates of a person's birth and death.

> The Oxford English Dictionary was first published under the editorship of James A. H. Murray (1888–1933).

Use parentheses to enclose cross-references to other parts of your paper or to enclose documentation.

The map (p. 4) shows the areas of heaviest rainfall.

Nick Carraway felt unsettled to see Gatsby at the end of his dock beckoning in the direction of a "single green light" (21).

Enclose numbers or letters that introduce items in a list within a sentence.

The dictionary provides (1) pronunciation, (2) etymology, (3) past meanings, and (4) usage citations for almost 300,000 words.

Place commas directly *after* a set of parentheses.

His favorite American author is Emily Dickinson (he refers to her as "my favorite recluse"), but he also appreciates Walt Whitman.

When a parenthetical sentence is not enclosed within another sentence, capitalize the first word and use end punctuation inside the closing parenthesis.

The countess of Dia is almost forgotten today. (She was quite well known in her own time.)

When a parenthetical sentence falls within another sentence, use no period, and do not capitalize the first word.

Uncle Henry (he is my mother's brother) has won two awards for his poetry.

38b Brackets

Brackets are used to enclose words that are added to or changed within direct quotations or, in special cases, to substitute for parentheses.

Use brackets to enclose small changes that clarify the meaning of a reference or of a word or to make quoted words read correctly within the context of a sentence.

E. B. White describes a sparrow on a spring day. "Any noon in Madison Square [in New York City], you may see one pick up a straw in his beak, and put on an air of great business, twisting his head and glancing at the sky."

Brackets are used to provide supplemental information to clarify the sentence.

E. B. White describes a spring day. "Any noon in Madison Square, you may see [a sparrow] pick up a straw in his beak, and put on an air of great business, twisting his head and glancing at the sky."

Brackets are used to change a pronoun (one) *to a more specific word* (sparrow) *since the writer has taken this single sentence out of context.*

White concludes by noting that the bird "[hopped] three or four times and [dropped] both the straw and the incident."

Brackets indicate a change of tense from present to past to better suit the writer's purpose of summary.

Use the Latin word *sic* ("such") within brackets to indicate that an error in quoted material was present in the original.

In its statement, the commission said that its new health insurance program "will not effect [*sic*] the quality of medial care for county employees."

Use brackets within parentheses to avoid double parentheses.

Theodore Bernstein explains that a person who feels sick is nauseated: "A person who feels sick is not nauseous any more than a person who has been poisoned is poisonous" ("Dos, Don'ts and Maybes of English Usage" [New York: *Times,* 1977]).

Use brackets when you change the capitalization to lowercase (or vice versa) from a quotation to fit correctly into your sentences.

When Henry David Thoreau said "[t]he mass of men lead lives of quiet desperation," he actually knew little about the conditions under which most Americans lived.

PARENTHESES, COMMAS, OR DASHES?

Parentheses, commas, and dashes can all be used to set off non-essential material within a sentence. Which you use depends on how far you wish to remove the information from central attention. In many cases, the choice amounts to a writer's judgment call.

◆ Use commas when the material being set off is closely related in meaning to the rest of the sentence.

A dusty plow, the kind the early Amish settlers used, hung on the wall of the old barn.

Dashes would also work well with this example.

◆ Use parentheses when the material being set off is not closely related and when you want to de-emphasize it.

Two young boys found an old plow (perhaps as old as the first Amish settlement) hidden in an unused corner of the barn.

Dashes or commas would also work well with this example.

◆ Use dashes when the material being set off is not closely related to the main sentence and you want to emphasize it.

The old plow—the one his great-grandfather had used—was still in good working order.

This example calls strongly for dashes.

39 DASHES, SLASHES, AND ELLIPSIS POINTS

Dashes, slashes, and ellipses represent alternative ways of representing breaks and pauses within prose sentences or poetic verses.

39a Dashes

Dashes set off explanations, definitions, examples, appositives, and other supplementary information, as well as interruptions and pauses in speech. In contrast to parentheses, they call attention to the material they set off and thus emphasize contrasts.

Dashes set off explanations, definitions, examples, or appositives within and at the end of sentences.

True democrats—small "d" democrats—believe in majority rule.

We did not notice the rain—it began so softly.

Dashes emphasize contrasts.

I haven't read many novels by European writers—not to mention those by Asian or African writers.

Dashes indicate a pause, interruption, or abrupt shift in thought.

"Well, I guess I was a little late—OK, an hour late."

"It's exciting to see an eagle—there's one now!"

Dashes with other punctuation

Do not capitalize the first word of a sentence enclosed by dashes within another sentence. If the enclosed sentence is a question or an exclamation, use a question mark or an exclamation point at the end.

The twenty-first century is here—who would have thought so little has changed?

The twenty-first century—and what a century it promises to be!—is here.

Do not use commas or periods immediately before or after a dash. Dashes are especially flexible punctuation marks, capable of substituting for periods and semicolons as well as commas and parentheses in fast, informal writing. But since speed and informality are sometimes frowned upon in academic writing, use them judiciously.

Ellipsis points   39b

Ellipsis points are three periods each preceded and followed by a space. They are used to mark the deliberate omission of words or sentences from direct quotations.

Use an ellipsis to indicate an omission within a sentence.

In *Drawing on the Right Side of the Brain,* Betty Edwards tells the reader, "You may feel that . . . it's the drawing that is hard."

If you are omitting the end of a sentence, use a period or other end punctuation before an ellipsis; it will look like four dots in a row. Do not space between the last word before the omission and the period.

Edwards says, "Drawing is not really very hard. . . . You may not believe me at this moment."

Use a whole line of spaced ellipsis points when you omit a line or more of poetry.

> She walks in beauty, like the night
> . . . .
> And all that's best of dark and bright
> Meet in her aspect and her eyes.

Use ellipsis points to indicate a pause or interruption in dialogue.

"The panther tracks come from that direction . . . but where do they go after that?" he wondered.

39c Slashes

The slash (/) is a slanted line used to separate poetry quoted in text, to indicate alternative choices, and to separate figures in certain situations.
    Use a slash, preceded and followed by a space, to mark the end of a line of poetry incorporated in text.

Shakespeare opens "The Passionate Pilgrim" with a seeming paradox: "When my love swears that she is made of truth, / I do believe her, though I know she lies."

Use a slash with no space before or after to separate alternatives.

an either/or situation

a pass/fail grading system

Use a slash to separate month, day, and year in a date given entirely in figures and to separate the numerator and the denominator in a typed fraction written entirely in figures.

7/16/99

 40 END PUNCTUATION

Periods, question marks, and exclamation points tell you that a complete thought, a sentence, has ended.

Periods   40a

Use a period at the end of a statement, a mild command, or a polite request.

Use a period, not a question mark, after an indirect question (a question that is reported but not asked directly).

I wonder who made the decision.

Use a single period to end the sentence when an abbreviation containing a period falls at the end of a sentence.

Her flight leaves at 6:15 a.m.

Use a period in most abbreviations.

Mr., Mrs., Ms., in., ft., yd., mi., etc., e.g., i.e., vs.

Dr., Rev., Msgr., Mon., Tues., Wed., Atty., Gov., Sen.

Jan., Feb., Mar., St., Ave., Rd., p., para., fig., vol.

Include a space between the abbreviated letters for an author's name. This rule is especially important in documenting citations according to APA style.

E. B. White

Do not use a space after the periods in abbreviations that stand for more than one word.

U.S., U.K., B.C., A.D., B.A., Ph.D., M.D.

Do not use periods with acronyms (words formed from initials and pronounced as words) or with abbreviated names of government agencies, corporations, and other entities.

NASA, NATO, AIDS, CNN, SAT, FBI, CIA, EPA, IRS, IRA, NCAA

40b Question Marks

Use question marks at the end of direct questions. (Direct questions are usually signaled either by *what, where,* or *why* or by inverted word order, with the verb before the subject.)

Where is Times Square?   How can I get there?

Use a question mark or a period at the end of a polite request. A question mark emphasizes politeness.

Would you please sit down?

Use a question mark when a sentence ends with a tag question— one that is added at the end—even though the independent clause is declarative.

This train goes to Times Square, doesn't it?

Use a question mark for a direction question in quotation marks, even when it is part of a declarative sentence. Put the question mark before the closing quotation mark, and use no other end punctuation. (See 34e.) Do not capitalize the first word identifying the speaker after a quotation unless that word is a proper name.

"Have we missed the train?" she wailed.

Use question marks after each question in a series of questions, even if they are not all complete sentences. (Capitalization is optional, but be consistent.)

Where did Mario go? To the library? To the cafeteria? To class?

Use a question mark after a direct question enclosed within dashes.

When the phone rang—was it 7 a.m. already?—I jumped out of bed.

Exclamation points   40c

Use an exclamation point to convey emphasis and strong emotion in sentences that are exclamations, strong commands, or interjections.

Wow! It's late!   Stop the train!

In direct quotes, place the exclamation point inside the quotation marks and do not use any other end punctuation.

"Ouch!" my brother cried. "That hurts!"

Use an exclamation point after an exclamation enclosed between dashes.

They told me—I couldn't believe it!—that I'd won.

In most college writing, understatement is preferred to overstatement; use exclamation points sparingly, if at all.

PART SIX

❧ ❧ ❧

EDITING: CONVENTIONS OF WRITTEN ENGLISH

Source: *The College Writer's Reference,* Third Edition by Toby Fulwiler and
Alan R. Hayakawa.

41 SPELLING

The conventions that govern spelling and the use of capital letters, hyphens, italics, numbers, and abbreviations help readers understand your meaning. The conventions that govern the preparation of every document, whether a two-page essay or a business letter, are equally important since a reader's first impression is often based on what a document looks like.

English spelling seems sometimes to defy reason. As the English language has borrowed and then absorbed words from other languages, it has assumed or adapted the spellings of the originals. Thus, pronunciation is often not a good key to spelling. The same sound may be represented in different letter combinations—such as with the long *e* sound in *meet, seat, concrete, petite, conceit,* and *piece.* Conversely, the same letter or letter combination can represent different sounds—such as the *a* in *amaze,* the *g* in *gorgeous,* and the *ough* in *tough, though,* and *through.*

Commonly confused words   41a

Homonyms

Homonyms are words with the same sound but different meanings: *great/grate, fair/fare.* Be especially careful when spelling similar-sounding words. It is particularly easy to confuse contractions with their homonyms—*it's* for *its* and *their* for *there* or *they're.*

One word or two?

Some words can be written as one word or two, and the form that is used can make a difference in meaning.

Similar spellings

Words spelled and pronounced alike are easy to misspell.

advice (noun)   human (of people)
advise (verb   humane (merciful)

312

breath (noun)   personal (pertaining to a person)
breathe (verb)   personnel (employees; staff)

chose (past tense)   perspective (angle of view)
choose (present tense)   prospective (in the future)

device (noun)   prophecy (noun)
devise (verb)   prophesy (verb)

HOMONYMS AND OTHER SIMILAR-SOUNDING WORDS

accept (receive)   always (at all times)
except (leave out)   all ways (all methods)

access (approach)   ascent (climb)
excess (too much)   assent (agree)

adapt (change)   assure (convince)
adopt (choose)   ensure (make certain)
                                 insure (indemnify)
affect (influence)
effect (result; bring about)   bare (uncovered)
                                 bear (carry; the animal)
allot (assign, distribute)
a lot (a large amount)   bazaar (market)
                                 bizarre (weird)
allude (suggest)
elude (escape)   birth (childbearing)
                                 berth (place of rest)
allusion (suggestion)
illusion (deception)   board (plank; food)
                                 bored (drilled; uninterested)
already (previously)
all ready (completely prepared) born (given birth to)
                                 borne (carried)
altar (church table)
alter (change)   break (smash, split)
                                 brake (stopping device)
altogether (entirely)
all together (all in one place) canvas (fabric)
                                 canvass (examine)

(continued)

capital (city; wealth)
capitol (building)

censor (prohibit)
censure (blame)
sensor (measuring device)

cite (mention)
site (place)
sight (vision)

coarse (rough)
course (way, path)

complement (make complete)
compliment (praise)

conscience (moral sense)
conscious (aware)

council (committee)
counsel (advice; adviser)

cursor (computer marker)
curser (swearer)

dairy (milk-producing farm)
diary (daily book)

dessert (sweet food)
desert (dry land)

dissent (disagreement)
descent (movement downward)

dual (having two parts)
duel (fight between two people)

dye (color)
die (perish)

elicit (draw forth)
illicit (improper)

eminent (noteworthy)
imminent (impending)

everyday (ordinary)
every day (each day)

exercise (activity)
exorcise (drive out)

fair (just; average; bazaar)
fare (food; fee)

faze (disturb)
phase (stage)

formerly (at an earlier time)
formally (according to a pattern)

forth (forward)
fourth (follows *third*)

forward (to the front)
foreword (preface)

gorilla (ape)
guerrilla (fighter)

hear (perceive)
here (in this place)

heard (perceived)
herd (group of animals)

heroin (drug)
heroine (principal female
    character)

(continued)

314

hole (opening)
whole (entire)

holy (sacred)
wholly (entirely)

immigrate (come in)
emigrate (leave)

its (possessive of *it*)
it's (contraction of *it is*)

know (be aware)
no (negative, not yes)

lead (metal)
led (guided)

lesson (instruction)
lessen (reduce)

lightning (electric flash)
lightening (making less heavy)

maybe (perhaps)
may be (could be)

meat (food)
meet (encounter)

miner (excavator)
minor (person under a given
    age)

pair (two)
pear (fruit)
pare (peel; reduce)

passed (went by)
past (an earlier time)

peace (absence of war)
piece (part, portion)

peer (look; equal)
pier (pillar)

plain (simple; flat land)
plane (flat surface; smooth off;
    airplane)

pray (ask, implore)
prey (hunt down; what is
    hunted)

principle (rule)
principal (chief, chief person;
    sum of money)

quiet (silent)
quite (really, positively, very
    much)

rain (precipitation)
reign (rule)

right (proper; entitlement)
rite (ritual)

road (path)
rode (past of ride)

scene (setting, stage setting)
seen (perceived)

sense (perception)
since (from that time)

shone (past of shine)
shown (displayed)

(continued)

sometime (at some time)	waist (middle of the torso)
some time (an amount of time)	waste (squander)
stationary (not moving)	weak (feeble)
stationery (writing paper)	week (seven days)
straight (not curved)	wear (carry on the body)
strait (narrow place)	where (in what place)
tack (angle of approach)	weather (atmospheric
tact (sensitivity, diplomacy)	conditions)
	whether (if, in case)
taut (tight)	
taught (past of teach)	which (what one)
	witch (sorceress)
than (word of comparison)	
then (at that time)	whose (possessive of *who*)
	who's (contraction of *who is*)
their (possessive of *them*)	
there (in that place)	write (inscribe, record)
they're (contraction of *they are*)	wright (builder)
	right (correct)
threw (past of *throw*)	
through (by way of)	your (possessive of *you*)
	you're (contraction of *you are*)
to (in the direction of)	yore (long ago)
too (also)	
two (the number)	

American versus British spellings

Use American spellings rather than British ones: *center,* not *centre; labor,* not *labour.* If you forget which is which, check your dictionary.

Basic spelling rules   41b

The *ie/ei* rule and its exceptions

The familiar rule that "*i* comes before *e* except after *c,* or when sounded like *ay* as in *neighbor* and *weigh*" holds true in most cases.

i before *e*: belief, field, friend, piece, priest,

ei after *c*: ceiling, conceive, deceit, deceive, receipt

ei sounding like "ay": eight, feign, freight, sleigh

Exceptions

ie after *c*: ancient, conscience, science, species

ei not after *c*: caffeine, counterfeit, either, feisty, foreign, forfeit, height, leisure, neither, seize, weird

SPELLING TIPS

Misspellings can undermine your credibility as a writer. In some cases, your reader will even misunderstand what you mean.

◆ Always consult a dictionary when you are in doubt about how to spell a word.

◆ When checking the spelling of an unfamiliar word, note its etymology (its origin and the history of its usage). This information will help you understand why a word is spelled in a particular way and thus fix the correct spelling in your mind.

◆ In your notebook or journal or in a file on your computer, keep a personal spelling list of difficult words you encounter. Check to see whether a new word shares a root, prefix, or suffix with a word you already know; the connection helps you learn the meaning, as well as the spelling, of the new word.

◆ Use the spelling checker on your word-processing program to proofread your papers. It locates transposed or dropped letters as well as misspellings.

◆ Proofread your work carefully, even when you use a spelling checker. If your spelling is right but the word is wrong, the computer can't help. For example, if you confuse *to, too,* and *two* or *its* and *it's,* the spelling checker won't catch the problem because it can't recognize the context in which the word is used.

Spelling rules for suffixes

A **suffix** is a letter or a group of letters added to the end of a word that changes its meaning and sometimes its spelling.

The suffixes -cede, -ceed, *and* -sede
The syllables *-cede, -ceed,* and *-sede* sound alike and are often confused.

-cede (most common): concede, intercede, precede

-ceed: exceed, proceed, succeed

-sede (appears in only one word): supersede

Suffixes after words ending in y
If the letter before the final *y* is a consonant, change the *y* to *i* before adding the suffix unless the suffix begins with *i.*

friendly, friendlier   happy, happily   apply, applying

Keep the *y* if the letter before the *y* is a vowel.

convey, conveyed   annoy, annoyed   pay, payment

Exceptions: dryly, shyly, wryly.

Suffixes after words ending in e
When the suffix begins with a consonant, keep the final *e* before the suffix.

sure, surely   polite, politeness   hate, hateful

Exceptions: acknowledgment, argument, judgment, truly, wholly, awful, ninth.

Suffixes after words ending in a consonant
When adding a suffix to a word ending in a consonant, do not change the spelling, even if a double consonant results.

Benefit, benefited   girl, girllike   fuel, fueling

Final -ly or -ally

The suffixes *-ly* and *-ally* turn nouns into adjectives or adjectives into adverbs.

Add *-ly* to words that do not end in *-ic*: absolutely, really.

Add *-ally* to words that end in *-ic*: basically, automatically.

PRONUNCIATION AND SPELLING

If you spell some words exactly as you pronounce them, you will probably misspell them. As you edit, try to pronounce each word in your mind the way it is spelled, not the way you normally say it. The following words can be troublesome.

accidentally	literature	recognize
arctic	mathematics	relevant
arithmetic	memento	roommate
athlete	mischievous	sandwich
candidate	nuclear	similar
congratulations	possibly	surprise
environment	prejudice (noun)	temperature
extraordinary	prejudiced (adjective)	tentative
February	probably	usually
interference	pronunciation	veteran
laboratory	quantity	Wednesday
library	realtor	wintry

Spelling rules for plurals

Most English nouns are made plural by adding *-s*. The following are exceptions to this rule.

Nouns ending in ch, s, sh, *or* x

Add *-es* to form the plural of most nouns ending in *ch, s, sh,* or *x*:

church, churches   glass, glasses   box, boxes

Nouns ending in y

Add *-s* to form the plural of nouns ending in *y* if the letter before the *y* is a vowel. Change the *y* to *i* and add *-es* if the letter before the *y* is a consonant.

day, days   alloy, alloys   melody, melodies

Nouns ending in o

Add *-s* to form the plural of most nouns ending in *o*.

video, videos   trio, trios   inferno, infernos

For a few nouns that end in an *o* preceded by a consonant, form the plural by adding *-es*.

hero, heroes   potato, potatoes

For other nouns that end in *o*, the plural can be formed either way.

zero, zeros, zeroes   tornado, tornados, tornadoes

Nouns ending in f *and* fe

Change the *f* to *v* and add *-es* to form the plural of some nouns ending in *f*.

leaf, leaves   self, selves   half, halves

Add *-s* to form the plural of other nouns ending in *f*.

brief, briefs   belief, beliefs   proof, proofs

For some but not all nouns ending in *fe*, change the *f* to *v* before adding *-s*.

wife, wives   knife, knives   safe, safes

Irregular and unusual plural forms

A few nouns form plurals without adding *-s* or *-es*.

woman, women   man, men   goose, geese
child, children   foot, feet   mouse, mice

A few words have the same form for singular and plural.

moose, moose   sheep, sheep   series, series

Plurals of proper nouns
Add -*s* to form the plural of most proper nouns.

the Chungs   the Kennedys   several Jennifers

Add -*es* when the plural ending is pronounced as a separate syllable.

the Bushes   the Lopezes   the Joneses.

Plurals of compound nouns
When a compound noun is written as one word, make only the last part of the compound plural: *newspapers, notebooks.*
When a compound noun is written as separate words or hyphenated, make the word plural that expresses the main idea, usually a noun: *attorneys general, brothers-in-law, bath towels.*

42 CAPITALIZATION

Capital letters mark the beginning of sentences and the first letters of names, titles, and certain other words. The first-person singular pronoun *I* (*I'm, I'll, I'd*) and the interjection *O* (*O best beloved* and *forgive us, O Lord*) are also capitalized.

42a Capitalization of the first word of a sentence

Use a capital letter at the beginning of a sentence or an intentional sentence fragment. Like this.
Capitalization is optional in a series of fragmentary questions, but be consistent.

What was the occasion? A holiday? A birthday?

Capitalization of quotations and lines of poetry   42b

Capitalize the first word of a quoted sentence.

> "We'd like to talk to you," she said.

Do not capitalize the first word of the continuation of a quotation that is interrupted.

> "Unfortunately," he said, "we don't sell coffee."

When you change the capitalization from a source to fit your sentences, enclose such changes in square brackets.

Poets make deliberate decisions about when and how they use capital letters. When quoting poetry, always follow the capitalization of the original.

> Frost's poem opens formally: "Whose woods these are, I think I know. / His house is in the village, though." Lucille Clifton's opens informally: "boys / i don't promise you nothing. . . ."

Proper nouns   42c

Capitalize the names of particular persons, places, or things.

> Mercedes Benz   Persian Gulf   Gulf of Mexico

Do not capitalize the articles, conjunctions, or prepositions that appear within such names.

Individual people and animals
Capitalize the names and nicknames of individual people and animals.

> Michael Jordan   Buffalo Bill   Black Beauty

Capitalize words describing family members when they are used as names.

> Mother, my mother   Aunt Carol, his aunt

Religions and their members, deities, and sacred texts
Capitalize the names of religions, members of a religion, religious sects, deities, and sacred texts.

Judaism, Jews   Protestant
Allah   the Bible

Nationalities, ethnic groups, and languages
Capitalize the names of nationalities, ethnic groups, and languages.

English   French   African American
Slavic   Hindustani   Caucasian

Titles
Capitalize formal and courtesy titles and their abbreviations when they are used before a name and not set off by commas.

Gen. Colin Powell, Professor Cox, Ms. Wu, President Lincoln, Dean Ball

Capitalize titles not followed by a name when they indicate high office.

the Queen of England, the President of the United States, the Mayor of New York City

Months, days of the week, and holidays
Capitalize the names of months, weekdays, and holidays.

August 12, 1914   Tuesday   Labor Day
Fourth of July   Thanksgiving

Do not capitalize numbers written out or the names of seasons.

the twentieth of April   spring

Geographic names, place names, and directions
Capitalize the names of cities, states, countries, provinces, regions, bodies of water, and other geographic features.

Little Rock, Arkansas   Mexico   Quebec   the Midwest
the Western Hemisphere   Lake Erie   the Grand Canyon
the Great Lakes

Capitalize common nouns like *river, street,* and *square* when they are part of a place name.

Rodeo Drive   Hudson River   Washington Square

Do not capitalize common nouns when two or more proper nouns precede them.

the Tigris and Euphrates rivers

Capitalize direction words when they indicate regions, but not when they indicate compass directions.

the West, westerly   the Southwest, toward the south

Institutions, organizations, and businesses
Capitalize the names of organizations and businesses.

Oberlin College   Federal Reserve Bank of New York
Nashville Chamber of Commerce

Historical documents, events, periods, and movements
Capitalize the names of historical documents and well-known events or periods.

the Constitution   the Bill of Rights   the French Revolution
the Civil War   the Stone Age

Movements in art, music, literature, and philosophy
Capitalize the names of historical periods and artistic or aesthetic movements.

the Renaissance   Impressionist painters   the Romantic
                                                 poets
the Baroque   the Age of Enlightenment   Logical Positivism

Ships, aircraft, spacecraft, and trains
Capitalize the names of individual vehicles.

Air Force One   the Titanic   Voyager
the City of New Orleans (train)

Derivatives of proper nouns
Capitalize words derived from proper nouns.

Newtonian physics   Marxist economics   Texans

Do not capitalize words derived from proper nouns that have taken generic and independent meanings.

french fries   herculean   quixotic

PROPER NOUNS VERSUS COMMON NOUNS

Capitalize proper nouns (the names of specific people, places, or things); do not capitalize common nouns (the names of general types of people, places, or things).

English, French	history, political science
Chemistry 2	chemistry
American Literature 23	American literature
Harvard University	a university
the College of Arts and Sciences	the arts and sciences
the School of Business	a school or college
Vice President Johnson	a vice president
Professor Jones	a professor
the Supreme Court	a court of law
Haymarket Square	a town square
Representative Smith	a legislator
California	a state
October	autumn
the Northwest	north, west
the Holy Bible	a bible
the Hebrew God	a god
Lake Champlain	a lake
Uncle John	an uncle

Titles   42d

Capitalize the first word, the last word, and all other words except articles, conjunctions, and prepositions in the titles and subtitles of books, plays, essays, stories, poems, movies, television programs, pieces of music, and works of art.

> *Pride and Prejudice, Beauty and the Beast, La Traviata,* "The Wasteland," *Guernica, The Sopranos*

Words joined by a hyphen are usually both capitalized, except for articles, conjunctions, and prepositions.

> Jack-in-the-Box   *The One-Minute Grammarian*

In writing academic papers, remember to underline or italicize published titles (books, periodicals) and put quotation marks around the titles of chapters, articles, stories, and poems within published works. (See 34c and 43a.)

Capitalization and punctuation   42e

Colons
Capitalization is optional after a colon that joins two independent clauses when the second clause contains the main point of the sentence.

> The senators' courage failed them: the health-care bill was dead for another decade.

Use capitals after a colon that introduces a numbered list of complete sentences.

> His philosophy can be reduced to three basic rules: (1) Think for yourself. (2) Take care of your body. (3) Never hurt anyone.

Parentheses and dashes
Capitalize the first word of a complete sentence set off by parentheses or dashes when it stands alone.

> In 1972 Congress attacked sex discrimination in sports by passing Title IX. (The changes made in 1974 are called the Bayh amendments.)

Do not capitalize the first word of a complete sentence set off by parentheses or dashes when it falls within another sentence.

On many campuses Title IX has increased the number of competitive sports offered to women—even opponents agree—but its effect on men's sports is difficult to assess.

43 HYPHENS

Hyphens link words or parts of words to create new concepts and thus new meanings. They can also separate words into parts to clarify meaning. In addition, hyphens have many conventional uses in numbers, fractions, and units of measure.

43a Hyphens at the ends of lines

Use a hyphen to break words that are too long to fit at the end of a line. The following guidelines will also help you determine how to hyphenate words.

Divide words only between pronounced syllables. Words of only one pronounced syllable—*eighth, through, dreamed, urged*—cannot be divided without suggesting an incorrect pronunciation.

Divide at prefixes or suffixes rather than dividing base words. Try to leave both parts of a word recognizable: not *an-tibody* but *anti-body*, not *ea-gerness* but *eager-ness*.

Don't leave just one letter at the end of a line or carry over only one or two letters to the next line.

A word with an internal double letter is usually divided between those letters (*syl-la-ble, wil-low*), but keep double letters together if they fall at the end of a base word and divide the word before a suffix (*access-ible, assess-ment*).

43b Hyphens after some prefixes

Use a hyphen when a prefix precedes a capitalized word or a date. The prefix itself is usually not capitalized: *pre-Columbian, pre-1994.*

Use a hyphen after a prefix attached to a term of two or more words: *post–World War II, anti–labor union.*

Use a hyphen in almost all cases after the prefixes *all-, ex-* (meaning "former"), *self-,* and *quasi-.*

all-inclusive   ex-convict   self-hypnosis   quasi-judicial

To prevent misreading, hyphens are often used when a prefix ends with the same letter that begins the base word: *anti-intellectual, co-ownership.*

Use a hyphen when two prefixes apply to the same base word and are separated by a conjunction. Add a space after the first hyphenated prefix.

We compared the *pre-* and *post-election* analyses.

Hyphens in compound words   43c

Many compound words (**closed compounds**) are written as one word: *workhorse, schoolteacher.* Other compounds are written as two separate words (**open compounds**): *hope chest, lunch break, curtain rod.* But some compounds are hyphenated: *great-grandson, stick-in-the-mud.*

Check the dictionary to see which compound words are written as one word and which are hyphenated. If you don't find a compound there, then it is written as two words.

Hyphenate compound nouns of three or more words: *mother-in-law, jack-of-all-trades.*

Hyphenate when two or more modifiers act as a single adjective before a noun: *late-night party, loose-leaf notebook.*

Do not hyphenate well-known compound terms: *post office box, high school student.*

Do not hyphenate words ending in *-ly: a highly paid worker.*

Numbers, fractions, and units of measure   43d

Hyphenate two-word numbers from *twenty-one* to *ninety-nine.* Do not hyphenate before or after the words *hundred, thousand,* or *million.*

fifty-seven	twenty-two thousand
two hundred fifty-seven	six hundred twenty thousand

Hyphenate between the numerator and denominator of a spelled-out fraction unless one of them is already hyphenated.

one-half   two-thirds   twenty-one fiftieths

Hyphenate when *feet, inches, miles, pounds* are used as modifiers.

My dump truck has a *nine-cubic-yard* bed.

Do not hyphenate when the unit of measure is used as a noun.

My dump truck holds *nine cubic yards* of manure.

Hyphenate ages when they are used as nouns or modifiers:

six-year-old child   my son, the six-year-old

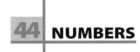 NUMBERS

When you use numbers to describe data and research findings that support your position, follow the conventions of the discipline in which you are writing. For general purposes, the following guidelines will help you decide when to spell out numbers and when to use figures.

44a Figures or spelled-out numbers?

Spell out numbers of one hundred or less and numbers that can be expressed in one or two words: *thirty students, three-fourths of the forest* but *517 students, 52,331 trees.*

Use a combination of words and figures for round numbers over one million: *The U.S. population exceeds 250 million.*

Spell out any number that begins a sentence: *Five students attended the concert.*

Treat numbers that readers must compare consistently: *Last year 87 cats and 114 dogs were adopted.*

In technical writing, use figures for numbers over nine and in all measurements: *3 pounds per square inch.*

SINGULAR AND PLURAL FORMS OF NUMBERS

Use the plural word for a number that is used as a plural noun without another number before it. You may need to add the word *of* after it.

The news reported only a few protesters, but we saw *hundreds*.

Dozens of geese headed south today.

When the word for a number is preceded by another number, use the singular form of the word, and do not use *of* with it.

There were approximately *two hundred* protesters.

At least *three dozen* geese flew over the lake today.

When a word expressing a unit of weight, money, time, or distance is used with another word to modify a noun, use the singular forms for both words.

It was a *three-hour* movie.

Conventional uses of numbers   44b

In all types of writing, convention requires the use of figures in certain situations.

DATES
>   11 April 1999   July 16, 1999   the year 1616

ADDRESSES
> 2551 Polk St., Apt. 3
> San Francisco, CA 94109

ABBREVIATIONS AND SYMBOLS
> 3500 rpm   37°C
> 65 mph $62.23
> 74%   53¢

If you spell out numbers, also spell out *percent, dollars,* and *cents: seventy-four percent, fifty cents, five dollars*

TIME
> 12:15   2330 hours

Numbers used with *o'clock, past, to, till,* and *until* are generally written out as words.

seven o'clock   twenty past one

DECIMALS AND FRACTIONS

2.7 seconds   35.4 miles

CROSS-REFERENCES AND CITATIONS

Chapter 12   line 25   act 3, scene 2

45 ABBREVIATIONS

Abbreviations are frequently used in tables, footnotes, endnotes, and bibliographies to help readers proceed through material quickly. The following abbreviations are acceptable in conventional and academic writing; scientific and technical writing may differ.

45a Abbreviated titles and degrees

Abbreviate titles of address when they precede a full name, except for *president* and *mayor,* which are never abbreviated.

Mr. Samuel Taylor   Dr. Ellen Hunter
St. Francis of Assisi   Prof. Ahmed Greenberg

Abbreviate titles and degrees that follow a name, such as *esq., M.D., LL.D., J.D.,* and *Ph.D.* Use either a title (such as *Dr.*) or a degree (such as *M.D.*), but not both.

Dr. Randall Marshall   Randall Marshall, M.D.

Abbreviate generational titles such as *Jr.* and *Sr.* When used in a sentence, they are set off by commas.

He talked to Thomas Burke, Jr., and to Karen Burke.

Do not abbreviate or capitalize titles that are not used with a proper name: *assistant professor of chemistry, doctor of internal medicine.*

Except for *Mr., Ms., Mrs.,* and *Dr.,* do not abbreviate titles that appear before a surname (last name) alone: *Professor Greenberg, Senator Braun, President Smith.*

Abbreviations with numbers   45b

Time

Use *A.M.* ("ante meridiem") or *P.M.* ("post meridiem") for specific times of day. You may also write *a.m.* or *p.m.* since capitalization is optional, but be consistent within one document.

3:45 p.m. (or P.M.)   12 noon

Year

Use *B.C.* ("before Christ") and *A.D.* ("anno Domini") for calendar years. Only *A.D.* precedes the year. To avoid religious reference, many writers substitute *B.C.E.* ("before the Common Era") and *C.E.* ("Common Era").

425 B.C. (or 425 B.C.E.)   A.D. 1215 (or 1215 C.E.)

Degrees, numbers, and units of measure   45c

Use *F* for degrees Fahrenheit and *C* for degrees Celsius (metric system measurement) when writing out temperatures. Use *no.* or *No.* for *number.* Use *mph* for *miles per hour, mpg* for *miles per gallon,* and *rpm* for *revolutions per minute.*

Whose address is No. 10 Downing Street?

The speed limit is 65 mph on the interstate.

In scientific and technical writing, abbreviate units of measure, usually without periods.

He added 200 mg of sodium cyanate to the beaker.

45d Symbols

Use symbols for degree (°), dollar ($), and percent (%) when they are used with figures. Spell out symbols in words when the figures are also spelled as words. Be consistent.

It was 30°C and sunny 75% of the time.

It was thirty degrees and sunny five percent of the time.

45e Abbreviated geographic names

Abbreviate geographic names when addressing mail. Use the U.S. Postal Service state abbreviations.

100 W. Glengarry Ave.
Birmingham, MI 48009

Do not abbreviate anything except the state name when presenting a full address in text. Do not abbreviate place names when you give a general address.

He lived at 11 West Sixth Street, Harrisburg, PA 17102.

She was born in Madison, Wisconsin.

45f Common Latin abbreviations

Use common Latin abbreviations in documentation and notes, but write out their English equivalents in your text.

ABBREVIATION	LATIN	MEANING
c. *or* ca.	*circa*	about
cf.	*confer*	compare
e.g.	*exempli gratia*	for example
et al.	*et alii*	and others
etc.	*et cetera*	and so forth
i.e.	*id est*	that is
N.B.	*nota bene*	note well

Acronyms and initials   45g

An **acronym** is a word made up of initials and pronounced as a word— *NATO* for *North Atlantic Treaty Organization,* for example. Acronyms are written with no periods and no spaces between the letters.

Most initial abbreviations, such as *CD* for *compact disc* or *JFK* for *John F. Kennedy,* are written with neither periods nor spaces between the letters. Some abbreviations for countries do use periods but no spaces: *U.S., U.K.*

Make sure that acronyms and initial abbreviations are familiar to your readers. If you have any doubts, give the full term the first time, followed by the abbreviation or acronym in parentheses.

> Commerce is governed by a set of treaties called the General Agreement on Tariffs and Trade (GATT).

> The National Collegiate Athletic Association (NCAA) posted new rules.

When you refer to the same organization a second time in your text, use the abbreviated version unless the initial reference is many pages earlier.

> Some have argued that the NCAA had no need for new rules.

AVOID ABBREVIATIONS IN FORMAL WRITING

In formal writing, spell out the full words you might abbreviate when writing informally. (Abbreviations are recommended for references and notes in research papers.)

◆ Days of the week and months: *Tuesday,* not *Tues.; December,* not *Dec.*

◆ Textual divisions: *page,* not *p.; Chapter,* not *Ch.* or *Chap.*

◆ Academic disciplines: *sociology,* not *soc; political science,* not *poly sci.*

◆ Academic institutions: *College of Arts and Sciences,* not *A&S*

◆ Academic titles: *professor,* not *prof.; doctor,* not *dr.*

◆ Personal names (unless authorized): *Robert,* not *Bob; Susan,* not *Sue*

◆ Holidays: *Christmas,* not *Xmas*

◆ Units of measurement: *quart,* not *qt.; pound,* not *lb.*

◆ Business names: *Company,* not *Co.; Corporation,* not *Corp.; Incorporated,* not *Inc.* (Do use abbreviations if part of the company name: *Johnson Bros. Inc.*)

46 | ITALICS AND UNDERLINING

To distinguish certain words in your text, use *italics*. In handwritten papers, <u>underline</u> words to indicate italics. In submitting manuscripts for publication, prefer underlining to italics.

46a Italics or underlining for titles

Check with your instructor if you are not certain whether to italicize or use underlining to indicate italics for published works in your written texts.

Use italics for the titles of longer published works.

- Books: *The Cat in the Hat, Moby Dick,* the *Principles of Geology*

- Plays: *Hamlet, The Zoo Story*

- Operas and other long musical works: *La Boheme,* Beethoven's *Seventh Symphony*

- Films: *The Godfather, Star Wars*

- Recordings: *Tapestry, The Greatest Hits of John Denver*

- Newspapers: the *New York Times*

- Magazines: *The New Yorker, Time, Newsweek*

- Television and radio series: *ER, Friends, Prairie Home Companion*

- Long poems considered to be independent works: *Leaves of Grass, The Wasteland*

- Works of art: *The Last Supper, Nude Descending a Staircase, Venus de Milo*

- Web sites: *Amazon.com, Encyclopaedia Britannica Online*

- Chapters, stories, poems, songs within longer published works: add quotation marks to indicate a work was published within a larger work. "The Black Cat" "Song of Myself" "Homer Meets Godzilla" (episode)

Do not use italics (or quotation marks) for titles of sacred works, parts of sacred works, ancient manuscripts, and public documents.

the Bible   the Bill of Rights   the Civil Rights Act

Italics or underlining for the names of individual trains, ships, and planes   46b

Use italics for the official names of individual trains, ships, airplanes, and spacecraft.

City of New Orleans (train)   the *Titanic* (ship)
Spirit of St. Louis (airplane)

Italics or underlining for foreign words   46c

Many words in English have been absorbed by the language and do not require italics. Recently borrowed foreign words do.

My favorite dish is lasagne.

Try the *pasticcio di faglioni.*

Use italics for the Latin names of plants and animals.

Homo erectus is an ancestor of modern humans.

Use italics for words or numbers that stand only for themselves and for letters used as symbols in mathematics and other disciplines.

the term *liberal*   to substitute y for u.

Italics or underlining for emphasis   46d

Use italics to indicate that a certain word or words should receive special attention or emphasis.

We all hear music in our heads, but how is music processed by the *brain?*

Be careful not to overuse italics. Too much emphasis of this sort can become monotonous and lose its impact.

Use italics to refer to a word as a word within a sentence.

The word *italics* is often used synonymously with the word *underlining* throughout this chapter.

PART SEVEN

❧   ❧   ❧

EDITING: GRAMMAR

Source: *The College Writer's Reference,* Third Edition, by Toby Fulwiler and Alan R. Hayakawa.

47 REVIEWING GRAMMAR

The **sentence,** a group of words expressing a complete thought, is the basic unit of speech and writing. Sentence grammar describes how sentences are organized and structured. It also describes the function of each word in a sentence. An understanding of grammar helps you identify and improve places where your writing may be confusing. It also helps you find nonstandard structures or usages that may distract the reader from your meaning.

Although grammar can be intimidating, it can be approached as a puzzle. One way to figure grammar out is to ask, "What kind of word is this?" Answers will name parts of speech: nouns, pronouns, verbs, adjectives, prepositions, conjunctions, and interjections. Another grammar question is "How is the word used in the sentence?" Answers will include subject, predicate, object, and complement. Finally, grammar asks, "What kind of sentence is this?" and answers with simple, compound, or complex sentences. The following three sections serve as a guide to help you answer these three questions.

Parts of speech   47a

A word's meaning and position in a sentence determine what part of speech it is. Some words change depending on the context in which they appear. For example, *ride* can function as a verb or a noun.

> They went for a *ride.*   *(noun)*

> They *ride* their horses.   *(verb)*

Look at the word as well as how it's used in the sentence to help you determine what part of speech it is. Use the following categories as a guide.

Nouns

Nouns are words that name persons, animals, places, things, or ideas: *woman, Flipper, Grand Canyon,* and *virtue* are all nouns.

Proper nouns name particular people, animals, places, or things: *Ralph Nader, Black Beauty, Kentucky, Catholicism.* They are almost always capitalized. Generic nouns, or common nouns, can apply to any member of a class or group: *scientist, horse, state, ship, religion.* They are generally not capitalized.

Concrete nouns refer to things that can be seen, heard, touched, smelled, or tasted: *butterfly, telephone, ice, fudge.* **Abstract nouns** refer to ideas or concepts that cannot be directly sensed: *nature, communication, temperature, temptation.*

Count nouns refer to one or more individual items that can be counted: *one book, two books.* They usually name something concrete, though some count nouns are abstract: *one idea, several ideas.* **Noncount nouns** refer to entities that either cannot be counted individually (*water, oil*) or are used in a sense that does not imply counting (*sand, money*). These are seldom made plural. Often such nouns are quantified by preliminary phrases: <u>grains of</u> sand, <u>pails of</u> water, <u>little</u> time, <u>enough</u> wood.

Collective nouns, such as *crowd, couple,* and *flock,* refer to groups of similar things.

Singular and plural nouns

Singular nouns refer to an individual person, place, or thing: *student, dorm, box.* **Plural** nouns refer to more than one: *students, dorms, boxes.* Adding *-s* or *-es* to the singular usually creates plural forms. However, some nouns change more completely from singular to plural status: *goose, geese; child, children; man, men; medium, media.* Other nouns remain the same regardless of number: *sheep, sheep.*

Possessive forms of nouns

When you want to indicate possession, ownership, or connections, you can usually add an apostrophe and an *-s* to a noun: *the student's paper, the school's mission.*

USING ARTICLES WITH NOUNS

Whether to use *a, an,* or *the* before a noun depends on the type of noun and the context in which it is used. Nouns are either count nouns or noncount nouns. **Count nouns,** which name things that can be counted, can be singular (*island, child, ratio*) or plural (*islands, children, ratios*). **Noncount nouns,** naming things that generally cannot be counted or quantified, usually cannot be made plural (*information, homework, justice, success*).

◆   You must use an article before a singular count noun unless the noun has a quantifier (*one*) or a possessive (*my, her*) before it.

 an island   the child   a ratio

Exceptions to this rule are singular proper nouns, which in most cases do not require an article.

 Italy   Pearl Street   Lake Erie

◆   Use *a* or *an* with a singular count noun when you have not specified one particular thing or individual.

> There is *a problem* with this approach.
>
> *Readers don't know what the problem is yet.*
>
> We all appreciate *an understanding friend.*
>
> *Any* understanding friend, *not a particular one.*

◆   Use *the* with a singular count noun in the following cases.
◆   The noun has already been mentioned.

> There is a problem with this approach. *The problem* is a subtle one.

◆   The noun is made specific by elements that follow it.

> *The problem* that I see with this approach is a subtle one.
>
> *The modifying clause* that I see with this approach *makes it clear that the writer is referring to one specific problem.*

◆   The noun is made specific by the context.

> I entered a large lecture hall. *The teacher* was standing behind a lectern. *The blackboard* seemed very far away.
>
> *In a lecture hall, there is likely to be only one teacher and only one blackboard.*

342

SOME NONCOUNT NOUNS

air	energy	love	smoke
alcohol	equipment	machinery	snow
art	fog	mail	stuff
beef	food	make-up	sugar
biology	freedom	mathematics	temperature*
candy	fruit	milk	traffic
cash	furniture	money	travel
cereal	garbage	news	truth
cheese	gasoline	noise	wind
clothing	homework	peace	wine
coffee	information	rain	wood
cold	jewelry	research	work
courage	knowledge	rice	writing
darkness	life	scenery	

◆   Think about these major groupings as a way to decide whether something is count or not.

Names for languages *(Japanese, Latin, Urdu)*

Areas of study *(environmental science, physics, history)*

Substances *(granite, water, oxygen, sugar)*

◆   Remember that some noncount nouns can also be countable when their usage switches from the general to the specific or when a concept can be measured or quantified.

analysis	iron	temperature
calculation	science	pressure
diamond	grain	growth

Pronouns

A pronoun is a substitute for a noun (or for another pronoun). The word that the pronoun replaces is called its **antecedent.**

If the assignment is long, it will require some planning.

PRONOUNS

PERSONAL

I, me, my, mine   we, us, our, ours
you, your, yours
she, her, hers
he, him, his   they, them, their, theirs
it, its

DEMONSTRATIVE

this	that	these	those

RELATIVE

that	whatever	whichever	whoever	whomever
what	which	who	whom	whose

INTERROGATIVE

what	which	who	whom	whose
whatever	whichever	whoever	whomever	

REFLEXIVE AND INTENSIVE

myself	yourself	himself	herself	itself
ourselves	yourselves	themselves		oneself

RECIPROCAL

each other	one another

INDEFINITE

all	each	many	none	somebody
any	either	more	no one	someone
anybody	everybody	most	nothing	something
anyone	everyone	much	one	what
anything	everything	neither	several	
both	few	nobody	some	

While antecedents often appear before the pronoun, they may also follow the pronoun.

ronoun　　　　antecedent

Because of its length, the assignment was a challenge.

Personal pronouns

Personal pronouns (*me, you, it, they,* and so on) refer to specific people, animals, places, things, or ideas. **Possessive pronouns** (*my, your, theirs*) indicate ownership.

She asked *me* to buy *her* bike.

Personal pronouns are categorized according to **person, number,** and **gender** (in third person singular).

	SINGULAR		PLURAL	
1ST PERSON	I, me	my, mine	we, us	our, ours
2ND PERSON	you	your, yours	you	you, yours
3RD PERSON			they, them	their, theirs
MASCULINE	he, him	his		
FEMININE	she, her	her, hers		
NEUTER	it	its		

Demonstrative pronouns

Demonstrative pronouns (*this, that, these, those*) point to a specific person, place, or thing. They may function as adjectives to modify nouns or substitute for nouns.

This classroom is bright and airy.　(This *modifies classroom.*)

This is the best classroom!　(This = *classroom.*)

Relative pronouns

Relative pronouns (*who, whom, whose, which,* and *that*) introduce dependent clauses that act as adjectives and *relate* back to antecedents (words occurring earlier in a sentence).

She chose the knife *that cut best.*　(That cut best *modifies* knife.)

Some relative pronouns (*whoever, whomever, whatever, what,* and *whichever*) introduce noun clauses rather than relating back to previous words in a sentence.

> He'll do *whatever he wants.*   (Whatever he wants *acts as the object of* do.)

Relative pronouns change form to show case.

Interrogative pronouns

Interrogative pronouns (*who, what, whose,* and so on) ask questions.

> *Who* is there?

> *Whose* essay is this?

Reflexive and intensive pronouns

Reflexive and **intensive pronouns** end in *-self* or *-selves* (*myself, yourself, themselves,* and so on). **Reflexive pronouns** show that the "doer" and the "done to" are the same person.

> *Dave* cut *himself* while shaving.   (Dave *and* himself *refer to the same person.*)

Intensive pronouns are used to emphasize, or "intensify," an antecedent.

> I talked to the president *herself.*

Unlike reflexive pronouns, intensive pronouns can be omitted without changing the sense of the sentence: *I talked to the president.* Reflexive and intensive pronouns change form to show person, number, and gender, just as personal pronouns do.

Reciprocal pronouns

Reciprocal pronouns (*each other, one another*) describe an action or state that is shared between two people, animals, places, things, or ideas. They can serve to substitute for or modify a noun.

> The investigators helped *one another* with the research.

> Students critiqued *each other's* papers.

Indefinite pronouns

Indefinite pronouns (*all, each, many, none,* and so on) refer to nonspecific persons, places, or things and therefore do not require an antecedent. Most are either always singular (*someone*) or always plural (*many*). They do not change form to show person, number, or gender.

Pronoun case

Case indicates the role a word plays in a sentence, whether it is a **subject,** an **object,** or a **possessive.** In the following examples, *Norm,* a proper noun, plays each role and is in a different case in each sentence. The masculine singular pronoun, in the correct case, substitutes for *Norm* following each example.

Norm led the class discussion.   (Norm *is the subject.*)

He led the class discussion.

The class applauded *Norm* for his hard work.   (Norm *is the object of* applauded.)

The class applauded *him* for his hard work.

It was *Norm's* turn to take this responsibility.   (Norm's *is in the possessive case because the turn belongs to him.*)

It was *his* turn to take this responsibility.

Just as nouns take on different roles, so do pronouns.

SUBJECTIVE		OBJECTIVE		POSSESSIVE	
SINGULAR	PLURAL	SINGULAR	PLURAL	SINGULAR	PLURAL
I	we	me	us	my, mine	our, ours
you	you	you	you	your, yours	your, yours
he, she, it	they	him, her, it	them	his; her, hers; its	their, theirs
who		whom		whose	
whoever		whomever			

When pronouns act as subjects, use **subjective case.**

We should leave now.   (We *is the subject.*)

It was *she* who wanted to leave.   (She *is the subject complement.*)

When pronouns act as objects, use **objective case.**

Whom did they choose?   (Whom *is the object of the verb* choose.)

The judging seemed unfair to *us*.   (Us *is the object of the preposition* to.)

Seeing *her* made the holiday complete.   (Her *is the object of the verbal* seeing.)

When pronouns indicate possession or connection, use **possessive case.** Some possessive pronouns act as adjectives (modifying nouns) while others act as nouns (as subjects or complements).

That is *my* book bag.   (My *modifies* book bag.)

That book bag is *mine*.   (Mine *is the same as, or subject complement to,* book bag.)

Verbs

A **verb** describes an action or state of being.

The student *registered* for the class.

The student *is* excited about the course.

Verbs change form to show person, number, tense, voice, and mood.

◆ **Person** indicates who performed the action: *I* write; *she* writes.

◆ **Number** indicates whether one or more performed the action: *he* sings; *they* sing.

◆ **Tense** indicates when the action was performed: *she* argues; *she* argued.

◆ **Voice** shows whether the sentence subject acts or is acted upon: she *paid* the bill; the bill *was paid*.

◆ **Mood** indicates the speaker's stance toward the action: *I am a millionaire; if I were a millionaire.*

Auxiliary verbs

In addition to a main verb in a sentence, **auxiliary** or **helping verbs** (forms of *be, do, have,* and so on) may appear to create a **verb phrase.**

main verb

After swimming for an hour, he decided to go home.

verb phrase

My oldest sister was doing a crossword puzzle.

The verb phrase consists of the main verb doing *and the auxiliary verb* was.

When used as auxiliaries, these verbs change to show person, number, and tense.

Other auxiliary verbs, known as **one-word modals** (*can, could, may, must, might, shall, should, would, will*) and **multiple-word modals** (*be able to, be going to, have got to, have to,* and so on) are also used as auxiliaries. While one-word modals do not change to show person, number, or tense, multiple-word modals often do change.

I *can sing,* and you *can dance.*

I *am able to sing,* and you *are able to dance.*

Transitive and intransitive verbs

Some verbs carry meaning all by themselves (**intransitive verbs**) while others need an object to complete the meaning (**transitive verbs**). Many verbs can work either way, depending on the context.

transitive verb

Joey grew tomatoes last summer.   (Tomatoes *is the object of* grew.)

intransitive verb

The tomatoes grew rapidly.   (Tomatoes grew *by themselves.*)

Linking verbs

Linking verbs (*be, become, seem*) and verbs describing sensations (*appear, look, feel, taste, smell, sound*) link the subject of a sentence to a **subject complement,** an element that renames or identifies the subject. Subject complements can be nouns or adjectives. Like an equal sign, linking verbs connect two equivalent terms.

Sue *is* nice.	Sue = nice
They *felt* tired.	They = tired
Jake *was* a recent graduate.	Jake = graduate

Voice

Verbs can show action in the **active voice,** where the subject of the sentence is the "doer."

active voice

The woman pushes the baby carriage.

When the subject of the sentence is "done to," the verb is in the **passive voice.**

passive voice

The baby carriage is pushed by the woman.

The "spotlight" is different in these two sentences; *woman* is the subject in the first, *baby carriage* in the second.

Verbals

Verbs can take on different forms to function as other parts of speech in sentences. These different forms are called **verbals.**

Cramming is a poor long-term study strategy.

Cramming *is a verbal functioning as a noun (subject).*

We had *boiled* eggs for breakfast.

Boiled *is a verbal functioning as an adjective to modify the noun* eggs.

This machine was designed *to last.*

To last *is a verbal used as an adverb to modify the verb* designed.

There are three different kinds of verbals, which have different forms and functions.

- **Gerund:** the *-ing* form of a verb functioning as a noun.

  I love *jogging* early in the morning.   (Jogging *serves as the direct object of* love.)

  The best exercise is *jogging.*   (Jogging *is the subject complement of* exercise.)

  My friends are so tired of my *jogging!*   (Jogging *is the object of the preposition* of.)

- **Participle:** present participle (ending in *-ing*) or past participle (ending in *-d, -ed, -en,* and so on) of a verb used as an adjective.

  He had no right *taking my pack.*   (Taking my pack *is a participial phrase modifying the noun* right.)

  Exhausted, the hikers decided to camp.   (Exhausted *modifies the noun* hikers.)

- **Infinitive:** *to* plus the base form of a verb used as a noun, an adjective, or an adverb.

  Her ambition is *to sing* at Carnegie Hall.   (To sing *is a noun acting as a subject complement to* ambition.)

  To have sung so well last night is something you should be proud of.   (*Note how the infinitive changes form to show tense.*)

After prepositions and certain verbs, the *to* of an infinitive does not appear; *to* is implied.

He did everything except wash the floor.

She let them visit their cousins.

Adjectives and adverbs

Adjectives and adverbs **modify** other words; they specify, say more about, and detail other words in sentences. To identify them, look at the words they modify.

Adjectives modify nouns and pronouns (and phrases and clauses used as nouns).

The hikers wanted *waterproof* parkas for the trip.

The adjective answers the question, "What kind of parkas?" and says more about the noun parkas.

They were *beautiful.*

The adjective answers "What were they like?" and says more about the pronoun They.

Adverbs modify verbs, adjectives, and adverbs (and verbals, clauses, and full sentences).

His judgment was made *hastily.*

The adverb answers "How was it made?" and says more about the verb was made.

The feathers are *quite* beautiful.

The adverb answers "How beautiful?" and says more about the adjective beautiful.

She sings *very* nicely.

The adverb answers "How nicely?" and says more about the adverb nicely.

Surprisingly, the band played for hours.

The adverb modifies the entire sentence.

Adjectives and adverbs can communicate degrees of comparison.

He lives in an *old* house.   (*A positive modifier makes no comparison.*)

It is *older* than mine.   (*A comparative modifier compares two things.*)

It is the *oldest* house in the country.   (*A superlative modifier distinguishes among three or more things.*)

Kinds of adjectives

Adjectives that describe attributes of something are called **descriptive**: *gray sky, beautiful garden.* Adjectives that specify are called **limiting**: *this sky, my garden.* **Limiting** adjectives include the **indefinite articles** (*a* and *an*) and the **definite article** (*the*). Use *a* when the following word begins with a consonant or long *u* sound (*a monster, a university*) and *an* when the following word begins with other vowel sounds (*an apron*).

Several types of pronouns can also serve as limiting adjectives when they are directly followed by a noun.

She is going to buy *her* dog today.
The personal pronoun her *modifies* dog.

She hasn't decided *which* dog she will pick.
The relative pronoun which *modifies* dog.

She likes *that* dog very much.
The demonstrative pronoun that *modifies* dog.

But *all* [the dogs] look cute to her.
The indefinite pronoun all *modifies the implied noun* dogs.

Numbers, nouns, and proper nouns can also be used as adjectives when followed directly by nouns: *two dogs, masonry contractor,* and *Alaskan crab* (note capitalization).

Kinds of adverbs

In addition to the adverbs noted above, which modify verbs, adjectives, and other adverbs, several special groups of words are also classified as adverbs.

No and *nor* are adverbs called **negators.**

We are *not* ready.

Conjunctive adverbs, such as *however* and *nevertheless,* link two independent clauses that are separated by a semicolon.

Sally wanted to say goodbye to Tom; *however,* the train was leaving.

Relative adverbs, such as *where, why,* and *when,* introduce adjective or adverb clauses.

We were visiting the house *where* I grew up.

COMMON PREPOSITIONS

aboard	below	in case of	past
about	beneath	including	regarding
above	beside	in front of	since
according to	besides	inside	through
across	between	in spite of	throughout
after	beyond	into	till
against	but	like	to
ahead of	by	near	together with
along	concerning	next to	toward
along with	despite	notwithstanding	under
among	down	of	underneath
apart from	due to	off	unlike
around	during	on	until
as	except	onto	up
as for	except for	on top of	upon
at	for	other than	up to
away from	from	out	via
because of	in	out of	with
before	in addition to	outside	within
behind	in back of	over	without

Prepositions

Prepositions show the relationship of a noun or pronoun to another part of a sentence. Pronouns "take objects" and, together with their objects, form **prepositional phrases.**

The cow jumped <u>*over* the moon.</u>

Over is a preposition, the moon is its object.

CHOOSING THE RIGHT PREPOSITION

Prepositional phrases can indicate time, location, place, or direction. Here is a list of common prepositions that begin such phrases.

TIME

at noon, *at* night, *at* breakfast time

in a year or month, *in* 1999, *in* the twenty-first century, *in* the afternoon, *in* the morning, *in* an hour or a specified time period

on a specific date or day: *on* Monday, *on* October 3

by a specific date or time and not later: *by* next Thursday, *by* Thanksgiving

during (within a particular time period): *during* the day, *during* the month, *during* this century

until (any time before and up to a specified point): *until* today, *until* 8:00, *until* now

LOCATION OR PLACE

at the table, *at* home, *at* school, *at* the corner, *at* the subway station

in an enclosed space, *in* Canada, *in* the world, *in* class, *in* the car

on the desk, *on* the radio, *on* the wall, *on* a plane

DIRECTION

arrive *from* somewhere: *from* Australia, *from* your house, *from* another planet

go *to* a place: *to* Canada, *to* school, *to* church

fall *off* something: *off* a bike, *off* the roof

travel *around* an area: *around* Europe, *around* town

snowboard *down* something: *down* the hill

English has one-word prepositions (*aboard*) and multiple-word prepositions (*except for*). Acquaint yourself with the list of common prepositions included here so that you can readily recognize them.

Conjunctions

Conjunctions are words that join two or more words, phrases, or clauses.

Coordinating conjunctions (*and, or, nor, for, but, yet,* and *so*) join equal or similar elements.

Bill *and* I went shopping.

The bus will take you to the market *or* to the theater.

Bill went to the market, *but* Clara went to the theater.

Correlative conjunctions (*either . . . or, neither . . . nor, both . . . and, not only . . . but also, whether . . . or*) always appear in pairs and join pairs of similar words.

Neither Jack nor his brother was in school this morning.

She *not only* sings *but also* dances.

Subordinating conjunctions (*after, although, because, before, if, unless, when, where,* and *while*) introduce ideas in dependent clauses that are less important than (or subordinate to) the ideas in main (or independent) clauses.

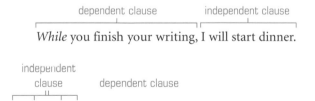

dependent clause   independent clause

While you finish your writing, I will start dinner.

independent
clause   dependent clause

I left *because* I was angry.

Conjunctive adverbs (*however, therefore, furthermore,* and so on) link independent clauses that are separated by a semicolon.

I am finished with the exam; *therefore,* I am leaving the class.

Interjections

Interjections are words that show surprise, dismay, or strong emotion. They are often "interjected" in speech or dialogue and typically require an exclamation point.

Ouch! That pipe is hot!

47b Elements of a sentence

The first section of this chapter looks at the puzzle "What kind of word is this?" This section explores "How is the word used in the sentence?" Sentences contain a **subject** (what or who the sentence is about) and a **predicate** (what the subject is doing). A subject may consist of a noun, a pronoun, or a group of words functioning as a noun, along with modifiers. A predicate contains the verb of the sentence along with its objects, its modifiers, and any complements or modifiers that refer to the subject.

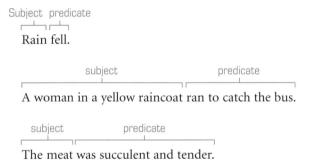

Subject predicate

Rain fell.

subject predicate

A woman in a yellow raincoat ran to catch the bus.

subject predicate

The meat was succulent and tender.

Subjects

The **simple subject** is the person or thing that performs the action of the predicate. Usually a noun or pronoun, it can also be a verbal, phrase, or clause used as a noun.

Long *shadows* crept along the lawn.　(*A noun as the subject*)

He looked exactly like a cowboy.　(*A pronoun as the subject*)

Singing pleases Alan.　(*A verbal—gerund—as the subject*)

To work hard is our lot in life.　(*An infinitive phrase as the subject*)

That Lily could dance amazed us all.   (*A clause as the subject*)

The **complete subject** consists of the simple subject and all words that modify or directly relate to it (adjectives, adverbs, phrases, or clauses).

> *Winning the last game of a dreadful season that included injuries, losing streaks, and a strike* was small consolation to the team.
>
> *Winning is a gerund used as the simple subject.* The last game *is the object of* Winning; of a dreadful season *is the prepositional phrase modifying* game; *and* that included injuries, losing streaks, and a strike *is a clause modifying* season. *This entire collection of words makes up the* complete subject.

A **compound subject** includes two or more subjects linked by a coordinating conjunction such as *and* or *or*.

> *Books, records, and videotapes* filled the room.

An **implied subject** is one that is not stated directly but may be understood.

> (*You*) Come to the meeting to learn about the preschool program.

Commands with verbs in the imperative mood, such as this one, often have the implied subject *you*.

Predicates

The **simple predicate** consists of the main verb of the sentence and any auxiliaries.

> The candidate who wins the debate *will win* the election.

The **complete predicate** consists of the simple predicate and all words that modify or directly relate to it. Objects and complements are part of the complete predicate, along with any modifiers, including phrases, clauses, and single words.

> The farmer *gave the pigs enough food to last the weekend.*
>
> *The verb* gave *is the simple predicate;* food *is the direct object of the verb, and* pigs *is the indirect object of the verb. The word* the *modifies* pigs, *and* enough *modifies* food. *The phrase* to last the weekend *also modifies* food.

A **compound predicate** includes two or more verbs for the same subject.

> At the beach we *ate* our picnic, *swam* in the surf, *read* to each other, and *walked* on the sand.
>
> *The sentence has four verbs—ate, swam, read, and* walked—*that share the same subject,* we.

Objects of verbs

A **direct object** receives the action of a transitive verb.

> The company paid its *workers* a day early.   (Workers *is the object of* paid.)

> She studied her *notes* all afternoon.   (Notes *is the object of* studied.)

Direct objects often fill in the missing *who* or *what* of the transitive verb: *Whom did the company pay? What did she study all afternoon?*

An **indirect object** is a person or thing to (or for) whom the verb is directed. It is either a noun or a pronoun that *precedes the direct object* of the sentence. (If this element is accompanied by a preposition, it becomes the object of the preposition and cannot be the object of the verb.)

Brett Favre threw Antonio Freeman the ball.

Indirect objects answer the question *To whom?* or *For whom?*: *To whom did Favre throw the ball?*

Complements

A **complement** renames or modifies a subject or object; it can be a noun, a pronoun, or an adjective.

A **subject complement** is a noun, a pronoun, or an adjective that renames or describes the subject of a sentence. It follows a linking verb— *be, become, seem, appear,* and so on—that joins two equivalent terms. Whatever appears before the linking verb is the subject; whatever appears after is the subject complement.

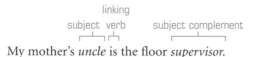

My mother's *uncle* is the floor *supervisor.*

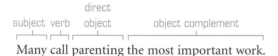

The floor *supervisor* is my mother's *uncle.*

A noun or pronoun used as a complement is sometimes called a **predicate noun:** *Judy is my sister.* An adjective used as a complement is sometimes called a **predicate adjective:** *She is very creative.*

An **object complement** follows a direct object and renames or modifies it.

Many call parenting the most important work.

Phrases

A **phrase** is a group of related words lacking a subject, a predicate, or both.

Verb phrase

A **verb phrase** consists of the main verb of a clause and its auxiliaries. It functions as the verb of a sentence.

The college has been having a difficult year.

Noun phrase

A **noun phrase** includes a noun or a pronoun, an infinitive, or a gerund serving as a noun, together with all its modifiers.

The famous and venerable institution is bankrupt.

Noun phrases may function as subjects, objects, or complements.

The college's president is distraught.   (*subject*)

He addressed *the board of trustees.*   (*object*)

They became *a terrified mob.*   (*subject complement*)

Verbal phrase

A **verbal phrase** contains a **verbal** plus any objects, complements, or modifiers. There are three kinds of verbals: infinitives, gerunds, and participles.

An **infinitive phrase** is built around an **infinitive,** the base form of the verb usually preceded by *to.* Infinitive phrases can function as nouns, adjectives, or adverbs. When they function as nouns, they are usually subjects, complements, or direct objects.

To raise a family is a noble goal.   (*an infinitive phrase used as a noun—subject*)

He has the duty *to protect his children.*   (*an infinitive used as an adjective to modify the noun* duty)

My father worked *to provide for his family.*   (*an infinitive used as an adverb to modify the verb* worked)

A **gerund phrase** is built around a **gerund,** the *-ing* form of a verb functioning as a noun. Gerund phrases always function as nouns—subjects, subject complements, direct objects, or objects of prepositions.

Studying these essays takes a lot of time.   (*gerund as subject*)

The key to success is *reading all the assignments.*   (*gerund as subject complement*)

My roommate likes *reading novels.*   (*gerund as direct object*)

She can forgive me for *preferring short stories.*   (*gerund as object of the preposition* for)

A **participial phrase** is built around a **participle,** either the present participle (end in *-ing*) or past participle (usually ending in *-ed* or *-d*), and always functions as an adjective.

Striking a blow for freedom, the Minutemen fired the "shot heard around the world." (*a participial phrase modifying the proper noun* Minutemen)

Prepositional phrase

A **prepositional phrase** consists of a preposition, its object, and any related modifiers.

prepositional phrase

The new book was hailed with great fanfare.

A prepositional phrase may function as an adjective or an adverb.

He knows the difficulty *of the task.* (*a prepositional phrase modifying the noun* difficulty *and therefore functioning as an adjective*)

She arrived *at work* a little early. (*a prepositional phrase modifying the verb* arrived *and therefore functioning as an adverb*)

Appositive phrase

An **appositive phrase** appears directly after a noun or pronoun and renames or further identifies it.

appositive phrase

Ralph Nader, a longtime consumer advocate, supports the new auto emissions proposal.

Absolute phrase

An **absolute phrase** modifies an entire sentence or clause. It consists of a noun or pronoun and a participle, together with any accompanying modifiers, objects, or complements.

absolute phrase

The opposition notwithstanding, the committee approved the resolution.

Clauses

A group of related words with a subject and a predicate is a **clause.** A clause that *can* stand alone as a complete sentence is called an **independent clause** or **main clause** of the sentence.

The moon rose.

main clause

The winner will be the candidate who best communicates with
the voters.

A clause that *cannot* stand by itself as a complete sentence is called
a **dependent clause** or **subordinate clause.** Because such a clause usually
begins with a subordinating conjunction (*because, when, unless,* and so
on) or a relative pronoun (*who, which, that,* and so on), it cannot stand
alone.

The little girl laughed *when the moon rose.*

The little girl laughed *can stand alone as a complete sentence, but* when the
moon rose *cannot.*

I assume *that the best candidate will win the election.*

I assume *can stand alone as a complete sentence, but* that the best candidate
will win the election *cannot.*

To make sense, dependent clauses must join independent clauses.
Dependent clauses can be classified as noun, adjective, or adverb clauses
depending on what role they play.

A **noun clause** is one used in the same way as a noun—as a subject, an object, or a subject complement. It is usually introduced by a
relative pronoun (*who, what, which,* and so on) or by a subordinating
conjunction (*how, when, where, whether, why*).

What I want is a good job.   (*a noun clause working as the subject of
the sentence*)

In class we learned *how we can improve our writing.*   (*a noun
clause working as the direct object of the verb* learned)

We wondered to *whom we should send them.*   (*a noun clause working as the object of the preposition* to)

An **adjective clause** modifies a noun or pronoun elsewhere in the
sentence. Most adjective clauses begin with relative pronouns such as
who, whose, or *that.* They can also begin with the relative adverbs *when,
where,* or *why* and are sometimes called **relative clauses.**

The book *that you reserved* is now available.   (*an adjective clause modifying the noun* book)

The graduating seniors, *who had just completed their exams,* were full of high spirits.   (*an adjective clause modifying the noun* seniors)

An **adverb clause** modifies a verb, an adjective, an adverb, or an entire clause. Adverb clauses tell *when, where, why,* or *how,* or they *specify a condition.* They are introduced by subordinating conjunctions such as *although, than, as,* or *since.*

The fish ride the tide *as far as it will carry them.*   (*an adverb clause modifying the verb* ride)

Now they can be caught more easily *than at any other time.*   (*an adverb clause modifying the adverb* easily)

If you get confused trying to identify the function of a particular clause, ask yourself what job it's doing in the sentence. If the clause functions as a subject, direct object, or subject complement, it is a **noun clause.** If it modifies a noun or pronoun, it is an **adjective clause.** If it modifies a verb, an adjective, an adverb, or an entire clause, it is an **adverb clause.** (Adjective and adverb clauses can also be called **modifier clauses.**)

Sentence classification and sentence patterns   47c

Sentences can be classified by function and by grammatical structure. They can also be described in terms of their sentence patterns.

Classifying sentences by function

Declarative sentences make statements. The normal word order for a declarative sentence is subject followed by predicate.

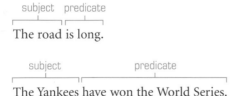

subject predicate

The road is long.

subject   predicate

The Yankees have won the World Series.

Word order is occasionally inverted.

predicate   subject

At the top of the hill stood a tree.

Interrogative sentences ask questions. They can be introduced by an interrogative pronoun, or the subject can follow part of the verb.

Who goes there?

Can pigs really fly?   (*The verb is* can fly.)

Imperative sentences make commands or requests. The subject, *you,* is typically not stated but implied. The verb form used for the imperative is always the base form.

Drive slowly.

Signal before changing lanes.

Exclamatory sentences exclaim (and usually end with an exclamation point).

Oh, how I hate to get up in the morning!

Classifying sentences by grammatical structure

Sentences are classified by grammatical structure according to how many dependent and independent clauses they contain.

A **simple sentence** consists of a single independent clause and no dependent clause. Some simple sentences are brief. Others, if they contain modifier phrases or compound subjects, verbs, or objects, can be quite long.

Marmosets eat bananas.

Benny and Griselda, marmosets at our local zoo, eat at least fifteen bananas a day, in addition to lettuce, nuts, oranges, and apples.

A **compound sentence** has two or more independent clauses and no dependent clause. The independent clauses are usually joined by a comma and a coordinating conjunction.

They grew tired of waiting, so they finally hailed a taxi.

A **complex sentence** contains one independent clause and at least one dependent clause.

The students assemble outside when the bell rings.

A **compound-complex sentence** contains at least two independent clauses and at least one dependent clause.

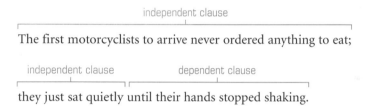

The first motorcyclists to arrive never ordered anything to eat;

they just sat quietly until their hands stopped shaking.

Understanding sentence patterns

Most independent clauses are built on one of five basic patterns.

1. The simplest pattern has only two elements, a subject and a verb.

    Nobody noticed.

Even when expanded by modifying phrases, the basic pattern of an independent clause may still be only subject-verb.

Heavy tropical rain fell Tuesday and Wednesday in the Philippines, causing mud slides and driving hundreds from their homes.

2. The next simplest pattern includes a subject, a verb, and a direct object.

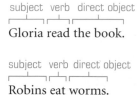

Gloria read the book.

subject verb direct object

Robins eat worms.

3. A third pattern is subject–verb–indirect object–direct object.

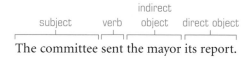

The committee sent the mayor its report.

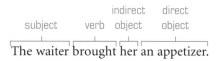

The waiter brought her an appetizer.

4. A fourth pattern is subject–verb–subject complement.

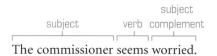

The commissioner seems worried.

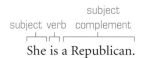

She is a Republican.

5. The fifth basic pattern is subject–verb–direct object–object complement.

His friends call him an achiever.

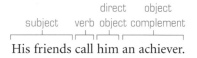

That makes him proud.

48 USING VERBS CORRECTLY

Good writing uses strong verbs. While verbs show action, they also can provide other information, much of which is included in the following box. When drafting and revising your work, select correct verb forms that best convey the meaning you intend.

TERMS USED TO DESCRIBE VERBS

Person indicates who or what performs an action.

1ST PERSON	the one speaking	*I read.*
2ND PERSON	the one spoken to	*You read.*
3RD PERSON	the one spoken about	*He reads.*

Number indicates how many people or things perform the action.

SINGULAR	one	*I think.*
PLURAL	more than one	*We think.*

Tense indicates the time of the action.

PRESENT	at this time	*I learn.*
PAST	before this time	*I learned.*
FUTURE	after this time	*I will learn.*

Mood expresses the speaker's attitude toward or relation to the action.

INDICATIVE	states a fact or asks a question	*You are quiet.*
IMPERATIVE	gives a command or a direction	*Be quiet!*
SUBJUNCTIVE	expresses a desire or requirement or states a condition contrary to fact	*I would be happier if you were quiet.*

Voice presents the subject as the "doer" (active) or "done to" (passive).

ACTIVE	The subject acts.	*She read the book.*
PASSIVE	The subject is acted on.	*The book was read by her.*

48a Standard verb forms

Except for the verb *be,* all English verbs have five forms. They are used to express the **tense** of a verb.

♦   To express present action

BASE FORM   I *act.*

-S FORM   He *acts.* She *acts.* It *acts.*

♦   To express past action

PAST TENSE (*-D* OR *-ED* + BASE FORM)

I *acted.*

PAST PARTICIPLE (FORM OF *BE* OR *HAVE* + PAST PARTICIPLE)

I *have acted.*

PRESENT PARTICIPLE (*-ING* + BASE FORM) EXPRESSES CONTINUING ACTION (IN PRESENT AND PAST TENSE)

I *am acting.*

I *was acting.*

Such changes in the verbs occur in regular verbs, while irregular verbs form the past tense and past participle in other ways.

SUMMARY OF VERB FORMS

BASE FORM	*-S* FORM	PAST TENSE	PAST PARTICIPLE	PRESENT PARTICIPLE
REGULAR				
act	acts	acted	acted	acted
seem	seems	seemed	seemed	seeming
IRREGULAR				
know	knows	knew	known	knowing
eat	eats	ate	eaten	eating
hit	hits	hit	hit	hitting

Using -s and -ed forms

Except for the verbs *be* and *have, -s* or *-es* is the ending for third person singular regular verbs in the **present tense.**

The baby *sleeps.*

Everyone at the party *dances.*

Though nonstandard usage is sometimes seen (dialects, informal talk, literary effect, and so on), academic writing ordinarily requires standard verb usage.

◆   He ~~don't~~ need to study.
      doesn't

The **past tense** of all regular verbs is created by adding *-d* or *-ed* to the base form.

◆   She ~~walk~~ her dog even though it was raining.
      walked

Irregular verb forms   48b

While regular verbs form the past tense and part participle by adding *-d* or *-ed,* irregular verbs do not follow this pattern and are consequently sometimes confusing. Some irregular verbs (including *bet, bid, burst, cost, cut, hit, quit*) do not change in any form.

I *hit* the ball now, but I *hit* it better yesterday. In the past, I have *hit* it even better.

Some others have a pattern of vowel changes.

I *ring* the bell today, and I *rang* it yesterday as I have *rung* it every morning.

These patterns are not, however, reliable enough to predict. Consult the following box when you revise and edit your work.

FORMS OF IRREGULAR VERBS

BASE FORM	PAST TENSE	PAST PARTICIPLE
arise	arose	arisen
awake	awoke, awakened	awakened, awoken
be	was, were	been
bear	bore	borne
beat	beat	beaten, beat
become	became	become
begin	began	begun
bend	bent	bent
bet	bet	bet
bid	bid	bid
bind	bound	bound
bite	bit	bitten
blow	blew	blown
break	broke	broken
bring	brought	brought
build	built	built
burst	burst	burst
buy	bought	bought
catch	caught	caught
choose	chose	chosen
cling	clung	clung
come	came	come
cost	cost	cost
creep	crept	crept
cut	cut	cut
deal	dealt	dealt
dig	dug	dug
dive	dived, dove	dived
do	did	done
draw	drew	drawn
dream	dreamed, dreamt	dreamed, dreamt
drink	drank	drunk
drive	drove	driven
eat	ate	eaten
fall	fell	fallen
feed	fed	fed
fell	felt	felt
fight	fought	fought

(continued)

BASE FORM	PAST TENSE	PAST PARTICIPLE
find	found	found
flee	fled	fled
fly	flew	flown
forbid	forbade	forbidden
forget	forgot	forgotten, forgot
forgive	forgave	forgiven
freeze	froze	frozen
get	got	gotten, got
give	gave	given
go	went	gone
grow	grew	grown
hang (suspend)	hung	hung
have	had	had
hear	heard	heard
hide	hid	hidden
hit	hit	hit
hold	held	held
hurt	hurt	hurt
keep	kept	kept
know	knew	known
lay (put)	laid	laid
lead	led	led
leap	leapt, leaped	leapt, leaped
leave	left	left
lend	lent	lent
let (allow)	let	let
lie (recline)	lay	lain
light	lit, lighted	lit, lighted
lose	lost	lost
make	made	made
mean	meant	meant
meet	met	met
mistake	mistook	mistaken
pay	paid	paid
prove	proved	proved, proven
quit	quit	quit
read	read	read
rid	rid	rid
ride	rode	ridden
ring	rang	rung

(continued)

BASE FORM	PAST TENSE	PAST PARTICIPLE
rise	rose	risen
run	ran	run
say	said	said
see	saw	seen
seek	sought	sought
send	sent	sent
set	set	set
shake	shook	shaken
shoot	shot	shot
show	showed	shown, showed
shrink	shrank	shrunk
sing	sang	sung
sink	sank	sunk
sit	sat	sat
slay	slew	slain
sleep	slept	slept
speak	spoke	spoken
spin	spun	spun
spit	spit, spat	spit, spat
spring	sprang	sprung
stand	stood	stood
steal	stole	stolen
stick	stuck	stuck
sting	stung	stung
stink	stank, stunk	stunk
strike	struck	struck, stricken
swear	swore	sworn
swim	swam	swum
swing	swung	swung
take	took	taken
teach	taught	taught
tear	tore	torn
tell	told	told
think	thought	thought
throw	threw	thrown
wake	woke, waked	woken, waked, woke
wear	wore	worn
win	won	won
write	wrote	written

Sit and *set, lie* and *lay*   48c

Because the forms of *sit* and *set* and *lie* and *lay* sound similar and are related in meaning, they are often confused. They are really very different.

Set and *lay* mean "to place" and need an object to complete their meaning (what are they placing?). They are **transitive verbs** and take a direct object.

direct object   direct object

I *set* the table each morning before I *lay* the mail on the desk.

Sit ("to be seated") and *lie* ("to recline") need no object to complete their meaning and are **intransitive verbs.**

I will *sit* outside for a while, but soon I'll want to *lie* down.

Lie and *lay* get particularly confused because the past tense of *lie* is *lay.* To use the correct verb, first establish your meaning: Are you setting or laying *something?* (Or are you just enjoying yourself sitting and lying down?). Refer to the following chart for help.

Be sure to use the correct form of each of these troublesome verbs.

◆   The books were just ~~laying~~ lying on the table.

◆   She asked me to come in and ~~set~~ sit with her a while.

SIT/SET AND *LIE/LAY*			
BASE FORM	PAST TENSE	PAST PARTICIPLE	PRESENT PARTICIPLE
sit (intransitive verb)	sat	sat	sitting
set (transitive verb)	set	set	setting
lie (intransitive verb)	lay	lain	lying
lay (transitive verb)	laid	laid	laying

48d Auxiliary verbs

Main verbs often require **auxiliary** or **helping verbs,** commonly forms of *be, have,* or *do.* Together, the auxiliary verb and main verb form a **verb phrase.**

```
            verb phrase
       ┌─────────┴─────────┐
    auxiliary   main verb
     ┌───┴───┐  ┌────┴────┐
```
Tyler has been working.

Auxiliary verbs do various jobs in sentences.

The student council *is considering* what to do.   (*present progressive tense*)

They *do want* to go to the conference.   (*emphasis*)

Has he *received* the blueprints?   (*question*)

He *does* not *intend* to leave without them.   (*negative statement*)

The blueprints *were delivered* on Friday.   (*passive voice*)

Forms of *have, do,* and *be* change to indicate tense.

have, has, had

do, does, did

be, am, is, are, was, were, being, been

I *have mended* a jacket that *had gotten* torn.

Modal auxiliaries

Can, could, may, might, must, shall, should, will, and *would* are used with a main verb to express condition, intent, permission, possibility, obligation, or desire. These modal auxiliaries cannot stand alone as a main verb; they always appear with the base form of the verb unless the context creates necessary meaning. They *do not* change form to show person, tense, number, or mood.

Staying in touch with friends *can become* difficult as we grow older.

Can she *dance?* Yes, she can.   (Dance *is understood here.*)

Using auxiliary verbs correctly

Standard English requires the auxiliary verb *be* or *have* with present participles and irregular past participles.

◆   Gina ^is^ running for student council.

◆   She ^has^ spoken to everyone about it.

A form of *be*—*is, are, was, were*—along with the main verb is needed to create the passive voice.

Each student *is given* a book at graduation.

Verb tense   48e

English has three simple tenses, three perfect tenses, and a progressive form for each of them. Descriptions follow.

The **simple present** tense describes regular actions or those occurring at the same time as the speaking.

He *looks* happy today. He usually *looks* content.

The simple present also is used to state general facts or truths and when writing about literature.

In *The Tempest*, the wizard Prospero *seems* to control the heavens.

The **simple past** tense describes actions completed in the past.

He *looked* a little depressed yesterday.

The **simple future** tense describes actions that will occur in the future or predictable events.

He *will look* different tomorrow.

Flowers *will* wilt if left unattended.

The three perfect tenses indicate *action completed by a specific time.* Using forms of *have* plus the past participle, they place that action in the present, past, or future.

The **present perfect** describes action completed in the past or a completed action still occurring.

She *has looked* for the file today.

She *has looked* for it every day this week.

The **past perfect** describes action completed before another past action took place.

She *had looked* for the file ten times before she found it.

The **future perfect** describes an action that will be completed at some specific time in the future.

Once she goes through the last drawer, she *will have looked* everywhere.

The three progressive tenses describe *continuing action* in the present, past, or future.

The **present progressive** describes ongoing action in the present.

She *is anticipating* the holidays.

The **past progressive** describes continuous action in the past with no specified end.

Before her father's illness, she *was anticipating* the holidays.

The **future progressive** describes continuous or ongoing action in the future, which often depends on some other action or circumstance.

Once her father is better, she *will be anticipating* the holidays again.

The three perfect progressive tenses describe action that continues up to a specific time of completion in the present, past, or future.

The **present perfect progressive** describes action that began in the past and still continues.

> He *has been looking* for a job since August.

The **past perfect progressive** describes ongoing action that was completed before some other action.

> Before he found work, he *had been looking* for a job since August.

VERBS THAT DO NOT HAVE A PROGRESSIVE FORM

Verbs that express action, processes, or events are called **dynamic verbs.** Such verbs can usually be used in a progressive -*ing* form to express an action in progress.

> I am *walking* through the park.

Other verbs express attitudes, conditions, or relationships. These are called **stative verbs,** and they cannot usually be used in a progressive -*ing* form.

> ◆ I am ~~believing~~ your story.
>   *believe*

COMMON STATIVE VERBS

admire	dislike	like	see
agree	doubt	look	seem
appear	hate	love	smell
believe	have	need	sound
belong	hear	own	taste
contain	imagine	possess	think
cost	include	prefer	understand
disagree	know	remember	want

Sometimes these verbs are used as dynamic verbs to describe an activity or a process. In these cases, the progressive form may be used.

> Don't bother me while I *am thinking.*

> I was agreeing with you until you started the argument.

The **future perfect progressive** describes continuous action that will be completed at some future time.

By August, he *will have been looking* for a job for six months.

Sequence of tenses

Verb tenses throughout a piece of writing must relate logically to one another. The dominant tense of a piece is its **governing tense,** which affects the choice of tense for every verb.

In sentences, many combinations of verb tenses are possible, but the *sequence of tenses*—the way in which one verb's tense relates to the tense of others nearby—needs to describe events accurately and to make sense.

present · future

I think that you will enjoy this movie.

I am thinking *this before you* enjoy *the movie.*

present · present

I know that you like foreign films.

I know this at the same time as you like *them.*

present · past

I believe that you misunderstood me.

I believe this after you misunderstood *me.*

Changing the tense of any verb can change the meaning of a sentence, so edit carefully for verb tense.

Sequence with infinitives and participles

The tense of an infinitive or participle must be in sequence with the tense of the main verb.

The **present infinitive** (*to* plus the base form of verb) can show action occurring at the same time as, or later than, the action of the main verb.

Some children *like to play* with educational toys.

Liking *and* playing *take place at the same time.*

The committee *plans to vote* on the proposal next week.
Voting *takes place later than* planning.

The **perfect infinitive** (*to have* plus the past participle) generally indicates action that occurred before the action of the main verb.

I *seem to have misplaced* my credit card.
Misplacing *it has already happened.*

The **present participle** (the *-ing* form of the verb) shows action occurring at the same time as the action of the main verb.

Working obsessively, he *wrote* late into the night.
He wrote *while obsessed.*

The **present perfect participle** (*having* plus the past participle) shows action completed before that of the main verb.

Having worked feverishly all night, at dawn he *saw* the sunrise.

The **past participle** shows action taking place at the same time as, or completed before, the action of the main verb.

Guided by instinct, the swallows *returned* as usual on March 19.
Guiding *and* returning *take place at the same time.*

Born in 1917, John F. Kennedy *became* the country's youngest president in 1961.
He was born *before he* became *president.*

Sequence for habitual actions and universal truths

When a dependent clause expresses a habitual action or a universal truth, the verb in the dependent clause stays in the present tense regardless of the tense in the independent clause.

He *told* me he *works* for Teledyne.

Copernicus *demonstrated* that the earth *revolves* around the sun.

Notice that shifting to the past tense in a dependent clause can suggest that something is not true or habitual.

He *told* me that he *worked* for Teledyne, but the company *had* no record of him.

Ptolemy *believed* the earth *was* the center of the universe.

48f Verb mood

English has three different "moods," each of which is used for different purposes.

The **indicative mood** states facts, opinions, or questions and notes things that have happened, are happening, or will happen.

He *believes* that the theory is valid.

The **imperative mood** commands and gives directives. It appears as the base form of the verb and omits the subject, which is understood to be *you*.

Sit down and *complete* these forms.

Knead the dough until it forms a ball.

The **subjunctive mood** expresses wishes, requirements, and conditions that the speaker knows not to be so. Different forms exist for present, past, and perfect subjunctive.

The **present subjunctive** is the same *base form of the verb* for all persons and number.

I asked that we *leave* early to avoid traffic.

I asked that she *leave* me alone.

The **past subjunctive** uses the *simple past tense* for all verbs except *be,* which always uses *were.*

If you *donated* more than a million dollars, your college would name a hall after you.

◆ If he ~~was~~ *were* willing to help, what would we ask him to do?

The **perfect subjunctive** uses *had* plus the past participle (the past perfect tense of a verb).

If he *had caught* the ball, the run would not have scored.

Using the subjunctive

Use the subjunctive in some idiomatic expressions.

Long live the queen!   as it were
if I were you   far be it from me

After **as if, as though,** *or* **if**

Use the subjunctive with dependent clauses beginning with *if, as if,* and *as though* that note conditions contrary to fact. Use the past or perfect subjunctive in these cases.

He screamed as though the house *were* on fire.

If it *were* sunny, he could go out.

When the *if* clause expresses an *actual* condition, use the indicative mood.

If the baseball game *has begun,* we will know where to find him.

Do not use conditional auxiliaries in *both* the dependent clause and the main clause.

◆   If I ~~could have~~ left earlier, I would have been on time.
        had

Use the subjunctive mood to express a wish, a requirement, or a request.

Use the past or perfect subjunctive in dependent clauses expressing wishes. (Sometimes the relative pronoun *that* is omitted.)

◆   I wished there ~~was~~ some way to help them.
        had been

Use present subjunctive after verbs that require *(ask, demand, insist, recommend, request, require, specify, suggest)*

◆   Courtesy requires that he ~~comes~~ in formal attire.
        come

◆   Barbara insisted she ~~goes~~ alone.
        go

48g Voice

The voice of a verb tells you whether the subject is the actor (**active voice**) or the receiver of the action (**passive voice**). Use the active voice for simpler, more direct language.

> She *read* the book.   (*active voice*)

> The book *was read* by her.   (*passive voice*)

49 | MAKING SUBJECTS AGREE WITH VERBS

Verbs must agree with their subjects in number (Are you talking about one or more than one?) and person (Who is the feature person or persons? I? You? She? He? It? We? They?).

49a Agreement of person and number

Matters of agreement between the subject and verb usually involve the addition of the letter *s* in the third person singular in the present tense.

	SINGULAR	PLURAL
1ST PERSON	I think.	We think.
2ND PERSON	You think.	You think.
3RD PERSON	He, she, it thinks.	They think.

Though the addition of the letter *s* in the third person singular works for many verbs in common usage, the verb *to be* has different forms in the present and past tenses.

PRESENT TENSE		PAST TENSE	
I am.	We are.	I was.	We were.
You are.	You are.	You were.	You were.
He/she/it is.	They are.	He/she/it was.	They were.

Some general rules:

♦ If the *subject* ends in *-s* or *-es* (usually indicating a plural noun), the verb probably shouldn't end in *-s*.

The *mansions seem* elegant.

- If the *verb* ends in *-s* or *-es* (usually indicating a singular verb), the subject probably shouldn't end in *-s* or *-es*.

The *mansion seems* elegant.

Nouns with irregular plurals—*children, men*—don't follow these rules, of course. These plurals still require a verb without an *-s* or *-es*.

The *children walk* home.

Another exception is nouns that end in *-s* but are singular.

Politics is a dirty business.

There are also some verbs that end in *s* in their base form. These verbs add *-es* for the third person singular in the present tense.

They *pass* my house on their way to school.

She *passes* my house on her way to school.

Interruptions between subject and verb 49b

Words placed between the subject and verb can be confusing. To determine what verb is needed, eliminate the interrupting words and test for the proper match.

- The bowl of apples ~~are~~ *is* very tempting.
  Reduce the sentence to The bowl . . . is very tempting. *The singular subject* bowl *takes the singular verb* is.

- Mr. Johnson, along with his children, ~~were~~ *was* waiting outside.
  Reduce the sentence to Mr. Johnson . . . was waiting outside. *The singular subject* Mr. Johnson *takes the singular verb* was.

When the subject follows the verb 49c

When subjects follow verbs in sentences, it is sometimes difficult to locate the subject and determine the proper agreement. Restore normal word order to the sentence to help you find the subject.

Underneath the freeway overpass (*huddle/huddles?*) a ramshackle collection of cardboard shelters.

Reverse the sentence to A ramshackle collection of cardboard shelters *huddles* underneath the freeway overpass. *The singular subject* collection *takes the singular verb* huddles.

Questions

In questions, part of the verb almost always precedes the subject. Find the subject and check for proper agreement.

Are those seats next to you empty?

Change the sentence to Those *seats* next to you *are* empty.

Expletives

When *Here* and *There* introduce sentences, they are never subjects. Look elsewhere in the sentence for the subject.

There are almost eight million stories in the Naked City.

Change to Almost eight million *stories are* in the Naked City.

When *it* is used in an expletive construction, it is considered the grammatical subject of the sentence. Singular, *it* is followed by a singular verb.

It is the workers, not management, who *want* this change.

49d Verb agreement and linking verbs

Linking verbs, such as *be, become, seem,* and *appear,* connect the subject of the sentence to a subject complement that renames, identifies, or describes the subject. As you edit sentences containing a subject complement, make sure the verb agrees with the subject, not the complement.

◆　Her hobbies ~~is~~ *are* the one thing that makes her happy.

◆　His promises to change ~~appears~~ *appear* to be a waste of breath.

49e Verb agreement with subjects joined by *and*

Two or more subjects linked by *and* (compound subjects) are almost always *plural* and take a plural verb.

Peter and Patrick play on the lacrosse team.

Exceptions:

◆ When the two joined words comprise a single entity, use a singular verb.

   Red beans and rice is my favorite dish.

◆ When all the parts of a compound subject refer to the same person or thing, use a singular verb.

   My *friend, partner, and mentor has* brought expertise to the firm.

◆ When *each* precedes singular subjects joined by *and*, use a singular verb.

   Each river, brook, and stream in the country *has suffered from pollution.*

◆ When *each* follows a compound subject, the subject and verb are plural.

   The *pianist and the singer each deserve* special praise.

Verb agreement with subjects joined by *or* and *nor*   49f

When parts of a subject are joined by *or, nor, either . . . or, neither . . . nor,* or *not only,* make the verb agree with the subject closest to it.

   Neither the researchers *nor* the *professor accepts* the results.
   The singular noun professor *is closer to the verb; use the singular verb* accepts.

   Neither the professor *nor* the *researchers accept* the results.
   The plural noun researchers *is closer to the verb; use the plural verb* accept.

Verb agreement with collective nouns   49g

Words that refer to groups of people, animals, or things (*couple, flock, crowd, herd, committee*) are called **collective nouns**. Because they generally refer to the group as a singular unit, they generally take singular verbs. They may take plural verbs when individual members of the group are highlighted.

> The *jury has reached* a verdict.
> *Here the group,* jury, *is considered one unit and takes the singular verb* has.

> The *jury have returned* home.
> *Here the group,* jury, *is considered a group of individuals and therefore takes the plural verb* have.

To avoid such confusion, replace the subject with one that is clearly plural.

> The *jurors were* anxious to return home.

Media, data, curricula, criteria, and *phenomena* look like singular words in English, but in fact, they are plural forms of words (from Greek and Latin sources) like *criterion* and *phenomenon.* These words should take *plural* verbs. Check your dictionary to see whether a noun that ends in *a* is a singular or plural.

◆   The media ~~has~~ continued to focus on crime even as data ~~shows~~ cities

[correction above: have]   [correction above: show]

are becoming safer.

The collective noun *number,* preceded by the article *the,* refers to a group as a single unit and takes a singular verb.

> The number of visitors *has* been small.

When *number* is preceded by the article *a,* it implies "more than one" or "several," and it takes a plural verb.

> A number of visitors *have* been enthusiastic about the new exhibits.

49h Verb agreement with indefinite pronouns

Indefinite pronouns do not refer to *specific* persons or things. Some indefinite pronouns (*someone, nobody, everything,* and so on) are always considered *singular* (and take a singular verb).

VERB AGREEMENT WITH NONCOUNT NOUNS

Count nouns name persons, places, or things that can be counted—*one* apple, *two* oranges. **Noncount nouns** refer to things that can't be counted—*oil*—or refer to things in a sense that does not imply counting—*money, sand.*

NONCOUNT NOUNS	ABSTRACTIONS	EMOTIONS	QUALITIES
equipment	behavior	anger	confidence
water	education	happiness	honesty
homework	health	love	integrity
money	knowledge	surprise	sincerity

A few noncount nouns appear to be plural because they end in the letter *s*, but they are actually singular. Examples are *mathematics*, *news*, and *physics*.

Noncount nouns are usually used in the singular—most have no plural form—and take singular verbs.

Public <u>transportation</u> in Atlanta <u>makes</u> getting around easy.

This <u>information</u> <u>is</u> intended to help you when you edit.

Someone <u>has been sleeping</u> in my bed.

Everybody <u>wears</u> a heavy coat in such cold weather.

Some of these pronouns (*few, many, others,* and so on) are always considered *plural* (and take a plural verb).

Luckily, *few* of the passengers *<u>were injured</u>.*

Several of the children *<u>want</u>* to be included.

Still other pronouns (*all, any, some,* and so on) can be either singular or plural, depending on their meaning and the nouns to which they refer. (See the box Common Indefinite Pronouns.)

All <u>are</u> required to take the exam.
The plural unspecific reference takes a plural verb.

388

All I have *is* a rough idea.

The singular unspecific reference takes a singular verb.

All is plural when it means "the entire group." It is singular when it means "everything" or "the only thing."

Though some controversy exists about the way it sounds, the word *none*, used alone, takes a singular verb.

The birds all escaped, and *none was* recaptured.

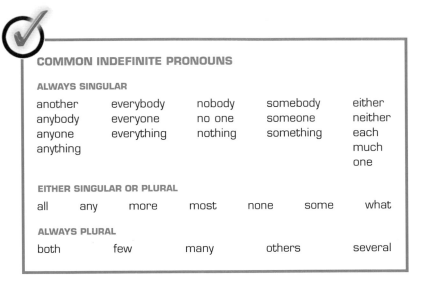

COMMON INDEFINITE PRONOUNS

ALWAYS SINGULAR

another	everybody	nobody	somebody	either
anybody	everyone	no one	someone	neither
anyone	everything	nothing	something	each
anything				much
				one

EITHER SINGULAR OR PLURAL

all	any	more	most	none	some	what

ALWAYS PLURAL

both	few	many	others	several

49i Verb agreement with *who, which,* and *that*

To determine whether a verb following one of the **relative pronouns** *who, which,* or *that* should be singular or plural, consider the word to which the pronoun refers (its **antecedent**).

Barb and Robin, *who* want to join the project, *have applied*.

Who refers to the plural Barb and Robin *and therefore takes the plural verb* have applied.

A bale of shingles *that slips* off the roof could hurt someone.

That refers to the singular noun bale *and therefore takes the singular verb* slips.

VERB AGREEMENT WITH QUANTIFIERS

FEW **AND** *A FEW*

> *Few*: "not many," "not enough"

> *A few:* "some," "several," "a small number"

Both take plural verbs.

> *Many* students *are taking* exams today. A few are out sick.

> *Few* *have failed* in past years.

LITTLE **AND** *A LITTLE*

> *Little*: "not much"

> *A little*: "some," "a small amount"

Both take singular verbs.

> *Little* *has been done* to address the problem of poverty.

> When it comes to jalapeños, *a little* *goes* a long way.

MOST **AND** *MOST OF THE*

> *Most*: "the majority"

Use a singular or plural verb, depending on the noun or pronoun it modifies or refers to.

> *Most* violence on TV *is* unnecessary.

> *Most* dogs *are tied up* when their owners are away.

> *Most of*, *most of the*: "the majority of"

Use a plural verb when followed by a plural noun or pronoun; use a singular verb when followed by a noncount noun or a singular pronoun.

> *Most of* our friends *encouraged* their children to read.

> *Most of the* neighborhood dogs *bark* in the morning.

Relative pronouns following *one of the* or *the only one of the* can be tricky. As a rule, *one of the* takes a plural verb and *the only one of the* takes a singular verb.

His wonderful laugh is *one of the* qualities that *endear* him to us.
plural

The voters believed that Tom was *the only one of the* candidates who *was* honest.
singular

49j Verb agreement with nouns ending in -s, with nouns that specify amounts, and with titles

Nouns ending in -s

Statistics, politics, economics, athletics, measles, news, acoustics, and *aesthetics* appear to be plural nouns, but all take singular verbs.

Economics is sometimes *called* "the dismal science."

Exception: When these nouns refer to specific instances or characteristics, they are considered plural and take a plural verb.

The *economics* of the project *make* no sense.

Nouns that specify amounts

Words describing amounts of *time* or *money, distances, measurements,* or *percentages* can take singular or plural verbs, depending on whether they refer to a singular unit (or sum) or a group of individuals (plural).

Fifteen *minutes is* too long to keep a class waiting.
Minutes *here is considered a block of time. The singular unit takes a singular verb.*

Fifteen *minutes fly* when you're having fun.
The plural minutes *takes a plural verb.*

Names or titles used as words

Names or titles involving more than one word are considered singular and take a singular verb.

Divine Secrets of the Ya-Ya Sisterhood was written by Rebecca Wells.

General Motors is an important employer in Michigan.

When a plural word is used as *a particular term*, use a singular verb.

Hyenas was what my father lovingly called us children.

 # 50 | USING PRONOUNS CORRECTLY

A pronoun is a stand-in for a noun that has been mentioned previously.

Sam lent me his *sweater*, but *it* was wrinkled.

It is the pronoun that refers back to the noun *sweater*. The noun to which a pronoun refers is called the pronoun's **antecedent.**

If you look carefully at the sentence above, you'll find that there are two other pronouns: *me* and *his*. While pronouns are frequently used in spoken and written language, they are also often the cause of confusion. This is partly because there are so many kinds of pronouns.

Personal pronouns substitute for specific persons or things.

Sally usually goes to the gym, but today *she* won't be able to.

Possessive pronouns show ownership.

That backpack is *mine*.

Reflexive pronouns return the reference to the person "doing" something.

John cut *himself* with the scissors.

Relative pronouns introduce dependent clauses that work as adjectives.

Josh and Sandra are the students *who* are leading the class this morning.

Interrogative pronouns introduce questions.

Who is going to the movies tonight?

Demonstrative pronouns indicate specific nouns and can also function as adjectives.

Don't pick *those* apples; *these* are riper.

Indefinite pronouns refer to nonspecific persons or things.

Everyone is working on this project.

Reciprocal pronouns refer to an action shared between two people, things, or ideas.

The investigators helped *one another* with the research.

Pronoun problems often surface in the following ways.

Reference: Is it clear to whom or what the pronoun refers?

Agreement: Does the pronoun agree with the noun to which it refers?

Case: When do you use *I* or *me*? *Who* or *whom*?

50a Pronoun Reference

The word to which a pronoun refers is called its **antecedent**. Problems occur when references are ambiguous, implied, or vague. To help clarify, state the antecedent explicitly.

Ambiguous reference (sentence can be read two ways)

Marco met Roger as he arrived at the gym.   (*When* who *arrived at the gym?*)

Clear reference

As Marco arrived at the gym, he met Roger.

Marco met Roger as Roger arrived at the gym.

Implied reference

◆   Interviews with several television newspeople made ~~it~~ seem like a fas-

    reporting

cinating career.

Because the writer is not explicit, the reader doesn't know what career seems fascinating.

Vague reference to *this, that,* **and** *which*

When used in simple sentences, these pronouns do not create problems. However, when they refer to a more general idea, they may need explicit clarification.

◆   No one has suggested taxing health care. This *tax* is unlikely.

Without this added word, it's not clear whether the suggestion or the tax is unlikely.

◆   She took the situation seriously, *a response* which I found laughable.

Without the explicit reference, it's not clear whether I found the situation or her response laughable.

Vague reference with *it, they,* **or** *you*

Though these pronouns are often clear when people are speaking, academic writing requires explicit reference.

◆   *According to* ~~It said on~~ the news this morning ~~that~~ the game was canceled.

◆   *The club doesn't* ~~They don't~~ let anyone in without a shirt or shoes.

Choosing *who, which,* **or** *that*

Use *who* for people or animals with names.

Black Beauty is a horse *who* lives in an imaginary world.

Use *which* or *that* for objects, ideas, and unnamed people or animals.

This is the policy *that* the administration wants.

He tried to rope the last steer, *which* twisted to avoid him.

WHICH

Clauses that begin with *which,* though they may add information, are not necessary to the meaning of the sentence.

> Laura's dog, *which* is very old, is a wonderful friend.
>
> *The dog happens to be very old, but the meaning here focuses on its being a good friend.*

Which used in this way introduces a **nonrestrictive modifier** and is always set off by commas.

THAT

Clauses that begin with *that* add information necessary to the meaning of the sentence.

> The dog *that got muddy* tramped through the house.
>
> *The dog's being muddy gives meaning to its tramping through the house.*

That always introduces a restrictive modifier.

Though *that* always introduces a restrictive modifier, *which* can be used to introduce a restrictive or a nonrestrictive modifier. To avoid confusion, some writers use *which* only for nonrestrictive modifiers.

WHO

Who may introduce both restrictive and nonrestrictive modifiers.

NONRESTRICTIVE	Americans, who eat a richer diet than Europeans, have higher rates of heart disease.
RESTRICTIVE	Americans who cut down on fatty foods may live longer than those who don't.

50b Pronoun-antecedent agreement

Personal pronouns should agree with their antecedents in number, person, and gender.

A pronoun is singular if *it* has a singular antecedent.

Pronouns are plural if *they* have plural antecedents.

When the tree fell, *it* shook the forest.

Mrs. Shaw held the door for *her* daughter.

Sexist pronouns

Agreement becomes problematic when pronouns refer to indefinite antecedents such as *anyone, someone,* and *everyone.* Since these pronouns can refer to either males or females, you must be careful in your use of pronouns that refer to these indefinite antecedents.

◆   If anyone needs to miss class, ~~he~~ *he or she* will need to contact the instructor.

This use of *he* is *not* acceptable since *he* refers only to males. To address this problem, consider the following alternatives.

Use the phrase *he or she* or *his or her.*

◆   If anyone needs to miss class, he *or she* will need to contact the instructor.

Revise the sentence using the plural *students* in place of the singular *anyone.*

◆   If ~~students needs~~ *students need* to miss class, ~~he~~ *they* will need to contact the instructor.

Eliminate personal pronouns altogether.

◆   If ~~anyone needs~~ *Students who need* to miss class, ~~he~~ will need to contact the instructor.

Agreement with antecedents joined by *and*

Pronouns referring back to a compound antecedent should be *plural.*

The book and the folders are in *their* places on the shelf.

Use a *singular* pronoun in the following cases.

◆   The compound antecedent is preceded by *each* or *every.*

Each book and folder is in *its* place on the shelf.

◆ The parts of the compound antecedent refer to the same person or thing.

As my *sociology professor and thesis advisor, she* helped me choose this semester's courses.

◆ Both parts of the compound antecedent refer to a single entity.

My favorite dish is rice and beans; *it* always tastes good on cold days.

Agreement with antecedents joined by *or* and *nor*

When all parts of an antecedent are *singular,* the pronoun referring to it is *singular.*

Either the assessor's *office* or the *court* will have to cut *its* budget.

When one part of the compound antecedent is *singular* and one is *plural,* make the pronoun agree with the antecedent closer to it.

Either the equipment failures or the bad *weather* will take *its* toll.
The singular pronoun its *refers to the singular—and closer—antecedent* weather.

Agreement with collective nouns

Use a single pronoun to refer to collective nouns (*couple, flock, crowd*) that are seen as a single group or unit.

◆ The flock rose suddenly from the pond and took up ~~their~~ *its* usual formation.

Use a plural pronoun to refer to collective nouns if members of the group are acting separately.

◆ The crew gathered ~~its~~ *their* belongings and prepared to leave the ship.

Agreement with indefinite pronouns

Words like *anyone, everyone, someone, anybody, everybody, somebody, anything, everything, something, either, neither, each, nothing, much, one,* and *no one* do not refer to a specific person, place, or thing. They are always singular and should take a singular pronoun.

Someone has left *his or her* notebook.

Neither of these books has *its* original cover.

The indefinite pronouns *few, many, both,* and *several* are always plural and therefore require a plural pronoun.

Few of the students have completed *their* work.

The indefinite pronouns *some, any, all, more, most,* and *none* can be singular or plural depending on their context.

In a survey of young voters, *some* said *they* were conservative.

The money is still in the safe. *Some* is still in *its* bags.

Pronoun case   50c

Since pronouns are stand-ins for nouns, they perform, as nouns do, different roles in sentences. These different roles are called *cases.* Use the **subjective case** of a pronoun for a person or thing that performs an action in the sentence.

She plays piano.

Use the **objective case** when a pronoun receives the action.

Bob gave the book to *her.*

Use the **possessive case** to show ownership.

My mom lives in the city.

	SUBJECTIVE	OBJECTIVE	POSSESSIVE
SINGULAR	I	me	my
	you	you	your
	he, she, it	him, her, it	his, her, its
PLURAL	we	us	our
	you	you	your
	they	them	their

Use the possessive pronouns above to precede a noun.

Megan is *her* sister.

However, use these possessive pronouns when no noun follows: *mine, yours, his, hers, its, ours, yours, theirs.*

The books are *mine.*

Compound subjects

Choosing the correct pronoun can be tricky when two or more words are joined. Test the sentence *without the added words* to determine the correct pronoun.

◆   Todd and ~~me~~ pruned the tall white pine.
    When you test the sentence as Me pruned the tall white pine, *it is clear that pronoun should be* I.

◆   Ralph, Otto, and ~~him~~ planned to go bowling.
    Remove Ralph *and* Otto. <u>Him</u> planned to go bowling *is not correct;* <u>he</u> planned to go bowling *is correct.*

Subject complements

Subject complements follow linking verbs and rename the subject or complete its meaning: *The winner was my dad. Winner* and *dad* are the same people, linked by the verb *was.* When there is a compound subject, use the subjective case for the pronoun.

It is *I* who is sorry.

◆   The real winners were my father and ~~me~~.

Compound objects

Two or more objects joined by *and, or,* or *nor* are considered **compound objects.** Use the objective case for each part of the construction.

◆   Just between you and ~~I~~, it's a fake.

◆   Give your donations to Nancy or ~~I~~.

Appositives

Appositives rename nouns or pronouns and must have the same case as the words they rename.

> It was the victors, Paul and *he,* who wanted to leave.
>
> *The appositive* Paul and he *renames* victors, *the subject complement, and is therefore in subjective case.*

> They asked the teachers, Barbara and *me,* to help out.
>
> *The appositive* Barbara and me *renames* teachers, *the direct* object *of the verb* asked, *and is therefore in the objective case.*

We or *us* **before a noun**

To determine which case to use, omit the noun and test for appropriate use.

◆   ~~Us~~ hikers were worried about the weather.
     _{We}

> *You wouldn't say, "Us were worried about the weather."*

◆   They told ~~we~~ hikers not to worry.
              _{us}

> *You wouldn't say, "They told we not to worry."*

Pronoun case with verbals

Participles, gerunds, and infinitives are called **verbals** because they are derived from verbs. Each of these can have objects. When a pronoun functions as an object of a verbal, use the objective case.

> I saw Robert greeting *him.*
>
> Him *is the object of the participle* greeting.

> Seeing *her* made the holiday complete.
>
> Her *is the object of the gerund* seeing.

> To know *him* is to love *him.*
>
> Him *is the object of the infinitives* to know *and* to love.

Pronouns before gerunds

Use the possessive case for pronouns preceding verbals used as nouns (gerunds).

◆   My
      ~~Me~~ leaving made them all sad.
            ^

Pronouns before infinitives
Use the objective case for pronouns preceding infinitives.

They want *her* to help.

It was hard for *him* to agree.

Pronoun case after *than* or *as*

If you are uncertain what case pronoun to use, construct test sentences to see which you mean.

She likes her dog better than (me/I?).

She likes her dog better than *I* (like her dog).

She likes her dog better than (she likes) *me*.

The different pronouns here mean two distinctly different things. In the first test sentence, *she* and *I* are both evaluating her dog; *she* and *I* are the subjects of the action. In the second test sentence, *she* is evaluating *me* and the *dog; me* and *her dog* are objects of the action. You need to be clear about what you intend when you choose your pronoun.

Who or *whom?*

The distinction between *who* and *whom* has all but disappeared from everyday speech, but in formal writing be more careful and use *who* for subjects and *whom* for objects.

In questions
When deciding whether to use *who* or *whom* in a question, turn the question into a statement by substituting *he* or *she* or *him* or *her*. If *he* or *she* fits, use *who*. If *him* or *her* fits, use *whom*.

Who had the authority to enter the building at night?

She *had the authority, so use* who.

When a pronoun (*him* or *her*) is the object of the verb or the object of the preposition, use *whom.*

To *whom* are you speaking?
You are speaking to him, *so use* whom.

In dependent clauses

When deciding whether to use *who* or *whom* in a dependent clause, check for the word's function within the clause.

◆   That woman, ~~who~~ ^{whom} I met last week, won the Noble prize for chemistry.

Whom *is the object of the verb* met, *even though it renames the subject of the main clause,* woman.

◆   She tells that same story to ~~whomever~~ ^{whoever} will listen.

Whoever *is the subject of* will listen. *The entire subordinate clause* whoever will listen *is the object of the preposition* to.

Using reflexive pronouns

Reflexive pronouns reflect the action of the sentence back to the subject.

John cut *himself* with the scissors.

I speak only for *myself,* not for my research partner.

Do not use reflexive pronouns as subjects.

◆   My partner and ~~myself~~ were invited to the reception.

51 | WORKING WITH ADJECTIVES AND ADVERBS

Adjectives and adverbs modify—they describe, identify, or limit the meaning of—other words. **Modifiers** can enrich description, transforming a simple sentence like *The hikers were lost* into a more engaging one like *The exhausted hikers were hopelessly lost.*

51a Adjective or adverb?

Adjectives modify (describe, identify, or limit) nouns or pronouns.

Hector is a *fine* father who has *gentle* hands and *abundant* patience

with *crying* babies.

He is *loving, careful,* and *dependable.*

Fine, gentle, abundant, *and* crying *are words that describe the nouns to which they're attached:* father, hands, patience, *and* babies. *Since they modify nouns, they're adjectives.* Loving, careful, *and* dependable *modify the pronoun* he *and are also adjectives.*

Adverbs modify verbs, adjectives, other adverbs, and sometimes whole clauses.

He *often* takes care of the baby at *truly* late hours and *nearly always*

quiets her *quickly.*

When attached to verbs, adverbs tell *when, where, how, why,* and *under what conditions* something happens (how often, to what degree). *Often, always,* and *quickly* modify verbs in the sentence above. When adverbs modify adjectives and other adverbs, they are used to intensify the words they modify. *Truly* modifies *late* (adjective); *nearly* modifies *always* (adverb) in the sentence.

Adverbs modifying whole clauses provide similar information (*when, where, how,* and so on).

Amazingly, he loves doing it.

As you can see, adjectives and adverbs are distinguished by what kinds of words they modify or what words they're attached to. When in doubt, look for the "anchor word," or the word they modify. If the anchor word is a noun or pronoun, the confusing word is working as and **adjective;** if the anchor word is a verb, an adjective, or an adverb, or if the word in question relates to an entire clause, it is working as an **adverb.**

Suffixes

Adjectives are often formed by adding endings such as *-able, -ful,* and *-ish* to nouns and verbs: *acceptable, beautiful, foolish.* Adverbs are often formed by adding *-ly* to an adjective: *nearly, amazingly, brilliantly.* However, an *-ly* suffix does not always mean that a word is an adverb. A number of adjectives end in *-ly: brotherly, friendly, lovely.* And many adverbs do not end in *-ly: always, here.*

Linking verbs and modifiers   51b

Adjectives usually come before nouns, but they can also come after a linking verb such as *be, become, appear, grow, seem, remind,* or *approve* to describe the subject (a subject complement). Since a subject complement modifies the subject—a noun or pronoun—it must be an adjective. If you are describing a *state of being,* as opposed to an action, use an adjective.

The ghost of Hamlet's father appears *anxious.*

The linking verbs *appear, look, smell, taste,* and *sound* can also function as action verbs. If you are describing an *action,* use an adverb.

The ghost of Hamlet's father appears *suddenly.*

(See 44a for more on linking verbs and modifiers.)

Commonly confused modifiers   51c

In casual speech, adjectives are often used instead of adverbs to modify verbs: *It fit real well* instead of *It fit really well.* Be sure to use the correct form of the following pairs in academic writing.

Bad and *badly*

Bad is an adjective and should be used only to modify nouns and pronouns: *bad food, bad assignment. Bad* is used as an adjective with linking verbs (see 44a), while *badly* is used to modify other verbs.

◆   She looked as though she felt ~~badly~~. *(bad)*

404

◆　　They were playing so ~~bad~~ ^{badly} that I left at halftime.

Good **and** *well*

Good is always an adjective. *Well* can be either an adjective meaning "healthy" or an adverb meaning "skillfully." *Good* and *well* are often confused in speaking, partly because they share the same comparative and superlative forms: *good, better, best; well, better, best.*

◆　　She is a very good singer, but can she sing ~~good~~ ^{well} enough to get the lead?

◆　　The hat looks ~~well~~ ^{good} on my mother.

Real **and** *really*

Real is used as an adjective meaning "genuine, true, not illusory." *Really* is an adverb meaning "truly" or "very."

Andrew is a *real* friend.

◆   He believed the interview was <del>real</del> *really* important to his job prospects.

Less **and** *fewer*

Less and *fewer* are both adjectives, but they function in different ways. *Less* describes something considered as a whole unit: *less hope, less money*. *Fewer* signifies quantities that can be counted: *fewer hopes, fewer dollars*.

◆   The house would lose *less* heat if *less* *fewer* windows were open.

Less can also be an adverb.

Sam was *less* successful as an actor than Brad because Sam delivered his lines *less* convincingly.

Comparatives and superlatives   51d

Adjectives and adverbs have three forms: the positive, the comparative, and the superlative. While the **positive** form of an adjective or adverb describes a particular property (*smart, funny*), the **comparative** compares that property between *two* people or things (*smarter, funnier*). The **superlative** form makes a comparison among *three or more* people or things (*smartest, funniest*). Some lengthy adjectives and most adverbs ending in *-ly* take *more* and *most* to form comparative and superlative forms. Negative comparisons are formed by using *less* and *least*.

POSITIVE	COMPARATIVE	SUPERLATIVE
big	bigger	biggest
fast	faster	fastest
good	better	best
careful	more careful	most careful
sharply	more sharply	most sharply
hopeful	less hopeful	least hopeful

Use the comparative to make a comparison between two people or two things, the superlative to compare three or more.

Which modifier you choose can tell a lot about what you're comparing.

Of the brothers, Joe was the *stronger* athlete.   (*There are two brothers.*)

Of the brothers, Joe was the *strongest* athlete.   (*There are at least three brothers.*)

Do not use double comparatives or superlatives. When forming comparatives, use either *-er* or *more,* not both. When forming superlatives, use either *-est* or *most,* not both.

◆   After eating, he felt ~~more~~ better.

IRREGULAR ADJECTIVES AND ADVERBS

POSITIVE	COMPARATIVE	SUPERLATIVE
good	better	best
well	better	best
bad	worse	worst
badly	worse	worst
ill	worse	worst
many	more	most
much	more	most
some	more	most
little*	less	least

*Little meaning "not much" is irregular. *Little* meaning "small" is regular: *little, littler, littlest.*

51e Avoiding double negatives

In English, one negative modifier (*no, not, never*) is sufficient to change the meaning of a sentence. When two negatives appear in the same sentence, they cancel each other out: *I didn't* have <u>no</u> money literally means I had some money. Eliminate double negatives.

◆   I ~~didn't have~~ no money.
         had

or

◆   I didn't have ~~no~~ money.
               any

52 | POSITIONING MODIFIERS

In English, word order can change meaning. For example, it makes a difference whether you say *the man ate the fish* or *the fish ate the man.*

While most of us put subjects and verbs in conventional order, problems in writing often involve modifiers: adjectives, adverbs, and phrases or clauses used as adjectives or adverbs. Since there might be more than one place in a sentence to put a modifier, it is important to connect the modifier clearly with what it is intended to describe or qualify. Otherwise, readers may misinterpret your meaning.

Repositioning misplaced modifiers   52a

Modifiers should point clearly to the words they modify. As a rule, related words should be kept together. A misplaced modifier can modify words or phrases other than the ones the writer intends: *We wanted our ordeal to end desperately.* Chances are, the writer did not want things to turn out badly, but rather he or she wanted very much (*desperately*) that the ordeal would end: *We desperately wanted our ordeal to end.*

Limiting modifiers

Put limiting modifiers such as *almost, even, hardly, just, merely, nearly, only, scarcely,* or *simply* directly before the words they modify. Notice how the meaning changes in the following sentences if the limiting modifier, *just,* is placed in front of different words.

They *just* want her to sing this song.

They want *just* her to sing this song.

They want her *just* to sing this song.

They want her to sing *just* this song.

52b Squinting Modifiers

Squinting modifiers seem to modify two things at once and can be confusing.

Students who follow directions *consistently* score well on tests.

To what is *consistently* connected? Are we talking about people *who consistently follow directions* or who *consistently score well?* Rewrite the sentence to clarify your intended meaning.

◆   Students who follow directions consistently score well on tests. [*consistently* inserted before "follow directions"]

◆   Students who follow directions consistently score well on tests. [*consistently* inserted before "score well"]

52c Dangling Modifiers

Dangling modifiers cause confusion since there is no clearly recognized noun that they modify. Consequently, the reader is left dangling as well.

Running through the rain, our clothes got soaked.

This sentence reads as if *our clothes* were *running through the rain;* however, the sentence suggests that "we" got wet, and it should be revised for clarity.

Place the subject (noun or pronoun) directly after the modifier, and supply new verbs if necessary.

◆   Running through the rain, our clothes got soaked. [*we got* inserted]

◆   Having completed her research, the paper earned her an A. [*she earned an A on* inserted]

◆   Still digging out from Thursday's snowfall, another storm is due on Sunday. [*residents prepared for* inserted]

Sometimes passive constructions in the main clause can leave introductory phrases floating with no subject to modify. To make your meaning clear, change the main verb to active voice.

◆ In studying the effects of cigarette smoking, monkeys ~~have been~~ ^*researchers have forced*^

~~forced~~ to inhale the equivalent of a hundred cigarettes a day.

Since monkeys have not been studying cigarette smoking, the meaning needs to be clarified.

Moving disruptive modifiers   52d

Disruptive modifiers distract readers by interrupting the flow of a sentence. Check for any disruptive modifier that splits an infinitive, divides a verb phrase, or needlessly separates major sentence elements.

Split infinitives

An infinitive consists of *to* plus the base form of a verb: *to fly, to grow, to achieve.* When a modifier comes between these two words, it is called a **split infinitive:** *to boldly go.* While we may often use such phrases in speech, they are considered awkward in formal writing.

◆ He promised to try diligently to avoid splitting infinitives.

You may need to change the construction of the sentence or some of the words when you correct confusing phrases.

◆ The director ~~wanted to vividly re-create~~ a bullfight for the second act. ^*planned a vivid re-creation of*^

Split verb phrases

A verb phrase consists of one or more **auxiliary verbs**—a form of *be, do,* or *have*—and a participle or the base form of a verb: *have been formed, does mention.* Lengthy interruptions between the two forms of a verb phrase can become unwieldy in writing and should be revised.

◆ ~~The Roanoke colony had, by~~ the time a supply ship arrived four years ^*By*^ *the Roanoke colony had* later, mysteriously disappeared without a trace.

Had plus *disappeared* has been split by a long phrase. Reunite the full phrase for clearer writing.

Separated sentence elements

Major sentence elements—subjects, verbs, objects, and complements—need to be near each other to make their relationships clear. At the same time, modifiers need to be near the sentence elements they modify. When these needs conflict, you have to make some choices based on your intended emphasis. Since there are no hard-and-fast rules about modifier placement, let the goals of clarity and precision guide your decisions.

◆ ~~Kentucky was, even~~ *Even* though many of its residents fought on the side of the Confederacy during the Civil War, *Kentucky was* never a stronghold of slavery.

or

◆ Kentucky was *never a stronghold of slavery,* even though many of its residents fought on the side of the Confederacy during the Civil War~~, never a stronghold of slavery.~~

PLACEMENT OF ADVERBS WITHIN VERB PHRASES

◆ When an adverb is used between elements of a verb phrase, it usually appears after the first auxiliary verb.

Our baseball stadium has *rarely* been filled to capacity.

◆ In questions, the adverb appears after the first auxiliary verb and the subject, but before the other parts of the verb.

In the past, have you *usually* found yourself writing a paper the day before it's due?

◆ When *not* negates another adverb, it should appear directly after the first auxiliary verb and before the other adverb.

This newspaper does *not usually* put sports on the front page.

Not *negates* usually; *the phase* not usually *means* "seldom."

◆ *Not* should appear after the adverb when it negates the action expressed by the main verb.

The senators have *often not* paid much attention to the voters who elected them.

Not *negates* paid.

53 ELIMINATING SENTENCE FRAGMENTS

A sentence is a group of words that expresses a complete idea. A **fragment** does not. Although fragments occur in everyday speech, they are seen as errors in academic writing. One kind of fragment neglects to tell what the sentence is about (the subject) or what happened (the verb).

> None of us understood the result. *Or even how it had happened.*

> *Seven graduate students in microbiology. Without any idea.*

Such fragments get in the way of clear and lucid writing and must be revised to make the writer's thoughts clear to the reader.

> Before we studied the 1948 election, none of us understood the result of the election or even how Truman's upset victory had happened.

> Seven graduate students are specializing in microbiology without any idea of the program's future.

Other fragments have a subject and verb, but because they contain a subordinating element, they cannot stand alone as independent clauses. To turn fragments into complete sentences, follow these strategies.

- Add the missing subject or verb to complete the sentence.

- Incorporate the fragment into a nearby sentence.

- If the fragment is a dependent clause, make it into an independent clause (a full sentence).

Often you can eliminate sentence fragments simply by repunctuating or by changing a few words (as examples above illustrate).

Fragments lacking verbs or subjects   53a

Providing missing elements

If a fragment lacks a verb or subject, you can simply add one.

RECOGNIZING FRAGMENTS

If you're unsure whether a group of words is a sentence fragment, ask yourself the following questions.

◆ Does it contain a verb? If not, it is a fragment.

◆ A controlled experiment *was conducted* comparing the effect of light on plants.

A gerund, an infinitive, or a participle without a helping verb cannot serve as the main verb of a sentence.

◆ Does it contain a subject? If not, it is a fragment.

◆ During the night, the protesters talked quietly and slept. *and* ~~And~~ prayed.

Certain sentences in the imperative mood (commands, orders, and requests) do not require explicit subjects: *Come at noon.* The subject is understood to be *you,* so an imperative sentence is not considered a fragment.

◆ Does it contain a subordinating word or phrase? If a group of words contains both a subject and a verb but is introduced by a **subordinating conjunction** (*until, because, after,* and so on) or a **relative pronoun** (*who, that, which*), it is a **dependent clause** and cannot stand alone as a complete sentence.

◆ None of the test plants bloomed during the experiment. *because* ~~Because~~ the time period was too limited.

◆ A fleet of colorful fishing boats *rocked* at anchor in the bay.

◆ The snowboarder cleared the rock ledge and flew out into space. *She spun* ~~Spun~~ twice in midair and sliced into the clean powder below.

Joining the fragment

Another solution is to incorporate the fragment part in a nearby sentence.

◆   Few employees held the company president in high regard. ~~Or~~ *or*
believed he could bring the business back to profitability.

With correction, employees *works as subject for* believed *as well as* held.

◆   Symbolism is an important technique in Alice Walker's "Everyday
~~Use." A~~ *Use," a* story that portrays cultural differences between generations.

Use a colon or a dash to join a list of examples to the sentence that
introduces it.

◆   Katherine Hepburn influenced a generation of current screen
actresses: Meryl Streep, Glenn Close, Sigourney Weaver, and Kathleen
Turner.

Dependent clause fragments   53b

Even though it contains both a subject and a predicate, a **dependent
clause** cannot stand alone as a sentence. Introduced by a **subordinating
conjunction** (such as *after, although, since, because, when, where,* or
whether) or a **relative pronoun** (*who, which,* or *that*), dependent clauses
by themselves are fragments.

To fix the situation, either create a new independent clause by
removing the subordinating word or attach the dependent clause to the
nearby independent clause it modifies.

◆   This is my cousin Jacob. ~~Who~~ *He* has never missed a day of school.

◆   The trees stood bare. ~~After~~ *after* the leaves had all fallen.

Intentional fragments   53c

Writers occasionally use fragments to create special effects—to reproduce the sound of spoken language or create dramatic emphasis.
Intentional fragments appear in fiction, personal essays, and narratives
and wherever dialogue is reproduced.

I knew that I was no legitimate resident of any world of ideas. I knew I couldn't think. All I knew then was what I couldn't do. All I knew then was what I wasn't, and it took me some years to discover what I was.

Which was a writer.

By which I mean not a "good" writer or a "bad" writer, but simply a writer, a person whose most absorbed and passionate hours are spent arranging words on pieces of paper.

—Joan Didion, "Why I Write"

If you use a fragment, think carefully about its effect and make sure that it seems intentional. Use it to create emphasis. When your point warrants disrupting readers' expectations, consider using a fragment. If it works.

54 ELIMINATING COMMA SPLICES AND FUSED SENTENCES

An **independent clause** includes a **subject** and **predicate** and can stand alone as a complete sentence because it expresses a complete idea.

Professional athletes can earn huge salaries.

Two independent clauses may be joined in one sentence if they are linked in a clear, conventional way.

◆ With a comma and a coordinating conjunction (*and, but, yet,* and so on)

◆ With a semicolon alone

◆ With a semicolon and a conjunctive adverb (*however, furthermore, instead,* and so on), or transitional phrase

◆ With a colon

These markers tell readers that a new idea is beginning and clarify the relationship between the ideas.

Two independent clauses that are joined (or "spliced") only by a comma make a **comma splice.**

independent clause   independent clause

**COMMA
SPLICE**
Professional athletes can earn huge salaries, some are paid

millions of dollars a year.

Seeing the comma after *salaries* without a coordinating conjunction, readers expect what follows to be part of the first clause rather than a new clause.

A **fused sentence** occurs when two independent clauses are joined without any marker.

independent clause   independent clause

**FUSED
SENTENCE**
Professional athletes can earn huge salaries some are paid

millions of dollars a year.

Following are several ways to eliminate comma splices and fused sentences from your writing.

◆ Use a comma and a coordinating conjunction to create a complete sentence.

◆ Use a semicolon, alone or with a conjunctive adverb or a transitional phrase, to create a complete sentence.

◆ Use a colon when the second clause illustrates the first.

◆ Divide the sentence into two sentences.

◆ Subordinate one clause to the other.

◆ Rewrite the sentence as one independent clause.

Which remedy you choose depends on the meaning you wish to convey, the length of the sentence, and the rhythm and wording of surrounding sentences. See the following box for specific examples.

Using a comma and a coordinating conjunction   54a

Coordinating conjunctions specify a relationship between equal grammatical elements: *and* (addition); *but* and *yet* (contrast); *so* and *for* (cause); *or* and *nor* (choice). To join independent clauses, use an appropriate coordinating conjunction preceded by a comma.

RECOGNIZING COMMA SPLICES AND FUSED SENTENCES

Comma splices and fused sentences often occur when two claus-es express ideas closely linked in the writer's mind. Here are some common writing situations in which such sentence errors occur.

◆   The second clause offers an example, explanation, or elaboration of the first.

◆   The tribes gathered every summer along the banks of the river ~~they~~ . They
fished and hunted and picked berries.

◆   The second clause contains a meaning that contrasts with the first.

◆   Everyone was asked to express an opinion on the plans, Mr. Johnson but
had to leave early.

◆   The subject of the second clause is a pronoun that renames the sub-ject of the first clause.

◆   The instructor asked us to write our thoughts down ~~she~~ said just to . She
write whatever came to mind as fast as we could.

◆   A conjunctive adverb or transitional phrase is incorrectly used to join two sentences.

◆   I remember playing with Ernest and Mike in fact I can barely remem-ber playing with anyone else.

◆   Maya Angelou has worked as an actress and director, her greatest but
success came as an autobiographer and poet.

54b Adding a semicolon

A semicolon after an independent clause signals that the following inde-pendent clause is just as important as the first one.

Semicolon alone

Two independent clauses may be joined with a semicolon alone only if the ideas in the clauses are closely and clearly related. If they are not, make them separate sentences or use a conjunction to clarify the relationship for the reader.

◆ For years the Federal Communications Commission has advocated legislation to allow competitive auctions for broadcast licenses ; so far, Congress has refused.

Semicolons are especially useful in sentences that contain more than two independent clauses.

◆ The sculpture was monstrous ; its surface was rough and pitted, and its colors were garish.

Here the semicolon clarifies the relationship among the three clauses. The second and third clauses together illustrate the point of the first clause.

Semicolon with a conjunctive adverb or transitional expression

Conjunctive adverbs (*finally, however,* and others listed in the box) and transitional expressions (*in fact, for example, among others,* and so on) can be used to join two independent clauses. To do so, you need a stronger mark of punctuation than a comma; use a semicolon.

◆ The rebel forces were never completely defeated ; moreover, they still controlled several strategic highland passes.

Use a semicolon with a transitional phrase like *in fact* or *for example.*

◆ Our friends helped us do so much work on Saturday ; in fact, we stacked two cords of wood.

Adding a colon   54c

Use a colon to join two independent clauses when the second clause explains, elaborates, or illustrates the first.

418

◆ My mother gave me one important piece of advice/never wear stripes with plaids.

54d Writing separate sentences

When one of the independent clauses is much longer, or different in structure, resolve the comma splice or fused sentence by writing two separate sentences.

◆ My last year of high school was an eventful one, ~~everything~~ *. Everything* seemed to be happening all at once.

54e Using subordination

Emphasize the main idea in your sentence, and place the less important idea in a dependent clause. Dependent clauses are introduced by subordinating conjunctions (*because, if, than, after, although, whenever, while,* and so on) or relative pronouns (*who, which, that*).

◆ *Because the* ~~The~~ rain had frozen as it hit the ground, the streets were slick with ice.

◆   The panel studied the issue ~~it~~ decided to recommend allowing the
        that

group to participate.

Creating one independent clause   54f

Collapse the two independent clauses in a fused sentence or comma
splice into one clause if they are close in meaning. If they have the same
subject, create a compound predicate.

◆   This book held my attention ~~it~~ gave a lot of information about the
        and

Renaissance.

Here the subject, book, *has two predicates:* held my attention *and* gave a lot
of information.

You can also turn one clause into a modifier clause.

◆   Mary Stewart steeps her stories in historic detail. ~~She is my favorite~~
        , my favorite author,

~~author.~~

55 ELIMINATING SHIFTS AND MIXED CONSTRUCTION

Readers are like bus riders: they like to know where they are being taken.
Good writers keep their passengers comfortable. They drive smoothly to
the expected destination, usually by a direct route.

Throughout a piece of writing, readers expect continuity in point
of view and references to time. Within sentences, they expect consis-
tency, with no puzzling shifts in the person and number of subjects, the
forms of verbs, or the way quotations are reproduced. There should
also be no twists and turns in grammar, logic, or sense.

Editing unnecessary shifts in person and number   55a

Unnecessary shifts in **person** often occur when pronouns are used in
sentences about groups or about unidentified people.

◆   When the researchers mixed the two chemicals, ~~you~~ *they* saw a surprising

reaction.

Some writers shift needlessly from third person (*he, she, it, one, they*) to second person (*you*) when trying to make a comprehensive statement.

◆   With the cost of prescription drugs spiraling upward ~~every~~ *one* day, you

can see that some regulation of the pharmaceutical industry is

inevitable.

Unnecessary shifts in **number** often occur with the use of pronouns. This error may occur when the writer is trying to avoid sexist use of the pronoun *he* or *his* to refer to an antecedent whose gender is indefinite. Make sure that pronouns match their antecedent in number.

◆   Every employee sets ~~their~~ *his or her* own work pace.

     Here employee *is singular, so the plural pronoun* their *does not match. A singular pronoun is required.*

55b Editing unnecessary shifts in tense

Tense places the action of the verb in time.

While a writer may use different tenses to show actions occurring at different times (*We will play tennis before we eat breakfast but after we have had coffee*), it is important to maintain a **governing tense** (the main tense of a piece of writing). Departures from the governing tense can be confusing and interfere with the writer's intentions (*When the letter arrived, it says nothing about the contract*).

The **literary present tense** is used to discuss literature or art. Once the literary present tense is established as your governing tense, be sure to maintain it.

◆   In *The Glass Menagerie*, Tom *realizes* how trapped he *is* after the

Gentleman Caller ~~departed.~~ *departs.*

55c Editing unnecessary shifts in mood

English verbs have three moods: the *indicative mood,* used for statements and questions; the *imperative mood,* used for commands, orders, and directions, and the *subjunctive mood,* used for wishes and for statements that are known to be not factual.

Watch for unnecessary shifts from the imperative to the indicative, particularly in instructions.

◆   First cover your work surface with newspapers, and then ~~you~~ make

sure your materials are within easy reach.

The indicative mood and the subjunctive mood often appear in the same sentence.

indicative   subjunctive

◆   My instructor *wishes* that I *were* more attentive.

Watch out for unnecessary shifts from the subjective to the indicative or the imperative.

◆   The contract requires that you *be* in Denver on July 1 and that you

~~must~~ be in Houston on August 1.

Editing unnecessary shifts in voice and subject   55d

The subject of an active-voice verb performs the verb's action: *He hit the ball.* The subject of a passive voice verb is acted upon: *The ball was hit by him.*

If a sentence has two verbs that share the same subject, it is acceptable to shift voice.

The students *completed* the project first and *were awarded* the prize.

Here completed *is the active verb and* were awarded *is the passive verb, but both share the same subject,* students.

Avoid shifting from the active to the passive voice (or passive to active) if it requires a change of subject.

◆   As we peered out of the tent, the waning moon ~~was seen~~ we saw through the

trees.

55e Editing unnecessary shifts between direct and indirect quotation

Direct quotations reproduce someone's *exact* words and are enclosed in quotation marks: *"I love my wife," he said.*

Indirect quotations paraphrase someone else's words and do not appear in quotation marks: *He insisted that he loved his wife.* Be consistent when using these.

◆ He said that he loved his wife and ~~"Why did~~ she ~~have~~ to leave ~~me?"~~
   wondered why   had   him.

◆ He insisted that he loved his wife and ~~why~~ did she have to leave ~~him?~~
   cried, "Why   me?"

There are several ways to revise a sentence whose clarity is jeopardized by one verb used to introduce indirect *and* direct quotations. Either use indirect quotation in both instances, quote less than the full sentence directly, or start a new sentence.

◆ Dr. Ryan claims that the play was composed before 1600 and ~~"It~~
   that
   it was written by
   ~~shows the clear hand of~~ Shakespeare."

◆ Dr. Ryan claims that the play was composed before 1600 and ~~"It~~
   that
   it "shows
   ~~shows~~ the clear hand of Shakespeare."

◆ Dr. Ryan claims that the play was composed before 1600 ~~and~~ "It
   . He says,

   shows the clear hand of Shakespeare."

55f Eliminating mixed constructions

A sentence that begins one way and then takes a turn in another way is called a **mixed construction.**

Using a grammatically unacceptable element as a subject or predicate causes a mixed construction. Prepositional phrases, for example, cannot serve as subjects of a sentence. Revise for clarity.

◆ *Listening*
   ~~By listening~~ closely and paying attention to nonverbal signals helps a

   doctor make a fuller diagnosis.

◆   *A doctor can make a fuller diagnosis by*
     ~~By~~ listening closely and paying attention to nonverbal signals ~~helps a~~
     ~~doctor make a fuller diagnosis.~~

Clauses beginning with subordinating conjunctions (*after, before, when, where, while, because, if, although,* or *unless*) that are used to modify cannot be the subject of a sentence. Revise the sentence by providing a new subject.

◆   *The doctor's status as*
     ~~Because the doctor is~~ an expert does not mean a patient should never
     question a diagnosis.

     Because the doctor is an expert *is not a proper subject; here the new subject is* The doctor's status.

Mixed constructions can occur with verbs also. A dependent clause, for example, cannot contain the main verb of a sentence. To edit such a sentence, either supply a new verb or change a verb already present so that it functions as the main verb.

◆   The fact that most patients are afraid to ask questions~~, which~~ gives
     doctors complete control.

     Here gives *becomes the main verb.*

Revising illogical constructions   55g

Though your meaning may seem very clear to you, the writer, it may not be as clear to the reader. If you find that some elements don't make sense, reduce your sentence to its most basic elements—subject and verb—to see where the problem lies.

◆   *Most*
     ~~The opinion of most~~ people believe that dogs make better pets than
     cats.

     Reducing the sentence to its basic subject and verb, we realize that opinion *cannot be the subject for* believe; *therefore, the sentence needs revision to make* people *the subject for* believe.

◆   Repeat offenders whose licenses have already been suspended for
     have their licenses
     drunk driving will ~~be~~ revoked.

It is not offenders *who will* be revoked *but rather* their licenses.

A **subject complement,** which follows a linking verb (*is, seems, appears,* and so on), must rename or comment on the subject. If it does not, you must revise the mixed construction.

◆ My father's favorite kitchen appliance is ~~using~~ the microwave oven.

Think of the sentence as an equation; kitchen appliance *is not the same as* using. *Revise for clarity.*

55h Eliminating faulty predication

A clause beginning with *when, where,* or *because* is used to modify and cannot work as a subject complement after a linking verb such as *is.*

◆ Pop art is ~~where an artist reproduces~~ based on images from commercial products and the popular media.

◆ In sudden-death ~~Sudden death~~ overtime ~~is when~~, the game is extended until one team scores.

Though often spoken, "The reason . . . is" often lapses into faulty constructions in writing. You must change one part of the sentence to match the other.

◆ ~~The reason little~~ Little has been done to solve the problem ~~is~~ because Congress is deadlocked.

◆ The reason little has been done to solve the problem is ~~because~~ that Congress is deadlocked.

PART EIGHT

ACADEMIC CONVENTIONS

Source: *The College Writer's Reference,* Third Edition, by Toby Fulwiler and Alan R. Hayakawa.

Each discipline in the academic community specifies a particular style to use in documenting research sources. English and the foreign languages use the format of the Modern Language Association (MLA). The social sciences, education, and business use the format of the American Psychological Association (APA). History and the fine arts use *The Chicago Manual of Style* (CMS), and the sciences use a variety of number systems. This handbook includes full explanations of the MLA, APA, and CMS systems, a brief description of the new *Columbia Guide to Online Style* (an optional system for citing Web-based research), and an overview of the number systems used in the physical and biological sciences.

The most common and economical form for documenting sources in research-based English papers is the MLA (Modern Language Association) system.

◆ All sources are briefly mentioned by author name in the text.

◆ A list of works cited at the end provides full publication data for each source named in the paper.

◆ Additional explanatory information written by the writer of the paper can be included in footnotes or endnotes.

The MLA system is explained in authoritative detail in the *MLA Handbook for Writers of Research Papers,* 5th ed. (New York: MLA, 1999) and on the MLA Web site <http://www.mla.org>.

Guidelines for formatting manuscripts   56a

The MLA guidelines for submitting college papers are fairly conservative and do not reflect the wealth of visually interesting fonts, type sizes, graphics, and other options available with most modern word-processing programs. If your instructor requests MLA format, follow the guidelines below. If your instructor encourages more open journalistic formats, use good judgment in displaying the information in your text.

Paper and printing

Print all academic assignments on 8½″ × 11″ white paper in a standard font (for example, Times New Roman, Courier) and type size (10 or 12 point) using a good-quality printer.

Margins and spacing

Allow margins of one inch all around. Justify the left margin only. Double-space everything, including headings, quoted material, and the Works Cited page. Indent five spaces for paragraphs.

Indent ten spaces for prose quotations of five or more lines or poetry of more than three lines. (Do not use quotation marks around these long quotations.)

Identification

On page 1, include your name, your instructor's name, the course title, and the date on separate lines, double spaced, flush with the upper left margin.

Title

Center the title on the first page, capitalizing key words only. If your instructor asks for strict MLA style, avoid using italics, underlining, quotation marks, boldface type, unusual fonts, or large type for the title. (MLA does not require a title page or an outline.) Double-space to the first paragraph.

Page numbers

Print page numbers in the upper right margin, one-half inch below the top of the paper. If following strict MLA format, include your last name before each page number to guarantee correct identification of stray pages (*Turner 1, Turner 2*).

Punctuation

One space is required after commas, semicolons, colons, periods, question marks, and exclamation points and between the periods in an ellipsis. (Double-spacing is optional after end punctuation.) Dashes are formed by two hyphens, with no extra spacing on either side.

Visual information

Label each table or chart as *Table 1, Table 2,* and so on. Label each drawing or photograph as *Figure 1* or *Fig. 2* and so on. Include a clear caption for each figure, and place it in the text as near as possible to the passage that refers to it.

DIRECTORY FOR MLA DOCUMENTATION GUIDELINES

IN-TEXT CITATIONS (56b)

1. Author identified in a signal phrase
2. Author not identified in a signal phrase
3. Two or more works by the same author
4. Unknown author
5. Corporate or organizational author
6. Authors with the same last name
7. Works in more than one volume
8. One-page works
9. Quotation from secondary source
10. Poem or play
11. More than one work in a citation
12. Long quotation set off from text
13. Electronic texts
14. Endnotes and footnotes

LIST OF WORKS CITED (56c)

DOCUMENTING BOOKS (56d)

1. Book by one author
2. Book by two or three authors
3. Book by more than three authors
4. Book by a corporation, an organization, or an association
5. Revised edition of a book
6. Edited book
7. Book with an editor and author
8. Book in more than one volume
9. One volume of a multivolume book
10. Translated book
11. Book in a series
12. Reprinted book
13. Introduction, preface, foreword, or afterword in a book
14. Work in an anthology or chapter in an edited collection
15. Essay or periodical article reprinted in a collection
16. Article in a reference book
17. Anonymous book
18. Government document
19. Dissertation, unpublished or published

(continued)

MLA

Guidelines for in-text citations   56b

The following guidelines explain how to include research sources in the main body of your text using MLA style.

Each source mentioned in your paper needs to be accompanied by a brief citation including the author's last name and the page number. These are placed either in the text itself or within parentheses. This in-text citation refers readers to the alphabetical list of works cited at your paper's end, listing full publication information about each source. The following examples illustrate the most common types of in-text citations.

1.   Author identified in a signal phrase

When you include the author's name in the sentence introducing the source, add only the specific page on which the material appeared, in parentheses following the information.

```
Carol Lea Clark explains the basic necessities for the
creation of a page on the World Wide Web (77).
```

Do not include the word *page* or the abbreviation *p.* before the number. The parenthetical reference comes before the period.

For a work by two or three authors, include all authors' names.

```
Clark and Jones explain. . . .
```

For works with more than three authors, list all authors or use the first author's name and add *et al.* (Latin abbreviation for "and others") without a comma.

```
Britton et al. suggest. . . .
```

2.   Author not identified in a signal phrase

When you do not include the author's name in your text, add it in parentheses along with the source page number. Do not punctuate between the author's name and the page number(s).

```
Provided one has certain "basic ingredients," the Web
offers potential worldwide publication (Clark 77).
```

For a work by two or three authors, include all authors' last names.

```
(Clark and Jones 15)
(Smith, Web, and Beck 210)
```

For works with more than three authors, list all authors' last names or list the first author only, adding *et al.*

```
(White et al. 95)
```

3. Two or more works by the same author

If your paper refers to two or more works by the same author, each citation needs to identify the specific work. Either mention the title of the work in the text or include a shortened version of the title (usually the first one or two important words) in the parenthetical citation. There are three correct ways to do this.

```
According to Lewis Thomas in Lives of a Cell, many
bacteria become dangerous only if they manufacture
exotoxins (76).
```

```
According to Lewis Thomas, many bacteria become dan-
gerous only if they manufacture exotoxins (Lives 76).
```

```
Many bacteria become dangerous only if they manufacture
exotoxins (Thomas, Lives 76).
```

Identify the shortened title by underlining (for books and other long works) or quotation marks (for short works, such as articles in periodicals) as appropriate. Put a comma between the author's last name and the title.

4. Unknown author

—— When the author of a work is unknown, give either the complete title in the text or a shortened version in the parenthetical citation, along with the page number.

```
According to Statistical Abstracts, in 1990 the
literacy rate for Mexico stood at 75 percent (374).
```

```
In 1990 the literacy rate for Mexico stood at 75
percent (Statistical 374).
```

5. Corporate or organizational author

When no author is listed for a work published by a corporation, foundation, organization, or association, indicate the group's full name either in the text or in parentheses.

```
(Florida League of Women Voters 3)
```

If the name is long, it is best to cite it in the sentence and put only the page number in parentheses.

6. Authors with the same last name

When you cite works by two or more different authors with the same last name, include the first initial of each author's name in the parenthetical citation.

```
(C. Miller 63; S. Miller 101-04)
```

7.   Works in more than one volume

Indicate the pertinent volume number for each citation before the page number, and follow it with a colon and one space.

```
(Hill 2: 70)
```

If your source is one volume of a multivolume work, do not specify the volume number in your text, but specify it in the Works Cited list.

8.   One-page works

When you refer to a work one page long, do not include the page number since that will appear in the Works Cited list.

9.   Quotation from a secondary source

When a quotation or any information in your source is originally from another source, use the abbreviation *qtd. in*.

```
Lester Brown of Worldwatch feels that international
agricultural production has reached its limit (qtd. in
Mann 51).
```

10.   Poem or play

In citing poems, name part (if divided into parts) and line numbers; include the word *line* or *lines* in the first such reference. This information will help your audience find the passages in any source where those works are reprinted, which page references alone cannot provide.

```
In "The Mother," Gwendolyn Brooks remembers "the chil-
dren you got that you did not get" (line 1).
```

When you cite up to three lines from a poem in your text, separate the lines with slash marks.

```
Emily Dickinson describes being alive in a New England
summer: "Inebriate of air am I / And debauchee of dew /
Reeling through endless summer days" (lines 6-8).
```

When you cite more than three lines, as a block quotation, indent ten spaces.

Cite verse plays using act, scene, and line numbers, separated by periods. For major works such as *Hamlet*, use identifiable abbreviations.

```
(Ham. 4.4.31-39)
```

11. More than one work in a citation

To cite two or more works, separate them with semicolons.

```
(Aronson, Golden Shore 177; Didion 49-50)
```

Note that more than one work by Aronson is cited in this paper, so the title is given as well.

12. Long quotation set off from text

To set off quoted passages of four or more lines, indent one inch or ten spaces from the left-hand margin of the text, double-space, and omit quotation marks. The parenthetical citation *follows* end punctuation (unlike citations for shorter, integrated quotations) and is not followed by a period.

```
Fellow author W. Somerset Maugham had this to say
about Austen's dialogue:
          No one has ever looked upon Jane Austen as a
          great stylist. Her spelling was peculiar and
          her grammar often shaky, but she had a good
          ear. Her dialogue is probably as natural as
          dialogue can ever be. To set down on paper
          speech as it is spoken would be very
          tedious, and some arrangement of it is nec-
          essary. (434)
```

13. Electronic texts

The MLA guidelines on documenting online sources are explained in detail online at <http://www.mla.org/set_stl.htm>.

Electronic sources are cited in the body of the text in the same style as print sources, by author, title of text or Web site, and page numbers. If no page numbers appear in the source, include section (*sec.*) number or title and/or paragraph (*par.*) numbers.

```
The Wizard of Oz "was nominated for six Academy
Awards, including Best Picture" (Wizard par 3).
```

However, Web pages commonly omit page and section numbers and are not organized by paragraphs. In such cases, omit numbers from your parenthetical references. (For a document downloaded from the Web, the page numbers of a printout should normally not be cited since pagination may vary in different printouts.)

```
In the United States, the birthrate per 1,000 people
has fallen steadily from 16.7 in 1995 to 14.6 in 1998
(Statistical).
```

14. Endnotes and footnotes

MLA style uses notes primarily to offer comments, explanations, or additional information (especially source-related information) that cannot be smoothly or easily accommodated in the text of the paper. In general, however, you should omit additional information, outside the main body of your paper, unless it is necessary for clarification or justification. If a note is necessary, insert a raised (superscript) numeral at the reference point in the text. Introduce the note itself with a corresponding raised numeral, and indent it.

Text with superscript

```
The standard ingredients for guacamole include avoca-
dos, lemon juice, onion, tomatoes, coriander, salt,
and pepper.[1] Hurtado's poem, however, gives this tra-
ditional dish a whole new twist (lines 10-17).
```

Note

```
       [1] For variations see Beard 314, Egerton 197, and
Eckhardt 92. Beard's version, which includes olives
and green peppers, is the most unusual.
```

Any published reference listed in the notes also appears in the Works Cited list.

Notes may come as **footnotes** at the bottom of the page on which the citation appears, or they may be included as **endnotes**, double spaced on a separate page at the end of your paper. Endnote pages should be placed between the body of the paper and the Works Cited list, with the title *Note* or *Notes.*

Conventions for the list of Works Cited   56c

Every source mentioned in the body of your paper should be identified in a list of works cited attached to the end of the paper using the following format.

- Center the title *Works Cited,* with no quotation marks, underlining, or boldface, one inch from the top of a separate page following the final page of the paper. (If asked to include works read but not cited, attach an additional page titled *Works Consulted.*)

- Number this page, following in sequence from the last text page of your paper. If the list runs more than a page, continue the page numbering in sequence, but do not repeat the title *Works Cited.*

◆ Double-space between the title and first entry and within and between entries.

◆ Begin each entry at the left-hand margin, and indent subsequent lines the equivalent of a paragraph indention (five spaces or one-half inch).

Order of entries

Alphabetize entries according to authors' last names. If an author is unknown, alphabetize according to the first word of the title (but do not use an initial *A, An,* or *The*).

Entry formats

Each item in the entry begins with a capital letter and is followed by a period. Each period is followed by one space. Capitalize all major words in the book and article titles. Underline published titles (books, periodicals); put quotation marks around titles of chapters, articles, stories, and poems within published works. Do not underline volume and issue numbers or end punctuation. Four variations on general formats are common.

BOOKS

ONE SPACE   ONE SPACE   ONE SPACE

Author(s). Book Title. Place of publication:

INDENT 5
  SPACES ——Publisher, year of publication.
                    ONE SPACE

JOURNAL ARTICLES

ONE SPACE   ONE SPACE   ONE SPACE, NO PUNCTUATION

Author(s). "Article Title." Journal Title volume

INDENT 5   ONE SPACE
  SPACES ——number (year of publication): inclusive page

numbers.

MAGAZINE AND NEWSPAPER ARTICLES

ONE SPACE   ONE SPACE   ONE SPACE, NO PUNCTUATION

Author(s). "Article Title." Publication Title date

INDENT 5   ONE SPACE
  SPACES ——of publication: inclusive page numbers.

ELECTRONIC SOURCES

```
         ONE SPACE            ONE SPACE
              |                    |
   Author(s). |"Title of Site." |Print source (same as
INDENT 5                 ONE SPACE            ONE SPACE
  SPACES ——— printed citation). |Description of site. |Date of
                          ONE SPACE
         electronic publication. |Page, paragraph, or sec-
                   ONE SPACE          ONE SPACE       NO PERIOD
         tion number. |Sponsoring body. |Date of access|

         <electronic address>.
```

AUTHORS

◆ List the author's last name first, followed by a comma and then the rest of the name as it appears on the publication, followed by a period. Never alter an author's name by replacing full spellings with initials or by dropping middle initials.

◆ For more than one author, use a comma rather than a period after the first author, and list the other authors' full names, first names first, separated by commas. Spell out the word *and* before the final author; do not use an ampersand (&). Put a period at the end.

◆ For more than one work by the same author, use three hyphens for the name after the first entry.

TITLES

◆ List full titles and subtitles as they appear on the title page of a book or in the credits for a film, videotape, or recording. Separate titles and subtitles with colons (followed by one space).

◆ Underline titles of entire books and periodicals.

◆ Use quotation marks around the titles of essays, poems, songs, short stories, and chapters or other parts of a larger work.

◆ Put a period after the title of a book or an article. Use no punctuation after the title of a journal, magazine, or newspaper.

PLACES OF PUBLICATION

◆ Places of publication are given for books and pamphlets, not for journals or magazines.

◆ Give the city of publication from the title page or copyright page. If several cities are given, use only the first.

◆ Use a colon to separate the place of publication from the publisher.

◆ For electronic sources, include the Internet address at the end of the entry in angle brackets (< >).

PUBLISHERS

◆ The name of the publisher is given for books and pamphlets. Shorten the publisher's name as described below under "Abbreviations." If a title page indicates both an imprint and a publisher (for example, Arbor House, an imprint of William Morrow), list both shortened names, separated by a hyphen (*Arbor-Morrow*).

◆ Use a comma to separate the publisher's name from the publication date.

DATE

◆ For books, give the year of publication, followed by a period.

◆ For other publications, give the year of publication within parentheses, followed by a colon.

◆ For newspapers, put the day before the month and year (*25 May 1954*) with no commas separating the elements.

◆ For magazines and newspapers, put a colon after the date.

◆ For electronic sources, include the date the site was accessed.

PAGE NUMBERS

◆ Page numbers are included for all publications other than books.

◆ Use a hyphen, not a dash, between inclusive page numbers, with no extra space on either side.

◆ Use all digits for ending page numbers up to 99 and the last two digits only for numbers above 99 (*130–38*) unless the full number is needed for clarity (*198–210*).

◆ If subsequent pages do not follow consecutively, use a plus sign after the last consecutive page number (*39+, 52–55+*).

◆ If no page numbers are available for electronic sources, include paragraph or section numbers.

ABBREVIATIONS

◆ To shorten a publisher's name, drop the words *Press, Company,* and so forth in the publisher's name (*Blair* for *Blair Press*). Use the abbreviation *UP* for *University Press* (*Columbia UP; U of Chicago P*).

◆ Use only the first name if the publisher's name is a series of names (*Farrar* for *Farrar, Straus & Giroux*). Use only the last name if the publisher's name is a person's name (*Abrams* for *Harry N. Abrams*).

◆ If no publisher or date of publication is given for a source, use the abbreviations *n.p.* ("no publisher") or *n.d.* ("no date").

◆ For periodicals, abbreviate months using the first three letters followed by a period (*Apr., Dec.*) except for *May, June,* and *July.* If an issue covers two months, use a hyphen to connect the months (*Apr.–May, June–Aug.*). (See model 20 below.)

Documenting books   56d

1. Book by one author

Thomas, Lewis. <u>Lives of a Cell: Notes of a Biology Watcher</u>.
        New York: Viking, 1974.

2. Book by two or three authors

Fulwiler, Toby, and Alan R. Hayakawa. <u>The Blair Handbook</u>,
        3rd ed. Upper Saddle River: Prentice, 2000.

Second and third authors are listed first name first. Do not alphabetize the authors' names within an individual Works Cited entry. The final author's name is preceded by *and*; do not use an ampersand (*&*). A comma always follows the inverted ordering of the author's first name.

3. Book by more than three authors

Britton, James, et al. <u>The Development of Writing Abilities
        11-18</u>. London: Macmillan, 1975.

With more than three authors, you have the option of using the abbreviation *et al.* (Latin for "and others") or listing all the authors' names in full as they appear on the title page of the book. Do not alphabetize the names within the Works Cited entry.

4. Book by a corporation, an organization, or an association

U.S. Coast Guard Auxiliary. <u>Boating Skills and Seamanship</u>.
        Washington: Coast Guard Auxiliary National Board,
        1997.

Alphabetize by the name of the organization.

5. Revised edition of a book

Hayakawa, S. I. <u>Language in Thought and Action</u>. 4th ed.
    New York: Harcourt, 1978.

6. Edited book

Hoy, Pat C., II, Esther H. Shor, and Robert DiYanni, eds.
    <u>Women's Voices: Visions and Perspectives</u>. New York:
    McGraw, 1990.

7. Book with an editor and author

Britton, James. <u>Prospect and Retrospect</u>. Ed. Gordon Pradl.
    Upper Montclair: Boynton, 1982.

The abbreviation *Ed.* when followed by a name replaces the phrase
Edited by and cannot be made plural. (See models 13 and 14.)

8. Book in more than one volume

Waldrep, Tom, ed. <u>Writers on Writing</u>. 2 vols. New York:
    Random, 1985-88.

When separate volumes were published in different years, use inclusive dates.

9. One volume of a multivolume book

Waldrep, Tom, ed. <u>Writers on Writing</u>, Vol. 2. New York:
    Random, 1988.

When each volume has its own title, list the full publication information
for the volume you used first, followed by information on the series
(number of volumes, dates).

Churchill, Winston S. <u>Triumph and Tragedy</u>. Boston:
    Houghton, 1953. Vol. 6 of <u>The Second World War</u>. 6
    vols. 1948-53.

10. Translated book

Camus, Albert. <u>The Stranger</u>. Trans. Stuart Gilbert. New
    York: Random, 1946.

11. Book in a series

Magistrate, Anthony. <u>Stephen King, The Second Decade</u>:
    Danse Macabre <u>to</u> The Dark Half. Twayne American
    Authors Series 599. New York: Twayne, 1992.

A book title appearing within another book's title is not underlined. Add
series information just before the city of publication.

12.   Reprinted book

Hurston, Zora Neale. <u>Their Eyes Were Watching God</u>. 1937.
     New York: Perennial-Harper, 1990.

Add the original publication date after the title; then cite information for the current edition.

13.   Introduction, preface, foreword, or afterword in a book

Selfe, Cynthia. Foreword. <u>Electronic Communication Across
     the Curriculum</u>. Ed. Donna Rice et al. Urbana: NCTE,
     1998. ix-xiv.

Atwell, Nancie. Introduction. <u>Coming to Know: Writing to
     Learn in the Intermediate Grades</u>. Ed. Nancie Atwell.
     Portsmouth: Heinemann, 1990. xi-xxiii.

14.   Work in an anthology or chapter in an edited collection

Donne, John. "The Canonization." <u>The Metaphysical Poets</u>.
     Ed. Helen Gardner. Baltimore: Penguin, 1957. 61-62.

Gay, John. <u>The Beggar's Opera</u>. 1728. <u>British Dramatists
     from Dryden to Sheridan</u>. Ed. George H. Nettleton and
     Arthur E. Case. Carbondale: Southern Illinois UP,
     1975. 530-65.

Lispector, Clarice. "The Departure of the Train." Trans.
     Alexis Levitin. <u>Latin American Writers: Thirty Stories</u>.
     Ed. Gabriella Ibieta. New York: St. Martin's, 1993.
     245-58.

Use quotation marks around the title of a poem, a short story, an essay, or a chapter. For a work originally published as a book, underline the title. Add inclusive page numbers for the selection at the end of the entry.

When citing two or more selections from one anthology, you may list the anthology separately under the editor's name.

Gardner, Helen, ed. <u>The Metaphysical Poets</u>. Baltimore:
     Penguin, 1957.

All entries within that anthology will then include only a cross-reference to the anthology entry.

Donne, John. "The Canonization." Gardner 61-62.

15.   Essay or periodical article reprinted in a collection

Emig, Janet. "Writing as Mode of Learning." <u>College
     Composition and Communication</u> 28 (1977): 122-28.

Rpt. in The Web of Meaning. Ed. Janet Emig. Upper
    Montclair: Boynton, 1983. 123-31.

Gannet, Lewis. Introduction. The Portable Steinbeck. New
    York: Viking, 1946. 1-12. Rpt. as "John Steinbeck's
    Way of Writing" in Steinbeck and His Critics: A
    Record of Twenty-five Years. Ed. E. W. Tedlock, Jr.,
    and C. V. Wicker. Albuquerque: U of New Mexico P,
    1957. 23-37.

Include the full citation for the original publication, followed by *Rpt. in*
("Reprinted in") and the publication information for the book. Add
inclusive page numbers for the article or essay found in the collection;
add inclusive page numbers for the original source when available.

16. Article in a reference book

"Behn, Aphra." The Concise Columbia Encyclopedia. 1998 ed.

Miller, Peter L. "The Power of Flight." The Encyclopedia
    of Insects. Ed. Christopher O'Toole. New York: Facts
    on File, 1986. 18-19.

For a signed article, begin with the author's name. For commonly known
reference works, full publication information and editors' names are not
necessary. For entries arranged alphabetically, page and volume numbers
are not necessary.

17. Anonymous book

The World Almanac and Book of Facts. New York: World
    Almanac-Funk, 2000.

Alphabetize by title, excluding an initial *A, An,* or *The.*

18. Government document

United States. Central Intelligence Agency. National Basic
    Intelligence Fact Book. Washington: GPO, 1999.

If the author is identified, begin with that name. If not, begin with the
government (country or state), followed by the agency or organization.
The U.S. Government Printing Office is abbreviated *GPO.*

19. Dissertation, unpublished or published

Kitzhaber, Albert R. "Rhetoric in American Colleges." Diss.
    U of Washington, 1953.

Use quotation marks for the title of an unpublished dissertation. Include the university name and the year. For a published dissertation, underline the title and give publication information as you would for a book, including the order number if the publisher is University Microfilms International (UMI).

Documenting periodicals   56e

20.   Article, story, or poem in a monthly or bimonthly magazine

```
Linn, Robert A., and Stephen B. Dunbar. "The Nation's
     Report Card Goes Home." Phi Delta Kappan Jan. 2000:
     127-43.
```

```
"From Beans to Brew." Consumer Reports Nov. 1999: 43-46.
```

Abbreviate all months except May, June, and July. Hyphenate months for bimonthlies (*July–Aug. 1993*). Do not list volume or issue numbers. If the article is unsigned, alphabetize by title.

21.   Article, story, or poem in a weekly magazine

```
Ross, Alex. "The Wanderer." New Yorker 10 May 1999: 56-53.
```

Note that when the day of the week is specified, the publication date is inverted.

22.   Article in a daily newspaper

```
Brody, Jane E. "Doctors Get Poor Marks for Nutrition
     Knowledge." New York Times 10 Feb. 1992: B7.
```

```
"Redistricting Reconsidered." Washington Post 12 May 1999: B2.
```

For an unsigned article, alphabetize by the title.

Give the full name of the newspaper as it appears on the masthead, but drop any introductory *A, An,* or *The.* If the city is not in the name, it should follow in brackets: *El Diario [Los Angeles].*

With the page number, include the letter that designates any separately numbered sections. If sections are numbered consecutively, list the section number (*sec. 2*) before the colon, preceded by a comma.

23.   Article in a journal paginated by volume

```
Harris, Joseph. "The Other Reader." Journal of Advanced
     Composition 12 (1992): 34-36.
```

If the page numbers are continuous from one issue to the next throughout the year, include only the volume number (always in Arabic numerals) and year. Do not give the issue number or the month or season. Note that there is no space between the closing parenthesis and the colon.

24. Article in a journal paginated by issue

```
Tiffin, Helen. "Post-Colonialism, Post-Modernism, and the
     Rehabilitation of Post-Colonial History." Journal of
     Commonwealth Literature 23.1 (1998): 169-81.
```

If each issue begins with page 1, include the volume number followed by a period and then the issue number (both in Arabic numerals, even if the journal uses Roman). Do not give the month of publication.

25. Editorial

```
"Gay Partnership Legislation a Mixed Bag." Editorial.
     Burlington Free Press 5 April 2000: A10.
```

If the editorial is signed, list the author's name first.

26. Letter to the editor and reply

```
Kempthorne, Charles. Letter. Kansas City Star 26 July
     1999: A16.
```

```
Massing, Michael. Reply to letter of Peter Dale Scott. New
     York Review of Books 4 Mar. 1993: 57.
```

27. Review

```
Kramer, Mimi. "Victims" Rev. of 'Tis Pity She's a Whore.
     New York Shakespeare Festival. New Yorker 20 Apr.
     1992: 78-79.
```

```
Lane, Anthony. Rev. of The Mummy. New Yorker 10 May 1999:
     104.
```

56f Documenting electronic sources

Electronic sources include both *databases,* available in portable forms such as CD-ROM, diskette, or magnetic tape, and *online sources* accessed with a computer connected to the Internet.

Databases

The Works Cited entries for electronic databases (newsletters, journals, and conferences) are similar to entries for articles in printed periodicals: cite the author's name; the article or document title, in quotation marks; the newsletter, journal, or conference title; the number of the volume or issue; the year or date of publication; and the number of pages, if available.

Portable databases are much like books and periodicals. Their entries in Works Cited lists are similar to those for printed material except that you must also include the following items.

◆ The medium of publication (*CD-ROM, diskette, magnetic tape*).

◆ The name of the vendor, if known. (This may be different from the name of the organization that compiled the information, which must also be included.)

◆ The date of electronic publication, in addition to the date the material originally may have been published (as for a reprinted book or article).

28.   Periodically updated CD-ROM database

```
James, Caryn. "An Army as Strong as Its Weakest Link." New
     York Times 16 Sep. 1994: C8. New York Times Ondisc.
     CD-ROM. UMI-Proquest. Oct. 1994.
```

If a database comes from a printed source such as a book, periodical, or collection of bibliographies or abstracts, cite this information first, followed by the title of the database (underlined), the medium of publication, the vendor name (if applicable), and the date of electronic publication. If no printed source is available, include the title of the material accessed (in quotation marks), the date of the material if given, the underlined title of the database, the medium of publication, the vendor name, and the date of electronic publication.

29.   Nonperiodical CD-ROM publication

```
"Rhetoric." The Oxford English Dictionary. 2nd ed. CD-ROM.
     Oxford: Oxford UP, 1992.
```

List a nonperiodical CD-ROM as you would a book, adding the medium of publication and information about the source, if applicable. If citing only part of a work, underline the title of the selected portion or place it within quotation marks, as appropriate (as you would the title of a printed short story, poem, article, essay, or similar source).

30.   Diskette or magnetic tape publication

```
Lanham, Richard D. The Electronic Word: Democracy,
     Technology, and the Arts. Diskette. Chicago: U of
     Chicago P, 1993.
```

```
Doyle, Roddy. The Woman Who Walked into Doors. Magnetic
     tape. New York: Penguin Audiobooks, 1996.
```

List these in the Works Cited section as you would a book, adding the medium of publication (for example, *Diskette* or *Magnetic tape*).

Online sources

Documenting a World Wide Web (WWW) or other Internet source follows the same basic guidelines as documenting other texts: cite *who* said *what, where,* and *when*. However, important differences need to be noted. In citing online sources from the World Wide Web or electronic mail, two dates are important: the date the text was created (published) and the date you found the information (accessed the site). When both publication and access dates are available, provide both.

Many WWW sources are often updated or changed, leaving no trace of the original version, so always provide the access date, which documents that this information was available on that particular date. Thus, most electronic source entries will end with an access date immediately followed by the electronic address: *23 Dec. 1999 <http://www.cas.usf.edu/english>*. The angle brackets < > identify the source as the Internet.

The following guidelines are derived from the MLA Web site <http://www.mla.org>. To identify a WWW or Internet source, include, if available, the following items in the following order, each punctuated by a period except the date of access.

- **Author** (or editor, compiler, or translator). Give the full name, last name first; include an alias, if available, for an unknown author.

- **Title.** Include titles of poems, short stories, and articles in quotation marks. Include the title of a posting to a discussion list or forum in quotation marks, followed by *Online posting*. Underline the titles of published sources (books, magazines, films, recordings).

- **Editor, compiler, or translator.** Include the name, if not cited earlier, followed by the appropriate abbreviation (*Ed., Com., Trans.*).

- **Print source.** Include the same information as for a printed citation.

- **Title** of the scholarly project, database, or Web site (underlined); if the source has no title, include a description such as *Home page*. Include the name of the editor if available.

◆ **Identifying number.** For a journal, include volume and issue numbers.

◆ **Date of electronic publication.**

◆ **Discussion list** information. Include the full name or title of the list or forum.

◆ **Page, paragraph, or section numbers.**

◆ **Sponsorship or affiliation.** Include the name of any organization or institution sponsoring the site.

◆ **Date of access.** Include the date you visited the site.

◆ **Electronic address.** Include the electronic address (URL) within angle brackets < >. To interrupt an electronic address at the end of a line, hit the return key, but do not hyphenate. Break an electronic address only after a slash.

31. Article in online database

```
Carlson, Margaret. "Stretches and Sighs: Gore's Fibs May Be
    Small Compared with Bush's, but They Drive Us Crazy."
    Time 16 Oct. 2000: 7 pars. Info Trac Web: Expanded
    Academic ASAP. Lansing Community Coll. Lib. 11 Oct.
    2001 <http://www.lcc.edu/library/iac.htm>.
```

32. Published Web site

```
Beller, Jonathon L. "What's Inside The Insider?" Pop
    Matters Film. 1999. 21 May 2000
    <http://popmatters.com/film/insider.html>.
```

33. Personal Web site

```
Fulwiler, Toby. Home Page. 2 Apr. 2000
    <http://www.uvm.edu/~tfulwile>.
```

The tilde (~) indicates a personal web address.

34. Professional Web site

```
Yellow Wall-Paper Site. 1995. U of Texas. 12 Dec. 1999
    <http://www.cwrl.utexas.edu/~daniel/amlit/
    wallpaper.html>.
```

35. Book

```
Twain, Mark. The Adventures of Tom Sawyer. Internet
    Wiretap Online Library. 4 Jan. 1998. Carnegie-Mellon
    U. 4 Oct. 1998 <http://www.cs.cmu.edu/Web/People/rgs/
    sawyr-table.html>.
```

36. Poem

Poe, Edgar Allan. "The Raven." American Review. 1845. Poetry
Archives. 8 Sep. 1998 <http://tqd.advanced.org/3247/
cgi-bin/dispoem.cgi?poet=poe.edgar&poem>.

37. Article in a journal

Erkkila, Betsy. "The Emily Dickinson Wars." Emily Dickinson
Journal 5.2 (1996): 14 pars. 8 Nov. 1998
<http://www.colorado.edu/EDIS/journal/index.html>.

38. Article in a reference database

"Victorian." Britannica Online. Vers. 97.1. 1 Mar. 1997.
Encyclopaedia Britannica. 3 May 1999
<http://www.eb.com:180>.

39. Posting to a discussion list

Beja, Morris. "New Virginia Woolf Discussion List." Online
posting. 22 Feb. 1996. The Virginia Woolf Society.
Ohio State U. 24 Mar. 1996
<gopher://dept.English.upenn.edu:70/0r0-1858-?Lists/
20th/vwoolf>.

40. E-mail or listserv message

Fulwiler, Toby. "A Question About Electronic Sources."
E-mail to the author. 23 May 2000.

Harley, Robert. "Writing Committee Meeting." Online posting. 24 Jan. 1999. UCLA. 25 June 1999.

Note that *e-mail* is spelled with a hyphen in MLA style.

41. Newsgroup (Usenet) message

Answerman (Mathes, Robert). "Revising the Atom." 2 Mar.
1997. 4 July 1997 <alt.books.digest>.

If you quote a personal message sent by somebody else, be sure to get
permission before including his or her address on the Works Cited page.

56g Documenting other sources

42. Cartoon, titled or untitled

Davis, Jim. "Garfield." Cartoon. Courier [Findlay, OH] 17
Feb. 1996: E4.

Roberts, Victoria. Cartoon. New Yorker 13 July 2000: 34.

43. Film or videocassette

Casablanca. Dir. Michael Curtiz. Perf. Humphrey Bogart and
Ingrid Bergman. Warner Bros., 1942.

```
Fast Food: What's in It for You. Prod. Center for Science.
    Videocassette. Los Angeles: Churchill, 1988.
```

Begin with the title, followed by the director, the studio, and the year released. You may also include the names of lead actors, the producer, and the like between the title and the distribution information. If your essay is concerned with a particular person's work on a film, lead with that person's name, arranging all other information accordingly.

```
Lewis, Joseph H., dir. Gun Crazy. Screenplay by Dalton
    Trumbo. King Bros., 1950.
```

44. Personal interview

```
Holden, James. Personal interview. 12 Jan. 2000.
```

Begin with the interviewee's name and specify the kind of interview and the date. You may identify the interviewee's position if relevant to the purpose of the interview.

```
Morser, John. Professor of Political Science, U of Wisconsin-
    Stevens Point. Telephone interview. 15 Dec. 1999.
```

45. Published or broadcast interview

```
Sowell, Thomas. "Affirmative Action Programs." Interview.
    All Things Considered. Natl. Public Radio. WGTE,
    Toledo. 5 June 1990.
```

```
Steingass, David. Interview. Counterpoint 7 May 1970: 3-4.
```

For published or broadcast interviews, begin with the interviewee's name. Include appropriate publication information for a periodical or book and appropriate broadcast information for a radio or television program.

46. Print advertisement

```
Cadillac DeVille. Advertisement. New York Times 21 Feb.
    1996, natl. ed.: A20.
```

Begin with the name of the product, followed by the description *Advertisement* and publication information for the source.

47. Unpublished lecture, public address, or speech

```
Graves, Donald. "When Bad Things Happen to Good Ideas."
    National Council of Teachers of English Convention.
    St. Louis. 21 Nov. 1989.
```

Begin with the speaker, followed by the title (if any), the meeting (and sponsoring organization, if needed), the location, and the date. If there

450

is no title, use a descriptive label (such as *Speech*) with no quotation marks.

48. Personal or unpublished letter

Friedman, Paul. Letter to the author. 18 Mar. 1998.

Personal letters and e-mail messages are handled nearly identically in Works Cited entries. Begin with the name of the writer, identify the type of communication (for example, *E-mail* or *Letter*), and specify the audience. Include the date written, if known, or the date received.

To cite an unpublished letter from an archive or private collection, include information that locates the holding (for example, *Quinn-Adams Papers. Lexington Historical Society. Lexington, KY*).

49. Published letter

King, Jr., Martin Luther. "Letter from Birmingham Jail." 28 Aug. 1963. Civil Disobedience in Focus. Ed. Hugo Adam Bedau. New York: Routledge, 1991. 68-84.

Cite published letters as you would a selection from an anthology. Specify the audience in the letter title (if known). Include the date of the letter immediately after its title. Place the page number(s) after the publisher information. If you cite more than one letter from a collection, cite the entire collection in the Works Cited list, and indicate individual dates and page numbers in your text.

50. Map

Ohio River: Foster, KY, to New Martinsville, WV. Map. Huntington: U.S. Army Corps of Engineers, 1985.

Cite a map as you would a book by an unknown author. Underline the title, and identify the source as a map or chart.

51. Performance

Bissex, Rachel. Folk Songs. Flynn Theater. Burlington, VT. 14 May 1990.

Rumors. By Neil Simon. Dir. Gene Saks. Broadhurst Theater, New York. 17 Nov. 1988.

Identify the pertinent details such as title, place, and date of performance. If you focus on a particular person in your text, such as the director or conductor, lead with that person's name. For a recital or individual concert, lead with the performer's name.

52. Audio recording

Young, Neil, comp., perf. <u>Mirror Ball</u>. In part accompanied
    by members of Pearl Jam. Burbank: Reprise, 1995.

Marley, Bob, and the Wailers. "Buffalo Soldier." <u>Legend</u>.
    Audiocassette. Island Records, 1984.

Depending on the focus of your text, begin with the artist, composer, or conductor. Enclose song titles in quotation marks, followed by the recording title, underlined. Do not underline musical compositions identified only by form, number, and key. If you are not citing a compact disc, specify the recording format. End with the company label, the catalog number (if known), and the date of issue.

53. Television or radio broadcast

"Emissary." <u>Star Trek: Deep Space Nine</u>. Teleplay by
    Michael Pillar. Story by Rick Berman and Michael
    Pillar. Dir. David Carson. Fox. WFLX, West Palm Beach.
    9 Jan. 1993.

If the broadcast is not an episode of a series or the episode is untitled, begin with the program title, underlined. Include the network, the station and city, and the date of the broadcast. The inclusion of other information such as narrator, writer, director, or performers depends on the purpose of your citation.

54. Work of art

Holbein, Hans. <u>Portrait of Erasmus</u>. The Louvre, Paris. <u>The
    Louvre Museum</u>. By Germain Bazin. New York: Abrams,
    n.d. 148.

Begin with the artist's name. Follow with the title, and conclude with the location. If your source is a book, also give pertinent publication information.

Student paper: MLA style   56h

The following paper was written by a first-year student, Andrew Turner, in response to an open topic assignment for an American literature survey course. The students were asked to present their research in MLA style, including a title page and an outline, which are optional under the MLA system. Notice that Andrew has chosen a full-sentence style for the outline. The title page and the outline page are unnumbered.

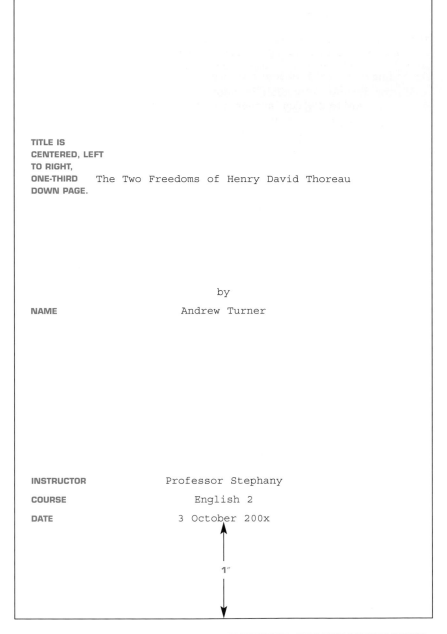

TITLE IS
CENTERED, LEFT
TO RIGHT,
ONE-THIRD   The Two Freedoms of Henry David Thoreau
DOWN PAGE.

by

NAME   Andrew Turner

INSTRUCTOR   Professor Stephany

COURSE   English 2

DATE   3 October 200x

1"

TITLE PAGE OF A STUDENT ESSAY IN MLA FORMAT (OPTIONAL) NOTE THAT MARGINS SHOWN
ARE ADJUSTED TO FIT SPACE LIMITATIONS OF BOOK. FOLLOW ACTUAL DIMENSIONS SHOWN
AND YOUR INSTRUCTOR'S DIRECTIONS.

The Two Freedoms of Henry David Thoreau

Thesis statement: The writings of Henry David Thoreau inspire modern readers by arguing for freedom from government intervention and freedom from social conformity.

    I. "Civil Disobedience" advocates political freedom while <u>Walden</u> argues for social freedom.

   II. "Civil Disobedience" ("CD") advocates freedom from government interference in daily life.
      A. The premise of "CD" is "That government is best which governs least."
      B. Thoreau is arrested for not paying poll tax and is put in jail.
        1. Thoreau protests war with Mexico and the institution of slavery.
        2. The doctrine of passive resistance is articulated in "CD."
      C. The case is made in "Slavery in Massachusetts" and "A Plea for John Brown."
      D. The influence of "CD" is felt throughout world.
        1. "CD" inspires Gandhi and King.
        2. "CD" is the basis for the British Labour Party platform.
        3. "CD" supports underground resistance to Nazi Germany.

 III. <u>Walden</u> (<u>W</u>) argues against social conformity and for simple living.
      A. Thoreau confronts the "essential facts of life."
        1. <u>W</u> provides an example of economical living.
        2. <u>W</u> provides an example of living alone.
      B. Thoreau lives deliberately at Walden Pond.
        1. Thoreau tends a bean patch.
        2. Thoreau chases loons.
      C. Living at Walden Pond is not an option today.

  IV. Thoreau's ideals inspire modern readers.

454

NAME Andrew Turner

INSTRUCTOR Professor Stephany

COURSE English 2

DATE PAPER DUE 3 October 200X

1/2″

1″

Turner 1

WRITER'S LAST NAME AND PAGE NUMBER APPEAR ON EACH PAGE.

DOUBLE SPACED

The Two Freedoms of Henry David Thoreau

Henry David Thoreau led millions of people throughout the world to think about individual freedom in a new way. During his lifetime, he attempted to live free of unjust governmental constraints as well as conventional social expectations.

WRITER OPENS WITH THESIS.

DO NOT JUSTIFY RIGHT-HAND MARGIN.

In his 1849 essay "On the Duty of Civil Disobedience," he makes his strongest case against governmental interference in the lives of citizens. In his 1854 book Walden: Or, Life in the Woods, he makes the case for living free from social conventions and expectations.

WRITER IDENTIFIES BY FULL TITLE THE TWO WORKS TO BE EXAMINED.

Thoreau opens "Civil Disobedience" with his statement that "that government is best which governs not at all" (222). He argues that a government should allow its people to be as free as possible, providing for the needs of the people without infringing on their daily lives. Thoreau explains:

ABBREVIATED TITLE IS USED AFTER WORK HAS BEEN IDENTIFIED BY FULL TITLE.

ONLY THE PAGE NUMBER IS NEEDED WHEN SOURCE IS INTRODUCED IN THE SENTENCE.

The government does not concern me much, and I shall bestow the fewest possible thoughts on it. It is not for many moments

INDENTED 10 SPACES BECAUSE QUOTATION IS MORE THAN 4 LINES

1″

Turner 2

MLA

SHORT TITLE IS ADDED TO PAGE NUMBER BECAUSE TWO WORKS BY THE AUTHOR APPEAR ON THE WORKS CITED PAGE.

that I live under a government.
("Civil" 238).

In other words, in his daily life
he attends to his business of eating,
sleeping, and earning a living and not
dealing in any noticeable way with an
entity called "a government."

Because Thoreau did not want his
freedom overshadowed by governmental regulations, he tried to ignore them.
However, the American government in 1845
would not let him. He was arrested and
put in the Concord jail for failing to
pay his poll tax--a tax he believed
unjust because it supported the government's war with Mexico as well as the
immoral institution of slavery. Instead of
protesting his arrest, he celebrated it
and explained its meaning by writing
"Civil Disobedience," one of the most
famous English-language essays ever
written. In it, he argues persuasively
that "under a government which imprisons

PAGE NUMBER ONLY (SENTENCE IDENTIFIES THE WORK)

any unjustly, the true place for a just
man is also a prison" (230). Thus the
doctrine of passive resistance was formed,
a doctrine that advocated protest against
the government by nonviolent means:

How does it become a man to
behave toward this American
government today? I answer that
he cannot without disgrace be
associated with it. I cannot
for an instant recognize that
political organization as my
government which is the
slave's government also. (224)

SIGNAL PHRASE INTRODUCES AUTHOR — According to Charles R. Anderson,
Thoreau's other writings, such as "Slavery
in Massachusetts" and "A Plea for Captain
John Brown," show his disdain of the
"[N]ortherners for their cowardice on con-
niving with such an institution" (28). he
wanted all free American citizens, North
and South, to revolt and liberate the
slaves.

In addition to inspiring his coun-
trymen, Thoreau's view of the sanctity of
individual freedom affected the lives of
PARTIAL QUOTATION IS WORKED INTO SENTENCE IN GRAMMATI-CALLY SMOOTH WAY. later generations who shared his beliefs
(King). "Civil Disobedience" had the
greatest impact because of its "worldwide
influence on Mahatma Gandhi, the British
Labour Party in its early years, the
underground in Nazi-occupied Europe, and

Turner 4

Negro leaders in the modern [S]outh"
(Anderson 30). In other words, for nearly
150 years, Thoreau's formulation of passive resistance has been a part of the
human struggle for freedom (Gandhi).

Thoreau also wanted to be free from
the everyday pressure to conform to society's expectations. He believed in doing
and possessing only the essential things
in life. To demonstrate his case, in 1845
he moved to the outskirts of Concord,
Massachusetts, and lived by himself for
two years on the shore of Walden Pond
(Spiller et al. 396-97). Thoreau wrote
Walden to explain the value of living
simply, apart from the unnecessary complexity of society: "Simplicity, simplicity, simplicity! I say, let your affairs
be as two or three, and not a hundred or
a thousand" (66). At Walden, he lived as
much as possible by this statement,
building his own house and furniture,
growing his own food, bartering for simple necessities, attending to his own
business rather than seeking employment
from others (Walden 16-17).

IDENTIFICATION OF WORK WITH MORE THAN THREE AUTHORS.

ABBREVIATED SHORT TITLE AFTER FIRST REFERENCE

SHORT TITLE IS INCLUDED BECAUSE MORE THAN ONE TITLE APPEARS ON WORKS CITED PAGE.

MLA

Living at Walden Pond gave Thoreau the chance to formulate many of his ideas about living the simple, economical life. At Walden, he lived simply in order to "front only the essential facts of life" (66) and to center his thoughts on living instead of on unnecessary details of mere livelihood. He developed survival skills that freed him from the constraints of city dwellers whose lives depended on a web of material things and services provided by others. He preferred to "take rank hold on life and spend [his] day more as animals do" (117).

PAGE NUMBERS SUFFICE WHEN CONTEXT MAKES SOURCE CLEAR.

BRACKETS INDICATE CHANGE IN WORDING SO PRONOUN CONFORMS TO SENTENCE GRAMMAR.

While living at Walden Pond, Thoreau was free to occupy his time in any way that pleased him, which for him meant writing, tending his bean patch, and chasing loons. He was not troubled by a boss hounding him with deadlines or a wife and children who needed support. In other words, "he wasn't expected to be anywhere at any time for anybody except himself" (Franklin). His neighbors accused him of being selfish and did not understand that he sought most of all "to live deliberately" (Walden 66), as he felt all people should learn to do.

Turner 6

Then as now, most people had more
responsibilities than Thoreau had, and
they could not just pack up their belongings and go live in the woods--if they
could find free woods to live in. Today,
people are intrigued to read about
Thoreau's experiences and are inspired by
his thoughts, but few people can actually
live or do as he suggests in Walden. In
fact, most people, if faced with the
prospect of spending two years removed
from society--from modern plumbing, automobiles, television, telephone, and
e-mail--would think of it as punishment
or banishment rather than freedom (Poger).

WRITER'S CONCLUSION REPEATS THESIS.

Practical or not, Thoreau's writings
have inspired countless people to reassess
how they live and what they live for.
Though unable to live exactly as he advocated, readers everywhere remain inspired
by his vision of independence, equality,
and, above all, freedom.

460

Works Cited

Anderson, Charles Roberts, ed. Thoreau's Vision: The Major Essays . Englewood Cliffs: Prentice, 1993.

Franklin, George. Professor of American Literature, Northfield College. Personal interview. 5 April 2000.

"Gandhi." Britannica Online . Vers. 97.1. 1 Mar. 1997. Encyclopaedia Britannica . 2 Mar. 1998 <http://www.eb.com:180>.

King, Jr., Martin Luther. "Letter from Birmingham Jail." 28 Aug. 1963. Civil Disobedience in Focus . Ed. Hugo Adam Bedau. New York: Routledge, 1991. 68-84.

Poger, Ralph. "A Postmodern Point of View." Home page. 2 Apr. 2000 <http://www.acu.edu/~rpoger>.

Spiller, Robert E., et al. Literary History of the United States: History . 3rd ed. New York: Macmillan, 1963.

Thoreau, Henry David. "On the Duty of Civil Disobedience." 1848. Walden and "Civil Disobedience ." 1854. New York: Signet-NAL, 1995. 222-40.

Turner 8

AUTHOR'S NAME IS NOT REPEATED. NAME IS REPLACED BY 3 HYPHENS FOLLOWED BY A PERIOD.

---. <u>Walden: Or, Life in the Woods</u>. New

York: Harcourt, 1987.

WRIT 121
Kyle Cervantes   Cervantes 1
February 21, 2002

Mental Block

> "Mental illness is the last great stigma of the
>   20th century."
> —David Satcher, former United State Surgeon
>   General (qtd. In Kaufman A3)

Imagine living every moment with a battle between positive and negative thoughts raging in your mind. These thoughts are completely distorted, much like the image of yourself in a funhouse mirror. The positive thoughts are blurred and vague, while the negative thoughts are focused to crystal clarity. Because of this uneven match-up, the negative thoughts always seem to have an edge on winning. I have been experiencing this mental battle for close to five years now. Every day is a struggle to maintain my self-esteem and happiness because I suffer from severe depression and generalized anxiety disorder. I am far from being alone in my suffering from these illnesses, though. Many others struggle with these disorders every day of their lives. These illnesses are difficult enough to manage internally without having to deal with the discriminating practices of those who do not take mental illness seriously. Though doctors and health officials alike acknowledge the seriousness of mental illness, there is still a good portion of society that continues to trivialize the effects of mental illness on its victims.

Fifty million Americans suffer from some type of mental illness every year, according to the very first surgeon general's report on mental health (Kaufman A3). According to the report, this translates into an astounding one in five people who suffered from a mental disorder in 1999 (Kaufman A3). While researching sources for this paper, most, if not all of the sources referenced referred to mental illness as nothing short of an epidemic. Former Health and Human Services Secretary Donna E. Shalala, during the same year as the report, called mental illness a "public health crisis" in the United States. She went on to state, "The fact is that it [mental illness] is the second-leading cause of disability and the second-leading cause of premature death in this country" (qtd. in AMA 23).

With top officials conveying such dire information, it's hard to believe many people still think mental illness can simply be shrugged off. A report published by the *American Journal of Psychiatry* about discrimination based on mental illness found that respondents in every category of mental disorders reported social, economic and discriminatory barriers (Druss et al 1490). Many times throughout high school I was confronted with teachers and administrators who refused to excuse my absences even with a doctor's note. One time a teacher actually confronted me and said that depression isn't an illness at all, but a way for lazy people to get out of doing things they don't want to do.

It's discriminatory practices such as these that make life incredibly difficult for mental health patients everywhere. The best example of discrimination occurs by insurance companies. Even though laws have been passed that require equal lifetime coverage for mental and physical health costs, this hasn't stopped collection of gouging co-payments and severe limits on what treatment patients may receive (Kaufman A3). The percentage of total health-care dollars going to mental health has been cut in half over the past decade, from

6.1% to 3.2% ("It's Your Problem" 26). The president-elect of the American Psychiatric Association, Paul S. Appelbaum, M.D., attributes this decline to, "a corporate culture of denial…[which] sanctions discriminatory insurance benefits for mental illness for most employees in this country" (qtd. in Applebaum A18). I am no longer taking medication for my illness, but when I was, insurance covered little to none of the cost of prescriptions and none of the cost of visiting a psychiatrist or counselor.

I believe that much of the discrimination towards sufferers of mental illness originates with the stigma that is attached to what some perceive as craziness. Sometimes, thoughts of padded rooms and straight jackets cloud rational thinking about the subject. This is an archaic view of mental illness that hinders some from seeking help. I have run into many people, including friends and family, who display classic symptoms of depression, yet they absolutely refuse to seek treatment because they are afraid of what others will think. I remember how I used to believe people would think I was crazy if they knew I suffered from a mental illness. The American Medical Association has done research on the topic and found that the stigma attached to mental illness, despite massive public education efforts, still persists and is the major cause preventing people from seeking assistance (23). Sometimes what people choose not to say tells more about the current viewpoint on mental illness than their actual opinions. While looking for evidence for to support my thesis, in every poll and interview that I looked through, there was a very distinct pattern

that emerged. Every time a person chose to discuss their
stories, they also chose to remain anonymous or use a pseu-
donym in fear that people they know would find out about
their illnesses.

There is a long way to go in the general education of
the public about mental illnesses and their effects on the
population. As long as the problem is downplayed by society,
people will continue to live with a dangerous disorder and
not seek out medical treatment. Mental disorders are just as
prevalent as physical medical disorders and should be treated
with the same amount of thought and acceptance. I don't
believe many people would approach a cancer patient and ask
them if they are faking their disease. Just because you
can't see the effects of a mental disorder doesn't make them
any less serious. Ideally, the outlook on mental health will
grow brighter as people become more educated on the subject.

Works Cited

American Medical Association. "Overcome Barriers to
Mental Health Care." *American Medical News.* 44.36(2001):23.
InfoTrac OneFile. Gale Group. Lansing Community Coll. Lib.,
Lansing. 20 Feb. 2002 http://galenet.galegroup.com.

Appelbaum, Paul S., M.D. "Mental Health Care: It's Time
for Parity" *The New York Times.* 24 July 2001: A18.

Druss, Benjamin G., M.D., M.P.H. et al. "Understanding
Disability in Mental and General Medical Conditions."
American Journal of Psychiatry. 157 (2000): 1485-1491.

"It's Your Problem Too." *Business Week.* 28 Feb. 2000:26.
InfoTrac OneFile. Gale Group. Lansing Community Coll. Lib.,
Lansing. 20 Feb 2002 <http://galenet.galegroup.com>.

Kaufman, Marc. "Mental Illness in America: 50 Million
People a Year." *The Washington Post.* 14 Dec. 1999: A3.

APA DOCUMENTATION

Most disciplines in the social sciences and related fields use the name-and-date system of documentation put forth by the American Psychological Association (APA). The disciplines of education and business also use this system. This citation style highlights dates of publication because the currency of published material is of primary importance in these disciplines. Because collaborative authoring is common in the social sciences, listing all authors is customary. For more about the foundations and purposes of the APA system, see the *Publication Manual of the American Psychological Association,* 4th ed. (Washington: APA, 1994) or the APA Web site <http://www.apa.org/>.

57a Guidelines for formatting manuscripts

The APA guidelines for submitting college papers are fairly conservative and do not reflect the wealth of visually interesting fonts, type sizes, graphics, and other options available with most modern word-processing programs. If your instructor requests strict APA format, follow the guidelines below. If your instructor encourages more creative formats, use good judgment in displaying the information in your text. The following guidelines describe the preparation of the main body of your paper.

Paper and printing

Print all academic assignments on 8½″ × 11″ white paper in a standard font (for example, Times New Roman, Courier) and type size (10 or 12 points) using a good-quality printer.

Margins and spacing

Allow margins of one inch all around. Justify the left margin only. Double-space everything, including headings, quoted material, and the References page. Indent five spaces or one-half inch for paragraphs.

For prose quotations of more than forty words, indent five spaces or one-half inch from the left margin. Do not use quotation marks to mark the beginning and ending of quoted passages; include page numbers in parentheses at the end of the passage (*pp. 34–41*).

Page numbers

Print page numbers in the upper right margin of all pages one-half inch below the top of the paper (including the title page and abstract page). APA format requires a shortened title (2 or 3 words) five spaces before each page number to guarantee correct identification of stray pages (*Green 1, Green 2*).

Title page

Attach a numbered title page to your paper. Center the title fifteen lines from the top; immediately below type your name, your instructor's name, the course name, and the date.

On the first full page of text, center the title, capitalizing key words only. If your instructor asks for strict APA style, avoid using italics, underlining, quotation marks, boldface, unusual fonts, or type for the title. Double-space to the first paragraph.

If you are not using a title page, include on page 1 your name, your instructor's name, the course title, and the date, double spaced on separate lines, flush with the upper left margin.

Abstract

Write a paragraph of seventy-five to one hundred words that states your thesis and the main supporting points in clear, concise, descriptive language. Avoid statements of personal opinion and inflammatory judgment. Attach the abstract immediately following the title page; center the word *Abstract* one inch from the top of the page; double-space. (Outlines are not required.)

Punctuation

One space is required after commas, semicolons, colons, periods, question marks, and exclamation points and between the periods in an ellipsis. Dashes are formed by two hyphens, with no extra spacing on either side.

Visual information

APA style requires the labeling of all tables (charts, graphs) and figures (drawings, photographs) included in the text: *Table 1*, *Fig. 2*, and so on. Include a clear caption for each, and place each of these elements in the text as near as possible to the passage it refers to. In your text, be sure to discuss the most important information or feature in each table or figure you include.

APA

468

DIRECTORY FOR APA DOCUMENTATION GUIDELINES

FORMATTING MANUSCRIPTS (57a)

IN-TEXT CITATIONS (57b)
1. Single work by one or more authors
2. Two or more works by an author published in the same year
3. Unknown author
4. Corporate or organizational author
5. Authors with the same last name
6. Quotation from an indirect source
7. More than one work in a citation
8. Web site
9. Specific information from a Web site
10. Long quotation set off from text
11. Footnotes

FORMATTING THE REFERENCE LIST (57c)

DOCUMENTING BOOKS (57d)
1. Book by one author
2. Book by two or more authors
3. More than one book by the same author
4. Book by a corporation, an association, an organization, or a foundation
5. Revised edition of a book
6. Edited book
7. Book in more than one volume
8. Translated or reprinted book
9. Chapter or article in an edited book
10. Anonymous book
11. Government document

DOCUMENTING PERIODICALS (57e)
12. Articles in a journal paginated by volume
13. Article in a journal paginated by issue
14. Magazine article
15. Newspaper article

DOCUMENTING ELECTRONIC SOURCES (57f)
16. CD-ROM
17. Computer software
18. Online journal articles

(continued)

APA

19. Document on a World Wide Web (WWW) site
20. E-mail and listserv messages

DOCUMENTING OTHER SOURCES (57g)
21. Film, recording, and other nonprint media
22. Interviews and other field sources

Guidelines for in-text citations   57b

The following guidelines illustrate how to cite source information in the main body of your paper using APA style.

1. Single work by one or more authors

Whenever you quote, paraphrase, or summarize material in your text, give both the author's last name and the date of the source. For direct quotations, provide specific page numbers. Page references in the APA system are always preceded, in text or in the reference list, by the abbreviation *p.* or *pp.* to designate single or multiple pages.

Supply authors' names, publication dates, and page numbers (when listed) in parentheses following the cited material. Do not repeat any of these elements if you identify them in the text preceding the parenthetical citation.

```
Exotoxins make some bacteria dangerous to humans
(Thomas, 1974).

According to Thomas (1974), "Some bacteria are only
harmful to us if they make exotoxins" (p. 76).

We need fear some bacteria only "if they make exotox-
ins" (Thomas, 1974, p. 76).
```

For a work by two authors, cite both names.

```
Smith and Rogers (1990) note that all bacteria that
produce exotoxins are harmful to humans.

All known exotoxin-producing bacteria are harmful to
humans (Smith & Rogers, 1990).
```

The authors' names are joined by *and* within your text, but APA convention requires an ampersand (*&*) to join authors' names in parentheses.

For a work by three to five authors, identify all the authors by last name the first time you cite a source. In subsequent references, list only the first author, followed by *et al.* ("and others").

> The most recent study supports the belief that alcohol abuse is on the rise (Dinkins, Dominic, & Smith, 1989).

> When homeless people were excluded from the study, the results were the same (Dinkins et al., 1989)

If you are citing a source by six or more authors, identify only the first author in all the references, followed by *et al.*

2. Two or more works by an author published in the same year

To distinguish between two or more works published in the same year by the same author or team of authors, place a lowercase letter (*a, b, c,* and so on) immediately after the date. This letter should correspond to that in the reference list, where the entries are alphabetized by title. If two entries appear in one citation, repeat the year.

> (Smith, 1992a, 1992b)

3. Unknown author

To cite the work of an unknown author, identify the first two or three words of the entry as listed on the References page. If the words are from the title, enclose them in quotation marks or underline them, as appropriate.

> <u>Statistical Abstracts</u> (1991) reports the literacy rate for Mexico at 75% for 1990, up 4% from census figures 10 years earlier.

> Many researchers now believe that treatment should not begin until other factors have been dealt with ("New Evidence Suggests," 1987).

4. Corporate or organizational author

Spell out the name of the authoring agency for a work by a corporation, an association, an organization, or a foundation. If the name can be abbreviated and remain identifiable, you may spell out the name only the first time and put the abbreviation immediately after it, in brackets. For subsequent references use only the abbreviation.

> (American Psychological Association [APA], 1993)
> (APA, 1994)

5. Authors with the same last name

To avoid confusion in citing two or more authors with the same last name, include each author's initials in every citation.

```
(J. M. Clark, 1994)
(C. L. Clark, 1995)
```

6. Quotation from an indirect source

Use the words *as cited in* to indicate quotations or information in your source that was originally from another source.

```
Lester Brown of Worldwatch believes that international
agriculture production has reached its limit and that
"we're going to be in trouble on the food front before
this decade is out" (as cited in Mann, 1993, p. 51).
```

7. More than one work in a citation

List two or more sources within a single parenthetical citation in the same order in which they appear in your reference list. If you refer to two or more works by the same author, list them in chronological order with the author's name mentioned once and the dates separated by commas.

```
(Thomas, 1974, 1979)
```

List works by different authors in alphabetical order by the author's last name, separated by semicolons.

```
(Miller, 1990; Webster & Rose, 1988)
```

8. Web site

When citing an entire Web site, not specific text or a figure, give the electronic address (URL) in your text.

```
To locate information about faculty at the University
of Vermont, visit the school's Web site
<http://www.uvm.edu>.
```

When the site's name and address are included in the text, no reference entry is needed.

9. Specific information from a Web site

Cite specific information (author, figure, table, paraphrased or quoted passage) from a Web site as you would a print source, by including the brief author/date information in the text or in parentheses, followed by complete information on the References page.

10.   Long quotation set off from text

Start quotations of forty or more words on a new line, and indent the block five spaces or one-half inch from the left-hand margin. Indent the first line of the second or any subsequent paragraphs (but not the first paragraph) five additional spaces. Double-space all such quotations, omit quotation marks, and place the parenthetical citation after any end punctuation, with no period following the citation.

11.   Footnotes

Footnotes provide additional information of interest to some readers but are also likely to slow down the pace of your text or obscure your point for other readers. Make footnotes as brief as possible. When the information you wish to add is extensive, present it in an appendix.

Number footnotes consecutively on a page following the References list on a page headed *Footnotes;* double-space, and indent the first line of each footnote as you would a paragraph.

57c Guidelines for the APA References page

All works mentioned in a paper should be identified in a reference list according to the following general rules of the APA documentation system.

Format

After the final page of the paper, title a separate page *References* with no underlining, italics, or quotation marks. Center the title one inch from the top of the page. Number the page in sequence with the last page of the paper.

Double-space between the title and the first entry. Also double-space both between and within entries. Set the first line flush with the left-hand margin.

Indent the second and all subsequent lines of an entry five spaces from the left margin in a hanging indent. (Exception: manuscripts submitted for publication to APA journals may use the paragraph indent format, with the first line indented five spaces and subsequent lines flush with the left margin—but these will be reset as hanging indents when published. Ask your instructor which is preferred.)

If your reference list exceeds one page, continue in sequence on an additional page or pages, but do not repeat the title *References.*

Alphabetize the list of references according to authors' last names, using the first author's last name for works with multiple authors. For entries by an unknown author, alphabetize by the first word of the title, excepting insignificant words (*A, An, The*).

Entry formats

Each item that begins with a capital letter is followed by a period and one space. Only the first word is capitalized in book and article titles, which are underlined. Three variations on general formats are the most common.

BOOKS

ONE SPACE   ONE SPACE   ONE SPACE

Author(s). (Year of publication). Book Title. City of

INDENT 5
SPACES —— publication: Publisher.

JOURNAL ARTICLES

ONE SPACE   ONE SPACE   ONE SPACE

Author(s). (Year of publication). Article title.

INDENT 5
SPACES —— Journal Title, volume number, inclusive page

numbers.

MAGAZINE AND NEWSPAPER ARTICLES

ONE SPACE   ONE SPACE

Author(s). (Year, month of publication). Article

INDENT 5
SPACES —— title. Publication Title, inclusive page

numbers.

AUTHORS

- List the author's last name first, followed by a comma and the author's initials (not first name).

- When a work has more than one author, list all authors in this way, separating the names with commas.

- For multiple authors of a single work, place an ampersand (*&*) before the last author's name.

- Place a period after the last author's name.

TITLES

- List the complete titles and subtitles of books and articles, but capitalize only the first word of the title and any subtitle, as well as all proper nouns.

- ◆ Underline the titles of books, magazines, and newspapers, but do not underline article titles or place quotation marks around them.

- ◆ Place a period after the title. Make sure punctuation is under-scored, also.

EDITION AND VOLUME NUMBERS

- ◆ For books, include the edition number, in parentheses, immediately following the title.

- ◆ For periodicals, include the volume number, underlined, immediately following the title.

PUBLISHERS

- ◆ List publishers' names in shortened form, omitting words such as *Company.*

- ◆ Spell out the names of university presses and organizations in full.

- ◆ For books, use a colon to separate the city of publication from the publisher's name.

DATES AND PAGE NUMBERS

- ◆ For magazines and newspapers, use a comma to separate the year from the month and day, and enclose the publication date in parentheses (*1954, May 25*).

- ◆ Give full sequences for pages and dates (*361–375*, not *361–75*), separating page numbers by a hyphen with no spaces.

- ◆ If pages do not follow consecutively (as in newspapers), include subsequent page numbers after a comma: *pp. 1, 16*. Note that *pp.* precedes the page numbers for newspaper articles but not for journal articles.

ABBREVIATIONS

- ◆ Abbreviate state and country names, but not months.

- ◆ Use U.S. postal abbreviations (*NY, VT, WI*) for state abbreviations, but omit them for cities well known for publishing: Baltimore, Boston, Chicago, Los Angeles, New York, Philadelphia, and San Francisco.

57d Documenting books

Following are examples of the reference list format for a variety of source types using standard APA hanging indent format.

1. Book by one author

Benjamin, J. (1988). <u>The bonds of love: Psychoanalysis,
    feminism, and the problem of domination.</u> New York:
    Prometheus.

2. Book by two or more authors

Zweigenhaft, R. L., & Domhoff, G. W. (1991). <u>Blacks in the
    white establishment? A study of race and class in
    America.</u> New Haven, CT: Yale University Press.

Include all authors' names in the reference list, regardless of the number
of authors associated with a particular work.

3. More than one book by the same author

List two or more works by the same author (or the same author
team listed in the same order) chronologically by year, earliest work first.
Arrange any such works published in the same year alphabetically by
title, placing lowercase letters after the dates. In either case, give full
identification of author(s) for each reference listing.

Bandura, A. (1969). <u>Principles of behavior modification.</u>
    New York: Holt, Rinehart, and Winston.

Bandura, A. (1977a). Self-efficacy: Toward a unifying theory
    of behavioral change. <u>Psychological Review, 84,</u> 191-215.

Bandura, A. (1977b). <u>Social learning theory.</u> Englewood
    Cliffs, NJ: Prentice Hall.

If the same author is named first but listed with different co-authors,
alphabetize by the last name of the second author. Works by the first
author alone are listed before works with co-authors.

4. Book by a corporation, an association, an organization, or a foundation

American Psychological Association. (1994). <u>Publication
    manual of the American Psychological Association</u> (4th
    ed.). Washington: Author.

Alphabetize corporate authors by the corporate name, excluding the
articles *A*, *An*, and *The*. When the corporate author is also the publisher,
designate the publisher as *Author*.

5. Revised edition of a book

Peek, S. (1993). <u>The game inventor's handbook</u> (Rev. ed.).
    Cincinnati: Betterway.

6. Edited book

```
Schaefer, Charles E., & Reid, S. E. (Eds.). (1986). Game
    play: Therapeutic use of childhood games. New
    York: Wiley.
```

Place *Ed.* or *Eds.,* capitalized, after the editor(s) of an edited book.

7. Book in more than one volume

```
Waldrep, T. (Ed.). (1985-1988). Writers on writing (Vols.
    1-2). New York: Random House.
```

For a work with volumes published in different years, indicate the range of dates of publication. If you referred to only one volume of a multivolume work, indicate only the volume cited.

```
Waldrep, T. (Ed.). (1988). Writers on writing (Vol. 2).
    New York: Random House.
```

8. Translated or reprinted book

```
Freud, S. (1950). The interpretation of dreams (A. A.
    Brill, Trans.). New York: Modern Library-Random House.
    (Original work published 1900)
```

The date of the translation or reprint is in parentheses after the author's name. Place the original publication date in parentheses at the end of the citation, with no period. In the parenthetical citation in your text, include both dates: (*Freud 1900/1950*).

9. Chapter or article in an edited book

```
Telander, R. (1996). Senseless crimes. In C. I. Schuster &
    W. V. Van Pelt (Eds.), Speculations: Readings in
    culture, identity, and values (2nd ed., pp. 264-272).
    Upper Saddle River, NJ: Prentice-Hall.
```

The chapter or article title is not underlined or in quotation marks. Editors' names are listed in normal reading order (surname last). Inclusive page numbers, in parentheses, follow the book title.

10. Anonymous book

```
Stereotypes, distortions and omissions in U.S. history
    textbooks. (1977). New York: Council on Interracial
    Books for Children.
```

11.   Government document

U.S. House of Representatives, Committee on Energy and
     Commerce. (1986). Ensuring access to programming for
     the backyard satellite dish owner (Serial No. 99-127).
     Washington: U.S. Government Printing Office.

For government documents, provide the higher department or governing agency only when the office or agency that created the document is
not readily recognizable. If a document number is available, list it in
parentheses after the document title. Write out the name of the printing
agency in full rather than using the abbreviation *GPO.*

Documenting periodicals   57e

In citing periodical articles, use the same format for listing author names
as for books.

12.   Article in a journal paginated by volume

Hartley, J. (1991). Psychology, writing, and computers: A
     review of research. Visible Language, 25, 339-375.

If page numbers are continuous throughout volumes in a year, use only
the volume number, underlined, following the title of the periodical.

13.   Article in a journal paginated by issue

Lowther, M. A. (1977). Career change in mid-life: Its
     impact on education. Innovator, 8(7), 1, 9-11.

Include the issue number in parentheses if each issue of a journal is paginated separately; do not use the abbreviation *p.* or *pp.*

14.   Magazine article

Garreau, J. (1995, December). Edgier cities. Wired, 158-163,
     232-234.

For nonprofessional periodicals, include the year and month (not abbreviated) after the author's name; do not use the abbreviation *p.* or *pp.*

15.   Newspaper article

Finn, P. (1995, September 27). Death of a U-Va. student
     raises scrutiny of off-campus drinking. The
     Washington Post, pp. D1, D4.

If an author is listed for the article, begin with the author's name, then list the date (spell out the month); follow the article title with the title of the newspaper. If there is a section number or letter, combine it with the page or pages, including continued page numbers as well, using the abbreviation *p.* or *pp.* If the name of the newspaper includes the word *the*, capitalize and underline it also.

57f Documenting electronic sources

APA conventions for documenting electronic sources such as CD-ROMs, diskettes, and magnetic tapes list author, date, and title followed by the complete information for the corresponding print source, if available.

16. CD-ROM

```
Krauthammer, C. (1991). Why is America in a blue funk?
     Time, 138, 83. Retrieved from UMIACH database
     (Periodical Abstracts, CD-ROM Item: 1126.00)
```

17. Computer software

```
HyperCard (Version 2.2) [Computer software]. (1993).
     Cupertino, CA: Apple Computer.
```

Provide the version number, if available, in parentheses following the program or software name. Add the descriptive term *Computer software* in brackets, and follow it with a period. Do not underline the names of computer programs.

Online sources

APA provides the following general format for listing online (World Wide Web or email) sources, which closely follow the conventions for their printed equivalent—*who, when,* said *what, where.* Check the APA Web site <http://www.apa.org/journals/webref.html> for updates.

Format for online publication

```
Author(s) (date of publication). Article or chapter title.
     Title of periodical, book, or site. Inclusive page or
     paragraph numbers. Date retrieved from [name of]
     Internet source: electronic address
```

18. Online journal articles

Kapadia, S. (1995, November). A tribute to Mahatma Gandhi:
    His views on women and social exchange [19 paragraphs].
    Journal of South Asia Women's Studies, 1 (1). Retrieved
    December 2, 1995 from the World Wide Web:
    http://www.shore.net/~india/jsaws

Indicate the number of paragraphs in brackets after the title. Note that
on-line is hyphenated in APA style. Do not add a period at the end of the
electronic address.

19. Document on a World Wide Web (WWW) site

Williams, S. (1996, June 14). Back to school with the quilt.
    AIDS Memorial Quilt Website. Retrieved June 14, 1996,
    from the World Wide Web: http://www.aidsquilt.org/
    newsletter/stories/backto.html

Chicago prep star Fields seriously injured in crash. (1996,
    February 27). ESPN Sportszone. Retrieved March 12, 1996,
    from the World Wide Web: http://www.sportszone.com/gen/
    top/0707241001.html

20. Email and listserve messages

Electronic conversations are not listed on the References page. Cite
email and listserve messages in the text as you would personal letters
or interviews.

R. W. Williams, personal communication, January 4, 1998.

Documenting other sources   57g

21. Film, recording, and other nonprint media

Curtiz, M. (Director). (1942). Casablanca [Film]. Hollywood,
    CA: Warner Bros.

Alphabetize a film listing by the name of the person or persons with primary responsibility for the product. Identifying information about this
person or persons, such as the director, should appear in parentheses.
Identify the medium in brackets following the title, and indicate both
location and name of the distributor (as publisher).

22. Interviews and other field sources

These are identified in the text in parentheses (name, place, date) but are
not listed on the References page. See model 20.

57h Informational research paper: APA style

The research essay "Green Is Only Skin Deep: False Environmental Advertising," by Elizabeth Bone, was written in response to an assignment to identify and explain one problem in contemporary American culture. She documented her essay according to the conventions of the American Psychological Association (APA). This sample includes a title page, an abstract, and an outline page; check with your instructor to find out whether these are required for course papers. Note that margins shown are adjusted to fit space limitations of book. Follow actual dimensions shown and your instructor's directions.

APA

ABBREVIATED TITLE (OPTIONAL)

Green   1

PAGE NUMBERING
BEGINS ON TITLE
PAGE.

TITLE PAGE IS
CENTERED AND
DOUBLE SPACED.

Green Is Only Skin Deep: TITLE
False Environmental Marketing

Elizabeth Bone   AUTHOR

Professor John Clark   INSTRUCTOR

English 1   COURSE

December 6, 200X   DATE

APA

ABSTRACT ON SEPARATE PAGE
FOLLOWING TITLE PAGE

Green   2

Abstract   HEADING CENTERED

NO
PARAGRAPH
INDENT

Most Americans consider themselves
environmentalists and favor supporting   DOUBLE
SPACED
environmentally friendly or "green"
companies. However, companies use a number
of false advertising practices to mislead
the public about their green practices and

THE
ABSTRACT
SUMMARIZES
THE MAIN
POINT OF
THE PAPER.

products by (1) exaggerating claims,
(2) masking false practices behind technical
terminology, (3) mis-sponsoring green
events, (4) not admitting responsibility for
real problems, (5) advertising green by
association, and (6) solving one problem
while creating others. Consumers must be
skeptical of all commercial ads and take the
time to find out the truth behind
advertising.

**OUTLINE ON A SEPARATE PAGE FOLLOWING ABSTRACT
AND CONFORMING TO TRADITIONAL OUTLINE FORMAT**   1/2″

1″   Green   3

Outline   HEADING CENTERED

I. Environmental consciousness is strong   DOUBLE
    in Americans.   SPACED

**ROMAN
NUMERALS
INDICATE
MAJOR
DIVISIONS.**

    A. Gallup poll finds 75% are envi-
        ronmentalists.

    B. False advertising betrays con-
        sumers.

II. Definitions are exaggerated by the
    media and government.

**LETTERS
INDICATE
SUBDIVISIONS
AND
SUBORDINATE
POINTS.**

    A. Biodegradable plastic is false
        advertising.

    B. Federal Trade Commission regulates
        definitions.

III. Terminology is highly technical.

    A. CFCs threaten our ozone layer.

    B. Chrysler advertising misleads us
        about chemicals.

IV. Some companies are green by sponsor-
     ship yet not green.

    A. Ford supports the Smithsonian
        Institute Ocean Planet.

    B. Ford is guilty of pollution in
        Michigan.

    **OUTLINE
    USES
    SENTENCE
    FORMAT.**

V. "It's not my problem."

    A. CFCs are not produced by natural
        gas.

    B. Natural gas causes other pollution.

APA

    VI. Many companies are green only by association.

        A. Advertising has nothing to do with product.

        B. Chevrolet logo implies relationship.

    VII. Some companies have a narrow focus in their environmentalism.

        A. Chevron employees do good in Mississippi.

        B. Chevron pollutes Santa Monica Bay.

    VIII. Environmental image does not match reality.

        A. Earth First! educates consumers.

        B. Federal Trade Commission regulates advertising.

        C. Consumers beware!

APA

Green   5

1/2″

TITLE IS REPEATED FROM TITLE PAGE

Green Is Only Skin Deep:

False Environmental Marketing

DOUBLE SPACED

A recent Gallup poll reported that 75% of Americans consider themselves to be environmentalists (Smith & Quelch, 1993). In the same study, nearly half of the respondents said they would be more likely to purchase a product if they perceived it to be environmentally friendly or "green." According to Smith and Quelch, since green sells, many companies have begun to promote themselves as marketing products that are either environmentally friendly or manufactured from recycled material. Unfortunately, many of these companies care more about appearance than reality.

AUTHOR'S NAME, DATE, AND PAGE NUMBERS ARE IN PARENTHESES

INFORMATIONAL THESIS IS AT END OF FIRST PARAGRAPH.

The most common way for a company to market itself as pro-environment is to stretch the definitions of terms such as "biodegradable" so that consumers believe one thing but the product delivers something else. For example, so-called biodegradable plastic, made with cornstarch, was introduced to ease consumers' fears that plastic lasts forever in the environment. However, the cornstarch plastic broke down only in specific controlled

FIRST EXAMPLE OF FALSE ADVERTISING IS INTRODUCED.

APA

laboratory conditions, not outdoors and not in compost bins. The Federal Trade Commission has updated its regulations to prevent such misrepresentations, so that now Glad and Hefty trash bags are no longer advertised as biodegradable (Carlson, Grove, & Kangun, 1993).

The use of technical terms can also mislead average consumers. For example, carbon fluoride compounds, called CFCs, are known to be hazardous to the protective layer of ozone that surrounds the earth, so their widespread use in air conditioners is considered an environmental hazard (Decker & Stammer, 1989). Chrysler Corporation advertises that it uses CFC-free refrigerant in its automobile air conditioners to appeal to environmentally concerned con- sumers ("Ozone layer," 1994). However, Weisskopf (1992) points out that the chemi- cal compounds that replace CFCs in their air conditioners pose other environmental hazards that are not mentioned.

Another deceptive greening tactic is the sponsoring of highly publicized envi- ronmental events such as animal shows, con- certs, cleanup programs, and educational

SECOND EXAMPLE IS GIVEN.

AUTHOR QUOTED BY NAME IN THE TEXT IS FOLLOWED BY PUBLICATION YEAR IN PARENTHESES.

TRANSITIONS KEEP THE READER ON TRACK.

APA

Green   7

exhibits. For example, Ocean Planet was a
well-publicized exhibit put together by the
Smithsonian Institution to educate people
about ocean conservation. Ford Motor Company
helped sponsor the event, which it then used
in its car advertisements: "At Ford, we feel
strongly that understanding, preserving, and
properly managing natural resources like our
oceans should be an essential commitment of
individuals and corporate citizens alike"
("Smithsonian Institution's Ocean Planet,"
1995, p. 14).

     While sponsoring the exhibit may be a
worthwhile public service, such sponsorship
has nothing to do with how the manufacture
and operation of Ford automobiles affect the
environment. In fact, Ford was ranked as
among the worst polluters in the state of
Michigan in 1995 (Parker, 1995).

     Some companies court the public by
mentioning environmental problems and
pointing out that they do not contribute to
those problems. For example, the natural
gas industry describes natural gas as an
alternative to the use of ozone-depleting
CFCs ("Don't you wish," 1994). However,
according to Fogel (1985), the manufacture

of natural gas creates a host of other environmental problems from land reclamation to carbon-dioxide pollution, a major cause of global warming. By mentioning problems they don't cause while ignoring ones they do, companies present a favorable environmental image that is at best a half truth, at worst an outright lie.

Other companies use a more subtle approach to misleading green advertising. Rather than make statements about environmental compatibility, these companies depict the product in unspoiled natural settings or use green quotations that have nothing to do with the product itself. For example, one Chevrolet advertisement shows a lake shrouded in mist and quotes an environmentalist: "From this day onward, I will restore the earth where I am and listen to what it is telling me" ("From this day," 1994). Below the quotation is the Chevy logo with the words "Genuine Chevrolet." Despite this touching appeal to its love of nature, Chevrolet has a history of dumping toxic waste into the Great Lakes (Allen, 1991). Has this company seriously been listening to what the earth has been telling it?

QUOTATION OF FEWER THAN 40 WORDS IS INTEGRATED INTO THE TEXT.

APA

Green   9

The most common manner in which companies attempt to prove they have a strong
environmental commitment is to give a single example of a policy or action that is
considered environmentally sound. Chevron
has had an environmental advertising campaign since the mid-1970s. In the 1990s the
company's ads featured Chevron employees
doing environmental good deeds (Smith &
Quelch, 1993). For example, one ad featured
"a saltwater wetland in Mississippi at the
edge of a pine forest . . . the kind of
place nature might have made," going on to
explain that this wetland was built by
Chevron employees ("The shorebirds who
found," 1990). However, LaGanga (1993)
points out that during the time this advertisement was running in magazines such as
Audubon, Chevron was dumping millions of
gallons of nasty chemicals (carcinogens and
heavy metals) into California's Santa
Monica Bay, posing a health risk to swim-
mers. The building of the wetland in one
part of the country does not absolve the
company for polluting water somewhere else.
    It should be clear that the environ-
mental image a company projects does not
necessarily match the realities of the

PAGE NUMBER IS NOT LISTED WHEN IT IS LISTED ON REFERENCES PAGE.

ELLIPSIS POINTS INDICATE MISSING WORDS IN QUOTATION.

APA

company's practice. The products made by
companies such as Chrysler, Ford, General
Motors, and Chevron are among the major
causes of air and water pollution: automobiles and gasoline. No amount of advertising can conceal the ultimately negative
effect these products have on the environment (Kennedy & Grumbly, 1988). According
to Shirley Lefevre, president of the New
York Truth in Advertising League:

> It probably doesn't help to single
> out one automobile manufacturer or
> oil company as significantly worse
> than the others. Despite small
> efforts here and there, all of these
> giant corporations, as well as other
> large manufacturers of metal and
> plastic material goods, put profit
> before environment and cause more
> harm than good to the environment.
> (personal communication, May 1995)

Consumers who are genuinely interested
in buying environmentally safe products and
supporting environmentally responsible companies need to look beyond the images
projected by commercial advertising in magazines, on billboards, and on television.

DOUBLE SPACED

INDENTED 5 SPACES

COLON IS USED TO INTRODUCE A LONG QUOTATION.

INTERVIEW CONDUCTED BY AUTHOR IS NOT LISTED ON THE REFERENCES PAGE.

APA

Green   11

Organizations such as Earth First! attempt
to educate consumers to the realities by
writing about false advertising and exposing
the hypocrisy of such ads ("Do people
allow," 1994), while the Ecology Channel is
committed to sharing "impartial, unbiased,
multiperspective environmental information:
with consumers on the Internet (Ecology,
1996). Meanwhile the Federal Trade
Commission is in the process of continually
upgrading truth-in-advertising regulations
(Carlson et al., 1993). Americans who are
truly environmentally conscious must remain
skeptical of simplistic and misleading commercial advertisements while continuing to
educate themselves about the genuine needs
of the environment.

SECOND CITATION OF MORE THAN THREE AUTHORS IS SHORTENED TO FIRST AUTHOR'S NAME AND *ET AL.*

THESIS IS REPEATED IN MORE DETAIL AT END.

1″

AUTHORS ARE LISTED ALPHABETICALLY.

References **HEADING CENTERED**

DOUBLE SPACED

Allen, F. E. (1991, March 10). Great Lakes cleanup enlists big volunteers. The Wall Street Journal, p. B1.

INITIALS ARE USED FOR FIRST AND MIDDLE NAMES.

Carlson, L., Grove, S. J., & Kangun, N. (1993). A content analysis of environ-mental advertising claims: A matrix methods approach. Journal of Advertising, 22(9), 27-39.

ONLY FIRST WORD AND PROPER NAMES ARE CAPITALIZED IN ARTICLE TITLE.

"P." OR "PP." IS NOT USED TO INDICATE PAGES IN A PROFESSION-AL JOURNAL

Decker, C., & Stammer, L. (1989, March 4). Bush asks ban on CFC to save ozone. Los Angeles Times, p. A1.

Do people allow themselves to be that gullible? (1994, September). Earth First! 9, 6.

DATE FOLLOWS AUTHOR (OR TITLE IF NO AUTHOR IS IDENTIFIED).

Don't you wish we could just do this to CFC's natural gas advertisement? (1994, December 7). Audubon, 12, 7.

The ecology channel. (1996). Retrieved November 20, 1997, from the World Wide Web: http://www.ecology.com

Fogel, B. (1985). Energy: Choices for the future. New York: Franklin Watts.

BOOK AND PERIODICAL TITLES ARE UNDERLINED.

From this day onward I will restore the earth where I am. (1994, November-

INDENTED 5 SPACES

December). [Chevrolet advertisement]. Audubon, 11-12, 18-19.

APA

Green   13

Kennedy, D., & Grumbly, T. P. (1988).
Automotive emissions research. In
Watson, A., Bates, R. R., & Kennedy,
D. (Eds.), Air pollution, the
automobile, and public health
(pp. 3-9). Cambridge, MA: National
Academy Press.

LaGanga, M. (1993, February 4). Chevron to
stop dumping waste near shoreline.
Los Angeles Times, pp. A1, A10.

The ozone layer has protected us for 1.5
billion years: It's time we returned
the favor. (1994, November-December).
[Chrysler advertisement]. Audubon,
11-12, 40-41.

Parker, L. (1995, March 28). GM, Ford among
top polluters in state. Detroit News,
p. A2.

The shorebirds who found a new wetland.
(1990, July). Audubon, 7, 38.

Smith, N. C., & Quelch, J. A. (1993).
Ethics in marketing. Boston, MA:
Richard D. Irwin.

Smithsonian Institution's Ocean Planet: A
special report. (1995, March).
Outdoor Life, 3, 13-22.

Weisskopf, M. (1992, February 23). Study
finds CFC alternatives more damaging
than believed. The Washington Post,
p. A3.

"P." OR "PP."
IS USED
FOR PAGE
NUMBERS IN
BOOKS OR
POPULAR
PERIODICALS.

TITLES OF
PERIODICALS
ARE
NORMALLY
CAPITALIZED.

TITLE IS
USED
WHEN NO
AUTHOR IS
IDENTIFIED
IN THE
SOURCE.

APA

58 WRITING FOR WORK

Businesses value efficiency and accuracy, and business communications mirror those objectives. Business writing should be simple, direct, and brief; it should convey correct information and conform to standard conventions; and it should be honest and courteous.

Audience is particularly important in business writing. Ask yourself who your readers are. What information do they already have? What else do they need to know? Who else might read what you have written? In general, adopt an objective and fairly formal tone.

58a Business letters

Business letters commonly request, inform, or complain, and they are often addressed to a reader unknown to the writer. State your purpose clearly, and provide all the information needed to make it easy for the reader to respond. All business letters include the following elements.

Paper   Business letters are typed on 8½″ × 11″ paper, one side only.

Format   Most business letters use block format; that is, every element of the letter is typed flush with the left margin.

Heading   Type the sender's address (but not name) and the date, single spaced, approximately one inch from the top of the first page. Spell out street and town names and months in full. Abbreviate state names using standard postal abbreviations. Include the zip code.

If you use letterhead stationery, type the date two lines below the letterhead address.

Inside address   Type the recipient's address two lines below the heading. (If the letter is very short, add space here so that the letter will be centered on the page.) Include the person's full name (and title, if appropriate), followed by her or his position (if needed); the name of the department or division within the company; the company name; and the full street, city, and state address.

When writing to an unknown person, always try to find out his or her name and its correct spelling, perhaps by calling the company switchboard. If you can find no name, use an appropriate title (*Personnel Director* or *Claims Manager*, for example) in place of a name.

Greeting   Type the opening salutation two lines below the inside address (*Dear Dr. Smith, Dear Mei Ling Wong*) followed by a colon. If you and the recipient are on a first-name basis, you may use only the first name alone (*Dear Mei Ling*).

If you do not know the recipient's name, use *To Whom It May Concern* or some variation of *Dear Claims Manager* or *Attention: Marketing Director* (the latter without a second colon). Avoid the old-fashioned *Dear Sir* or *Dear Sir or Madam*.

Body   Begin the body of the letter two lines below the greeting. Single-space within paragraphs; double-space between paragraphs. Do not indent the first line of a paragraph.

If your reason for writing is clear and simple, state it directly in the first paragraph. If it is absolutely necessary to detail a situation, provide background, or supply context, do so in the first paragraph or two; then move on to state your purpose.

If your letter is more than a page long, type the addressee's last name, the date, and the page number flush with the right margin at the top of each subsequent page.

Closing   Type the complimentary closing two lines below the last line of the body of the letter. The most common closings are *Sincerely, Cordially, Yours truly, Respectfully yours* (formal), and *Best regards* (informal). Capitalize only the first word of the closing, and follow it with a comma.

GUIDELINES FOR BUSINESS WRITING

Your reader's time, as well as your own, is valuable.

◆   Get to the main point quickly. Avoid unnecessary information and repetition.

◆   Write in simple, direct language. Keep your sentences straightforward and readable.

◆   Choose the active voice over the passive.

◆   Use technical terminology and jargon sparingly. Write out complete names of companies, products, and titles. Explain any unusual terms.

◆   Avoid emotional or offensive language and sexist constructions. Always be courteous, even when lodging a complaint.

◆   Use numbers or descriptive headings to help readers locate information quickly.

◆   Use graphs, charts, and other illustrations when they convey information more clearly than words.

Signature   Type your full name, including any title, four lines below the closing. Sign the letter with your full name (or just your first name if you have addressed the recipient by first name) in blue or black ink in the space above your typed name.

Additional information   You may provide additional brief information below your signature, flush with the left margin. This may include recipients of copies of the letter (*cc: Jennifer Rodriguez*); the word *Enclosures* (or the abbreviation *enc.*) to indicate that you are also enclosing additional material mentioned in the letter; and, if the letter was typed by someone other than the writer, the writer's initials and the typist's initials (*TF/jwl*).

58b Memos

Memos are short (one-page) efficient (to the point) communications written between and among employees in the same institution or business. The purpose of a memo is to address a topic—usually a single topic—in order to get something done. Memos are commonly written to call meetings, ask questions, initiate actions, and remind readers about policies or forthcoming events.

Memos are often written to people who already know each other, so the voice is commonly informal, though the voice you use will depend on your relationship to the receiver—more informal to friends, more formal to people you know less well.

The idea of a memo is to provide as much information as possible, quickly, in the least amount of space, so that the most basic information (audience, author, date, purpose) is presented at the beginning of the message—a form borrowed by e-mail for the same reasons. A memo starts like this:

To:
From:
Date:
Subject: (or Re: for "in reference to")

If a memo is to be copied to other parties, a *cc:* line is added to the bottom with the recipients' names.

58c The conventions of e-mail

E-mailing to friends and family is one thing; e-mailing to instructors or business associates is something else. Writing an e-mail message to someone you know well is like writing a friendly letter: e-mail is informal (Hey John!), full of your personality (Hmm) and often funny (☺), and it takes common experiences for granted (Remember last July . . .). In other words, for written conversations—e-mail or otherwise—among people who know and trust each other, there are no fixed conventions. However, when you send messages to inform or query people you don't know well, especially if something important is at stake (the clarity of an assignment, the closing of a deal), keep the following conventions in mind.

- **Keep it brief.** People are impatient reading long messages on computer monitors; the longer the text, the more likely people will skim.

- **Keep it informal.** People expect e-mail to be informal and friendly— *I* and *you* and contractions are expected—but they also expect to see full sentences and normal capitalization and punctuation.

- **Read your audience.** As with every other communication, adjust your writing style according to who will read it; if you don't know your audience, follow the conventions carefully.

- **Get to the point.** E-mail should be purposeful, direct, and to the point. Use the message line to indicate your subject.

- **Limit the scope.** Focus on a single point or issue. Your respondent may miss something important if you include too many items.

- **Number items.** If it's important to address several issues or questions in a single e-mail, number them so the points are clear and don't get lost at the receiving end.

- **Check often.** E-mail is fast and efficient only if it's checked regularly; if e-mail is an expected mode of communication, check it daily.

- **Reply promptly.** E-mail has caught on quickly in our culture because it's so much faster than conventional mail. Replies are best made the same or the following day.

- **Reread once.** Because e-mail is fast, people don't spend a lot of time revising it. However, you'll save yourself some embarrassment by proofreading each message before sending it.

- **Reply purposefully.** It's annoying to receive e-mail meant for others; double-check your address line before sending a message.

◆ **Be kind and courteous.** Address people by name (*Hi, Robyn*); end with a salutation (*Thanks for your help*); and don't "flame" with angry, insulting messages you'll regret later.

◆ **Respect privacy and copyright.** Don't forward messages or publish copyrighted material without permission.

58d Résumés

A résumé is a brief summary of an applicant's qualification for employment. It outlines education, work experience, and other activities and interests so that a prospective employer can decide quickly whether or not an applicant is a good prospect for a particular job. If your résumé is attractive to an employer, the potential employer will usually contact you to set up a personal interview.

Try to tailor your résumé for the position you are seeking by emphasizing experience that is most relevant to the job. Preparing a résumé on a computer lets you revise it easily and quickly.

A résumé is usually sent out with a cover letter that introduces the applicant, indicates the position applied for, and offers additional information that cannot be accommodated on the résumé itself. A résumé should be brief and to the point, preferably no more than one page long. (If relevant experience is extensive, more than one page may be acceptable.) Résumé formats vary, but most include the following information.

Personal information   Résumés begin with the applicant's name, address, and phone number, usually centered at the top. An e-mail address and cell phone number may also be included.

Objective   Many college résumés include a line summarizing the applicant's objective, either naming the specific job sought or describing a larger career goal.

Education   Most first-time job applicants list their educational background first because their employment history is limited. Name the last two or three schools you attended (including dates of attendance and degrees), starting with the most recent. Indicate major areas of study. If your grade point average is high, list it, and if you've received awards, list them—a résumé is not the place to be modest.

Work experience   List all relevant jobs, most recent first, including company name, dates of employment, and a brief job description or list of duties. Use your judgment about listing jobs at which you had difficulties with your employer.**Work experience**   List all relevant jobs, most recent first, including company name, dates of employment, and a brief job description or list of duties. Use your judgment about listing jobs at which you had difficulties with your employer.

Special skills or interests   Mention special skills, interests, or activities that provide additional clues about your abilities and personality. You may want to conclude with the line "References available on request."

References   At the end of your résumé, you have two choices: either (1) include the statement "References available on request" or (2) provide the names, addresses, and phone numbers of two or three people—teachers, supervisors, employers—whom you trust to give a good reference for you. (Make sure you get their permission first, however.)

The advantage of the first method is that the employer must indicate an interest in you by contacting you about references, which lets you know where you stand. The advantage of the second is that employers have all the necessary information in one package to make a decision about interviewing you.

Write a cover letter to your résumé as a business letter, pointing out special features of your background or elaborating upon experience and interest for which there is no room on the résumé proper.

STATE ABBREVIATIONS

Use the U.S. Postal Service abbreviations (capitalized, with no periods) for the names of the fifty states and the District of Columbia only on mail, in full addresses in text, or in documentation. Spell out these names in the text of a paper or letter.

STATE	ABBREVIATION	STATE	ABBREVIATION
Alabama	AL	Missouri	MO
Alaska	AK	Montana	MT
Arizona	AZ	Nebraska	NE
Arkansas	AR	Nevada	NV
California	CA	New Hampshire	NH
Colorado	CO	New Jersey	NJ
Connecticut	CT	New Mexico	NM
Delaware	DE	New York	NY
District of Columbia	DC	North Carolina	NC
Florida	FL	Ohio	OH
Georgia	GA	Oklahoma	OK
Hawaii	HI	Oregon	OR
Idaho	ID	Pennsylvania	PA
Illinois	IL	Rhode Island	RI
Indiana	IN	South Carolina	SC
Iowa	IA	South Dakota	SD
Kansas	KS	Tennessee	TN
Kentucky	KY	Texas	TX
Louisiana	LA	Utah	UT
Maine	ME	Vermont	VT
Maryland	MD	Virginia	VA
Massachusetts	MA	Washington	WA
Michigan	MI	West Virginia	WV
Minnesota	MN	Wisconsin	WI
Mississippi	MS	Wyoming	WY

SAMPLE BUSINESS LETTER

```
     405 Martin Street
     Lexington, Kentucky 40508   HEADING
     February 10, 200x

     Barbara McGarry, Director
     Kentucky Council on the Arts   INSIDE ADDRESS
     953 Versailles Road
     Box 335
     Frankfort, Kentucky 40602

     Dear Ms. McGarry:   GREETING

     John Huff, one of my professors at the University  BODY,
     of Kentucky, recommended that I write to you        NO
     regarding openings in the Council's internship      INDENTS
     program this summer. I would like to apply for
     one of these positions and have enclosed my
     résumé for your consideration.

     As you will note, my academic background combines
     a primary concentration in business administra-
     tion with a minor in the fine arts. My interest
     in the arts goes back to childhood when I first
     heard a performance by the Lexington Symphony,
     and I have continued to pursue that interest ever
     since. My goal after graduation is a career in
     arts administration, focusing on fund-raising and
     outreach for a major public institution.

     I hope you'll agree that my experience, particu-
     larly my work with the local Community Concerts
     association, is strong preparation for an intern-
     ship with the Council. I would appreciate the
     opportunity to discuss my qualifications with you
     in greater detail.

     I will call your office within the next few weeks
     to see about setting up an appointment to meet
     with you. In the meantime, you can reach me at
     the above address or by phone at 555-4033.
     Thank you for your attention.

     Sincerely,
                                  CLOSING
     Chris Aleandro                SIGNATURE

     Chris Aleandro


     enc.                          ADDITIONAL INFORMATION
```

```
                    Chris Aleandro
                   405 Martin Street
              Lexington, Kentucky 40508
                    (606) 555-4033


Objective: Internship in arts administration
```

Education
```
University of Kentucky: 1999 to present.
        Currently a sophomore majoring in business
        administration with a minor in art history.
        Degree expected May 2004.
Henry Clay High School (Lexington, KY): 1995 to 1999.
        College preparatory curriculum, with emphasis in
        art and music.
```

Related Work Experience
```
Community Concerts, Inc.: 1999 to present.
        Part-time promotion assistant, reporting to local
        director. Responsibilities include assisting
        with scheduling, publicity, subscription/
        ticketing procedures, and fund-raising. Position
        involves general office duties as well as heavy
        contact with subscribers and artists.
Habitat for Humanity: September to November 1999.
        Co-chaired campus fund-raising drive that
        included a benefit concert, raising $55,000.
Art in the Schools Program: 1997-1999.
        Volunteer, through the Education Division of the
        Lexington Center for the Arts. Trained to conduct
        hands-on art appreciation presentations in grade
        school classrooms, visiting one school a month.
```

Other Work Experience
```
Record City: 1996 to 1998 (part time and summers).
        Salesclerk and assistant manager in a music
        store.
```

Special Skills
```
Word processing (Macintosh and Windows)
Desktop publishing
Web page design
Photography
```

References: Available on request.

NOTES ON USAGE

Like every other aspect of editing, good usage—selecting the most appropriate word for your purpose and context—seldom involves clear-cut distinctions and unvarying rules. Even language authorities do not agree on the acceptability of all usages. Where disagreement does exist, writers have greater liberty to make their own choices. For example, although some writers prefer to use *farther* only for physical distances and *further* for differences of degree, the two words have in fact been used interchangeably for hundreds of years.

You should strive to use words carefully and correctly, since your use of language shows how well you understand your material and reflects on the overall quality of your education.

This glossary provides information about many of the most frequently confused or misused words. Some usages listed here are acceptable or common in contexts other than formal academic writing. For example, **nonstandard** usages (such as *anyways* for *anyway*) reflect the speech patterns of particular communities but do not follow the conventions of the dominant American dialect. **Colloquial** usages (such as *flunk* for *fail* or *totally* meaning *very*) are often heard in speech but are usually inappropriate for academic writing. **Informal** usages (such as using *can* and *may* interchangeably) may not be acceptable in formal research essays or argument papers. Except as noted, this glossary recommends usage as found in formal academic writing.

a, an   Use *a* before words that being with a consonant sound (*a boy, a history, a shining star*) even if the first letter of the word is a vowel (*a useful lesson*). Use *an* before words that begin with a vowel sound (*an antelope, an hour, an umbrella*).

accept, except   *Accept* is a verb meaning "to receive" or "to approve" (*I accept your offer*). *Except* is a verb meaning "to leave out" or "to exclude" (*He excepted all vegetables from his list of favorite foods*) or a preposition meaning "excluding" (*He liked to eat everything except vegetables*).

adapt, adopt   *Adapt* means "to adjust" or "to accommodate"; it is usually followed by *to* (*It is sometimes hard to adapt to college life*). *Adopt* means "to take into a relationship" (*My parents are adopting another child*) or "to take and use as one's own" (*I have adopted my roommate's habit*).

adverse, averse   *Adverse* is an adjective meaning "unfavorable" or "unpleasant," generally used to describe a thing or situation (*Adverse weather forced us to cancel the game*). *Averse*, also an adjective, means "opposed to" or "feeling a distaste for" and usually describes feelings about a thing or situation; it is usually followed by *to* (*We are averse to playing on a muddy field*).

advice, advise   *Advice* is a noun meaning "recommendation" or "information given." *Advise* is a verb meaning "to give advice to" (*I advise you to take my advice and study hard*).

affect, effect   *Affect* as a verb means "to influence" or "to produce an effect" (*That movie affected me deeply*). *Affect* as a noun means "feeling" or "emotion," especially in psychology. *Effect* is commonly used as a noun meaning "result," "consequence," or "outcome" (*That movie had a profound effect on me*); it is also used as a verb meaning "to bring about" (*Dr. Jones effected important changes as president*).

aggravate   *Aggravate* is a verb meaning "to make worse." *Aggravate* is sometimes used colloquially to mean "to irritate" or "to annoy," but in formal writing use *irritate* or *annoy* (*I was irritated by my neighbors' loud stereo; my irritation was aggravated when they refused to turn it down.*)

all ready, already   *All ready* means "fully prepared" (*The children were all ready for bed*). *Already* means "previously" (*The children were already in bed when the guests arrived*).

all right, alright   The two-word spelling is preferred; the one-word spelling is considered incorrect by many.

all together, altogether   *All together* means "all gathered in one place" (*The animals were all together in the ark*). *Altogether* means "thoroughly" or "completely" (*The ark was altogether too full of animals*).

allude, elude   *Allude* is a verb meaning "to refer to something indirectly"; it is usually followed by *to* (*Derek alluded to the rodent infestation by mentioning that he'd bought mousetraps*). *Elude* is a verb meaning "to escape" or "to avoid" (*The mouse eluded Derek at every turn*).

allusion, illusion   *Allusion* means "an indirect reference" or "the act of alluding to, or hinting at, something" (*Derek's allusion to lunchtime was not lost on his companions*). *Illusion* is a noun meaning "misapprehension" or "misleading image" (*Mr. Hodges created an optical illusion with two lines*).

a lot   *A lot* should be written as two words. Although *a lot* is used informally to mean "a large number" or "many," avoid using *a lot* in formal writing (*The prisoners had many* [not *a lot of*] *opportunities to escape*).

although, while   *Although* means "despite the fact that." The primary meaning of *while* is "at the same time that." In formal writing, do not substitute *while* for *although* (*Although* [not *while*] *John did the grocery shopping, he wished Mary would sometimes help.*) See *since*.

a.m., p.m., or A.M., P.M.   Use only with numbers to indicate time (6:30 P.M.), not as a substitute for *morning, afternoon, evening,* or *night.*

among, between   *Among* should be used when discussing three or more individuals (*It was difficult to choose among all the exotic plants*). *Between* is used when discussing only two individuals (*There were significant differences between the two candidates*).

amount, number   *Amount* should be used to refer to quantities that cannot be counted or cannot be expressed as a single number (*Fixing up the abandoned farmhouse took a great amount of work*). *Number* is used for quantities that can be counted (*A large number of volunteers showed up to clean out the abandoned farmhouse*).

an   See *a, an.*

and/or   *and/or* is used in technical and legal writing to connect two terms when either one or both apply (*Purchasers must select type and/or size*). Avoid this awkward phrasing by using the construction "*a or b or both*" (*Students may select chemistry or physics or both*).

anxious, eager   *Anxious* is an adjective meaning "worried" or "uneasy" (*Lynn is anxious about her mother's surgery*). Do not confuse it with *eager*, which means "enthusiastic," "impatient," or "marked by strong desire" (*I am eager* [not *anxious*] *to leave*).

anybody, anyone, any body, any one   *Anybody* and *anyone* are singular indefinite pronouns that refer to an unspecified person (*Anybody may apply for the new scholarship. Anyone on the hill could have seen our campfire*). *Any body* and *any one* are noun phrases consisting of the adjective *any* and the noun *body* or the pronoun *one*; they refer to a specific body or to a single member of a group (*Each child may select any one toy from the toy box*).

anyplace, anywhere   In formal writing, do not use *anyplace*; use *anywhere* instead (*We could not find the game piece anywhere* [not *anyplace*]).

anyways, anywheres   Use the standard terms *anyway* and *anywhere*.

as   *As* may be used to mean "because" (*We did not go ice skating as the lake was no longer frozen*), but only if no confusion will result. For example, *We canceled the meeting as only two people showed up* could mean that the meeting was canceled at the moment when the two people showed up or because only two showed up.

as, as if, like   To indicate comparisons, *like* should be used only as a preposition followed by a noun phrase to compare items that are similar but not equivalent (*Ken, like his brother, prefers to sleep late*). In formal writing, *like* should not be used as a conjunction linking two clauses. Use *as* or *as if* instead (*Anne talks as if* [not *like*] *she has read every book by Ernest Hemingway*).

assure, ensure, insure   *Assure* is a verb meaning "to reassure" or "to convince" (*The lawyer assured her client that the case was solid*). *Ensure* and *insure* both mean "to make sure, certain, or safe," but *insure* generally refers to financial certainty (*John hoped his college degree would ensure him a job, preferably one that would insure him in case of injury or illness*).

as to   Do not use *as to* as a substitute for *about* (*We had questions about* [not *as to*] *the company's affirmative action policies*).

averse   See *adverse, averse*.

awful, awfully   *Awful* is an adjective meaning "inspiring awe." In formal writing, do not use it to mean "disagreeable" or "objectionable." Similarly, the adverb *awfully* means "in an awe-inspiring way"; in writing, do not use it in the colloquial sense of "very."

awhile, a while   The one-word form *awhile* is an adverb that can be used to modify a verb (*We rested awhile*). Only the two-word form *a while*, that is, the article *a* and the noun *while*, can be the object of a preposition (*We rested for a while*).

bad, badly   *Bad* is an adjective, so it must modify a noun or follow a linking verb, such as *be, feel,* or *become* (*John felt bad about holding the picnic in bad weather*). *Badly* is an adverb, so it must modify a verb (*Pam played badly today*).

being as, being that   *Being as* and *being that* are nonstandard expressions for *because* (*Anna withdrew from the tournament because* [not *being as*] *her shoulder was injured*).

beside, besides   *Beside* is a preposition meaning "by the side of" or "next to" (*The book is beside the bed*). *Besides* can be used as a preposition meaning "other than" or "in addition to" (*No one besides Linda can build a good campfire*). *Besides* can also be used as an adverb meaning "furthermore" or "in addition" (*The weather is bad for hiking; besides, I have a cold*).

between   See *among, between*.

breath, breathe   *Breath* is a noun (*I had to stop to catch my breath*); *breathe* is a verb (*It became difficult to breathe at higher elevations*).

bring, take   The verb *bring* describes movement from a distant place to a nearer place; the verb *take* describes movement away from a place (*Dr. Gavin asked us to bring our rough sketches to class; she said we may take them home after class*).

burst, bust   *Burst* is an irregular verb meaning "to break open, apart, or into pieces." Its past tense and past participle are both *burst; bursted* is nonstandard and should not be used (*Lee burst the balloon with the point of a pen*). *Bust* is an informal verb meaning "to burst," "to break," and "to arrest"; avoid it in formal writing.

but, however, yet   Each of these words should be used alone, not in combination (*We finished painting the house, but* [not *but however*] *there was still much work to do*).

can, may   In informal usage, *can* and *may* are often used interchangeably to indicate permission. But in formal writing, only *may* should be so used (*May I borrow your dictionary?*). *May* is also used to indicate possibility (*It may snow* *tomorrow*); *can* is used only to indicate ability (*I can see much better with my new glasses*).

capital, capitol   *Capital* is an adjective meaning "punishable by death" (*capital punishment*) or is used to refer to uppercase letters (*A, B*). As a noun it means "accumulated wealth" (*We will calculate our capital at the end of the fiscal year*) or "a city serving as a seat of government" (*Albany is the capital of New York*). *Capitol* is a noun indicating a building in which lawmakers meet (*The civics class toured the state capitol last week*).

censor, censure   *Censor* is a noun or verb referring to the removal of material that is considered objectionable. *Censure* is a verb meaning "to blame or condemn sternly" (*Plans to censor song lyrics have been censured by groups that support free speech*). *Sensor* is a monitoring device, such as a photoelectric cell, that responds to a stimulus, such as light; other commonly used sensors respond to heat, sound, and movement.

cite, site   *Cite* is a verb meaning "to quote for purposes of example, authority, or proof" (*Tracy cites several legal experts in her paper on capital punishment*). *Site* as a noun means "place or scene" (*Today we poured the foundation on the site of our future home*). As a verb it means "to place or locate" (*The house was carefully sited to take advantage of the view*).

climactic, climatic   *Climactic* is an adjective derived from *climax*; it refers to a moment of greatest intensity (*In the climactic scene of the play, the murder's identity is revealed*). *Climatic* is an adjective derived from the noun *climate*; it refers to weather conditions (*Some people fear that climatic changes are caused by environmental pollution*).

compare to, compare with   *Compare to* means "to liken" or "to represent as similar" (*Jim compared our new puppy to an unruly child*). *Compare with* means "to examine to discover similarities or differences" (*We compared this month's ads with last month's*).

complement, compliment   *Complement* is a verb meaning "to fill out or complete"; it is also a noun meaning "something that completes or fits with" (*The bouquet of spring flowers complemented the table setting*). *Compliment* is a verb meaning "to express esteem or admiration" or a noun meaning "an expression of esteem or admiration" (*Russ complimented Nancy on her choice of flowers*). As a noun, *complement* means a set (*The ship's complement of sails included two mains, a spinnaker, a genoa, and a storm jib*). The noun *compliment* means a flattering remark or action (*The team voted her captain, which she took as a compliment*).

compose, comprise   *Compose* means "to constitute or make up"; *comprise* means "to include or contain" (*Only eight members compose this year's club; last year's comprised fifteen*).

conscience, conscious   *Conscience* is a noun referring to a sense of right and wrong (*His conscience would not allow him to lie*). *Conscious* is an adjective meaning "marked by thought or will" or "acting with critical awareness" (*He made a conscious decision to be more honest*).

contact   *Contact* is often used informally as a verb meaning "to get in touch with," but it should not be used this way in formal writing. Use a verb such as *write* or *telephone* instead.

continual, continuous   *Continual* means "recurring" or "occurring repeatedly" (*Liz saw a doctor about her continual headaches*). *Continuous* means "uninterrupted in space, time, or sequence" (*Eventually we grew used to the continuous noise*).

council, counsel   *Council* is a noun meaning "a group meeting for advice, discussion, or government" (*The tribal council voted in favor of the new land-rights law*). As a noun, *counsel* means "advice" or "a plan of action or behavior" (*The priest gave counsel to the young men considering the priesthood*). It can also refer to a legal representative (*The company's legal counsel denied comment on the lawsuit*). *Counsel* may also be used as a verb meaning "to advise or consult" (*The priest counseled the young man*).

criteria   *Criteria* is the plural of *criterion*, which means "a standard on which a judgment is based" (*Many criteria are used in selecting a president, but a candidate's hair color is not an appropriate criterion*).

data   *Data* is the plural of *datum*, which means "an observed fact" or "a result in research." Some writers now use *data* as both a singular and a plural noun; in formal usage it is still better to treat it as plural (*The data indicate that a low-fat diet may increase life expectancy*).

different from, different than   *Different from* is preferred to *different than* (*Hal's taste in music is different from his wife's*). But *different than* may be used to avoid awkward constructions (*Hal's taste in music is different than* [instead of *different from what*] *it was five years ago*).

differ from, differ with   *Differ from* means "to be unlike" (*This year's parade differed from last year's in many ways*). *Differ with* means "to disagree with" (*Stephanie differed with Tom over which parade was better*).

discreet, discrete   *Discreet* is an adjective meaning "prudent" or "modest" (*Most private donors were discreet about their contributions*). *Discrete* is an adjective meaning "separate" or "distinct" (*Professor Roberts divided the course into four discrete units*).

disinterested, uninterested   *Disinterested* is an adjective meaning "unbiased" or "impartial" (*It will be difficult to find twelve disinterested jurors for such a highly publicized case*). *Uninterested* is an adjective meaning "indifferent" or "unconcerned" (*Most people were uninterested in the case until the police discovered surprising new evidence*).

don't   *Don't* is a contraction for *do not*, not for *does not*. The contraction for *does not* is *doesn't* (*He doesn't* [not *don't*] *know where she's living now*).

due to   *Due to* is an adjective phrase that is generally used after forms of the verb *be* (*The smaller classes were due to a decline in enrollment*). In formal writing, *due to* should not be used as a prepositional phrase meaning "because of" (*Class size decreased because of* [not *due to*] *a decline in enrollment*).

each   *Each* is singular (*Each goes in its own place*).

effect   See *affect, effect*.

e.g.   *E.g.* is the Latin abbreviation for *exempli gratia*, which means "for example." In formal writing, use *for example* or *for instance*.

elicit, illicit   *Elicit* is a verb meaning "to draw forth" or "to bring out" (*The investigators could not elicit any new information*). *Illicit* is an adjective meaning "unlawful" or "not permitted" (*The investigators were looking for evidence of illicit drug sales*).

elude   See *allude, elude*.

emigrate, immigrate   *Emigrate* means "to leave one's country to live or reside elsewhere" (*His grandparents emigrated to Israel*). *Immigrate* means "to come into a new country to take up residence" (*His grandparents immigrated to the United States*).

eminent, imminent   *Eminent* means "lofty" or "prominent" (*Her operation was performed by an eminent surgeon*). *Imminent* means "impending" or "about to take place" (*The hurricane's arrival is imminent*).

ensure   See *assure, ensure, insure*.

enthused, enthusiastic   In formal writing, *enthused*, a past-tense form of the verb *enthuse*, should not be used as an adjective; use *enthusiastic* (*Barbara is enthusiastic* [not *enthused*] *about her music lessons*).

especially, specially   *Especially* is an adverb meaning "particularly" or "unusually" (*The weather was especially cold this winter*). *Specially* is an adverb meaning "for a special reason" or "in a unique way" (*The cake was specially prepared for Sandy's birthday*).

etc.   An abbreviation for the Latin expression *et cetera*, *etc.* means "and so forth." In formal writing, avoid ending a list with *etc.*; indicate that you are leaving items out of a list with *and so on* or *and so forth*. Use *etc.* alone, not with *and*, which is redundant.

eventually, ultimately   Although these words are often used interchangeably, *eventually* means "at an unspecified later time," while *ultimately* means "finally" or "in the end" (*He knew that he would stop running eventually, but he hoped that he would ultimately win a marathon*).

everybody, everyone, every body, every one   *Everybody* and *everyone* are singular indefinite pronouns that refer to an unspecified person (*Everybody wins in this game*). *Every body* and *every one* are noun phrases consisting of the adjective *every* and the noun *body* or the pronoun *one*; they refer to each individual body or each single member of a group (*Every one of these toys must be picked up*).

except   See *accept, except.*

expect   *Expect* means "to anticipate or look forward to." Avoid using it colloquially to mean "to think or suppose" (*I suppose* [not *expect*] *I should go study now*).

explicit, implicit   *Explicit* means "perfectly clear, direct, and unambiguous" (*Darrell gave me explicit directions to his house*). *Implicit* means "implied" or "revealed or expressed indirectly" (*His eagerness was implicit in his cheerful tone of voice*).

farther, further   Although these words are often used interchangeably, some writers prefer to use *farther* to refer to physical distances (*Boston is farther than I thought*) and *further* to refer to quantity, time, or degree (*We made further progress on our research project*).

fewer, less   *Fewer* is an adjective used to refer to people or items that can be counted (*Because fewer people came to the conference this year, we needed fewer programs*). *Less* is used to refer to amounts that cannot be counted (*We also required less space and less food*).

finalize   Many writers avoid using *finalize* to mean "to make final." Use alternative phrasing (*We needed to complete* [not *finalize*] *plans*).

firstly, secondly, thirdly   These expressions are awkward; use *first, second,* and *third.*

former, latter   *Former* is used to refer to the first of two people, items, or ideas being discussed, *latter* to refer to the second (*Monet and Picasso were both important painters; the former is associated with the Impressionist school, the latter with Cubism*). *Former* and *latter* should not be used when referring to more than two items; use *first* and *last* instead.

further   See *farther, further.*

get   The verb *get* has many colloquial uses that should be avoided in formal writing. *Get* can mean "to provoke or annoy" (*He gets to me*), "to start" (*We should get going on this project*), or "to become" (*She got worried when he didn't call*). *Have got to* should not be used in place of *must* (*I must* [not *have got to*] *finish by five o'clock*).

goes, says   The verb *goes* is sometimes used colloquially for *says,* but avoid this usage in formal writing (*When the coach says* [not *goes*] *"Now," everybody runs*).

good and   *Good and* should not be used for *very* in formal writing (*My shoes were very* [not *good and*] *wet after our walk*).

good, well *Good* is an adjective; it should not be used in place of the adverb *well* in formal writing (*Mario is a good tennis player; he played well* [not *good*] *today*).

hanged, hung *Hanged* is the past-tense and past-participle form of the verb *hang* meaning "to suspend by the neck until dead" (*Condemned prisoners were hanged at this spot*). *Hung* is the past-tense and past-participle form of the verb *hang* meaning "to suspend" or "to dangle" (*All her clothes were hung neatly in the closet*).

hardly, scarcely *Hardly* and *scarcely* are adverbs meaning "barely," "only just." Do not use phrases like *can't scarcely* and *not hardly* in formal writing; these are double negatives (*I can scarcely* [not *can't scarcely*] *keep my eyes open*).

has got, have got These are colloquial expressions; in formal writing use simply *has* or *have* (*He has* [not *has got*] *his books packed*).

have, of The auxiliary verb *have* (not *of*) should be used in verb phrases beginning with modal auxiliaries such as *could, would,* and *might* (*We could have* [not *could of*] *gone to the concert*).

he/she, his/her When you require both female and male personal pronouns in formal writing, use *he or she* (or *she or he*) and *his or her* (or *her or his*). (For more on avoiding sexist language, see 28c.)

herself, himself, itself, myself, ourselves, themselves, yourself, yourselves These are reflexive or intensive pronouns and should be used only to reflect the action of a sentence back toward the subject (*He locked himself out of the apartment*) or to emphasize the subject (*I myself have no regrets*). Do not use these pronouns in place of personal pronouns such as *I, me, you, her,* or *him* (*He left an extra key with Bev and me* [not *myself*]).

hisself *Hisself* is nonstandard; use *himself*.

hopefully *Hopefully* is an adverb meaning "in a hopeful manner" (*The child looked hopefully out the window for her mother*). In formal writing, do not use *hopefully* to mean "I or we hope that" or "It is hoped that" (*I hope that* [not *Hopefully*] *Bob will remember his camera*).

hung See *hanged, hung.*

i.e. *I.e.* is an abbreviation for the Latin phrase *id est,* which means "that is." In formal writing, use *that is* instead of the abbreviation (*Hal is a Renaissance man; that is* [not *i.e.*], *he has many interests*).

if, whether Use *if* in a clause that refers to a conditional situation (*I will wear my new boots if it snows tomorrow*). Use *whether* (or *whether or not*) in a clause that expresses or implies an alternative (*I will decide whether to wear my boots when I see what the weather is like*).

illusion See *allusion, illusion.*

immigrate See *emigrate, immigrate.*

imminent See *eminent, imminent.*

implicit See *explicit, implicit.*

imply, infer *Imply* is a verb meaning "to express indirectly" or "to suggest"; *infer* is a verb meaning "to conclude" or "to surmise" (*Helen implied that she had time to visit with us, but we inferred from all the work on her desk that she was really too busy*). A speaker implies; a listener infers.

incredible, incredulous *Incredible* is an adjective meaning "hard to believe"; *incredulous* is an adjective meaning "skeptical" or "unbelieving" (*My parents were incredulous when I told them the incredible story*).

infer See *imply, infer.*

ingenious, ingenuous *Ingenious* means "resourceful" or "clever" (*Elaine came up with an ingenious plan*). *Ingenuous* means "innocent" or "simple" (*It was a surprisingly deceptive plan for such an ingenuous person*).

in regards to *In regards to* is an incorrect combination of two phrases, *as regards* and *in regard to* (*In regard to* [or *As regards;* not *In regards to*] *the first question, refer to the guidelines you received*).

inside, inside of; outside, outside of The prepositions *inside* and *outside* should not be followed by *of* (*The suspect is inside* [not *inside of*] *that building*).

insure See *assure, ensure, insure.*

invitation, invite *Invitation* is a noun; *invite* is a verb (*I will invite her to the party and hope she will accept the invitation*). Do not use *invite* as a noun (*Thanks for the invitation* [not *invite*]).

irregardless, regardless Do not use the nonstandard *irregardless* in place of *regardless* (*We will have the party regardless* [not *irregardless*] *of the weather*).

is when, is where Avoid these awkward expressions in formal writing to define terms (*Sexual harassment refers to* [not *is when someone makes*] *inappropriate sexual advances or suggestions*).

its, it's *Its* is the possessive form of the pronoun *it; it's* is a contraction for *it is* (*It's hard to tear a baby animal away from its mother*).

kind, sort, type *Kind, sort,* and *type* are singular nouns; each should be used with *this* (not *these*) and a singular verb (*This kind of mushroom is* [not *these kind of mushrooms are*] *expensive*. The plural forms—*kinds, sorts,* and *types*—should be used with *these* and with a plural verb (*These three types of envelopes are the only ones we need*).

kind of, sort of   In formal writing, avoid using the colloquial expressions *kind of* and *sort of* to mean "somewhat" or "rather" (*My paper is rather* [not *kind of*] *short; my research for it was somewhat* [not *sort of*] *rushed*).

later, latter   *Later* means "after some time"; *latter* refers to the second of two people, items, or ideas (*Later in the evening Jim announced that the latter of the two guest speakers was running late*). See *former, latter*.

lay   See *lie, lay*.

lead, led   As a verb, *lead* means "to go first" or "to direct"; as a noun, it means "front position" (*Hollis took the lead in organizing the files*). *Led* is the past-tense and past-participle form of the verb *lead* (*He led me to the cave*).

learn, teach   *Learn* means "to gain knowledge or understanding"; *teach* means "to cause to know" or "to instruct" (*Tonight James will teach* [not *learn*] *us a new dance step; I hope we can learn it quickly*).

leave, let   *Leave* means "to depart"; it should not be used in place of *let*, which means "to allow" (*When you are ready to leave, let* [not *leave*] *me give you a ride*). The expressions *leave alone* and *let alone*, however, may be used interchangeably (*I asked Ben to leave* [or *let*] *me alone while I worked on my paper*).

led   See *lead, led*.

less   See *fewer, less*.

liable, likely   *Liable* means "inclined" or "tending," generally toward the negative (*If you don't shovel the sidewalk, you are liable to fall on the ice*). *Liable* is also a legal term meaning "responsible for" or "obligated under the law" (*The landlord is liable for the damage caused by the leak*). *Likely* is an adjective meaning "probable" or "promising" (*The school board is likely to cancel classes if the strike continues*).

lie, lay   The verb *lie* meaning "to recline" or "to rest in a horizontal position" has the principal forms *lie, lay, lain*. *Lie* should not be confused with the transitive verb *lay*, which means "to put or set down" and is followed by an object; the principal forms of *lay* are *lay, laid, laid* (*Lay the blanket on this spot and lie* [not *lay*] *down; She laid the book next to the spot where he lay on the bed*).

like   See *as, as if, like*.

likely   See *liable, likely*.

loose, lose   *Loose* is an adjective meaning "not securely attached"; it should not be confused with the verb *lose*, which means "to misplace," "to fail to keep," or "to undergo defeat" (*Be careful not to lose that loose button on your jacket*).

lots, lots of   *Lots* and *lots of* are colloquial expressions meaning "many" or "much"; avoid them in formal writing (*The senator has much* [not *lots of*] *support; she is expected to win many* [not *lots of*] *votes*).

man, mankind   These terms were once used to refer to all human beings. Now such usage is considered sexist; use terms such as *people, humanity,* and *humankind* instead (*What has been the greatest invention in the history of humanity* [not *mankind*]*?*).

may   See *can, may.*

may be, maybe   *May be* is a verb phrase (*Charles may be interested in a new job*); *maybe* is an adverb meaning "possibly" or "perhaps" (*Maybe I will speak to him about it*).

media   The term *media,* frequently used to refer to various forms of communication such as newspapers, magazine, television, radio, is the plural form of the noun *medium*; it takes a plural verb (*Some people feel that the media were responsible for the candidate's loss*).

moral, morale   *Moral* is the message or lesson of a story or experience. (*The moral is to treat others as you wish to be treated*). *Morale* is the mental condition or mood of a person or group (*The improvement in the weather lifted the crew's morale*).

most   In formal writing, do not use *most* to mean "almost" (*Prizes were given to almost* [not *most*] *all the participants*).

myself   See *herself, himself. . . .*

neither   The pronoun *neither* is singular (*Neither of my parents is able to come this weekend*).

nor, or   *Nor* should be used with *neither* (*Neither Paul nor Sara guessed the right answer*); *or* should be used with *either* (*Either Paul or Sara will drive me home*).

number   See *amount, number.*

of   See *have, of.*

off of   Use *off* alone; *of* is not necessary (*The child fell off* [not *off of*] *the playground slide*).

OK, O.K., okay   All three spellings are acceptable, but this colloquial term should be avoided in formal writing (*John's performance was all right* [or *adequate* or *tolerable,* not *okay*], *but it wasn't his best*).

on account of   In formal writing, avoid *on account of* to mean "because of" (*The course was canceled because of* [not *on account of*] *lack of interest*). Also see *due to.*

outside, outside of   See *inside, inside of; outside, outside of.*

passed, past   *Passed* is the past-tense form of the verb *pass* (*She passed here several hours ago*). *Past* may be an adjective or a noun referring to a time before the present (*She has forgotten many details about her past life*).

penultimate   See *ultimate, penultimate.*

per   The Latin term *per* should be reserved for commercial or technical use (*miles per gallon, price per pound*) and avoided in other formal writing (*Kyle is exercising three times each* [not *per*] *week*).

percent, percentage   The term *percent* refers to a specific fraction of one hundred; it is always used with a number (*We raised nearly 80 percent of our budget in one night*). Do not use the symbol % in formal writing. The term *percentage* is more general and is not used with a specific number (*We raised a large percentage of our budget in one night*).

perspective, prospective   *Perspective* is a noun meaning "a view"; it should not be confused with the adjective *prospective* meaning "potential" or "likely" (*Mr. Harris's perspective on the new school changed when he met his son's prospective teacher*).

phenomena   *Phenomena* is the plural of the noun *phenomenon*, which means "an observed fact, occurrence, or circumstance" (*Last month's blizzard was an unusual phenomenon; there have been several such phenomena this year*).

plenty   *Plenty* means "full" or "abundant"; in formal writing, do not use it to mean "very" or "quite" (*The sun was quite* [not *plenty*] *hot*).

plus   *Plus* is a preposition meaning "increased by" or "with the addition of" (*With wool socks plus your heavy boots, your feet should be warm enough*). Do not use *plus* to link two independent clauses; use *besides* or *moreover* instead (*Brad is not prepared for the advanced class; moreover* [not *plus*], *he can't fit it in his schedule*).

precede, proceed   *Precede* is a verb meaning "to go or come before"; *proceed* is a verb meaning "to move forward or go on" or "to continue" (*The bridal attendants preceded the bridge into the church; when the music started, they proceeded down the aisle*).

pretty   In formal writing, avoid *pretty* to mean "quite" or "somewhat" (*Dave is quite* [not *pretty*] *tired this morning*).

principal, principle   *Principal* is an adjective meaning "first" or "most important"; it is also a noun meaning "head" or "director" or "an amount of money" (*My principal reason for visiting Gettysburg was my interest in the Civil War. My high school principal suggested the trip*). *Principle* is a noun meaning "a rule of action or conduct" or "a basic law" (*I also want to learn more about the principles underlying the U.S. Constitution*).

proceed   See *precede, proceed*.

quotation, quote   *Quotation* is a noun, and *quote* is a verb. Avoid using *quote* as a noun (*Sue quoted Jefferson in her speech, hoping the quotation* [not *quote*] *would have a powerful effect on her audience*).

raise, rise   *Raise* is a transitive verb meaning "to lift" or "to increase"; it takes a direct object (*The store owner was forced to raise prices*). *Rise* is an intransitive verb meaning "to go up"; it does not take a direct object (*Prices will rise during periods of inflation*).

rarely ever   Do not use *rarely ever* to mean "hardly ever"; use *rarely* alone (*We rarely* [not *rarely ever*] *travel during the winter*).

real, really   *Real* is an adjective meaning "true" or "actual" (*The diamonds in that necklace are real*). *Really* is an adverb, used informally to mean "very" or "quite"; do not use *real* as an adverb (*Tim was really* [not *real*] *interested in buying Lana's old car*). In formal writing, it is generally best to avoid using *really* altogether.

reason is because   *Reason is because* is redundant; use *reason is that* or *because* instead (*The reason I am late is that* [not *because*] *I got stuck in traffic. Yesterday I was late because* [not *The reason I was late yesterday was because*] *I overslept*).

reason why   *Reason why* is redundant; use *reason* alone (*The reason* [not *The reason why*] *we canceled the dance is that no one volunteered to chaperone*).

regardless   See *irregardless, regardless*.

relation, relationship   *Relation* is a connection or association between things; *relationship* is a connection or involvement between people (*The analyst explained the relation between investment and interest. The relationship between a mother and child is complex*).

respectfully, respectively   The adverb *respectfully* means "in a respectful manner" (*The children listened to their teacher respectfully*). The adverb *respectively* means "in the order given" (*The sessions on Italian, French, and Spanish culture are scheduled for Tuesday, Wednesday, and Thursday, respectively*).

rise   See *raise, rise*.

says   See *goes, says*.

scarcely   See *hardly, scarcely*.

sensual, sensuous   *Sensual* means "arousing or exciting the senses or appetites"; it is often used in reference to sexual pleasure (*His scripts often featured titillating situations and sensual encounters*). *Sensuous* means "experienced through or affecting the senses," although it generally refers to aesthetic enjoyment or pleasure (*Her sculpture was characterized by muted colors and sensuous curves*).

set, sit   *Set* is a transitive verb meaning "to put" or "to place"; it takes a direct object, and its principal forms are *set, set, set* (*Mary set her packages on the kitchen table*). *Sit* is an intransitive verb meaning "to be seated"; it does not take a direct object, and its principal forms are *sit, sat, sat* (*I sat in the only chair in the waiting room*).

shall, will   In the past, *shall* (instead of *will*) was used as a helping verb with the first-person subjects *I* and *we*. Now *will* is acceptable with all subjects (*We will* *invite several guests for dinner*). *Shall* is generally used in polite questions (*Shall we go inside now?*) or in legal writing (*Jurors shall refrain from all contact with the press*).

since *Since* should be used to mean "continuing from a past time until the present" (*Carl has not gone skiing since he injured his knee*). Do not use *since* to mean "because" if there is any possibility that readers will be confused about your meaning. For example, in the sentence *Since she sold her bicycle, Lonnie has not been getting much exercise,* the word *since* could mean either "because" or "from the time that." Use *because* to avoid confusion.

sit See *set, sit.*

site See *cite, site.*

so, so that The use of *so* to mean "very" can be vague; use *so* with a *that* clause of explanation (not *Gayle was so depressed,* but *Gayle was so depressed that she could not get out of bed*).

somebody, someone, something These singular indefinite pronouns take singular verbs (*Somebody calls every night and hangs up; I hope someone does something about this problem soon*).

someplace, somewhere Do not use *someplace* in formal writing; use *somewhere* instead (*The answer must lie somewhere* [not *someplace*] *in the text*).

some time, sometime, sometimes The phrase *some time* (an adjective and a noun) means "a length of time" (*We have not visited our grandparents in some time*). *Sometime* is an adverb meaning "at an indefinite time in the future" (*Let's get together sometime*); *sometimes* is an adverb meaning "on occasion" or "now and then" (*Sometimes we get together to talk about our assignments*).

sort See *kind, sort, type.*

stationary, stationery *Stationary* is an adjective meaning "not moving" (*All stationary vehicles will be towed*). *Stationery* is a noun meaning "writing materials" (*Karen is always running out of stationery*).

supposed to, used to Both of these expressions consist of a past participle (*supposed, used*) followed by *to.* Do not use the base forms *suppose* and *use* (*Ben is supposed* [not *suppose*] *to take the garbage out; he is used* [not *use*] *to his mother's reminders by now*).

sure, surely In formal writing, do not use the adjective *sure* to mean "certainly" or "undoubtedly"; use *surely* or *certainly* or *undoubtedly* instead (*It is certainly* [or *surely;* not *sure*] *cold today*).

sure and, try and *Sure and* and *try and* are colloquial expressions for *sure to* and *try to,* respectively; avoid them in formal writing (*Be sure to* [not *and*] *come to the party. Try to* [not *and*] *be on time*).

take   See *bring, take.*

teach   See *learn, teach.*

than, then   *Than* is a conjunction used in comparisons (*Dan is older than Eve*). *Then* is an adverb indicating time (*First pick up the files and then deliver them to the company office*).

that   See *that, which* and *which, who, that.*

that, which   A clause introduced by *that* is always a restrictive clause; it should not be set off by commas (*The historical event that interested him the most was the Civil War*). Many writers use *which* only to introduce nonrestrictive clauses, which are set off by commas (*His textbook, which was written by an expert on the war, provided useful information*); however, *which* may also be used to introduce restrictive clauses (*The book which offered the most important information was an old reference book in the library*). (See 46i.)

their, there, they're   *Their* is the possessive form of the pronoun *they* (*Did they leave their books here?*). *There* is an adverb meaning "in or at that place" (*No, they left their books there*); it may also be used as an expletive with a form of the verb *be* (*There is no time to look for their books*). *They're* is a contraction of *they are* (*They're looking all over for their books*).

theirselves   *Theirselves* is nonstandard; always use *themselves.*

then   See *than, then.*

'til, till, until   *Till* and *until* are both acceptable spellings; *'til*, however, is a contraction and should be avoided in formal writing (*We will work until we are finished; you should not plan to leave till then*).

to, too, two   *To* is a preposition often used to indicate movement or direction toward something (*Nancy is walking to the grocery store*). *Too* is an adverb meaning "also" (*Sam is walking too*). *Two* is a number (*The two of them are walking together*).

toward, towards   *Toward* is preferred, but both forms are acceptable.

try and   See *sure and, try and.*

type   In colloquial speech, *type* is sometimes used alone to mean "type of," but avoid this usage in formal writing (*What type of* [not *type*] *medicine did the doctor prescribe?*). Also see *kind, sort, type.*

ultimate, penultimate   *Ultimate* literally means "the last." In formal writing, do not use it in the colloquial sense of "the best" (*the toughest challenge*, not *the ultimate challenge*). *Penultimate* is also sometimes used to mean "the best," but it means "next to last."

ultimately   See *eventually, ultimately.*

uninterested   See *disinterested, uninterested.*

unique   *Unique* is an adjective meaning "being the only one" or "having no equal." Because it refers to an absolute, unvarying state, it should not be preceded by a word that indicates degree or amount, such as *most, less,* or *very* (*Her pale blue eyes gave her a unique* [not *very unique*] *look*). The same is true of other adjectives that indicate an absolute state: *perfect, complete, round, straight,* and so on.

until   See *'til, till, until.*

usage, use   The noun *usage* means "an established and accepted practice or procedure" (*He consulted the glossary whenever he was unsure of the correct word or usage*). Do not substitute it for the noun *use* when the intended meaning is "the act of putting into service" (*Park guidelines forbid the use* [not *usage*] *of gas grills*).

used to   See *supposed to, used to.*

utilize   The verb *utilize*, meaning "to put to use," is often considered inappropriately technical for formal writing. It is generally better to use *use* instead (*We were able to use* [not *utilize*] *the hotel kitchen to prepare our meals*).

wait for, wait on   *Wait for* means "to await" or "to be ready for." *Wait on* means "to serve"; in formal writing they are not interchangeable (*You are too old to wait for* [not *on*] *your mother to wait on you*).

way, ways   Do not use *ways* in place of *way* when referring to long distances (*Los Angeles is a long way* [not *ways*] *from San Francisco*).

well   See *good, well.*

where   *Where* is nonstandard when used in place of *that* (*I read that* [not *where*] *several of the company's plants will be closed in June*).

where . . . at, where . . . to   *Where* should be used alone, not in combination with *at* or *to* (*Where did you leave your coat?* [not *Where did you leave your coat at?*] *Where are you going next?* [not *Where are you going to next?*]).

whether   See *if, whether.*

which   See *that, which.*

which, who, that   Use the relative pronoun *which* to refer to places, things, or events; use *who* to refer to people or to animals with individual qualities or given names; use *that* to refer to places, things, or events or to groups of people (*The parade, which was rescheduled for Saturday, was a great success. The man who* [not *which*] *was grand marshall said it was the best parade that he could remember*). *That* is also occasionally used to refer to a single person (*Beth is like the sister that I never had*). (See 46i.)

while   See *although, while.*

who   See *which, who, that.*

who, whom, whoever, whomever   Use *who* and *whoever* for subjects and subject complements; use *whom* and *whomever* for objects and object complements (*Who revealed the murderer's identity? You may invite whomever you wish*). (See 47c.)

who's, whose   *Who's* is a contraction of *who is* (*Who's coming for dinner tonight?*). *Whose* is the possessive form of *who* (*Whose hat is lying on the table?*).

will   See *shall, will.*

-wise   The suffix *-wise* indicates position or direction in words such as *clockwise* and *lengthwise*. In formal writing, do not add it to words to mean "with regard to" (*My personal life is rather confused, but with regard to my job* [not *jobwise*], *things are fine*).

yet   See *but, however, yet.*

your, you're   *Your* is the possessive form of the pronoun *you* (*Your table is ready*); *you're* is a contraction of *you are* (*You're leaving before the end of the show?*).

EDITING SYMBOLS

ABB	abbreviation	PASS	passive voice
ADJ	adjective	REF	pronoun reference
ADV	adverb	REP	repetitious
AWK	awkward	S–V AGR	subject-verb agreement
BIAS	biased language	SHIFT	distracting shift
CAP, ≡	capital letter	SLANG	slang
CASE	pronoun case	SP	spelling
CLICHE	cliché	SP OUT	spell out
COH	coherence	SUB	subordination
CONCL	conclusion	T	verb tense
COORD	coordination	TONE	tone
CS	comma splice	TRANS	transition
D	diction	??	unclear
DEV	development	VERB	verb
DIR	indirect	W	wordy
DM	dangling modifier	'	apostrophe
EMPH	emphasis	[]	brackets
FRAG	sentence fragment	:	colon
FS	fused sentence	,	comma
HYPH	hyphen	$\frac{1}{M}$	dash
INC	incomplete construction	. . .	ellipsis points
		!	exclamation point
ITAL	italics (underlining)	() parens	parentheses
JARG	jargon	⊙	period
LC	lowercase letter	?	question mark
MIXED	mixed construction	" "	quotation marks
MM	misplaced modifier	;	semicolon
MOOD	verb mood	/	slash
MS	manuscript	⌒	close up space
NUM	number	#	add space
OPEN	opening	^	insert
¶	paragraph	⟶	delete
//	parallelism	∼ tr	transpose
P	punctuation	X	obvious error
P–A AGR	pronoun-antecedent agreement		

INDEX

writing with, 54–55
Concession, transitional words or phrases indicating, 166
Concise summaries, 230
Concise writing, 242–48
Conclusions, 229–31
Concrete nouns, 252, 340
Concrete words, 256
Conferences, 60–61
Confirming, as reading strategy, 13, 14
Conflict, opening with, 151–52
Conjunctive adverbs, 234–35
    correcting comma splices, 417
    linking independent clauses, 352, 355
    list of, 418
    semicolons with, 282, 417
Connotation, 258–59
conscience, conscious, 507
Consonants, 317
contact, 508
continual, continuous, 508
Contractions, 290
Coordinate adjectives, 276
Coordinating conjunctions, 234, 355
    items in series and, 275
    joining independent clauses, 415–16
    parallel structures and, 242
Coordination, 232, 234–36
    combining sentences and, 241
    equal ideas, 234–35
    related ideas, 235–36
Correlative conjunctions, 234, 355
council, counsel, 530
Count nouns, 340, 342, 387
Creative writing, 38–39
    experimenting with form, 39
    intensifying experience, 38–39
criteria, 508
Critical essays. *See* Interpretive writing
Critical reading, 14–21
Critical thinking, 11
Cross-references, 203
    punctuating, 300

D

-d, -ed, verb tense and, 369
Dangling modifiers, 408–09
Dashes, 307

capitalization and, 325–26
transition suggested by, 167
with other punctuation, 303
with supplementary information, 302
data, 508
Databases:
    MLA documentation of, 444–48
Dates:
    commas with, 278
    MLA documentation style, 438
    numbers in, 329
    parentheses with, 299
Daybooks. *See* Journals
Days of week, capitalization of, 322
Declarative sentences, 363–64
Defensiveness, avoiding, 58
Defining, in explanatory writing, 104–105
Definite articles, 352
Deities, capitalizing, 322
Delayed-thesis organization, 37
Demonstrative pronouns, 343, 344, 392
Denotation, 256–57
Dependent clauses, 233, 238, 281
    fragments and, 412, 413
    habitual actions/universal truths and, 379–80
    mixed constructions and, 423
    sentence elements, 362
    who/whom in, 401
Describing, in explanatory writing, 105–106
Descriptive adjectives, 352
Descriptive grammar, 259
Design. See Document design
Details
    adding, 143
    opening with, 153
Dialogue, 294
    starting a, 69–70
Diaries. *See* Journals
Dictionaries, 253–54, 316
different from, different than, 508
differ from, differ with, 508
DIOLOG, 188
Direct address, 276–77
Directions, capitalizing, 322
Direct objects, 346–47, 358
    gerund phrases as, 360
    noun clauses as, 363

ESL INDEX

A

a, an, the, articles, 341
Academic writing, 257
Adjectives, order of, 404
Adverbs, 410
Articles, nouns and, 341–42

C

Conjunctions, subordinating, 239
Count nouns, 341–42

D

Dependent clauses, 239
Descriptive grammar, 259
Direction, prepositions and, 354
Dynamic verbs, 377

G

Grammar:
    perscriptive *versus* descriptive,
        259

I

Independent clauses, 239
–ing, dynamic verbs and, 377

J

Journal writing, 226

L

Location, prepositions and, 354

M

Money units, 329

N

Noncount nouns, 341–42, 387
Nouns:
    articles with, 341
    count/noncount, 341–42, 387–88

number forms, 329
    plural, 329
Number forms, 329
Numbers, singular and plural, 329

P

Particle. See Phrasal verbs
Phrasal verbs, 257–58
Place, prepositions and, 354
Plagiarism, 216
Plural number forms, 329
Prepositions:
    guidelines for choosing, 354–57
    list of, 353
    with verbal phrases, 257
Perscriptive grammar, 259

Q

Quantifiers, 389

S

Singular number forms, 329
Stative verbs, 377
Subject–verb agreement, 387–88
Subordinating conjunctions, 239

T

Time:
    number forms for, 329
    prepositions with, 354
Transitional expressions, 226

V

Verb phrases, 410
Verbs:
    agreement with noncount nouns,
        387
    dynamic, 377
    phrasal, 257–58
    stative, 377

W

Weight units, 329